Mesa Verde's Secret Garden

Mesa Verde's Secret Garden

A History of Managing the Backcountry and Wilderness of a National Park

Christopher Barns

UNIVERSITY OF NEW MEXICO PRESS | ALBUQUERQUE

Library of Congress Cataloging-in-Publication Data
Names: Barns, Christopher, 1950– author.
Title: Mesa Verde's secret garden : a history of managing the backcountry and wilderness of a national park / Christopher Barns.
Description: Albuquerque : University of New Mexico Press, 2025. | Includes bibliographical references and index.
Identifiers: LCCN 2024028325 (print) | LCCN 2024028326 (ebook) | ISBN 9780826367662 (paperback) | ISBN 9780826367679 (epub) | ISBN 9780826367686 (pdf)
Subjects: LCSH: Wilderness area monitoring—Colorado—Mesa Verde National Park. | Wilderness areas—Colorado—Mesa Verde National Park. | Cultural property—Protection—Colorado—Mesa Verde National Park. | Mesa Verde National Park (Colo.)—History.
Classification: LCC F782.M52 B37 2025 (print) | LCC F782.M52 (ebook) | DDC 978.827—dc23/eng/20240711
LC record available at https://lccn.loc.gov/2024028325
LC ebook record available at https://lccn.loc.gov/2024028326

Founded in 1889, the University of New Mexico sits on the traditional homelands of the Pueblo of Sandia. The original peoples of New Mexico—Pueblo, Navajo, and Apache—since time immemorial have deep connections to the land and have made significant contributions to the broader community statewide. We honor the land itself and those who remain stewards of this land throughout the generations and also acknowledge our committed relationship to Indigenous peoples. We gratefully recognize our history.

Cover photograph: courtesy of Nick Dunlap on Unsplash
Designed by Felicia Cedillos
Composed in ITC New Baskerville

In honor of
James M. Copeland
archaeologist and friend
(not necessarily in that order)

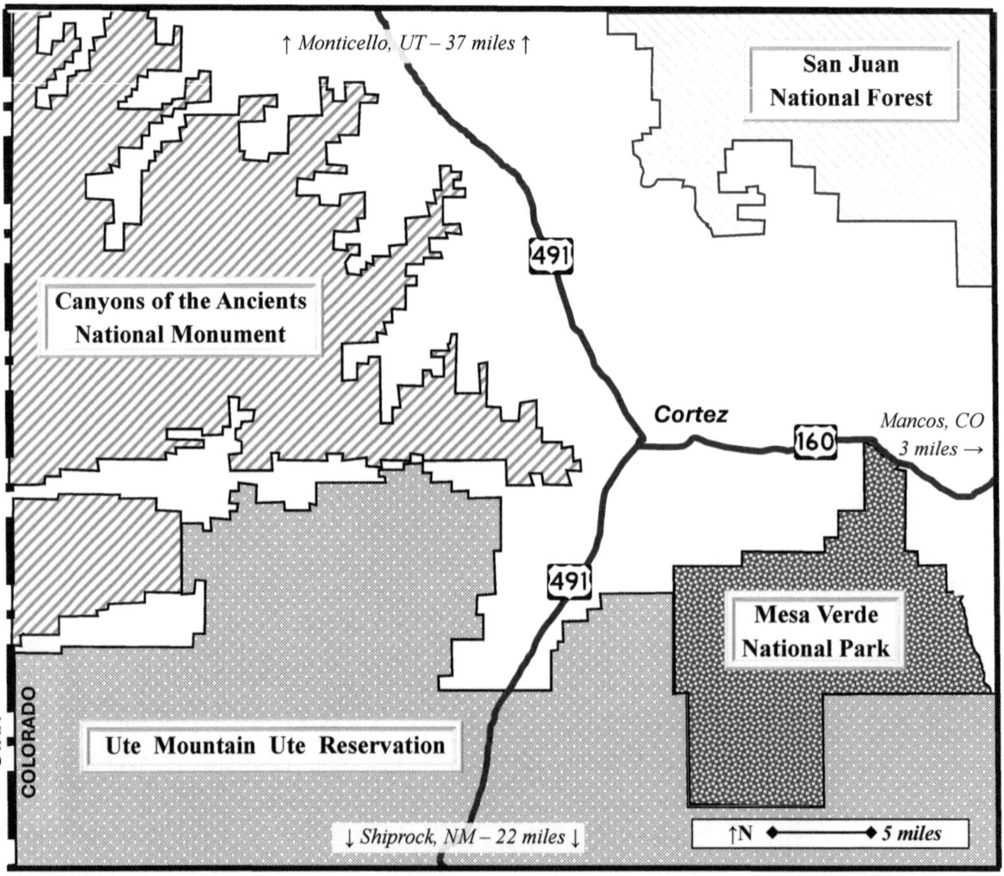

Mesa Verde National Park and the area surrounding Cortez, Colorado.

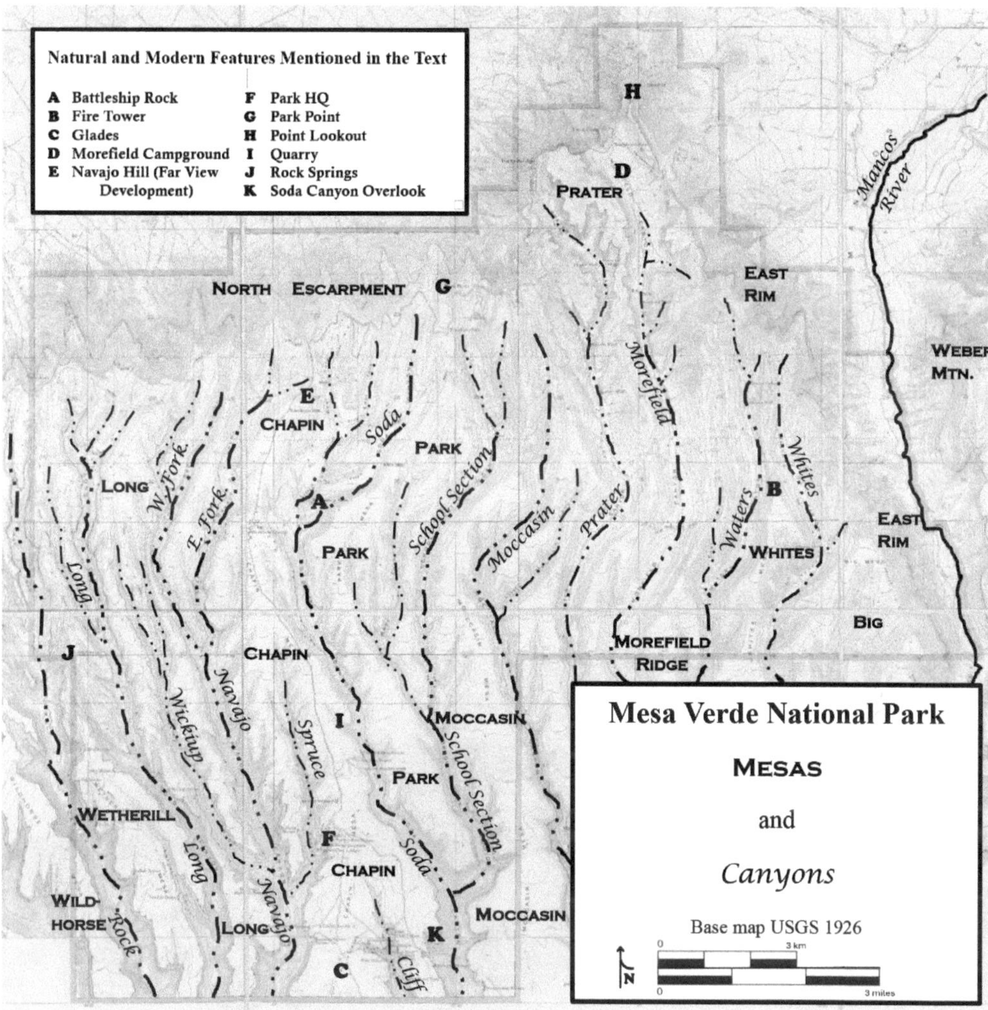

Natural and Modern Features Mentioned in the Text
A Battleship Rock
B Fire Tower
C Glades
D Morefield Campground
E Navajo Hill (Far View Development)
F Park HQ
G Park Point
H Point Lookout
I Quarry
J Rock Springs
K Soda Canyon Overlook
Mesa Verde National Park
Mesas
and
Canyons
Base map USGS 1926
North Escarpment
Prater
East Rim
Weber Mtn.
Mancos River
Chapin
Park
Long
Whites
Big
Morefield Ridge
Moccasin
Wetherill
Wild-horse
Soda
School Section
Morefield
Waters
Navajo
Wickiup
Spruce
Cliff
Rock
W. Fork
E. Fork

Contents

Acknowledgments

How often have I read an author's acknowledgments, and seen the book's editor mentioned? Almost always, and I used to think that it was a nice gesture born out of polite duty. I can't speak for another author, but that is not the reason I must begin by thanking Brenton Woodward at the University of New Mexico Press. I will forever be indebted to him for his belief in, advocacy for, and perceptive comments on *Mesa Verde's Secret Garden.* Without him, this book would be nothing more than a pile of electrons gathering dust in some remote corner of my laptop.

Next, I want to thank the current staff at Mesa Verde National Park. In this book I am quite critical of some of their predecessors. That should not be construed as denigrating anyone at Mesa Verde with whom I have had the pleasure to work. We may disagree about proper stewardship of the Park's Wilderness and backcountry, but their commitment to Mesa Verde is unquestioned.

Of critical importance to me, this book would not have been possible without the professional assistance, friendship, inspiration, and provocation of many people throughout my career. Some of these people have been long-time friends as well as coworkers; some crossed my path only for a moment, but at a critical juncture; some are no longer here to share our love of Wilderness. But all are important to me:

Peter Appel, Steve Archibald, Cheryl Armstrong, Gertrude Burnap, Steve Boutcher, Tom Caples, Tom Carlson, Dru Carr, Elvin Clapp, Jim Copeland, Julie Decker, Tim Devine, Steve DoBell, Marietta Eaton, Joel Farrell, Eric Finstick, Susan Fox, Wayne Freimund, Lora Anderson Gale, Faith Gemmill, Jean Craighead George, Ilyse Gold, Kari Gunderson, Greg Hansen, Dave (Wendell) Harmon,

Doug Hawes-Davis, Jeff Jarvis, Tim Knopp, Greg Kroll, Jim Kurth, Peter Landres, Dave Lime, Adrienne Lindholm, Karen Lindsey, Tim Manns, Fred Matt, Leo McAvoy, Linda Merigliano, Connie Myers, George Nickas, Martin Nie, Rebecca Oreskes, Mike Pool, Ellis Richard, Don Rodriguez, Nancy Roeper, Chris Roholt, Chris Ryan, Mike Salamacha, Deb Salt, Doug Scott, Yvette Silva, Rich Simmons, Emily Simpson, James Sippel, Press Stephens, Ken Straley, Ralph Swain, Jim Walters, Ed Zahniser, and Sandi Zellmer.

Finally, and most importantly, my love and thanks go to Kathleen Stachowski: "you are my home." I look forward to however much of the next twenty-five years we might be blessed to share.

Foreword

Real history is made up from the documents
that were not meant to be published.[1]

The genesis of this book took place in the office of the Superintendent of Mesa Verde National Park in the summer of 2017.

My wife and I had recently moved back to the Four Corners a few years after I had retired from the staff of the interagency Arthur Carhart National Wilderness Training Center in Missoula, Montana. I had been a wilderness specialist at Carhart for over fifteen years, and Cliff Spencer, then the Mesa Verde superintendent, was a participant in the last course geared toward upper-level wilderness managers that I helped teach.

So, I came to Cliff asking if there was some volunteer work I could do to help Mesa Verde that would take advantage of my expertise. Cliff had invited Allan Loy to the meeting. Allan is extremely knowledgeable in wilderness stewardship, but his time is also tremendously overcommitted to tasks of higher priority to the Park. They thought I might help get the Park's Wilderness Character Monitoring program off the ground.

For ten years I had been on several different teams under the leadership of Peter Landres at the Aldo Leopold Wilderness Research Institute, trying to figure out how to objectively measure whether an agency managing wilderness areas was assuring "the preservation of their wilderness character" as required by Section 2(a) of the Wilderness Act of 1964. I was eager to help the Park but foresaw one problem—I knew Mesa Verde completely ignored one of the essential qualities of wilderness character.

Of the 806 wilderness areas designated by Congress as of 2024, Mesa Verde is the only land-based area that prohibits all recreational use (there are nine others where recreational use is not allowed—small islands managed by the U.S. Fish and Wildlife Service). I wondered how to track changes in wilderness recreation when such use was banned—not only in the designated wilderness, but also in the areas the Park deemed eligible for designation that had not yet been acted on by Congress where, by National Park Service policy, existing wilderness character was to be preserved.

Allan informed me that there were no additional lands eligible for wilderness designation—not because they didn't exist, but because the Park had never gotten around to doing the required inventory. Congress had directed the Park to go through such a process when the Wilderness was designated in 1976, but it hadn't even been started forty-one years later. The inventory had been on their program of work for a few years, but there simply were higher priorities.

Seeing the opportunity of a lifetime, I offered to start just such an inventory. Cliff agreed, and I spent portions of the next three years wandering around the otherwise-closed Mesa Verde backcountry looking for wilderness eligibility. The experience was . . . well, words are insufficient.

As preparation for the inventory, I needed access to the Park's historical files—trying to determine how the staff arrived at the decision to keep the Mesa Verde Wilderness closed to the public.

What I found was astounding. And it led to this book.

The documents in the Mesa Verde Research Library proved an incredibly rich source for deciphering the mindset of the staffs who worked in the Park over the years. These included not only public documents from decades past, but also internal drafts, staff meeting notes, memoranda, personal letters, and other correspondence. Of particular interest was the marginalia on a wide variety of documents. Occasionally the author of these comments identified her- or himself, often they did not. Sometimes the author is readily apparent—such as when long-time Superintendent Jesse Nusbaum used his distinctive green ink; other times, authorship is a matter of conjecture.

The research occasionally was laborious. Dr. Tara Travis, then the Supervisory Museum Curator, was exceptionally helpful in assisting me to navigate the filing system. But by the library's rules, I was allowed to view only one file at a time, and Tara's assistant, Sam Denman, devoted what must have seemed to him like years of his life retrieving one file after another for me. There were hundreds.

An added difficulty presented itself when I'd come across a memo with the words "see the attached map." There never was a map attached. They had been separated at the time of filing, with all the maps stored in a section of the research files that had not yet been systematically arranged. Besides, I was not authorized to view any maps that weren't in the public domain—another example of just how extraordinarily secretive the management of Mesa Verde is. Frustrating for me, but the secrecy is not entirely without reason.

This exploration resulted in *Mesa Verde's Secret Garden: A History of Managing the Backcountry and Wilderness in a National Park*. This work addresses the changes in management of the Mesa Verde National Park backcountry and Wilderness—primarily from the point of view of park administration, though the stewardship of this resource cannot be separated from the cultural and biophysical components of the landscape that led Mesa Verde to be designated a National Park in the first place.

Mesa Verde's Secret Garden is arranged chronologically from the time of the Park's designation in 1906 to the present, with a concluding chapter exploring "The Path Forward." The book's structure examines the early tendency to "garden" Mesa Verde—that is, to manipulate the natural conditions and processes to create a Park that managers considered more aesthetically pleasing, which decreased over time as managers learned that "preservation" was more a matter of ecology than scenery. Simultaneously, the desire to keep the backcountry (and Wilderness) a "secret" increased, from the earliest days when exploration by the public was encouraged, to the total prohibition of the present day.

Through this history, Mesa Verde emerges as a prime example of the conflicts often seen as inherent between the stewardship of what appear to be opposing resources. It is customary for disputes to be expected when trying to balance preservation and resource extraction. But here, as in other parks and wilderness areas with exceptionally important cultural components, there arises a friction between wilderness preservation and cultural preservation, both of which are mandated, to varying degrees, by legislation. The National Wilderness Preservation System, created by the Wilderness Act of 1964, must be managed in concert with the National Historic Preservation Act. And vice versa. What it means to "preserve" a natural area (including wilderness, with its required public access) or a cultural area have changed over the decades, and stewardship tenets continue to evolve. *Mesa Verde's Secret Garden* tracks these changes in Mesa Verde and offers questions to guide stewardship of a unified preservation in the future.

This book does not address the centuries of management undertaken by the indigenous Ancestral Puebloans. This was their home, and is still considered as such by their descendants, whose interests in current management are reflected in this book's conclusion. It does not detail many of the actions taken by people of European ancestry who moved though the Mesa Verde landscape for the decades prior to the area being designated a National Park, except to address the ways in which the "free-for-all" behavior in those days directly impacted early federal management. This should not be taken as minimizing or an excuse for the gross mistreatment of the Native Americans of this area—actions which are outside the scope of this book. Nor does it cover the encroachment on (and eventual taking of) Ute lands with the Park's designation in 1906—part of the lands to which the Utes had already been restricted by treaties only a few decades before. The Park's relationship with its Ute neighbors post designation of the Park is covered throughout, as part of this administrative history.

Those interested in the era prior to the Park's designation are directed to *American Indians & National Parks*, by Keller and Turek;

Duane Smith's *Mesa Verde National Park: Shadows of the Centuries*; and *Mesa Verde National Park: The First 100 Years*, edited by Houk and Marcovecchio.[2] In addition, though stewardship of the National Forests and National Parks is substantially different, those interested in the decision-making process involving policy and management outcomes for contested resource allocation, including public participation in land use planning decisions, should read *An Open Pit Visible from the Moon*, by Adam Sowards.[3]

Abbreviations and Terminology

For ease in reading the text, a series of common abbreviations and rules of usage have been incorporated.

In general, where used in this work, the following terms carry the meanings indicated here:

archeology: The spelling more generally used by the National Park Service, which is therefore the spelling usually used here. Certain scientists refer to their profession as "**archaeology,**" and where they are being quoted, that spelling is retained.

backcountry: An area not highly developed (e.g., through building roads) to facilitate visitation by the public. In some backcountry locations the level of development or other management considerations may be disqualify an area as wilderness. In other words, all wilderness areas are backcountry, but not all backcountry areas are eligible to be designated wilderness or are managed as such. In Mesa Verde, just what constitutes the Park's "backcountry" has changed over time—most notably with the development of Wetherill Mesa moving from "backcountry" to "frontcountry," changing its treatment. Readers familiar with the Mesa Verde "backcountry" in the first two decades of the twenty-first century will recognize it as the portions of the Park that are closed to all public entry. The backcountry/wilderness comparison is discussed further in the introduction.

designated wilderness: An unnamed or otherwise not specific area designated as such by Congress.

Director: The Director of the National Park Service. Directors of other agencies are so identified.

DSC: The Denver Service Center of the NPS.

Far View: Either the cluster of cultural sites in the middle of Chapin Mesa or the Park development farther north. The term is spelled as two words for consistency, even though specific internal documents may refer to either as "Farview."

Mesa Verde: Mesa Verde National Park. If the greater landform is meant, that will be indicated or referred to as the Mesa Verde cuesta. Mesa Verde is often abbreviated **MEVE,** even though that abbreviation is a modern one that is absent in earlier documents. Frequently, "Mesa Verde" is used to describe the Park's management staff or personnel—as in "Mesa Verde issued a Foundation Document in 2015." Likewise, "**the Park**" can refer to either Mesa Verde National Park or its management personnel, depending on context.

Morefield: The spelling currently used for a variety of landforms and areas in Mesa Verde. In various documents and on USGS maps it is spelled "Morfield." For consistency, the current preferred spelling is used throughout this work, regardless of the spelling in the original document.

Regional Director: The senior management official having jurisdiction over Mesa Verde and other units of the National Park System in a given portion of the country and to whom the Superintendent reports. The location of the Regional Director's office and the subset of units over which s/he has jurisdiction has changed repeatedly. Those specifics are usually omitted in this work. It may be abbreviated **RD.**

Regional Office: The NPS office with direct responsibility over MEVE. The name and location of this office has changed several times over the decades, and those distinctions are neither made nor cited in this work. It may be abbreviated **RO.**

Superintendent: Used to designate the most senior management official stationed at MEVE, even though the official title (and additional responsibilities) has changed over the decades. Superintendents at other NPS units are identified by name and full title.

Wilderness (with a capital *W*): A specific area designated as such by Congress.

wilderness (with a lowercase *w*): An area that possibly possesses the characteristics of wilderness listed in Section 2(c) of the Wilderness Act of 1964, whether or not it has been designated as Wilderness by Congress. This is more specific than the romantic term "wilderness" as used by many authors in the nineteenth century, and different from the vague pejorative straw man erected by several current wilderness critics. For more detail, see "Wilderness, wilderness character, and how they differ from backcountry" in this book's introduction.

Common abbreviations include:

BLM: Bureau of Land Management
FWS: United States Fish & Wildlife Service
NPS: National Park Service
USDA: United States Department of Agriculture
USDI: United States Department of the Interior
USGS: United States Geological Survey

Other abbreviations in the text are defined at their initial use.

Mistakes in spelling, grammar, or punctuation within quotations have been corrected without comment, unless to do so might fundamentally change the original meaning. In addition, simple changes in punctuation and capitalization have been made for ease of reading where such changes do not affect the meaning of the original.

Certain terms used in historical documents are retained for accuracy of citation, even though those terms would not otherwise appear. These include "Anasazi" rather than "Ancestral Puebloans"; "Indian" rather than "Native American," "indigenous American," or "First People"; "man" rather "humans"; and "ruins" as opposed to "dwellings" or "sites."

Introduction

The management history of the Mesa Verde backcountry and wilderness is checkered. For the first several decades of the Park's existence, wilderness appreciation at Mesa Verde was no different than throughout most of the country—that is, though various separate qualities may have been valued, the whole of wilderness, and the complex meanings associated with it, simply were not considered. The backcountry was visited to a greater or lesser degree and managed for a variety of values; wilderness was an undifferentiated concept. This changed with the designation of formal wilderness areas elsewhere in the country, accompanied by a congressionally mandated set of management proscriptions not found in undifferentiated backcountry. At that point, the wilderness concept was actively denied at Mesa Verde, and then, after eventual designation of the Mesa Verde Wilderness, became subject to a somewhat benign neglect. As will be detailed in chapter 6, "Mission 66 and the Wilderness Bill," much of this has to do with the historical antipathy of the National Park Service toward designated wilderness in general and the specific opposition to designation by the Mesa Verde staff during the original wilderness evaluation in the late 1960s and early 1970s, covered in chapter 8, "Mesa Verde Meets the Wilderness Act: The Fight over Wilderness Designation."

In one way, this relationship with wilderness is to be expected at Mesa Verde—and to some extent it may be appropriate. This park, in contrast with all other National Parks created prior to Mesa Verde's establishment in 1906, was not designated to protect natural wonders. Rather, it was "the first, and . . . still the only, national park in the United States created to preserve archaeological values."[1] In his seminal history of the National Park Service, John Ise pointed out that the bill creating Mesa Verde National Park said nothing about the wildlife or any other wilderness natural resource.[2] The emphasis on the cultural resources of Mesa Verde was so pervasive that in the 1931 publication *National Parks Portfolio,* the chapter on Mesa Verde has over twenty pictures of antiquities, and then advises the reader with a photograph captioned "Most of Mesa Verde's travel is by motor." The accompanying photograph is of a car on a dirt road along a beautiful creek—one found nowhere in the Park. Apparently, that made no difference—the "ruins" were all labeled correctly.[3]

Even publications specific to Mesa Verde that were published after the Mesa Verde Wilderness was designated in 1976 have given short shrift to wilderness. Archeologists Robert and Florence Lister wrote a Mesa Verde guidebook for the Park concessioner eleven years after the Mesa Verde Wilderness was designated; there is no mention of wilderness.[4] Duane Smith's important history ignores the wilderness designation altogether, and in discussing park management after the time of this designation, Smith makes one oblique reference to "wilderness resources and values."[5] In 2003, in the epilogue to a volume on the natural history of piñon-juniper woodlands, Mesa Verde Natural Resources Branch Chief George San Miguel wrote of "management considerations" for conservation; he made no mention of the Park's Wilderness.[6] The Mesa Verde Museum Association's celebration of the park's centennial devotes one paragraph to the subject.[7]

Archeologist Jim Copeland was working as an NPS employee at Mesa Verde when its wilderness was designated, and yet was unaware of it at the time; wilderness historian Mark Harvey worked at Mesa Verde for four years shortly after the Park's wilderness designation and had no idea any part of the park was designated wilderness.[8]

Roderick Nash and Craig Allin, in their great works of wilderness history, make no mention of the wilderness in Mesa Verde.[9]

In 2024, the Park's brochure mentions the existing wilderness for the first time, forty-eight years after designation. The text appears to be an addendum and does not mention that the Mesa Verde Wilderness is closed to the public, nor are the boundaries of the three units of the Wilderness shown on the Park map.

For everyone concerned, the Mesa Verde Wilderness seems an afterthought.

So, what *is* wilderness? More specifically, what is wilderness in Mesa Verde? How does it differ from backcountry, and how was the Mesa Verde backcountry used—and not used—prior to Wilderness designation? What was the designation process, and why—given the opposition of so many—did there come to be any wilderness designated at Mesa Verde in the first place? How have both the Mesa Verde Wilderness and the remaining backcountry been managed since Wilderness designation? And how might the Wilderness and backcountry be managed going forward? *Mesa Verde's Secret Garden* seeks to answer these questions.

At its most basic, the NPS defines "backcountry" as "a generic descriptor for areas of a park unit outside of highly developed frontcountry zones." With no legal definition, it informally describes the undeveloped areas of a park. In backcountry areas "facilities and road access are limited, and dispersed recreational opportunities in a natural setting are reached primarily by a network of trails." Though a backcountry area may exhibit wilderness character, there is no statutory mandate to maintain it that way unimpaired into the future. However, in the NPS, "Backcountry acreage that has been inventoried and found eligible for formal study is to be managed for nondegradation of wilderness values until a study can be completed."[10]

There is considerable misunderstanding about what conditions are required for an area to be considered for designation as Wilderness, and what such a designation means for an area after it is designated. The common understanding of "wilderness" is not the same as the statute's legal definition.

The conditions and requirements of designated wilderness, as described below, create a specific wilderness character, and "each agency administering any area designated as wilderness shall be responsible for preserving the wilderness character of the area and shall so administer such area for such other purposes for which it may have been established as *also* to preserve its wilderness character" (emphasis added).[11] Landres et al. distilled fifteen years of working with the idea of wilderness character and how to monitor it into a three-component "holistic concept": "Biophysical environments primarily free from modern human manipulation and impact"; "Personal experiences in natural environments relatively free from the encumbrances and signs of modern society;" and "Symbolic meanings of humility, restraint, and interdependence in how individuals and society view their relationship to nature."[12]

If this sounds subjective, it is. The subjectivity of wilderness was recognized early in its theoretical history. In 1926, Aldo Leopold wrote Benton MacKaye, calling wilderness "a point of view, not a piece of land." Sigurd Olson, wilderness champion of the northern canoe country, wrote: "The real significance of wilderness is a cultural matter. . . . It has to do with the human spirit." More recently, wilderness educator Leo McAvoy wrote: "We cannot afford to be objective. The need for wilderness is no more objective or measurable than the need for love, but it is there and it is real." And Faith Gemmill, former member of the Gwich'in Steering Committee in northern Alaska, summed up: "If there was no wilderness, I think humankind would be lost. Without these places, we would be cold, hard. We wouldn't have any real foundation. . . . Anybody can have that connection if they're open to that connection. And I think that it's vital to our spirituality."[13]

This suite of ideals encompasses both tangible and intangible values and may be found in lands other than those designated as wilderness, including many backcountry areas. But only in those designated lands is the wilderness character protected by law, codified by Congress in the Wilderness Act of 1964, where "wilderness" is defined:

> A wilderness, in contrast with those areas where man and his own works dominate the landscape, is hereby recognized as an area

> where the earth and its community of life are untrammeled by man, where man himself is a visitor who does not remain. An area of wilderness is further defined to mean in this chapter an area of undeveloped Federal land retaining its primeval character and influence, without permanent improvements or human habitation, which is protected and managed so as to preserve its natural conditions and which (1) generally appears to have been affected primarily by the forces of nature, with the imprint of man's work substantially unnoticeable; (2) has outstanding opportunities for solitude or a primitive and unconfined type of recreation; (3) has at least five thousand acres of land or is of sufficient size as to make practicable its preservation and use in an unimpaired condition; and (4) may also contain ecological, geological, or other features of scientific, educational, scenic, or historical value.[14]

From this definition, five "qualities" have been identified that, taken together, represent the essential tangible aspects of wilderness character found in the statutory definition of wilderness, reflected in on-the-ground conditions in wilderness and the outcomes of wilderness stewardship. These qualities are required to be addressed in designated wilderness but are often found in areas other than those designated by Congress as a Wilderness. They may be useful in assessing management options in non-wilderness backcountry areas, and it may be appropriate to manage for these qualities in areas that are not legally designated wilderness if agency policy requires that the area be managed to preserve its wilderness character.[15]

The qualities of wilderness character are discussed below one at a time, but it must be kept in mind that the character of any wilderness is greater than the sum of these five qualities. The qualities form a unified physical, social, and managerial setting, which provides scientific, cultural, educational, and economic values to society. In addition, psychological, spiritual, ethical, democratic, and other intangible values also benefit both the individual and society. The symbiotic interaction of all these values is what the 1964 Wilderness Act describes as the "benefits of an enduring resource of wilderness."[16]

Note that in comparing the definition found in the Wilderness Act with the five qualities described below, any reference to size has been eliminated. In general, the size of a Wilderness is not subject to managerial discretion. Congress dictates the size of an area with its designation, and the managing agency must preserve its wilderness character at whatever size Congress mandates.[17]

The "qualities" of wilderness character are:

1. Untrammeled

A wilderness is "essentially unhindered and free from the intentional actions of modern human control or manipulation." That is, it is wild. This is the quality that most clearly separates wilderness from backcountry. A backcountry area may be wild in fact, but only in a Wilderness is it wild by law.

No other concept in the Wilderness Act is so misunderstood. "Untrammeled" is not to be confused with "pristine," as many critics of the Act claim. Wilderness areas are not conceived as so-called "virgin America"—places unmanipulated by humans in the past. Not only had many areas now designated as Wilderness been heavily manipulated by Native Americans (such as in Mesa Verde), but some had been mined or logged in the late nineteenth and even early twentieth centuries. This point cannot be stressed too heavily: "Untrammeled" is a forward-looking term, one that refers (at least legally) from the moment of designation into the future, not to some condition of the land in the past.

Consequently, managing a wilderness as "untrammeled" does not mean "return to the way the land was managed by the First People." The original human inhabitants manipulated the land—sometimes dramatically—in ways necessary for physical sustenance. Such manipulations today would usually be incompatible with the purpose of Wilderness.

In addition, the qualifier "intentional" is important. The effects of some unintentional actions (such as air pollution) certainly degrade wilderness character. For the most part, these are out of the control of the land manager and are accounted for in the "natural" quality.

What would an untrammeled Mesa Verde wilderness look like? Ideally, there would be no intentional manipulation of the biophysical environment, including any plant or animal species, no intentional alteration of the physical environment, and no interference with natural processes, such as fire. "If ecological processes operate essentially uncontrolled within the wilderness frame of reference, the results, whatever they might be, are desirable by definition. The object is not to stop change, nor to recreate conditions as of some arbitrary historical date, nor to strive for favorable change in big game populations or in scenic vistas. The object is to let nature 'roll the dice' and accept the results with interest and scientific curiosity."[18] Or, as Howard Zahniser, primary author of the Wilderness Act, wrote, "In Wilderness we are guardians, not gardeners."[19] *Mesa Verde's Secret Garden* tracks how the Park Service's willingness (and rationales) to "garden"—to manipulate the biophysical environment—have changed over time.

2. Natural

A wilderness is "protected and managed so as to preserve its natural conditions." Certainly, many backcountry areas are predominantly natural, and are often protected as such through agency policy. In many ways, wilderness areas are a refuge for the "other nations, caught with ourselves in the net of life and time."[20]

However, determining what is "natural" is not always easy, and it can be quite difficult to determine the direction or amount of change that is or is not "natural." It is perhaps easier to identify what is *not* natural. In 1963, the Leopold Report found "Americans have shown a great capacity for degrading and fragmenting native biotas. So far, we have not exercised much imagination or ingenuity in rebuilding damaged biotas. It will not be done by passive protection alone."[21]

What would a natural Mesa Verde backcountry or wilderness look like? Ideally, there would be a complete assemblage of indigenous species—and absence of non-indigenous species—with thorough compositions, functions, structures, and interactions between biotic and abiotic components. Variability and change would occur, with ecological systems evolving at a pace and direction uninfluenced by modern humans or their technology. However, ecological systems inside wilderness are affected by actions taken outside wilderness, the most obvious being the artificial flow of the Mancos River at the Park's eastern boundary. *Mesa Verde's Secret Garden* follows the Park Service's evolving concern for—and attention to—what is "natural."

3. Undeveloped

A wilderness is "essentially without . . . improvements or the sights and sounds of modern human occupation." Here, too, many backcountry areas are relatively undeveloped, though there may be greater development in a backcountry than is expected in a designated wilderness, and wilderness areas have an explicit screen built into the law that must be applied for an improvement to be legal.

The Wilderness Act's section 4(c) prohibits physical developments (such as structures, installations, and both permanent and temporary roads) as well as temporal developments (that is, where the wilderness is "developed" for the duration of the use of a prohibited tool—such as motor vehicles, motorized equipment, and mechanical transport).[22]

Of course, humans are defined as toolmakers, yet in 1939 Aldo Leopold noted that modern tools have enabled humans "to make changes of unprecedented violence, rapidity, and scope." Almost twenty years later, Zahniser wrote that our approach to wild land should be one of humility and respect: we need "areas of the earth within which we stand without our mechanisms that make us immediate masters over our environment."[23]

An exception exists: Some otherwise-prohibited tools and developments may be used if they can pass the screen of being "necessary to meet minimum requirements for the administration of the area for the purpose of this Act"[24]—that is, the permission must be for the least amount of an otherwise-prohibited use that would be necessary (not just convenient) for preserving one or more of the qualities of wilderness character. As Zahniser noted, in the determination of necessity, restraint and humility are key.

What would an undeveloped Mesa Verde backcountry or wilderness look like? Ideally, no physical or temporal developments would be necessary—or, at least, in wilderness no unnecessary development would be present. *Mesa Verde's Secret Garden* documents a variety of developments that have been proposed over time, and their potential impacts on recreational opportunities, the biophysical environment, and the resource of wildness.

4. Solitude or Primitive and Unconfined Recreation

In a wilderness, recreational opportunities occur "in an environment that is relatively free from the encumbrances of modern society, and for the experience of the benefits and inspiration derived from self-reliance, self-discovery, physical and mental challenge, and freedom from societal obligations." In a backcountry area, the level of use may be too high to reasonably expect solitude, or, conversely, unlike in a wilderness, there may be no recreational use allowed at all. A wilderness need not offer both "solitude" and "primitive and unconfined recreation" (though it may supply both), but at least one or the other must be present.

What would an outstanding opportunity for solitude or primitive and unconfined recreation in a Mesa Verde backcountry or wilderness look like? For the sake of brevity, throughout this book this quality often will be simplified to just "recreation," though that term should encompass its most inclusive concepts—not just an individual having fun, but also possibly having an experience that "re-creates" the appreciation for and affinity with the natural world and the human inhabitants that came before. Ideally, such recreational use would have no significant negative impacts on the other qualities of the wilderness resource. *Mesa Verde's Secret Garden* notes the changes over time in the recreational opportunities provided by the Park Service in the Mesa Verde backcountry as it was increasingly made off-limits.

5. Other Features of Value

A wilderness may have "important elements or 'features' that are not covered by the other four qualities." As cited earlier, the Wilderness Act specifically lists the possible presence of "ecological, geological, or other features of scientific, educational, scenic, or historical value."

Wilderness areas are not required to have any of these Other Features, but if present they are no less important than any of the four required qualities. Of course, backcountry areas may also have these features of value and, where present, are just as rigorously protected though policy or the application of other laws.

What would protecting the other features of value in a Mesa Verde backcountry or wilderness look like? In a Mesa Verde wilderness, of course, the dominant features of value are the outstanding cultural attributes and their archeological context for which the area was originally designated a National Park, and so "archeology" or "cultural resources" will be used as the shortened terms for this quality. Where different features of value are discussed, they will be specifically mentioned. In an ideal Mesa Verde wilderness, archeological resources would be protected for their scientific value, cultural patrimony, inspiration, and intrinsic value. *Mesa Verde's Secret Garden* chronicles the changes over time since the Park's designation in how various cultural resources have been valued, and how that influenced the management of the backcountry and wilderness.

It should be apparent there may be inherent conflicts when trying to preserve certain qualities.

The word "ideal" appears in each of the paragraphs discussing the five qualities of a wilderness area's character. Sometimes an ideal quality is impossible to meet. For example, no ecosystem on earth meets the criterion of being "uninfluenced by modern humans or their technology." Such an ecosystem becomes aspirational rather than an absolute necessity in wilderness, and managers strive toward this goal, cognizant of their limitations.

Sometimes the ideal of two qualities conflict. For example, look at a common instance of "gardening": one could not remove non-native species to make an area more natural without intentionally manipulating the environment, making the area less untrammeled. In cases like this, the short-term degradation of one quality is often deemed acceptable as a requirement of the verifiable long-term improvement of another quality. Such a trade-off might be considered in limiting recreation (which the Act calls to be "unconfined") to protect certain natural or other features of value, such as cultural resources. These limits reach their extreme when managing for "secrecy."

Of particular importance to Mesa Verde, there can be a tension in managing tangible cultural resources in a wilderness that is, by law, managed for seemingly contradictory purposes.

Since "untrammeled" refers to the "earth and its community of life," it may seem there is generally no conflict with preserving distinct tangible cultural remains—unless one were to try to replicate the intensive management undertaken by the Ancestral Puebloans prior to their departure from the mesa. Approaching the nexus of the "earth and its community of life" and tangible cultural remains from a different point of view may reveal that the two are inseparable. This concept is discussed further in the conclusion, "The Path Forward."

Likewise, seen one way, cultural sites generally have no impact on the natural quality except in the limited area of the site itself. But from that different point of view, changes to a site over time are every bit as natural as changes in native vegetation. This, too, is explored more in the concluding chapter.

Cultural remains frequently include structures, and their maintenance (if undertaken) may require the use of tools prohibited by The Wilderness Act, as discussed above. In this case, there is conflict with the undeveloped quality of wilderness, but since the cultural feature itself may be part of the character of the wilderness, the tradeoff between preservation and keeping the area undeveloped can be appropriate. The question then changes from whether managers *can* stop the weathering of these features, to whether they *should* do so. How do stewards of these resources decide?

Finally, recreational use is compatible with the preservation of cultural resources if that use does no undue damage. In fact, the presence of cultural meaning can significantly enhance visitor experiences.

Mesa Verde's Secret Garden looks at how the backcountry and wilderness have been managed throughout Mesa Verde's modern history by focusing on each of the qualities of wilderness character. Although separating the five qualities is useful for analysis, it does not reflect on-the-ground management reality. Management decisions often affect multiple qualities. For example, previous efforts to manipulate the Park's ecosystem by killing native porcupines made the area less natural *and* less untrammeled. Building a new trail may improve recreational opportunities, but doing so would make the area more developed and may negatively impact other features of value.

Management decisions are often obvious in relation to the quality which is most impacted—positively or negatively. However, this is not always possible, and several qualities might be affected, and managers sometimes have trouble dissecting the multiple effects. The wilderness resource is one of synergy, and impacts across multiple qualities are the rule, not the exception. Moreover, there are some decisions that affect the very idea of wilderness as a whole, rather than primarily one or two qualities. These may not be explicitly called out in the text.

Even though Mesa Verde was originally designated as a National Park because of its Other Features of Value, the archeological resources in the backcountry cannot be—nor should be—separated from the whole of the wilderness resource. This should be apparent from the discussion above and is considered in analyzing the management of the area's wilderness character over time.

Finally, while the management of Mesa Verde's backcountry is examined through the lens of the qualities of wilderness, it should not inferred that these qualities legally should have been the focus of management attention prior to designation in 1976 of the Mesa Verde Wilderness, nor even after that date in the portions of the Park not designated as Wilderness (though this may be required by NPS policy, as noted above).[25] However, even though preserving these qualities may not have been legally required, they nonetheless may be measures of good stewardship. Of course, hindsight is 20/20, and what constitutes management acknowledged as good stewardship has changed over the decades.

CHAPTER ONE

Mesa Verde National Park

The Earliest Years

1906–1916

MESA VERDE NATIONAL PARK was designated on June 29, 1906. At that time, six major national parks had been designated: Yellowstone, Yosemite, Sequoia, General Grant (in 1940, Grant would become part of Kings Canyon National Park), Mount Rainier, and Crater Lake.[1] They had been created to protect everything from vast, superlative scenery, to iconic groves of unique trees—parts of the country's natural history. Mesa Verde was different. Set aside not for sublime views or biological wonders, but instead for the cultural remains of ancient Americans, this key difference has colored management at Mesa Verde ever since.

At the same time the Mesa Verde National Park bill was being considered, and spurred in large part by the depredations in the Park briefly discussed below, the Antiquities Act was signed by President Roosevelt on June 8, 1906. It provides for presidential "proclamations" to set aside as National Monuments areas with "historic landmarks, historic and prehistoric structures, and other objects of historic or scientific interest," which would be "confined to the smallest area compatible with [their] proper care and management." It also initiates a process for the scientific "examination of ruins, the excavation of archaeological sites, and the gathering of objects of antiquity upon the lands."[2]

"Preservation from Injury or Spoliation"

Legislation was already before Congress to designate Mesa Verde a National Park, not a National Monument. The Mesa Verde designation, Public Law 59–353, directs the Secretary of the Interior to prescribe regulations for "the preservation from injury or spoliation of the ruins and other works and relics of prehistoric or primitive man within said park." Like the Antiquities Act, it also provides penalties for theft or any willful disturbance of the evidence "of an ancient civilization or other property." Any person doing so would be guilty of a crime with serious (for the day) consequences—fines up to one thousand dollars or twelve months in prison, or both, at the discretion of the judge. There is no mention of the preservation of any other resources in the Park, though the "other property" might be inferred to incorporate the protection of other resources. It wasn't until 1928 that the Park was given the explicit requirement to protect "animals and birds in the park from capture or destruction, and to prevent them from being frightened," and to preserve "natural curiosities or wonderful objects."[3]

From the very beginning, management of Mesa Verde was primarily concerned about impacts to cultural resources. National Park historian Richard Sellars pointed out similarities between the appropriation of cultural and natural resources: the unrestrained removal of thousands of cultural objects paralleled the rampant extraction of natural resources, such as timber and minerals, that was taking place throughout the West.[4]

Mesa Verde was far from immune to artifact removal, nor was it the only location where cultural remains were carted off by visitors. However, prior to the Antiquities Act and the Park's designation, such activities were not illegal. Many participants were open about their participation; John Wetherill listed almost twenty people he knew to have systematically "worked" the cultural sites throughout the Four Corners. His family originally had Mesa Verde to themselves, where almost every room in Cliff Palace "paid us for working." Many sites were so rich in archeological remains that Wetherill's brother-in-law, Charles Mason, claimed that returning to a room that had been worked two or three times previously could still yield a profit. Even fifty years later, Jesse Nusbaum, long-time Superintendent of Mesa Verde, was appalled by the amount of "archeological loot" collected by the Wetherill family, though it should be noted that Nusbaum did not paint them all with the same brush, holding John in considerably higher esteem. But at least many of the Wetherill collections found their way to the Universities of California and Pennsylvania. The "work" of countless others ended up on private mantelpieces.[5]

The more visible—and famous—sites, were hardest hit. Excavations conducted by J. Walter Fewkes for the Smithsonian Institution found rooms and middens already plundered. Park Superintendent Hans Randolph reported further damage: walls demolished to let in light, beams used for firewood, and dwellings that had been so thoroughly ransacked that he believed little material of scientific value remained.[6]

The very earliest archeological surveys in Mesa Verde, conducted by Edger Hewett, were of the cliff dwellings and paid little attention to sites on mesa tops and in canyons. They certainly are unspectacular when compared to the cliff dwellings, yet they came to be seen as essential in understanding the people who lived in Mesa Verde, even as the emphasis was—and continues to be—on the cliff dwellings. In the Park's second Annual Report, Superintendent Randolph referenced the work of excavation and repair of several named cliff dwellings. He also advocated for similar work to be undertaken at less conspicuous sites throughout the park, including what he believed were burial mounds.[7]

Vandals, too, eventually learned the "value" of the mesa-top sites. Scientific excavation of one trash mound uncovered evidence of just how thorough the early vandalism had been. Stray bones were uncovered, with adult, juvenile and baby burials jumbled together in evidence of repeated random digging.[8]

Degradation of Mesa Verde's cultural resources did not magically end in 1906. In a unique bifurcation of management responsibilities, archeological work was conducted under the authority of the Smithsonian Institution, while the Park's administration under the Department of the Interior was primarily concerned with recreational developments, relegating protection of the cultural resources somewhat less effective than if there had been unified management. At first, attempts to protect them were largely limited to placing signs informing the public about the penalty for destroying the ruins. Astonishingly, Superintendent Randolph claimed, "Since the establishment of the park there has not been found a single act of vandalism, and no unlawful excavations have been attempted." This certainly must have been a statement born out of either ignorance or—perhaps more likely—self-aggrandizement. Subsequent Superintendents would make similar claims to buff up their job approval.[9]

Superintendent Jesse Nusbaum is perhaps a more reliable judge. (Though after reading much of his work, one gets the impression Jesse was not above polishing his own reputation.) He believed that while the Nordenskiöld and the Wetherill-Mason parties undoubtedly collected some sherds along with whole pots, the only plausible explanation for the scarcity of decorated sherds is that they attracted the attention of visitors. In addition, inadvertent damage to the structures was inevitable, with visitors breaking down walls as they climbed into rooms to be ransacked.[10]

"Hotels and Creature Comforts"

At the time of designation, Mesa Verde National Park was, in essence, all backcountry. Archeological research was conducted under the purview of the Smithsonian Institution, so for the earliest Park's managers, development of access was just as important—or more so—as protection of the archeology. The initial Acting Superintendent, William Leonard, complained about the condition of the "pony trails," overgrown with juniper and piñon. In his first report to the Secretary of the Interior, only fourteen months after the Park had been designated, Acting Superintendent Charles Werner devoted four of his five pages to development (roads, trails, ladders, cabins, water sources), and only one page on the repair of the "ruins." The Park's first permanent Superintendent, Hans Randolph, made a list of recommendations in his initial report to the Secretary of the Interior. At the top of the list was building roads to the principal dwellings, since few travelers were willing to take the long, difficult horseback trip, up a steep and seemingly dangerous trail, to reach them.[11]

Access was an issue throughout the National Parks, though as early as 1912 the British Ambassador to the United States warned of overdevelopment: "There are plenty of roads for the lovers of speed and noise, without intruding on these few places where the wood nymphs and water nymphs ought to be allowed to have the landscape to themselves."[12]

In Mesa Verde, the pace of development was slow. Three years after Randolph's recommendation to the Secretary for an entrance road, it still had not been built. Acting Superintendent Richard Wright urged its construction, proclaiming that when the entrance road was finished it would "open the door, so long *locked by the fastnesses* [sic] *of the wilderness,* to the mystic and fascinating country of the cliff dwellers" (emphasis added). The next year, Superintendent Shoemaker promised that a safe and scenic entrance road "not equaled in any State in the Union" would soon be finished.[13]

Naturally, the emphasis on development was stressed by local citizens. The *Daily News* out of Denver proclaimed, "To the timid traveler the wonders of the Mesa Verde have been, under present conditions, almost inaccessible, but the establishment of the national park will change the tortuous trail to a system of good roads and in time [will provide] hotels and creature comforts."[14]

This kind of boosterism was perfectly in line with Interior Department goals, which included granting concession contracts for first-class hotels that would be built in harmony with their surroundings. But ten years after Mesa Verde's designation, due to difficult access and being so far from population centers or without direct rail connection, it was the least visited National Park.[15]

Development beyond Chapin Mesa was envisioned early in the Park's history. The cost of a road to the Wetherill Mesa sites would be prohibitive, so it was decided a horse trail from Spruce Tree House should be built. By 1915, as it became clear the automobile was going to become the Park's transportation of choice, cost became less of an impediment, and a road was proposed from the head of Navajo Canyon over to Rock Springs.[16]

However, safety and control over visitors, with an eye to protecting the cultural resources for which the Park had been designated, were always important. The first Park regulations, dated March 19, 1908, state, "Persons without archeological permits who wish to visit and enter the ruins shall in all cases be accompanied by a park ranger or other person duly authorized by the Superintendent." Peabody House, now called Square Tower House, was closed due to resource impacts and the danger inherent in the hazardous access trail that traversed a rock outcrop where visitors had to use the shallow steps carved by Ancestral Puebloans.[17]

"All Underbrush Should Be Properly Burned"

At the time (and as will be seen, for many decades after), the thought of keeping a National Park undeveloped wasn't considered, and keeping recreational opportunities primitive was not necessary. That there might be a park, or even a portion of one, left deliberately untrammeled—totally wild—was a concept even more foreign to managers at Mesa Verde, or to the people beginning to build a Park Service at the national level, than the idea of keeping it undeveloped. It was more appropriate to "garden" a park to achieve whatever natural-*appearing* landscape would be most pleasing, and in the early years management of a park's natural resources were a means to increase tourism. Managers across the country defined "natural conditions" to be the nature that they desired, and took actions including predator control and other manipulations, such as stocking fish in previously fishless waters or supplemental feeding to increase the number of "game" animals. The first Director of the National Park Service, Stephen Mather, declared the favored animals, in their "undisturbed majesty and serenity," were part of the scenery.[18]

The Chief Geographer of the United States Geological Survey, Robert Bradford Marshall—charter member of the Sierra Club and early supporter of National Parks (and not related to Wilderness Society cofounder Bob Marshall)—advanced a policy that was to haunt the National Park System for decades and indirectly impacts Mesa Verde to this day: protecting the "enormous timber resources" of the parks from fire. Most of the early acts creating the parks allowed the Secretary of the Interior to sell timber to protect or "improve" the park. "Steps should be taken toward accomplishing this cleaning up at the earliest practicable date. All underbrush and rubbish should be properly burned off."[19]

"Many Thousand Head of Cattle Could Be Pastured"

And yet, in the Mesa Verde garden, the earliest managers had a blind spot when it came to one of the most pervasive impacts to the naturalness of the area—the presence of grazing livestock. In this, they were not alone among park advocates and managers. There was widespread grazing in Yosemite and Sequoia, where herds of sheep and cattle were degrading the landscape. In fact, Chief Geographer Marshall was remembered as claiming, "A certain amount of grazing in those areas where it will not interfere with the campers' privileges is perfectly proper."[20]

At Mesa Verde, for many years prior to designation, large portions of the Park were used by local cattlemen as summer range. By the time the Park was established, Jesse Nusbaum claimed it was already over-grazed.[21] Some of these animals—cattle, sheep, and horses—were an inevitable result of the presence of privately owned lands within the Park, called "inholdings." In addition to private land held along most of the Mancos River bottom on the east boundary, there were three homesteads in the wider valley bottoms of Prater, Morefield, and Waters Canyons, named for the owners of the inholdings. These had been established before the Park was set aside and were the so-called "base properties" for controlling grazing on the adjacent public lands.

Originally, grazing was supposed to be forbidden in the Park, and animals found within the boundaries were supposed to be impounded. Park records are not clear as to whether enforcement regulations were never made final, or were simply ignored. Nevertheless, historian Ricardo Torres-Reyes estimated that from 1906 through 1911, at least 2,150 cattle and 600 to 2,400 sheep grazed each season on park lands without permit or control, and he asserted that every Superintendent prior to 1921 was an avid defender of the grazing interests.[22]

The first of the Superintendents to show just how friendly one could be to local commercial interests was Randolph. He said the law setting aside Mesa Verde was defective because it did not include the right to lease lands for coal mining and grazing. Doing so would provide important revenue for Park maintenance, since coal deposits were known in the area, and there was a demand by locals to open the area to mining.[23]

Even before a legislative "remedy" to allow grazing was enacted, Randolph installed windmills over wells on the three private holdings and put windmills over newly dug wells near the heads of East Navajo and the west fork of Little Soda Canyons. Among Randolph's shadier dealings, temporary park ranger James Frink gave the Superintendent half of his salary in exchange for grazing privileges in the park.[24]

In 1910, Congress passed the legislation that Randolph had argued for in his Annual Report the previous year. The Deficiency Appropriation Act (Public Law 61–267) included language to allow the Secretary of the Interior to grant leases and permits for or development of the resources in the Park, as long as the leases did not include any of the prehistoric sites nor inhibit public use.

This law had not resulted from the desires of local economic interests alone. Chief Geographer Marshall asserted that "many thousand head of cattle could be pastured each season in the various national parks with no resulting damage." The cattle, he argued, "would keep the trails open and eat the underbrush." Perhaps most importantly, "Such a policy would remove much of the present attitude of criticism against the Government for withdrawing these lands from use of any kind save as pleasure grounds."[25]

Superintendent Richard Wright issued the first grazing permits in Mesa Verde, as well as coal mining leases.[26] Fortunately for the Park, only one of these leases was commercially developed, the Todd Mine, and that tract was removed from the Park in 1913 by a boundary adjustment in Public Law 63–4.

It wasn't long before Park officials noticed that sheep—at Mesa Verde and elsewhere—were destroying the grasses as they ate, seeming to validate John Muir's decades-long reference to them as "hoofed locusts." By the end of 1913, the Secretary informed Superintendent Shoemaker that the sheep were to be excluded from all national parks.[27]

Cattle, however, remained, and Park administration became increasingly entwined with cattle interests. Superintendent Rickner even had a herd of his own, and apparently allowed the cattle of friends to graze for free, while using the Ancestral Puebloan structure in the Far View Sites on central Chapin Mesa known as Mummy Lake for water.[28]

"*Hamlet* with the Royal Dane Left Out"

In addition to removing the Todd Mine from the Park, Public Law 63–4 was the first of many attempts to change the boundaries of the Park to better preserve the actual ancient cliff dwellings in the area, which the original Act in 1906 missed. Virginia McClurg, one of the early promoters of designating the Park and a leader of the Cliff Dwellers Association, compared the error of the boundary "with that of a play of *Hamlet* with the royal Dane left out."[29] In 1913 the Park was extended approximately 14,520 acres to the south on what was now the western half of the Park. In supposed compensation to the Utes, from whose reservation this new extension was taken, the Act deleted roughly 10,080 acres on the Park's far west and transferred it to the Ute tribe. Originally, the 1906 designation had granted the Secretary of the Interior control over the archeology in a five-mile buffer around the designated Park. The 1913 expansion apparently obviated the need for federal control to the south, and relinquished control over the buffers to the west, north, and east. With the boundary adjustment, it was thought the Park would gain jurisdiction over the most notable and important sites, while the buffer zone, "contains no ruins of magnitude or unusual importance." Prior to the law's passage, Superintendent Randolph had proposed to enlarge the Park along the five-mile strip lying east of Mancos Canyon. Randolph's preference was ignored, only to resurface almost seventy-five years later.[30]

The unilateral taking from the Utes would create problems much earlier.

"One of Our Finest Parks"

The first National Park Conference was held in Yellowstone in September of 1911. Part of the rationale for this seminal event was to address the assertion by Secretary of the Interior Walter L. Fisher that attendance at the parks had not increased as it should have. Congressional appropriations had been paltry, he reasoned, because of indifference of the traveling public. Change in Congressional funding would only come with increased use of the parks, which in turn depended on vastly improved visitor accommodations. It was a solution which spawned a philosophy that was a major factor guiding the National Park Service for the next fifty years.[31]

Between the designation of Mesa Verde and this conference, one additional park, Glacier, had been designated by Congress. However, the Antiquities Act had been used by Presidents Roosevelt and Taft to create thirty National Monuments. Over half of these were considered natural wonders, and varied greatly in size, from Natural Bridges in Utah (originally only 120 acres) to Grand Canyon National Monument in Arizona Territory (over 800,000 acres). The cultural monuments—from prehistoric sites to early Spanish missions to a battlefield from the so-called Indian Wars of the 1870s—were, on average, much smaller (though Chaco National Monument was over 20,000 acres).[32]

At the conference, Chief Geographer Marshall, who elsewhere championed development, took exception to Mesa Verde's designation as a national park. He had visited two months prior to the conference and found "there is nothing in this park to make it of national importance save the cliff dwellings." He claimed there was no opportunity for camping and that the scenery was so unremarkable it needed no protection. His recommendation was to change Mesa Verde's status by creating a national monument out of small areas around the ruins and converting the remaining land into a national forest. It is unclear if Marshall knew most of the important cliff dwellings were on land carved out of the Ute reservation, and could have been returned.[33]

A few hours after Marshall's disparaging comments, he was rebutted by Acting Superintendent Richard Wright. Wright claimed that Mesa Verde, if properly managed, should rank among the most important of the parks, "a position which its quaint and mystic contents, its natural beauty, and its historical value fully justifies."[34]

Wright was not alone in this assessment. Not long after, Director Mather agreed:

> The natural features of the park itself are distinctively scenic, and, of course, it is remarkably unique because of its ancient buildings and relics of a past civilization. Everything about the Mesa Verde combines to make it one of our finest parks, and hence worthy of the best attention of the Federal Government.[35]

Why wasn't Mesa Verde turned into a Monument as Chief Geographer Marshall insisted was appropriate? Was Mesa Verde's archeology simply too outstanding for the "lesser" designation? Or was its elevated status secured by sublime scenic beauty? Honest appraisal makes the latter seem unlikely. Yet the archeological resources cannot be separated from their environment. Even by the end of its first decade of existence, there was already a tension at Mesa Verde National Park between managing cultural and natural resources that would define its stewardship for over one hundred years.

CHAPTER TWO

Mesa Verde and the Birth of the National Park Service

1916–1921

MESA VERDE WAS THE seventh National Park designated. By 1916, there were fifteen National Parks and eighteen National Monuments. These "earth monuments" were seen as America's way to compete with the centuries-old civilizations of Europe. America might not have a Notre Dame, but it has Yellowstone and Yosemite. At Mesa Verde, the monuments were made by humans, so perhaps this place was close to Notre Dame after all.[1]

"A Workable Mandate"

On August 25, 1916, President Woodrow Wilson signed what is known as the National Park Service Organic Act (Public Law 64–235). In designating a system of national parks, Section 1 of the law defines their purpose: "to conserve the scenery and the natural and historic objects and the wild life therein and to provide for the enjoyment of the same in such manner and by such means as will leave them unimpaired for the enjoyment of future generations."

This phrase, the so-called "dual mandate," has guided NPS management principles ever since despite its inherent ambiguities. In later years, this clause created a certain amount of conflict between conservation and use. Richard Sellars has clarified this "perpetual tension . . . between leaving the parks and monuments 'unimpaired' (which implies minimal manipulation and intrusion) versus developing them for public use and enjoyment (which often involves extensive manipulation and intrusion)." The idea that The Organic Act "sets forth an impressive, unambiguous resource preservation mandate" is a relatively recent interpretation coming out of the growing environmental awareness of the 1950s, '60s, and '70s.[2]

At the time of the Organic Act's passage, Director Stephen Mather stated that the parks would provide "the greatest good to the greatest number." Three problems are not addressed by this simple equation. First, what is to be considered "good"? Second, who would be counted and who would be left out of "the greatest number"? However, the third and most essential problem is how does one decide which takes precedence—the "good" or the "number"? It is impossible to maximize both variables. Eventually, park managers would have to decide which was more important—a decision that might vary on a case-by-case basis or over time. At the most basic level, the "dual mandate" of the Organic Act—conservation and use—requires a similar decision on which takes precedence.[3]

However, at the low visitation numbers during the first years of the Park Service, and particularly at Mesa Verde, what is now often seen as paradox was then what has been called "a workable mandate." Protecting the scenery was equivalent to protecting the "natural objects." Secretary of the Interior Franklin Lane advocated expanding park boundaries to complete their "scenic need," and Mather's assistant, Horace Albright, advocated admitting new parks to the System based on the "quality of scenic beauty required by National Park standards."[4]

At Mesa Verde, even though the fundamental purpose was the preservation of cultural resources, the Organic Act apparently expanded it to include conservation of scenery, natural objects, and wildlife. (As noted in the previous chapter, this direction was made explicit in 1928 with passage of Public Law 70–317.) This implies the fundamental dilemma that Mesa Verde managers have wrestled with ever since: How can all the cultural and natural resources in Mesa Verde be preserved unimpaired and yet enjoyed by present and future generations?

"Roads and Trails Like Switzerland's"

At first, there seemed to be little conflict between preservation and use. Recreation meant development, and the original interpretation of the 1916 law didn't change that. Director Mather was quite explicit: "Our national parks are practically lying fallow, and only await proper development to bring them into their own." In fact, there was a fear that without an adequate transportation infrastructure, the public would not support scenic preservation. He thought each of the parks should have one major road penetrating into the heart of the scenic backcountry, which would still leave large areas in a natural state that could be accessed only by trails. Robert Sterling Yard, a newspaper man turned adman for the parks and the Park Service's Chief of the Educational Division, went further than his boss: "We want our national parks developed. We want roads and trails like Switzerland's. We want hotels of all prices from lowest to highest. . . . We want good fishing. We want our wild animal life conserved and developed." The NPS administration was so intent on catering to tourists, Mather approved golf courses in Yellowstone and Yosemite. They were never built.[5]

For Mesa Verde in particular, the relative inaccessibility of the mesa was already seen as a problem. Mather's 1917 Annual Report noted that in addition to funds for excavation, "the other greater [*sic*] need of Mesa Verde was a new road for ascending the mesa." Multiple access routes were considered. Superintendent Rickner proposed a road from Spruce Tree Camp (in the vicinity of the current Park headquarters on Chapin Mesa) south to the Mancos River, and then west to connect with the road between Cortez and Shiprock, shortening the commonly used access to the area by about seventy-five miles.[6]

Opening up the wonders inside the Park was a related effort. The 1919 Superintendent's Annual Report advocated for a road down Wetherill Mesa past Rock Springs to access more of the park for tourists so they could "visit and explore all the finest ruins in the park, many of which are now beyond the reach of any but the hardiest travelers."[7]

In keeping with Mather's recommendation that parks build ten miles of trail for every mile of road, trails at Mesa Verde were being developed, too. The trail to the base of Square Tower House, which had relied on footholds carved out by the Ancestral Puebloans, was made safer by blasting a new section of trail and installing a handrail. A trail was extended from near Cliff Palace south below the mesa rim a few hundred yards to Sunset House, and another cleared around the southern end of Chapin Mesa, though Navajo, Soda, and Cliff Canyons, to Inspiration Point—far south onto the Ute lands.[8]

One of the features in the western portion of the Park to receive the greatest interest was the natural bridge below Spring House. Long recognized as the only such feature in the Park, it has a span of ninety feet and reaches twenty-five feet above the ground. It was an extremely popular destination, despite the rugged travel required to reach it. The feature proved so popular that Rickner had a trail built to Spring House from the headquarters area campground, suitable for travel by foot or saddle horse. One visitor's self-published book includes a photograph of unexcavated Spring House, extolling its virtue as an example of what undiscovered sites would look like, and calls attention to the natural bridge below. In fact, on the simple Park map accompanying the 1920 Superintendent's Annual Report, the Natural Bridge is the westernmost feature identified, and Spring House isn't shown at all.[9]

The increase and eventual ebb of recreational development and access in the Mesa Verde backcountry/wilderness is one of the major themes running through the history of the Park.

"These Animals Should Be Killed Off"

The drive toward development was coupled with a policy of manipulating the environment—gardening—to a desired condition. Section 3 of the Organic Act, parts of which are now often overlooked, permits the destruction of plants and animals (such as predators) deemed to be "detrimental to the use" of parks; allows livestock grazing when "not detrimental" to a park's primary purpose; and allows

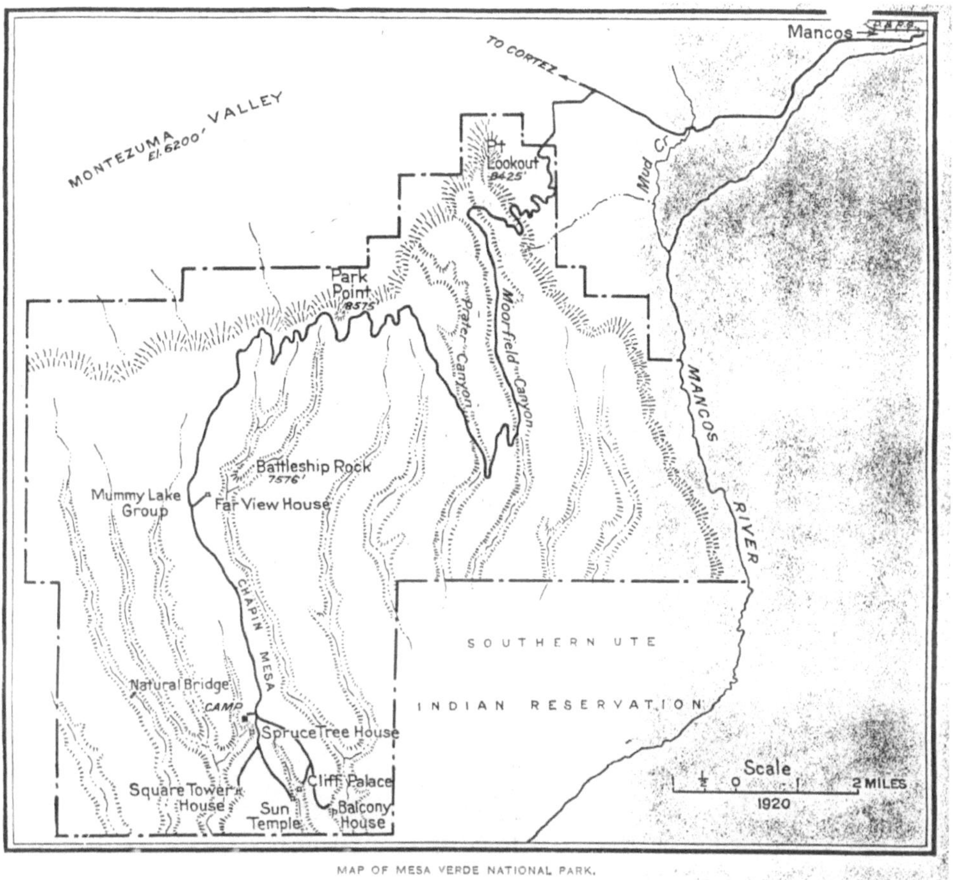

Figure 1. This 1920 map accompanying the Superintendent's Annual Report shows what were considered the major tourist attractions in Mesa Verde at the time. The "Natural Bridge" is the farthest west feature of note.

timber to be cut and sold to control insect infestations or otherwise improve the scenery.[10]

Mesa Verde Superintendent Rickner noted that "game" animals were on the increase, with deer overwintering in the Park. However, since mountain lions also were increasing in or near the park, "These animals should be killed off, for they keep the deer from increasing as they would otherwise do." In fact, it seemed the primary driver for fencing the Park was to turn it into an ideal game preserve. This would mean not only killing the predators but also introducing bison and elk in addition to the native deer and bighorn sheep, as well as growing hay to feed them in bad winter weather.[11]

Conflicting with this idea of Mesa Verde as a "game preserve" was the continuing presence of domestic cattle. In retrospect, Jesse Nusbaum said that cattle grazing had devastated the Park, and their removal would be consistent with the Organic Act's Section 3. Superintendent Rickner had followed Superintendent Randolph's lead in grazing his own animals within the Park (without fee, of course) and issued permits for an additional 1,320 head. Rickner's personal interest may explain his rather astonishing claim to the NPS Director that "There is no one feature of the drive [along the park road] that has caused so much favorable comment from tourists than the occasional glimpse of a bunch of cattle near the watering places. More photographs have been attempted of cattle seen along the drive than almost any other feature of the park." It wasn't until the next decade that permitted grazing was terminated. To be fair, the idea that cattle were a tourist attraction was held even by Aldo Leopold—at least early in his career.[12]

"A Day of Revelry in the Park"

Rickner's sketchy management, as evidenced by his relationship with cattle grazing, also seems to have pervaded his protection of Mesa Verde's cultural resources. Every year in his report to the Director, he included variations on how well order had been maintained, and that there was no vandalism or other rule violations. Yet Torres-Reyes relates the experience of a visitor who stayed at the Spruce Tree Camp for four months in 1920, while Rickner was still Superintendent: "It was the customary thing [for local area residents] to make Sunday a day of revelry in the park, with young people crawling over the walls of the repaired buildings, and willfully destroying such portions as had deteriorated and were frail. They also scratched and wrote their names everywhere." Torres-Reyes goes on to quote the visitor directly: "'I stood in the waiting room in the [Park's] hotel and saw visitors enter with their arms filled with pottery and skeletal materials, which probably were turned over to Mr. Jeep. How he disposed of them later I do not know, but I have heard rumors that they were sent out of the park to the individuals who collected them.'"[13]

The "Mr. Jeep" referenced was the son-in-law of Superintendent Rickner. Nusbaum asserted that whenever Jeep learned that Fewkes was going to excavate a ruin, he took fellow NPS employees to plunder the site before Fewkes could get to it. The looted artifacts were on exhibit in the Park museum, and Jeep claimed the collections were his personal property. Perhaps most egregious, Jeep had made an exceptional discovery in 1915—Daniels House, on the southwest side of Long Mesa, which at the time remained the park's only cliff dwelling known to remain unlooted. Jeep took from it a dozen intact corrugated jars, several stone axes, and other artifacts. They joined his stash in the museum.[14]

In 1917, Director Mather sent his assistant, Horace Albright, to Mesa Verde in order to investigate complaints that had come to the Director's attention. Albright found an administration ruled by nepotism, with Jeep excavating and selling artifacts, and with "about the same attitude toward the park that his father-in-law, the Superintendent, has."[15]

Clearly, a different kind of Superintendent was needed.

"There Is a Limit"

Rickner did, however, see something in Mesa Verde that has echoed down through the decades since his superintendency. In his Annual Report of 1918, he wrote, "Leaving the Mancos-Cortez highway, the traveler turns his back on all signs of the improvements of civilization. He steps at once into an unbroken wilderness where the road on which he is traveling is the only mark of man's handiwork."[16] Of course, the policy of development would encroach on that "unbroken wilderness" to bring the marvels of Mesa Verde to the public. To be sure, neither Rickner nor other officials in the Park Service at the time had in mind a concept of wilderness that was to be enunciated just one year later.

On December 6, 1919, a meeting took place in Denver between two Forest Service employees—a ranger from New Mexico, and a landscape architect from Colorado—that would change management of federal lands. Arthur Carhart, the landscape architect, summarized his meeting with Aldo Leopold in the "Memorandum for Mr. Leopold, District 3."

They had expressed concern over the proliferation of "man-made improvements" throughout the National Forests. While they recognized the Forest Service obligation to maximize return to the American people, they believed that a monetary equation was insufficient in the case of aesthetics. Carhart told Leopold of his recent revelation at Trapper's Lake in north central Colorado, where he had been sent to plot summer homes. The two men came to this conclusion:

> There is a limit to the number of lands of shorelines on the lakes; there is a limit to the number of lakes in existence; there is a limit to the mountainous areas of the world. And in each one of these situations there are portions of natural scenic beauty which are God-made, and the beauties of which, of a right, should be the property of all people.[17]

In this, Carhart was contradicting the proclamation of Gifford Pinchot, the first Chief of the U.S. Forest Service: "The first duty of the human race is to control the earth it lives upon," and "The first principle of conservation is development, the use of natural resources now existing on this continent for the benefit of people who live here now." Rather, it is likely Carhart was reflecting the early ecological proclamations of George Perkins Marsh, who looked at European civilization and concluded: "Man is everywhere a disturbing agent. Wherever he plants his foot, the harmonies of nature are turned to discords." Marsh, a Republican Congressman from Vermont, was far from alone in this assessment. Among the more influential Congressmen of the next generation, John F. Lacey—Republican from Iowa and champion of the Antiquities Act of 1906—was concerned about the misuse and waste of natural resources. He condemned the greed that would destroy a forest if it could be turned into money and warned that if such destruction were to continue, the earth would become "as worthless as a sucked orange."[18]

However, Leopold and Carhart had a concrete proposal: preserving some areas from human development would return a greater total value to people. Importantly, they suggested that all the preserved areas need not be scenically superlative. Contrary to the prevalent sentiment in the Park Service, it wasn't the visual attractiveness to a visitor that was paramount, but the simple opportunity to get into undeveloped country. Even simply for undeveloped country to *exist.*[19]

In January of 1921, Carhart attended the National Parks Conference and tried to convince the attendees that by using the ideas he had been working out with Leopold, the national forests could provide important recreational needs. In a response, National Park Service Director Stephen Mather argued that the national forests should not try to imitate the national parks. Mather even admitted he had personally intervened with the chairman of the House Appropriations Committee to see that Forest Service recreational development went unfunded.[20]

Mather did not succeed, and the idea of wilderness took root. It touched Mesa Verde almost two decades later and came in full force another three decades after that.

CHAPTER THREE

The Nusbaum Decade

1921–1931

DURING THE EARLY YEARS of the Park Service, many of the Superintendents were holdovers from a time when the positions were filled by a process of political patronage. Park Service Director Stephen Mather believed that many Superintendents were completely ineffectual. His assistant, Horace Albright, was blunt: these were "incompetent men appointed as politicians."[1]

Mesa Verde appeared to have one of the worst. In the autumn of 1920, after hearing alarming reports about what was going on, Mather decided to visit the Park to see for himself. Jesse Nusbaum, relating the event to Herbert Evison over forty years later, said what Mather found "was so distressing that Mr. Mather decided the only way it could be corrected was to terminate that Superintendent as soon as he could find the person who was completely qualified. . . . In other words, a very competent and broad administrator."[2]

Naturally, Nusbaum was just that administrator.

Jesse Nusbaum was born in Greeley, Colorado, in 1887. He first came to the Four Corners at the age of twenty with the Archaeological Institute of America to photograph sites in the area. Among the Mesa Verde files are several pictures of locations within what is now Canyons of the Ancients National Monument, managed by the BLM, and Hovenweep National Monument, managed by the Park Service. The Smithsonian sent him back in 1910 to survey and stabilize Mesa Verde's Balcony House—a task he undertook without training or prior experience, and with astonishing success. In earlier excavations at Mesa

Verde, Fewkes had the habit of removing artifacts without concern for site maintenance or restoration, but Nusbaum took a more responsible approach. It whetted his appetite for serious archeology, which took him to study at George Washington University and then excavate and collect for New York's Museum of the American Indian.[3]

"The Most Competent Qualified Men Available"

Colorado Senator Lawrence Phipps had intended to continue the practice of approving Park Service appointments in his state. But, according to Nusbaum, Mather told Phipps that he intended "to replace political-appointed Superintendents with the most competent qualified men available, regardless of political pressures and affiliations, as he was now doing for Mesa Verde." The way park Superintendents were selected was to be changed—not just at Mesa Verde, but throughout the Park Service. In general, Mather chose either landscape architects or engineers to be Superintendents for guiding park development. But Nusbaum was different.[4]

Designating Jesse Nusbaum as Superintendent brought together the archeology program and visitor services in a way that Mesa Verde (or any other park) had not previously experienced. It had been the Service policy not to grow its own scientific expertise, but hiring an archeologist to run Mesa Verde was an exception. The most obvious expression of this was Nusbaum's own project in 1926 to re-excavate Step House Cave on Wetherill Mesa. In addition, he worked on Moccasin Mesa (including Bone Awl House, outside the Park boundary), and several other sites on Wetherill which had been visited by Nordenskiöld and the Wetherills. Despite difficult access, he found these had been severely pot-hunted, and most of the cultural objects had been removed.[5]

He also recognized the increasing importance of mesa-top sites. Since they were not as stunning (or obvious) as the cliff dwellings, they had—for the most part—been subject to less pot-hunting. Consequently, in 1929 a team arrived from Gila Pueblo in Arizona, led by Harold S. Gladwin, to survey the mesa tops and canyon bottoms.

These less-looted sites provided Gladwin an opportunity to make representative collections of pottery to help establish a ceramic chronology, while the occasional foreign sherds would help trace Mesa Verdean trade connections in the greater Southwest.[6]

"There Was No Control Whatever"

Under Nusbaum, there was also an increased drive to protect the resources as the enabling legislation had directed. Forty years later he recalled, "The first thing I noted was that there was no control whatever for the protection and preservation of the ruins. Anybody that came into the Park could drive their car any place they wanted to go." From the time of the earliest tourists until Nusbaum stopped the practice in 1921, "visitors had the liberty of picking up whatever sherds they desired, and few failed to collect sherds."[7]

Despite these alarming statements, his first official report to the Department of the Interior stated there were "only a few minor infringements"—a statement repeated in the reports of 1922 and 1923.[8] Was Nusbaum exaggerating the problems when retelling the story years later to make himself look good? Or was he minimizing the impacts at the time to give the impression that he had everything under control? Was the truth somewhere in between? Other evidence in the Park, as well as comparisons with other areas outside Mesa Verde, suggest his alarming statements made in later years on this point were not embroidered.

"Grazing Will Be Terminated on the National Park"

Chief among Nusbaum's struggles to make the Park more natural was his ongoing effort to eliminate livestock grazing. As noted in the previous chapter, Section 3 of the Organic Act allowed grazing to continue if "not detrimental" to a park's primary purpose. While the primary purpose at Mesa Verde was the preservation of archeology, Nusbaum was appalled that the overgrazed condition he had noted when he first came to Mesa Verde in 1910 had gotten worse.[9]

The grazing operations which were of most concern had base properties (that is, land that served as the base of operations for the livestock use, usually associated with a source of water) on three inholdings. These consisted of 320 acres in Prater Canyon originally homesteaded by William F. Prater; 160 acres in Morefield Canyon homesteaded by Josiah J. Morefield; and 160 acres in Waters Canyon owned by Roy C. Waters. Nusbaum recalled telling the permittees, "I am going to propose that you reduce your cattle grazing by 20 percent over a period of five years, each year. That means that at the end of the fifth year, grazing will be terminated on the National Park." One year, Nusbaum accepted the Waters Canyon inholding rather than a grazing fee, but buying out the other two was too expensive for the federal budget; even though the grazing on the Park ended, those inholding properties remained private until the 1940s.[10]

The result from ending grazing to the Park's ecosystem astonished even Nusbaum. Bare ground became covered in grasses, marsh conditions returned to Prater Canyon, and honeysuckle came back so thick that "you had trouble driving a pick-up car into it and breaking your way through it." Importantly, he claimed, "It has been fine ever since."[11]

However, this was not the end of the pressure to commercially graze Mesa Verde. A banker from Mancos tried to get a grazing lease by saying the tall grass (a result of grazing elimination) was a fire hazard and that the Park would burn if it weren't grazed. "I resisted his every move successfully, stating that the majority of fires in the park during my regime were caused through the carelessness of stockmen and Southern Ute Indians, largely from their unextinguished campfires and live cigarette butts."[12]

Then, in 1930, while Nusbaum was on detail at the Laboratory of Anthropology in Santa Fe, his Chief Clerk, R. A. Devlin, wrote about Clarence Teague, who had just bought edgeholdings (privately owned land within a park boundary but not completely surrounded by park lands) along the Mancos River corridor on the eastern boundary of the Park. Acting on Nusbaum's authority (though without his knowledge), Devlin asked Teague if he wanted to exchange this land to the government for a grazing privilege elsewhere within the Park. Teague expressed some interest and indicated he would want to graze in the Whites Canyon section on the east side of the Park. This, Teague asserted, would not interfere with any part of the Park where tourists would possibly come. Devlin then wrote the NPS Director, relating the situation and adding that Teague would talk with his partner on the Prater Canyon inholding, Frank Stevens, to see if they wanted to exchange that land as well for a similar grazing privilege.[13]

Nusbaum was not pleased by Devlin's initiative. He immediately wrote the Director. "It has been difficult to get other grazing out of the park, and this proposition should not be accepted." He cited the improved natural conditions as justification for the permanent exclusion of grazing, not just in Mesa Verde, but throughout the entire Park System.[14]

Director Albright agreed, writing back to Devlin that he needed to call off the deal with Teague. There was no legal authority to offer this exchange, he said, and it would be "contrary to the [now] well-established policy of eliminating grazing on the park lands."[15]

Grazing was to come up again during World War II. And the idea that the eastern portion of Mesa Verde was expendable "trade-bait" would resurface in the future as well. In part, that was due to the effects of cattle along the Mancos River. Before livestock grazing there had been a "jungle of underbrush" with "hundreds of beaver skins being taken out of this region by early trappers." But "a half century of domestic stock grazing has changed the whole picture, until this land is practically worthless."[16]

"The First Elk Ever Seen"

The problem with feral livestock seems to have started during this era. Nusbaum reported that horses, burros, and cattle were often encountered and that they seemed to fear humans more than wild animals. Their populations seemed relatively stable, despite authorized attempts at capture and removal by the cattlemen as well as Utes and Navajos.[17]

Nusbaum also paid greater attention to the natural wildlife than his predecessors had. "The first elk ever seen in the park made his appearance near the head of Navajo Canyon August 15, and traveled for 2 miles in front of a Ford car." "Two small bears were noted on the park this season for the first time. Coyotes are numerous, likewise bobcats, occasionally a wolf; kit foxes, swifts [swift foxes], ring-tailed cats, porcupines, and badgers are often seen."[18]

However, natural species and processes continued to be manipulated for aesthetics. Torres-Reyes reported that it became "necessary" to initiate predator control to protect the deer from mountain lions, coyotes, and bobcats. This was common throughout the national parks at the time, justified by claiming the predators were "detrimental to the use" by the public. After all, Roger Toll, whose Superintendency at Yellowstone overlapped with Nusbaum's at Mesa Verde, had proclaimed a herd of antelope was "more valuable than a herd of coyotes," and it was ungulates, not predators, that were "the type of animal the park was for."[19]

In Nusbaum's words, "Coyotes are very plentiful notwithstanding our efforts to eradicate them." Given coyote biology—the animal increases litter size in response to population reductions—it is no wonder he was disappointed. Controlling predators became a more serious undertaking, and Nusbaum wanted the State of Colorado to send a mountain lion hunter to the park to kill a variety of predatory animals in the mistaken belief that "the game itself is the property of the State" and so it was their responsibility.[20]

Predator control was not the only form of trammeling. Three tame deer from Yosemite were brought to the park headquarters in the belief they would be more apt to stay in view for tourists than the Park's native, more wild deer.[21]

"Gardening" natural processes was not limited to animals. Among Nusbaum's recommendations was funding to cut and burn piñon trees that had been attacked by beetles. Without prompt action, he feared the piñon forests would disappear, and the Park would lose "one of [its] most attractive features." By 1929, a comprehensive forestry policy was developed that became the basis for future forestry management: protecting the park trees against fire, insects, and diseases.[22]

Perhaps the most famous interference with nature during this period was the beginning of the Park's crusade against porcupines who were killing scenic trees along the roads and at cliff dwellings. In his history of the animal in Mesa Verde, Nusbaum called it "an invasion" and blamed it on three factors: 1) overgrazing on adjacent valley range lands; 2) clearing piñon/juniper forests from farmlands north and west of Cortez; and 3) lumbering the ponderosa pine on the Dolores watershed. Whether these were legitimate causes is debatable, but Nusbaum did note the futility of attempting to control porcupine damage through limited, localized control. Nusbaum's antipathy toward the animal was even captured in an undated poem by an unattributed author (though likely a staff member) found in the Nusbaum Collection of the MEVE archives. The poem is titled "Ode to an Arboreal Pig," and creates a pseudo-Latin name for the beast: *Porkyswine nusbaumensis.*[23]

"This Long-Awaited Development"

During this decade, the Park Service continued to emphasize development to satisfy the demand they had created. In his 1918 outline of policy, Secretary Lane had indicated the Park Service should offer a "national playground system" to be made accessible "by any means practicable," and that individual parks should cooperate with tourist bureaus, automobile associations, and local chambers of commerce. This attitude no doubt informed Aldo Leopold's rant in "The River of the Mother of God": "And of all the foolish roads, the most pleasing is the one that 'opens up' some last vestige of virgin wilderness. . . . [F]rom the throats of a thousand luncheon clubs, and Chambers of Commerce, and Greater Gopher Prairie Associations rises the solemn chant 'There is No God but Gasoline and Motor is His Prophet!'"[24]

In 1922, The System's park Superintendents drafted a policy statement on development. While worrying about over-building, they believed that without facilities a park would be "merely a wilderness, not serving the purpose for which it was set aside, not benefitting the general public." Developments on Chapin Mesa were part of Nusbaum's plan for Mesa Verde, including building "a first-class hotel" to meet the demands of the public visiting Mesa Verde in ever-increasing numbers, as well as a park museum that went beyond a simple array of items on shelves such as had been displayed earlier. Other parks had museums prior to Nusbaum's at Mesa Verde, but none came up to his standards of professionalism, and he insisted a park museum was every bit a "national repository" as the Smithsonian.[25]

Recreational development was integral to the Park's long-range planning and took into account the preservation of the archeological resources that were Nusbaum's primary concern. "I planned and laid out roads . . . on the rim as much as possible, because I realized that looking at a ruin, the ruin doesn't deteriorate. People could stop there with field glasses and look, and they began finding ruins in places they had never seen . . . so it would keep them . . . looking for ruins from the rim, rather than tramping through them." Leopold criticized this attitude, too, in a 1925 article for *Sunset Magazine*: "If we think we are going to learn by cruising around the mountains in a Ford, we are largely deceiving ourselves."[26]

Nusbaum must have realized there was a valuable visitor experience besides just looking at a cliff dwelling or "tramping" through one. In his first year, signs were placed on the existing trail from Spruce Tree over to Spring House and the Natural Bridge on Long Mesa. The inclusion of the Natural Bridge gives a further measure of interest in this feature. Nusbaum projected that the trail be continued over to Rock Springs and Wetherill Mesa, opening to tourists this area of the Park with its "many fine ruins, one of which nearly rivals Cliff Palace in size and interest."[27]

The next year, three additional trails were built: one from Cliff Palace across the head of Cliff Canyon to Sun Temple; one from Square Tower House south to Casa Colorado and Inaccessible House; and a third from Square Tower House heading northwest a short distance to Little Long House.[28] Today, these trails either no longer

Figure 2. The Natural Bridge (near the center of the picture, in front of a pine tree) below Spring House (at the top of the picture). September 2020.

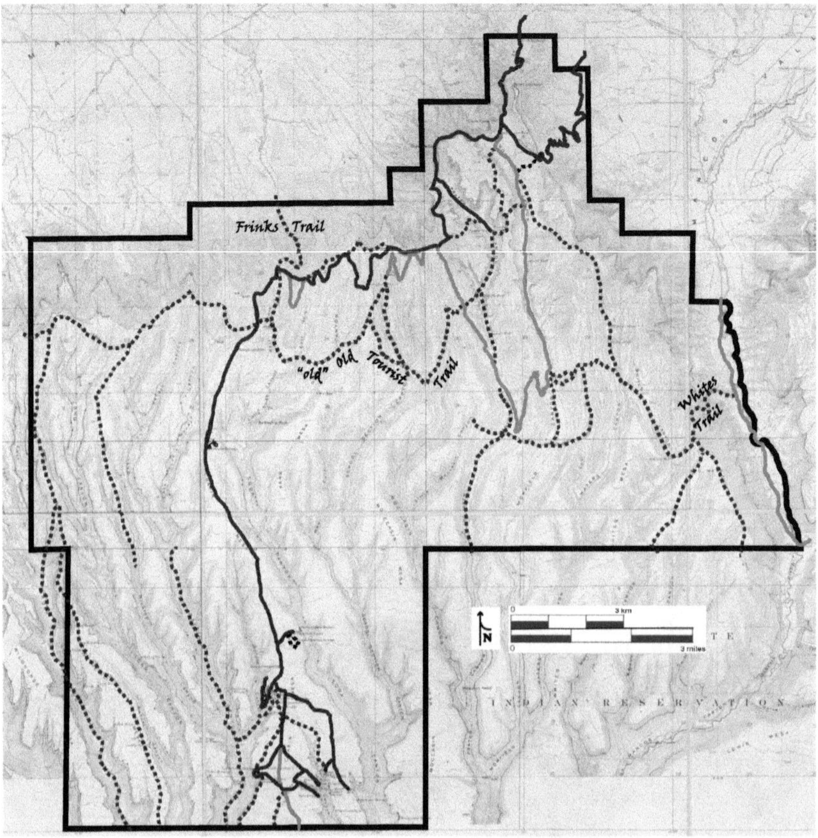

Figure 3. 1926 USGS map of Mesa Verde. For comparison purposes with later maps, the base map has been edited to show primary roads in solid black lines, secondary roads in gray lines, and trails in black dotted lines. Portions of roads and trails outside the Park boundary (thick black line) are not shown. Frinks Trail, Whites Trail, and the "old" Old Tourist Trail are added annotations. Compare with Figures 8, 9, 13, 17, and 43.

exist or are closed to the public. Casa Colorado and Inaccessible House are now—and were then—on the Ute's portion of Chapin Mesa but visiting these sites from Mesa Verde was common until the boundary was taken more seriously later in the century.[29]

By the end of 1923, the Park had finished the Rock Springs Trail from Spring House to Wetherill Mesa and "the wonderful ruins of

Mug House, Jug House, Kodak House, Long House, Double House, Ruin Sixteen, Step House, and Pinnacle Tower. [Construction included] foot trails over the cliffs to the ruins. This long-awaited development opens up the greatest group of ruins on the park outside of the Chapin Mesa group." It is unlikely that foot trails were constructed to all those sites, but this does indicate a desired level of access. In addition, both the "Soda Canyon Winter Trail" and "Navajo Canyon Trail" were widened and brushed out. Within ten years the Navajo Canyon Trail was barely passable.[30]

The 1926 USGS map of Mesa Verde indicates a trail up Navajo Canyon from the southern boundary to the junction of the West and East Forks of Navajo, but the only part of this that receives regular use now is the portion of a few hundred yards that is followed on the trail from Headquarters to Spring House. The map also shows a trail up Wickiup Canyon which by 1934 had disappeared under rockslides and tree growth. Though the route was apparently redeveloped in later years, this is evidence of how quickly routes on Mesa Verde can be lost—a fact readily apparent in the Park today. The "Soda Canyon Winter Trail" is likely the old route that heads north from the Mancos River and climbs out of Soda Canyon onto Moccasin Mesa at Bone Awl House, all south of the Mesa Verde boundary.[31]

The following year, the Superintendent again heralded the Rock Springs Trail. "This trail opens to the visitors dozens of hitherto practically unknown ruins on the west side. . . . None of the ruins on this trail have been excavated and repaired, [and] the number of ruins accessible by trail within the park has been more than doubled." He also touted for a second time the short foot trail from Square Tower House to the (unexcavated) Little Long House, as well as two wholly new trails. One of these went from Cedar Tree Tower on Chapin Mesa to a series of prehistoric dams that had been discovered during the previous season. Another trail was roughed out from Park headquarters to the elaborate pictographs on a rock formation then called "Pictograph Point." This trail—to what is now referred to as Petroglyph Point, as the glyphs are carved, not painted—was finally built twelve years later. In the ongoing theme of claiming credit for another's work, Assistant Superintendent Thomas J. Williams also cited completion of the Petroglyph Point trail under his watch.[32]

By 1927, Nusbaum reported a total of fifty miles of trail. A patrol cabin with water development had been built at Rock Springs, but Nusbaum thought no additional development on Wetherill Mesa would be necessary. "Unless we find it impossible to handle all visitors to ruins from Spruce Tree Camp [at Park headquarters], I trust that this area will forever remain a trail district."[33]

"Interesting Trips Take from a Week to 10 Days"

At this time, the pack-stock concessioner became more regulated, offering scheduled trips to several locations, some of them outside the Park: Spring House via Spruce Tree, Navajo, and Wickiup Canyons; Casa Colorado and Inaccessible House via Navajo Rim Trail; the Mouth of Long Canyon via Spruce Tree and Navajo Canyons; Mancos River via Lower Glades and Soda Canyon Tip-Off (south of the Park); Upper Navajo Canyon Ruins via Navajo Canyon Trail.[34]

The voluminous park brochure of 1930 lists all those scheduled trips, plus goes on to mention, "There are several much longer [nonscheduled] 1-day trips to more distant parts of the park area that can be taken by experienced riders only." Continuing the practice of offering trips outside the Park, the brochure offers trips to the sites in Mancos Canyon "perched on presumably inaccessible cliffs, hundreds of feet above the bed of the river" and to several named sites in the Canyon bottom, which can be "reached only by trail." For the truly adventurous, the Mesa Verde Pack & Saddle Company offered three-day rides to Rock Springs and the "Wetherill Mesa Ruins, which . . . have not been excavated or repaired. . . . Other equally interesting trips take from a week to 10 days." Presumably, the concessioner was exempt from the camping restrictions for the general public: "In order to preserve the natural scenery of the park and to provide pure water and facilities for keeping the park clean, permanent camp sites have been set apart for tourists visiting the park in their own conveyances, and no camping is permitted outside the specially designated sites."[35]

In addition to camping restrictions, rules on how a visitor could actually see the dwellings were explained—though not always in the clearest fashion. Visitors to the "ruins" had to be accompanied by a park ranger "or other person duly authorized by the superintendent." Presumably, the employees of the concessioner constituted "duly authorized" persons. But just what constituted a "ruin"? In his 1930 Annual Report, Nusbaum noted: "Under the present procedure, all the visitors to the ruins must be accompanied by ranger guides." But elsewhere in his Annual Report, the reference is to visitors being guided through "the *major* ruins." (emphasis added), and he wrote of developing more trails as "a real inducement to visitors to enjoy the more remote regions and interesting ruins of the park."[36]

In any event, the backcountry at large was open to exploration, and exploration was encouraged.

> Visitors who view the Mesa Verde from the automobile roads gain but an inkling of the weird beauty and surprises which this area holds for the more adventurous. Trail or hiking trips along the rim rock bordering the deep canyons lead to spectacular ruins not seen from any of the roads. The large Wetherill Mesa and Rock Springs groups of ruins can be reached only by trail. Likewise the ruins of the Mancos Canyon . . . are reached only by trail. Each turn and twist of the trail reveals entrancing vistas of rugged canyons, sheer cliffs, great caves, hidden ruins, distant mountains, tree-covered mesas, or open glades.[37]

For Nusbaum, "Particularly gratifying is the fact that park visitors now realize that the scenic aspects of the area are equally as important to visitors as the ruins themselves and that greater emphasis should be given this feature of the park area."[38]

Nusbaum had manipulated the ecosystem of Mesa Verde during his tenure, and he certainly did not want this garden to be a secret.

CHAPTER FOUR

The Great Depression and the CCC

1931–1942

THE GREAT DEPRESSION STARTED in October 1929. At first, rural America was spared from the worst effects of this calamity, and the National Parks fared surprisingly well. System-wide appropriations were up in 1930 by over three million dollars, and in 1931 appropriations doubled. Gifts to buy inholdings topped one million dollars. Nationwide, visitation remained stable. At Mesa Verde, visitation increased—up 15 percent in 1930 and another 7 percent in 1931—and among the developments, sufficient money was in the budget to enlarge the museum.[1]

"A Party Can Spend Several Days Profitably"

Trails that had been started in the 1920s were upgraded. Spring House, not yet excavated, was accessible on foot or by horse, and was one of the most popular destinations in the Park that could not be reached by automobile. The trail needed improvement; it was enlarged to four feet wide and grades reduced to a maximum of 15 percent, making it easier for horse travel, for people to walk side-by-side, and to facilitate the use of a ten-horsepower tractor to oil and maintain the route. The result was beautiful as well as functional, with attractive retaining and head walls constructed by a skilled Navajo construction crew. A more primitive trail continued on to provide access to Long Canyon and Wetherill Mesa. "The distance is short enough so that a party can make the trip in one day or, on

Figure 4. A skilled Navajo crew built this trail with exceptional stonework ca. 1930. Compare with Figures 6 and 12. October 2020.

account of the richness of material, a party can spend several days profitably in the territory opened up by this new piece of trail."[2]

The *Mesa Verde Notes* of July 1931 promoted horse trails throughout the Park, which "wind over a large part of the mesa rim and through most of the major canyons, offering both short and long rides in practically any direction one wishes to go" and singled out in detail the route to Spring House and the Natural Bridge, calling the formation "a thing uncommon; no one should miss seeing it."[3]

In August 1932, the young wild lands vagabond and would-be artist Everett Ruess visited Mesa Verde. He complained to his diary that he couldn't see the dwellings on his own but had to go in an auto caravan with a ranger. Having traveled to Mesa Verde by horse and foot, Ruess cadged rides with tourists on the interpreter-led tours and was sufficiently impressed to create what David Roberts, who chronicled Ruess's travels, called "one of his best blockprints": Square Tower House from the common viewpoint on the Chapin Mesa rim.[4]

Despite the constraints Ruess found at first, somehow he was able

Figure 5. Everett Ruess leaning out of a window at the west end of Long House, August 1932. Photographer unknown.

to make a four-day excursion to Wetherill Mesa, and Roberts related that he spent his nights in a ranger cabin. Presumably, this must have been the cabin at Rock Springs, and Rusho, an earlier chronicler of Ruess's travels, says the young man's diary indicated he was in the company of a park ranger. Ruess visited many of the sites on Wetherill; Roberts repeated them, editorializing, "The entries read like a laundry list of ruins knocked off: 'On to Kodak House.' 'Jug House ruin.' 'Over to No. 11. Couldn't get in.'" This diary entry implies Ruess had entered these other sites. Roberts continued, "Occasionally, Everett elaborates: 'Went to No. 16. Upper terrace well preserved—fine doors. Skeleton ex. preserved. Fondled skull.'" Among the photographs in *Finding Everett Ruess* is one of the young man jauntily thrusting his torso out of the second-story window of what the picture's caption refers to as "probably in Mesa Verde." It is obviously the tower at the west end of Long House. Someone else must have been present to take Ruess's picture. Was this his ranger friend? Whoever it was must have used his own camera, as Ruess's was ruined when his horse slipped into the Mancos River a few days before he entered the Park. It is not known how the photograph came to be in his family's possession, but it seems unlikely that Ruess's adventures on Wetherill Mesa were unique.

"The Country Must Be Accessible and Available"

Jesse Nusbaum had stepped down as Mesa Verde's Superintendent in 1931 to become director of the Laboratory of Anthropology in Santa Fe, New Mexico. In 1932, the new MEVE Superintendent, C. Marshall Finnan, developed a six-year program for park projects. Among them:

> Rock Springs trail (5 mi): The west side of the park contains some of the finest, most extensive and best preserved of the unexcavated cliff dwellings in the entire area. The entire western portion of the park will be kept in a natural and primitive state, so the construction of automobile roads is not contemplated. However, the country must be accessible and available to those visitors desiring to inspect and study the ruins of the area. . . . We now have a splendid trail from headquarters to Spring House Ruin. . . . The trail proposed . . . will extend from the terminus of the present trail to the Rock Springs cabin.[5]

Two years later, the next Superintendent, Ernest P. Leavitt, made a similar pitch for public access to encourage more tourists to see Spring House and beyond. To entice visitors, he recommended developing a stop for water and lunch at Rock Springs, so they would be refreshed before seeing the Wetherill Mesa sites.[6]

However, two years after that, another memo written on behalf of the NPS Deputy Chief Architect to the Director stated: "There is already a low standard trail in this location. As any relocation of this trail is apt to cause a bad scar, it is proposed that approval be withheld on this project until the location can be further studied."[7]

In the end, it is not clear exactly when the trail from Spring House to Rock Springs was developed to the high level it finally attained, nor who was responsible for which stages of development. What is clear is the desire by Mesa Verde management across several Park administrations to facilitate foot and horse access to Long and Wetherill Mesas.

"Splendid Trails Lead in All Directions"

Then the Great Depression became more severe. By 1932, across the Park System, budgets were cut. Attendance dropped. At Mesa Verde, visitation was down over ten percent—the greatest decline since the automobile facilitated access to the Park. Given the financial constraints as the Depression deepened, how could the Park possibly accomplish any of its planned developments?[8]

The answer came on March 31, 1933, with the passage of the Emergency Conservation Work (E.C.W.) Act, which created what came to be known as the Civilian Conservation Corps (CCC), designed to relieve the problems associated with widespread unemployment by developing "useful public works." These included protecting forested lands from fires, insects and diseases, and the construction and maintenance of trails and fire roads. This was a gift of labor for the National Park Service. The men would be housed, clothed, and fed, receive medical care and a small allowance—all at no cost to the parks—to be directed at projects already the preferences of park managers.[9]

The young men employed through that Act provided Mesa Verde with a no-cost workforce bigger than at any time before or since. It was the perfect opportunity for seriously gardening nature to improve the Park's scenery.

The first enrollees in the CCC (also frequently referred to as

"ECW boys") arrived at Mesa Verde on May 27, 1933. By the time the last enrollee left the Park in early 1942, between 3,000 and 4,000 "CCCers" had worked for six-month shifts in the Park. Most of their construction projects were directed in the developed "front country," much of it still visible today: many of the paths and buildings in the headquarters area; the Park Point fire lookout; the old campground and campfire arena near Park headquarters on the edge of Spruce Canyon; and some of the furniture and the famous dioramas formerly on display in the Chapin Mesa Museum. Thousands of "man-days" were expended on the labor-intensive and meticulous landscaping of the entrance road, as well as trying to maintain the troublesome Knife Edge section.[10]

Some recreational development was planned for what would then have been considered backcountry. The trail to Painted Kiva House, below the east rim of Chapin Mesa near Cedar Tree Tower, was reworked to change it from a trail for what was termed "active people," to one more suited to the average visitor. Trails to Casa Colorado and Pool Canyon (south of the Park boundary on Chapin Mesa) were improved to provide a circle trip "for short horseback rides, or for a tramp for those so inclined." The eastern portion of the Park was seen as a possible region for horse use, with trails from Morefield to Weaver Canyon and down the East Rim to the Mancos River, which would "prolong the stay of many a visitor who would otherwise remain just long enough to view the cliff dwellings."[11]

It appears much of the development was dual-purpose. Trails for patrols and fire suppression were necessary "and in certain areas can be used as horse-back trails for tourists; a cistern [should be constructed at Rock Springs and] made available to trail parties." A trail was planned from the draw near the quarry (see the map on page vii) over Park and Moccasin Mesas connecting with existing trails on the east side, and one built west of Far View House leading down into Navajo Canyon so the concessioner's horses could have access to additional grazing. The local CCC newsletter, *The Cliff Dweller*, reported this trail would also make it possible "for the tourist to enjoy the wonders there without having to fight his way down into the canyon."[12]

Figures 6 and 7. The trail constructed by the CCC from nearby Far View Sites down into Navajo Canyon (above, June 1935, National Park Service), has stood the test of time (below, October 2020). Compare with Figures 4 and 12.

There is some evidence that trails for conservation purposes were funded more easily than Public Works Physical Improvement Projects. This may have given impetus to officially describing trail projects as multipurpose: for "fire protection and police patrols, and for use of park visitors." "We wish to brush out a number of the old Ute Indian trails [for] fire suppression and patrol work. . . . These trails would also be of great value in tourist work, [allowing] the possibility of seeing new and previously inaccessible ruins." In addition, the language of the E.C.W. project proposals differed between horse trails described as being built for "fire and protective patrols," and truck trails built "for use of fire and administrative patrols *only*" (emphasis added).[13]

The Park brochures of the mid-to-late 1930s emphasized recreational opportunities, the 1935 version repeating the text found in the 1930 brochure cited above.[14]

The 1937 pamphlet was even more detailed on possibilities for the vacationer. Sites specifically mentioned included this enticement: "Such great ruins as Spring House, Long House, Kodak House, Jug House, Mug House, and Step House, as well as all of the ruins in the more remote canyons, can be reached by trail only." Horseback trips were offered: "Splendid trails lead in all directions. Large, unexcavated ruins, magnificent canyons and mesas off the beaten path unfold the charm of this primitive region. Rates are very reasonable." Foot travel, too, was encouraged. "Hikes to any section of the park can be arranged for with the park naturalist. If sufficient numbers enroll for such hikes, a naturalist guide will be provided. Do not venture away from the headquarters area unless accompanied by a guide or after first having secured permission from a duly authorized park officer. In making these trips it is important that the hiker prepare himself with proper footwear, as the trails are very precipitous in places."[15]

In other words, get permission, and the Park is yours to explore. In preserving Mesa Verde, the Park balanced the opportunity for discovery with a new restriction: it was now explicitly illegal to enter a cliff dwelling "unless accompanied by National Park Service employees."[16]

"The Most Disastrous Forest Fire"

Resource management emphasis shifted with the fires of 1934. The Wickiup Point Fire started July 11 and burned 287 acres. It was followed a week later by the more severe Wildhorse Fire that burned 4,318 acres, though much of it outside the Park. It was (somewhat hyperbolically) referred to by Chief Ranger Crouch as "the most disastrous forest fire in the history of the region." By the end of the month, NPS Acting Associate Director Hillory Tolson reported having received notification from Superintendent Leavitt that the Park was going to request E.C.W. funding for the construction of lookouts and truck trails for fire suppression. Tolson pushed back, dismissing the request as the product of someone "unfamiliar with normal conditions" and not recognizing that the fires were simply the product of unusual circumstances. He claimed "the record of recent years has shown that the normal danger of large fires to be very light" if caught quickly. He concluded that it would be ill-advised to build truck trails because of one bad fire year.[17]

In return, the Chief Ranger argued that if suppression was to be quick, as Tolson had wanted, the Park had too many remote sections that could not be reached without construction of these requested routes. Crouch asked which would be preferable: "an eight-foot scar across the landscape in two directions, or an area of 4500 acres which has been burned so badly that it is doubtful if anything will grow naturally in it during a generation?" His knowledge of fire impacts is suspect, but he concluded: "It is apparent to all concerned that Mesa Verde has not been patrolled in the past as it should have been [due to] the almost total lack of means of getting into the outlying areas of the park."[18]

Tolson was mistaken in his Mesa Verde fire history. Though the 1934 fires may have been the first major burns since the Park was designated, Park Service Associate Forester L. F. Cook noted at the time there was strong evidence of large fires in the past: the many charred stumps and large areas of oak and brush. Cook's letter to the NPS Chief Forester went on to enumerate the hardships of fighting fires on Mesa Verde: the difficulty in travel due to the topography (mesas separated by deep canyons), lack of water, and high winds during summer. He believed these physical constraints were compounded by issues outside the Park boundaries, accusing the Utes of being "notoriously careless with fire, and . . . very prone to set fires for supposedly improving their range."[19]

Cook was insistent that the truck trails be closed to the public since he felt the use by visitors would increase the risk of fire in the area. Jesse Nusbaum, however, had a different perspective, writing from his office in Santa Fe that motorized access by tourists would not necessarily be a fire risk, but would be a risk to the cultural resources. While Nusbaum advocated for access by hikers and horse, automobile tourists appeared to be entirely different.[20]

In the end, truck trails were proposed for the unnamed mesa west of Chapin Mesa, down Park Mesa, and as an extension of the Morefield Canyon truck trail to the east. The proposed road on Park Mesa was never built.[21]

The previously proposed trail from the quarry over Park and Moccasin Mesas was now a top priority. It would efficiently provide access to the canyon bottoms, even if truck trails were built down each mesa, and was necessary since any fire in those areas might quickly threaten the developments on Chapin Mesa.[22]

The Superintendent's Annual Report summarized the Park's position: "What happened on Wickiup and Wildhorse Mesas could easily happen on any other mesa in this region. If this fire had been on Chapin Mesa, our park would have been ruined. [We need] lookout towers, truck trails, and fire trails by which men and equipment can be quickly moved from park headquarters to the various sections of the park where fires originate." As part of fire suppression planning, the NPS Engineer looked at alternatives for what the Park had identified as its top priority trail, connecting Chapin and Moccasin Mesas: one over Park Mesa, and one around its southern end. The route over the mesa was recommended, even though more difficult to construct, because of its shorter length and greater fire protection for Park Mesa.[23]

However, the fundamental question remained as to whether any of these truck and horse trails were in the best interest of the Park. The antidevelopment sentiment was captured by the Acting Chief Assistant of the Washington Office's Wildlife Division in a memo to the Associate Director:

> It has also been expressed numerous times by members of the Service who have spent any length of time in the mesa that one of the chief elements of its charm is in its undeveloped primitive character. . . . It is my sincere belief that of all of the parks in the entire system, Mesa Verde could best afford to be without additional truck trails and lookouts, and that, on the other hand, this is the one park where such elements . . . would be most destructive of park values.[24]

Nevertheless, the Park administration continued to push for greater fire protection, focusing on routes made accessible to trucks. The Assistant Engineer from the Service's San Francisco office noted, "There is considerable lack of interest in horse trails just now. After more important matters are settled, they can be taken up." In mid-1936, the E.C.W. Work Program Outline included proposed improvement of a truck trail across the North Rim and down Wetherill Mesa to Rock Springs, and another continuing down Morefield Canyon and over to Whites Canyon. Authority to work on the West Side Truck Trail to Wetherill Mesa was finally given in 1940 and, consistent with the use of other truck trails, it was to be used only for Park administration.[25]

"Nature Goes to Extremes if Left Alone"

Road construction may have been delayed over concerns about excessive development, but the direction the Park was taking was unmistakable. As was consistent throughout most of federal land management at the time, fires were not seen as an agent of natural ecological change, but as a threat to the values for which the area was established. Torres-Reyes reported that from 1939 to 1969, the last year prior to his writing, Mesa Verde firefighters extinguished 200 fires. However, as early as 1935 biologist Adolph Murie not only opposed the total suppression of most fires across the entire National Park System, he objected to frequent post-fire "salvage logging" as destroying natural habitat. His views were opposed by Lawrence Cook, head of forestry in the western parks: "Nature goes to extremes if left alone." Humans had already modified nature, hence "compensatory management" was required. Cook had the last word. The garden needed to be tended.[26]

The gardening of Mesa Verde increased in varied ways. Manipulation of natural species and processes had been undertaken from the Park's earliest days, but now there was a workforce enabling managers to do so on a grand scale. Now it might be possible to control not only fire, but other natural processes, and the ample labor supplied by the CCC was perfect tool.

The first recorded CCC work project at Mesa Verde was controlling tent caterpillars in June of 1933. "Over a period of seven days, my crew of eleven men gathered and burned 9,398 caterpillar tents, an average of 122 tents per man per day. This enormous number of tents, which represented approximately 500,000 caterpillars, were taken from only a small area [along the entrance road]." *The Cliff Dweller* boasted, "The value of [eradicating pests] is not obviously apparent, but future generations will appreciate the fact that the work was done, preserving the natural beauty of the park for their enjoyment."[27]

Bark beetles, too, were seen as degrading the Park's aesthetics. Trees infected with the *Ips* beetle were removed so visitors would see the Park's forest in what the Superintendent at the time called "as nearly a natural, untouched condition as possible."[28]

The war on porcupines continued: a Park survey found damage to piñon and ponderosa pines was reaching "alarming proportions." The Park estimated that porcupines killed ten times as many trees as were killed by bark beetles, and a "porcupine crew" of CCC enrollees went out at night with flashlights to shoot them.[29]

Undesirable plants—both native and exotic—were targeted for elimination, including poison ivy along trails and Russian thistle and other exotic weeds along roads.[30]

Introducing or augmenting species or resources believed to be insufficient at the Park became feasible, too. Chief among these was the ponderosa pine, whose decline was blamed on dry years leading to poor seed production, and the ever-present porcupine menace. It became the NPS policy to prevent the ponderosa from disappearing at Mesa Verde. In a valiant attempt at gardening, the Acting Chief Ranger proposed planting 15,000 three-year-old seedlings on "barren slopes," claiming it could be done in two weeks by a crew of fifty men. One thousand ponderosas were planted along the North Rim as a trial to see if survival rates warranted further plantings in the future.[31]

After the fires of 1934, planting greatly increased. E. P. Meinecke, a forest pathologist from the USDA, advised that "A very large area had dropped in park value to nothing, and it would take many years before it could be lifted out of a stale, sheer ugliness. The forest itself would not come back for centuries." Some biologists disagreed with that assessment and suggested that nature be allowed to "take its course" since the plants that would reestablish on their own would form an early successional stage valuable for wildlife. This ecological view did not prevail. Between 1935 and the end of 1941, 238,190 piñon and juniper seedlings were planted, primarily on the burned area of the 1934 fire. Survival was negligible, but the Park went ahead with additional test plots, trying to figure out what method of reforestation would improve their results.[32]

At the same time, until the trees took hold, the area was sown with native plants. There was concern that not enough native seed could be obtained, so any deficiency would be made up by sowing wheat—out of sight of tourists. In the end, 160 acres of wheat were planted on Wetherill Mesa, but the plants did poorly.[33]

Gardening went beyond controlling undesirable species and manipulating vegetation. There were plans to develop eight ponds for fish and wildlife by building dams to store rain and floodwater.

They were to be built in Morefield, School Section, and Navajo Canyons, which would make keeping them filled easier and were great locations "for the benefit of tourist observation." It was optimistically estimated that to build these eight dams would take two months for a crew of twenty men. In August, construction started on the first of these in Morefield Canyon in the vicinity of the current sewage ponds. The crew built a dam approximately eighty feet long, twenty feet wide, and ten feet high. Brush was cleared; badger and prairie dog holes were filled. "Great interest and enthusiasm on this project was shown by both foremen and boys." It took about a month to complete the first dam.[34]

Soon after the completion of this first dam, the whole project came under criticism, and in the end only one of these developments was built. The criticism was not because the Park would be supplying an artificial water source and unnaturally trammeling the area. After all, the area was managed as a garden, not a wild place. The criticism was one of practicality, as it appeared that the dams would not hold water except for short periods immediately following rains. Supplemental water remained desirable—the question was how to deliver it. The Superintendent decided he wanted "seven wells developed, and windmills put up, as I feel that this is the only sure source of continuing water supply."[35]

Even George Meléndez Wright, the great wildlife biologist of the early years of the Park Service, wrote in favor of manipulating the biophysical environment of Mesa Verde: planting ponderosa pines to benefit the turkeys which he thought should be reintroduced, as should bighorn sheep. On the other hand, he thought porcupine "control" should occur only if "necessary." He favored developing water sources for wildlife—though he was opposed to predator control. Wright argued that "Mesa Verde National Park needs the natural faunal picture to supplement the archeological story presented. The wildlife of the Mesa at the time of the cliff dwellers was as much a part of their civilization as the artifacts and buildings. Without the wildlife there could have been no Mesa Verde culture. . . . Mountain sheep, deer, all the fur bearers, turkeys, grouse, and all the other forms of native wildlife of the Mesa should be there today. We have not yet begun to realize the wildlife possibilities of this park."[36]

"A Book of Facts Without an Index"

While the enrollees in the CCC provided the labor to develop the Park and trammel Nature, there was some thought that they might also be engaged in assisting with archeological projects, as was the case at other parks. The 1934 fires exposed many previously unknown sites, supporting the belief that the vast cultural richness of Mesa Verde was far from being known. No complete survey of the Park had been made, and the total number of "ruins" was a matter of speculation, though it had become obvious that mesa-top sites must far outnumber cliff dwellings. But lack of funding during the Depression years had greatly slowed necessary research. In 1935, Park Naturalist Paul Franke suggested using CCC recruits as the labor to conduct a Park-wide comprehensive archeological survey that would focus on these less obvious buildings. He was distressed to realize that, now knowing of their existence, the data on the mesa-top sites were fragmentary and scattered, "like a book of facts without an index."[37]

Franke's 1935 survey project never happened, but his plans were used years later when a survey was eventually funded. (In addition, he advocated for the necessity for conducting a rapid survey soon after an area burned. Following the Park's next major fire in 1959, archeologists were sent into the area to record the exposed ruins.) Whether the CCC recruits would have been appropriate for the task is questionable, though at least one worker reported he did such work. By 1938, Mesa Verde's Junior Park Naturalist noted that the "CCC boys" were damaging Spring House with digging in kivas and removing several of the large pieces of corrugated pottery. Archeological work was not included in Nusbaum's 1938 list of projects for the CCC.[38]

In short, archeological research had taken a backseat to development and manipulations facilitated by the abundant free labor and subsidized budgets.

"Adam and Eve Were Expelled from Their Garden of Eden"

There remains to be introduced one important advancement from this decade.

On January 21, 1935, 1,700 miles east of Mesa Verde, a group of wilderness advocates met to form The Wilderness Society "for the purpose of fighting off invasion of the wilderness and of stimulating . . . an appreciation of its multiform emotional, intellectual, and scientific values." In many ways, it was a rejection of urbanization of America as an unqualified good. Benton MacKaye, one of the founders and "father" of the Appalachian Trail, wrote: "The modern metropolis . . . depends on tentacles rather than on roots." They chose Robert Sterling Yard as their first president. Yard was a former NPS employee (the first Chief of the Educational Division), who had turned away from his earlier boosterism for road development (see chapter 2) and had been a founder of the National Parks Association.[39]

Jesse Nusbaum, who returned to Mesa Verde as Superintendent for a second time in 1936, could not have helped but be familiar with some of Yard's writings, perhaps including the "Summons to Save the Wilderness," appearing in the first issue of The Wilderness Society's magazine, *The Living Wilderness.* Yard had criticized the "popular craze and administrative fashion" of the NPS in building "all the highways possible everywhere," thereby having "decimated" the "primitive." He concluded, "The fashion is to barber and manicure wild America as smartly as the modern girl. . . . Wilderness is a natural resource having the same basic relationship to man's ultimate thought and culture as coal, timber, and other physical resources have to his material needs." The founders of The Wilderness Society believed wilderness was "a human necessity, not a luxury." Importantly, Yard followed up on Carhart and Leopold's idea that wilderness did not have to be scenic.[40]

In 1938, Nusbaum addressed the American Planning and Civic Association's Conference on National Parks in Washington, DC. His remarks, titled "Wilderness Aspects of National Parks," were reprinted in *Mesa Verde Notes.* He picked up on Yard's "popular craze" and maintained no one could have predicted the problems created by the rapid spread, volume, and speed of automobile traffic. Moreover, demands for vehicle access threatened the preservation ideals of the Service. What was needed was an immediate survey of undeveloped park land, and the establishment of wilderness areas which would be closed to visitors' automobiles. He went further:

> I cannot overemphasize the desirability of not opening up more of park areas to motorized travel. . . . The inherent desire of humankind to tarry, relax and seek new inspiration in areas of surpassing natural beauty and charm has been markedly lessened by the tempo of modern life. . . . [Man] superficially views the passing panorama of scenic splendor at maximum allowable speeds, his tempo for rest, relaxation and wilderness enjoyment being geared apparently to the speed of his car.[41]

This realization is striking when compared with Nusbaum's 1962 interview with Evison, noted above, where he talked of his rationale for placing roads on the rim of the Mesa Verde canyons during his first stint as Superintendent. Then, additional roads were seen as an appropriate diversion of visitors who consequently would not need to visit one of the cliff dwellings they had just seen from their car. He likely thought that somehow offering a substitute—if inferior—experience was justifiable because it would satisfy many visitors without taxing the wide variety of resources present.

But even in 1938, Nusbaum noted that the problem was more than automobiles. Recognizing the trend that the Wilderness Act of 1964 would later simply refer to in Section 2(a) as "growing mechanization," he wrote: "From [humanity's] primitive beginnings . . . we have progressively perfected [tools for] damaging [wilderness] character. Each oncoming generation expands and refines the instruments of potential wilderness destruction. It, therefore, becomes increasingly imperative that we aggressively strengthen the safeguards to wilderness preservation."[42]

Nusbaum also saw that wilderness preservation was not solely about preserving recreational experiences, but of protecting "natural elements," and he weighed in on the appropriate role of the National Parks in preserving wilderness as the only areas recognized for this purpose, adding, "The perpetuation and preservation, unimpaired, of wilderness values of national parks continue as its most potent ideals and functional objectives."[43]

Ironically, less than twenty years later when just such a law to preserve wilderness values was introduced in Congress, the Park Service strongly opposed being included. Details of this opposition are discussed in chapter 6.

Speaking explicitly about Mesa Verde, Nusbaum said, "Since road development has been restricted to a single entrance highway traversing the North Rim and to Chapin Mesa . . . [the Park] remains largely a wilderness of precipitous canyons and intervening mesa lands, enhanced by revealed and undisclosed human history."[44]

One of the most telling of Nusbaum's observations on the preservation of wilderness character can be found in this statement on the dangers of modernity:

> [We will not] expel humankind from publicly owned primitive wilderness areas as Adam and Eve were expelled from their Garden of Eden, but we can prescribe primitive modes of travel and use, [hoping that] will definitely restrict the extent of further impairment.[45]

Yet "expelling" people from their Garden is exactly what happened in Mesa Verde over the coming decades.

"Physical Development of Mesa Verde Has Far Outrun the Scientific Study"

By the end of 1941, stewardship of Mesa Verde National Park had settled into a predictable pattern.

Acting Superintendent Thomas Williams included in a Master Plan the following proposed actions in summarizing the Park's management: killing porcupines where trees have "a high aesthetic value"; revegetating areas that have been affected by "unnatural causes [such as] the forest fire." Approximately one million transplanted trees were deemed necessary since natural reproduction was almost nonexistent. He spent five pages on "Tree Insect Pest Control," including the native species *Ips* beetle, oak looper, and tent caterpillar.[46]

Six pages were devoted to "Forest Fire Control." Some of his writing concerned fire origins. He debunked the myth that most of the fires in the past had been due to the Utes burning trees and shrubs to increase forage and noted that Mesa Verde had twenty-nine fires in the past six years—lightning strikes that were all subject to immediate suppression. He noted that smoking was prohibited while on horseback and that the Navajo workers were permitted to take sweat baths only after reporting the location. To help control fires he was still advocating for a trail across Park Mesa, continuing "to Prater Canyon [*sic*] where it would join the east side truck trail."[47]

Williams summarized Mesa Verde management direction: "The duties of the [fire] protective organization are to prevent any new fire scars, to control every fire before the heat of the second day, and to hold each fire to its original acreage, that the beauties of the Mesa Verde shall remain unimpaired for future generations. Therefore, the detection, suppression and prevention of forest and brush fires will take precedence for the ranger force and other employees over all other work in the Park except the preservation of human life."[48]

Control over natural processes was paramount.

As for visitor services, Williams wrote that foot and horse trails went everywhere in the Park, thereby allowing visitors access to the "lesser-known reaches" of Mesa Verde. The Park's trail system map at the time is of insufficient quality to be reproduced here, but it indicates existing or planned trails down Rock Canyon, Wetherill Mesa, Long Mesa, Wickiup Mesa, and Navajo Canyon in the west. In the east, routes are shown from the East Rim down to the Mancos River south of the Park boundary via Big Mesa and the Wheeler Trail, and down the Whites Trail route off the side of the East Rim within the

Park. An existing route was shown from the Truck Trail north through Waters Canyon to Morefield, and one planned from the high point on that route returning to the Truck Trail along the East Rim. In addition to the Old Tourist Trail from Far View east to Morefield Canyon, the planned trail across lower Park Mesa meeting that existing trail on Prater Ridge was indicated.[49]

Trails and truck routes for fire protection and boundary patrol were planned throughout the park. However, expanded visitor amenities were planned to be limited to trails, rather than further development for motor vehicles. Roads for the public would be limited to Chapin Mesa. More roads were unnecessary given the trail system and would complicate patrolling.[50]

Archeological research had taken a hit during the financial devastation of the Depression. According to A. R. Kelly, Chief of the Washington Office Archeologic Sites Division, "It is generally conceded that the physical development of Mesa Verde has far outrun the scientific study which appears desirable in so large and outstanding an archeological area."[51]

Then, on December 7, 1941, everything changed.

CHAPTER FIVE

World War II and the Recovery

1942–1956

AMERICA'S INVOLVEMENT WORLD WAR II had four major impacts on the National Park Service. First, the men in the CCC left to go to war or were hired by war-related industries, followed soon after by many of the park employees. Full-time staff in the Park Service dropped from over 5,100 at the start of the war to approximately 1,500 by its end. Second, there was a drive to open up parks for the resources needed to fuel the war effort. Only eight days after the declaration of war on Japan, Secretary Harold Ickes went so far as to direct the Interior agencies for a "full mobilization of the Nation's natural resources for war . . . to serve our military," with the important caveat of "saving all that we can of such resources for future generations." Third, budgets were immediately slashed by 50 percent to prosecute the war and were further reduced by a total of almost 80 percent by war's end. The Service was merely hoping to keep the system intact, ready for a return to "normal" after the war was over—whenever that would be. And finally, attendance plummeted as gasoline rationing made travel increasingly difficult. Across the System, attendance decreased by over 70 percent in two years. At Mesa Verde, the drop was greater, due to the Park's remoteness and the difficulty of travel. Visitation dropped by 70 percent in 1942 and another 65 percent in 1943. On the other hand, this remoteness, along with the Park's relatively small size and the nature of its resources, also contributed to insulating the Park from military uses occurring at many other units in the System: as training areas or bombing ranges, camps for prisoners of war, or convalescent centers for American servicemen.[1]

"A System of Self-Guided Trails"

With the loss of personnel at Mesa Verde—even the entrance station wasn't staffed after 1942—the Park instituted what it referred to as "a system of self-guided trails," though they appear to have been more closely akin to short trails accessing mesa-top sites and wayside exhibits. These allowed for the presentation of interpretive information without the presence of a scarce ranger-naturalist. Ranger-led tours to the major ruins continued at specific times. Apparently, "visitors welcomed the greater freedom permitted by this self-guiding system." Demand for saddle-horse trips was so low that this service was entirely suspended during the 1944 and 1945 seasons.[2]

"Control of Wildlife"

Visitor services may have been reduced, but somehow the remaining employees managed to continue gardening the Park. Nusbaum returned for his third tour of duty, this time as Acting Superintendent for John McLaughlin. He continued his personal vendetta against the porcupine and gave orders that they should be shot if found along park roads or in the vicinity of major ruins. He eventually was stymied, despite his constant complaining that the continuing damage was "severe and parkwide, alarming, and deplorable," because he was informed by the Regional Office that authority for any "control of wildlife" would have to be secured from the Secretary of the Interior. He did, however, continue to direct the use of blowtorches to kill tent caterpillars on bitterbrush, and had "splendid success" using chemicals to kill "noxious perennials." The target plants included poison ivy and Mexican whorled milkweed, both native species.[3]

Not all manipulations made the Park so obviously less natural. Merriam turkeys were reintroduced as part of an effort to duplicate the significant components of Mesa Verde's prehistoric community of wildlife as recommended by George Wright in the previous decade. At first, the transplant was deemed successful without any control of predators or supplemental feeding. Within a few years, however, the ten birds that had been released at the head of Prater Canyon either did not survive or drifted out of the park.[4]

Plans were made to reintroduce another member of the prehistoric ecosystem, Rocky Mountain bighorn sheep. Evidence at the time indicated that they had lived on the mesa until the late 1890s, when they were extirpated as a result of indiscriminate hunting by settlers moving into the area. In early 1946, fourteen bighorns were released at Park headquarters. A year later, tracks were seen along the Mancos River, and seven animals were counted. They seemed to have left the Park to take up residence on Weber Mountain but would come to the Mancos for water.[5]

"A Little of the Worst of It"

The greatest threat to the Park during these war years came from a familiar source.

During the First World War, livestock interests had tried to get National Parks open to grazing. This was not an issue at Mesa Verde, as grazing was already permitted there at the time, and it wasn't until the 1920s that Nusbaum had closed grazing in most of the Park. However, early during World War II, sheep- and cattlemen again tried to force access to parks across the System as part of the wartime effort to increase meat production, and Mesa Verde was in the crosshairs. The Mancos Cattlemen's Association petitioned the Secretary of the Interior to open the Park for grazing 1,000 head of cattle in both the spring and fall, claiming doing so was needed due to the depleted condition of forage in the nearby National Forest summer range and the seasonal limitations necessary at higher elevations. Most of all, they claimed it would be their patriotic response to the war effort.[6]

A hearing by a subcommittee of the Senate Committee on

Public Lands and Surveys was held in November 1942, in Grand Junction, Colorado, under the chairmanship of Senator Pat McCarran of Nevada. After ten years in the Senate, McCarran was on his way to become arguably the most influential member of Congress, apparently a vindictive bigot who would "accept no organization that he didn't hold in his hand." In particular, he "didn't like the parks or any federal reservations," but rarely did public officials so blatantly express their biases as he did in Grand Junction: "I want to be entirely fair in the matter, and at the same time I want to give the Park Service a little of the worst of it." The portion of the hearing that concerned grazing in Mesa Verde featured opposing testimonies from Acting Superintendent Nusbaum, with Ira Kelly, representing the Cattlemen's Association. Kelly spoke first, claiming that in the past "the entire 77,000 acres" of the Park had been grazed—increasing the size of the Park by 50 percent. While acknowledging the Park had been set aside to protect the prehistoric ruins, he claimed there were only "two ruins on the Mesa it would be possible for cattle to get into." He also admitted that while the request was originally for the duration of the war, "we see no reason why it should not be continued."[7]

Included in the transcript of the hearing is a letter from NPS Director Drury. He estimated the area suitable for grazing in Mesa Verde to be 9,000 acres (a number that must have come from Nusbaum) and included an important declaration. Despite Secretary Ickes's offer at the beginning of the war to open up the parks, "None of the national parks . . . have been opened to additional grazing, and since the start of the war we have received only one request for the opening of one unit of the National Park System."[8]

In response to Kelly and under critical questioning from McCarran, Nusbaum disputed Kelly's figures on the number of ruins susceptible to damage from cattle, went through a lengthy history of grazing management in the Park, presenting photographs of how the vegetation at select locations had rebounded after having no cattle grazing for fifteen years. Of particular importance was his quoting current Secretary of the Interior Ickes: "'It is a part of sound national park policy, not to permit grazing by domestic livestock in areas set aside for recreation.'"[9]

Nusbaum's recollection of how the hearing ended deviates from the congressional record. This may well have been the result of the intervening years, as in 1962 he told his interviewer, Herb Evison, that the hearing was "in the late 30s"—it was in 1942—and that "I was on the stand for about two hours-and-a-half"[10]—it actually takes a little over an hour to read aloud the entire Mesa Verde section of the hearing, including the testimonies of Ira Kelly and Chief Ranger Faha, in addition to Nusbaum's. Moreover, in the interview with Evison, Nusbaum said that when he finished, McCarran said in response, "We have here a superintendent of an area who is doing everything he can to protect and preserve his area. It was a condition in which overgrazing caused it to go downhill so far. He has restored it. The purpose of it is a national park and to protect and preserve that vegetation. For that reason, I cannot entertain any hope of the cattlemen to reenter Mesa Verde."[11]

However, the hearing record shows quite a different summation. In the transcript, Nusbaum said he merely relied on his superiors' directives. Park Service Director Newton Drury had ordered that throughout the System commercial uses—mining, logging, and grazing—might possibly be permitted for the war effort, but only as a last resort and with the further stipulation that the activities had to be mitigated to reduce their impacts. Nusbaum explained to the Senator: "I can only operate under the policy." To which McCarran immediately responded that he was not criticizing Nusbaum for standing by Park Service policy. He was telling Nusbaum what the result of that policy would be: ignoring "the voice of the people" would turn the public so strongly against the Service that no more National Parks would be designated.[12]

McCarran then told Kelly that grazing wouldn't be allowed in any one park that would be contrary to a System-wide policy—unless there was an outstanding reason for the exception. McCarran looked hard for sufficient justification, drawing an analogy with the parks in the National Capital Region, beautiful, but now covered with temporary buildings housing war facilities. Washington "has had to give way from the aesthetic to the essential." He went on to suggest that at a time of rationing beef, aesthetic sensibilities may have to take a temporary backseat.[13]

Ultimately, try as he might, McCarran could find no "outstanding reason," though shortly after the war his position was supported from a surprising source. Citing a visit to the Park by Forest Service range management experts, NPS Associate Regional Director E. T. Scoyen noted that the "protected range in a national park has some value. . . . This is a form of use we should not only encourage but promote at every opportunity." Mesa Verde Superintendent Rose had a different interpretation of the Forest Service visit: "Forest Service officials stated that . . . we have probably the finest example of range *recovery* . . . to be found in the entire Southwest" (emphasis added).[14]

Scoyen's opinion did not prevail, and commercial livestock grazing never returned to Mesa Verde. Long before his 1962 interview, Nusbaum made sure that credit was given where he thought it due:

> I literally sweat blood here for many years finally to terminate grazing on Mesa Verde National Park lands by 1928, successfully defending that termination . . . against banking, grazing, and political pressures opposing me. . . . Beginning April 1942, I again sweat blood in building up defenses for Mesa Verde and the Service generally, defending in mid-November before the Senate Subcommittee, the principle of no grazing in national parks.[15]

"We Have No Money; We Can Do No Harm"

The decade after the war brought challenges throughout the National Park System. When the CCC program disappeared and many parks' personnel were drafted, maintenance and other aspects of park management suffered. But with the drastic drop in visitation occurring at the same time, the losses to the workforce were not particularly noticeable. After the war, however, attendance skyrocketed, more than doubling between 1945 and 1947, and the Park Service was ill-prepared. Initially, national budgets were directed into the Cold War, then the "hot" war in Korea; FDR's New Deal was all but forgotten.[16]

The budgetary shortfalls led to antiquated facilities so poorly maintained that they became a disgrace. In 1948, Director Newton B. Drury, by nature conservative and less interested in development than many other directors—before or since—reassured a group of Sierra Club leaders who were concerned about the Service's development plans: "We have no money; we can do no harm." Things deteriorated so badly that by 1953, Bernard DeVoto wrote a blistering essay in *Harper's Magazine* entitled "Let's Close the National Parks." He called out the deplorable conditions of the parks, their facilities, and the living arrangements of employees. His solution, drastic and only semi-hyperbolic: "The national park system must be temporarily reduced to a size for which Congress is willing to pay [and] held in trust for a more enlightened future."[17]

It would take until 1956 for a new initiative to change the dynamics of Service funding.

"Along the Rim Rocks and into the Canyons"

After the War, the infrastructure at Mesa Verde was stretched, but perhaps not nearly as badly as some other parks due, possibly, to inherently lower levels of use. However, visitation vastly increased postwar. Fewer than 13,000 visitors came in 1945. Within the next ten years, visitation increased more than ten-fold. Park staff kept up as best they could.[18]

In 1946, anticipating the increased interest in automobile touring of the parks, the AAA wrote to Mesa Verde to approve or correct their proposed wording for a brochure. The submitted text largely parroted the Park's brochure. The copy in the Mesa Verde files has notes added in Nusbaum's green ink, showing no corrections in the following: "Hikes to any section of the park may be arranged for with the park naturalist. Horseback trips may be taken along the splendid trails that lead in all directions, to large, unexcavated ruins, magnificent canyons and mesas off the beaten paths. . . . All prices include guide service. Pack Trips may be arranged (two days' notice is required). [Price] includes a guide-cook and all equipment." Nusbaum's response contained other corrections, but none concerning hiking or horseback trips.[19]

That year, a visitor self-published his account of visiting Mesa Verde.[20] He noted that the scenery and wildlife at Mesa Verde could never compete with other national parks, but he raved about the opportunities to visit the Park's cultural sites. These opportunities went far beyond the guided tours and the developed sites on Chapin Mesa at the Far View Group and Cedar Tree Tower, and he wrote, "numerous others may be visited by horsepower or legpower." He hiked three-and-a-half miles through woodland between the main highway and the head of Wickiup Canyon. He then quoted the Park's booklet: "'All of the mesa tops and wider canyon bottoms are dotted with ruins. . . . Countless hundreds of these ruins are to be seen.'"

The Park's brochure at the time emphasized that "One rule is rigidly enforced: <u>Visitors are not permitted to enter any cliff dwelling unless accompanied by a ranger</u>" (emphasis in the original). However, "This rule does not apply to ruins on the mesa tops, and visitors who have registered at the park entrance checking station or the museum may visit these ruins any time during daylight hours." (This phrasing is hereinafter referred to as "prohibition boilerplate.") Overnight stays were not allowed without being on a horseback trip with the Park's outfitter. Otherwise, the Park was open—as long as the visitor had a permit—to see "spectacular views and ruins" not otherwise visible, while the brochure noted that "Most trails require strenuous exertion on the part of the hiker."[21]

In 1949, landscape architects in the Regional Office created a map of existing and proposed trails in Mesa Verde. While it contains some obvious errors, it shows an extensive system, promoted in the Park brochures of the time.[22]

The short 1952 brochure contains the prohibition boilerplate. Camping was restricted to the free campground, but the brochure included "Trails for Hikers—Opportunity to visit many unusual

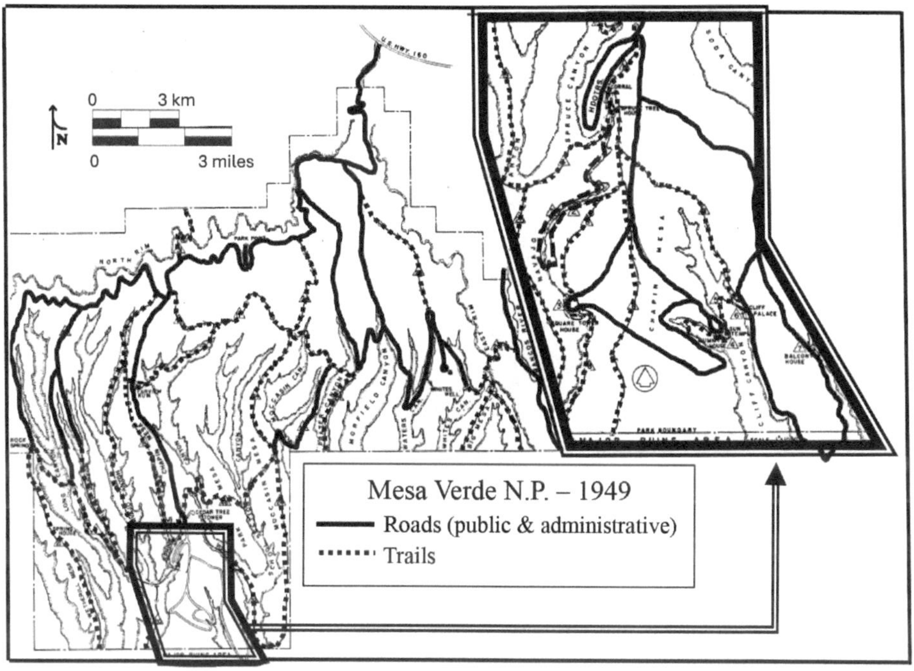

Figure 8. 1949 map of roads and trails. The original did not differentiate between public and administrative roads. In the inset at right, it shows routes near "the main ruins area" not detailed on the main map. For visual clarity, the inset of routes near the Park headquarters has been omitted, as has the planned (but not yet built) tunnel though Prater Ridge. Compare with Figures 3, 9, 13, 17, and 43.

points and outlying ruins is offered to those interested in hiking. Information and necessary permits may be obtained at the museum."[23]

The 1954 brochure is more detailed. The prohibition boilerplate was featured under "Preservation of the Ruins." In "What to Do in the Mesa Verde," wording was used similar to the 1947 brochure: "Hiking and horseback trips along the rim rocks and into the canyons lead to spectacular views and ruins that cannot be seen from the roads. Most trails require strenuous exertion, and because of the danger of getting lost, hikers must obtain maps and a permit before

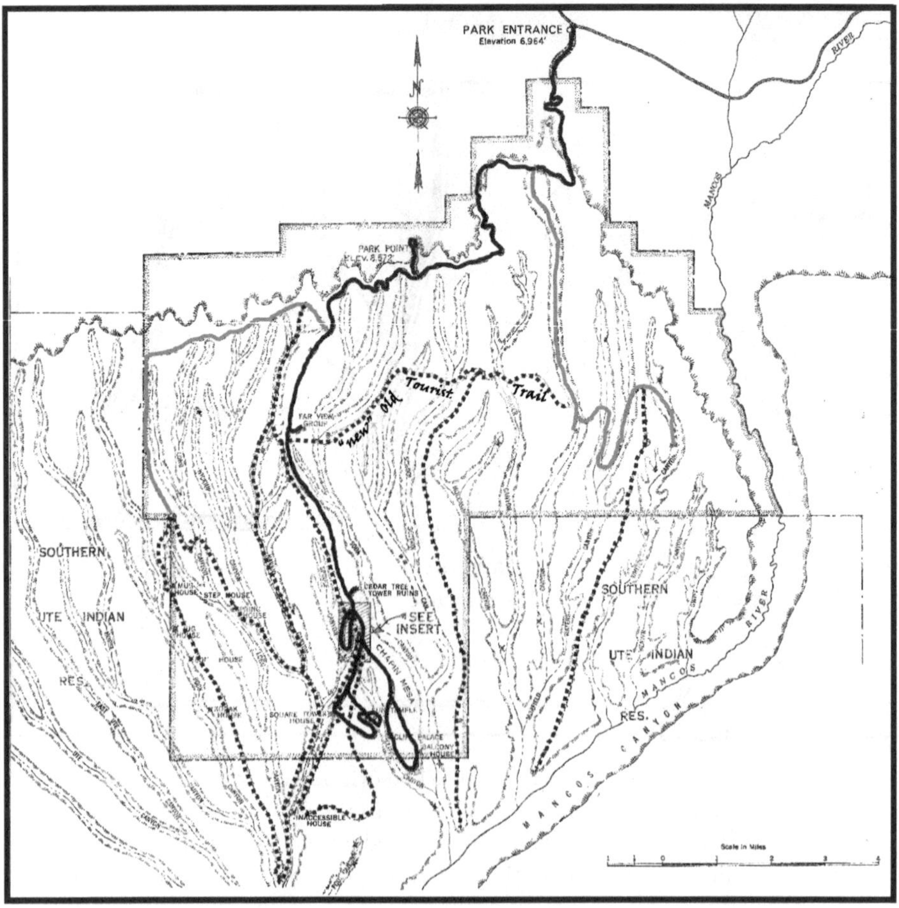

Figure 9. This map was page 8 in the Park's brochure given to all visitors (MEVE-PB 1954). For visual clarity, the insert referenced on the map has been omitted. The "new" Old Tourist Trail is an added annotation. Compare with Figures 3, 8, 13, 17, and 43.

leaving the headquarters area" (emphasis in original). "Saddle horses, especially trained for mountain trails, may be rented by the hour or day, and reasonable rates include the service of a guide. . . . A guide-cook accompanies each [overnight pack trip] party, and each person is furnished with a saddle horse, bed, canteen, slicker, and food."[24]

The public map in the 1954 brochure shows numerous trail opportunities for the visitor. East/west trails include the Old Tourist

Trail from Morefield Canyon to Far View Group and the trail from Headquarters on Chapin Mesa past Spring House and over to Rock Springs. North/south trails are shown on Whites Mesa from the "Emergency Truck Trail" to the promontory overlooking the Mancos Canyon (about five miles into the Ute lands); from the Old Tourist Trail down Moccasin Mesa (also to a point on Ute land overlooking the Mancos); a loop from Square Tower House south onto the Ute lands to Inaccessible House and returning through The Glades; a trail the entire length of Navajo Canyon, with a side trail down from Far View Group; and a route from Rock Springs, south on Wetherill Mesa, far past the Park boundary all the way to the Mancos River.

The Park's planning document at the time clearly stated, "Foot trails are provided between all points of interest. Horse trails are of length and diversity sufficient for both day and overnight trips. No major additions or deletions are contemplated." In fact, all the visitor amenities at the Park seemed complete: "No major or minor developed areas other than those existing are contemplated."[25]

"Irreplaceable Assets"

With the increase in visitation and access available throughout the Park, vandalism was a great concern—perhaps not as serious as in the early days, but a problem to be addressed nonetheless, and some violations boggle the mind. A husband and wife were caught in the act, and their admission included these excuses: "The only place we dug was up in the cave." "I was interested in fossils. I took some with a permit at Petrified [Forest National Park] and turned them in. Would have done the same here." "I don't think we did anything that the park wouldn't have done anyway."[26]

Part of the problem with the theft of antiquities stems from its tacit acceptability in that era, which the Park tried to counteract. On at least one Cortez High School field trip, "A special effort was made to discourage pot-hunting, an activity in which many of the students indulge." Nusbaum was quoted in an article in *Empire Magazine* that "Only recently over in northern Arizona, an archeologist returned to an important ruin to complete his excavation and found a group of 22 Boy Scouts digging up souvenirs. The scoutmaster, ignorant of the law, was chagrinned to learn that he was supervising his young charges in an act of criminal vandalism." More astonishing, "Local chambers of commerce and tourist lodges which advertise that there are lovely ruins nearby just waiting to be excavated. Some of them even provide guides and digging tools."[27]

However, Nusbaum believed that deliberate acts of vandalism were really quite rare. Instead, he felt the danger to the Park's archeological resources was due to either carelessness or—even more usual—simple overuse. It was these latter concerns that gave rise to routing visitors past, rather than through, Cliff Palace. He concisely summarized the concern and mandate for places like Mesa Verde:

> The vegetative cover and the wildlife of an area are renewable resources; and given proper protection, they tend to perpetuate themselves. Conversely, archeological ruins are irreplaceable assets; they represent the home and structures of vanished peoples. Therefore, such ruins must be given the highest form of protection from avoidable damage and deterioration.[28]

By the mid-1950s the primary alcove sites at Mesa Verde were protected by ranger guides, where they were inspected and cleaned each week during the heavy-use season. Extensive access to the backcountry was allowed through a permitting process.[29]

"Preservation, In All Its Naturalness"

Another major change at Mesa Verde in the postwar years was an initial consideration of holistic management, as was happening elsewhere in the System—and as George Wright had tried to convince the Service to consider some twenty years earlier.

The draft introduction of the Park's 1952 Master Plan Development Outline says that although the Park was designated as a significant archeological area, the biology and geology (and scenery) of

Mesa Verde were also of interest and importance. The primary guideline for development was to make the sites available to the public to the greatest extent while preserving the Park's significant values. The Master Plan had set out its own dual mandate for Mesa Verde. First, maximum protection for the Park's archeological resources "so that these priceless assets may be perpetuated unimpaired." Second, "preservation, in all its naturalness without material impairment, of the unique canyon-mesa scene and atmosphere which enfold these ruins."[30]

The draft was revised by the Regional Office. In his rebuttal comments to the RO's revision, Superintendent Rose emphasized the dual principles. He noted that the biophysical components mentioned in the Statement of Significance were dropped by the Regional Office when the plan got to the section listing General Themes of Development. Rose recognized that archeology had to be the Park's priority, but questioned a plan that stated the biophysical components were significant, yet the archeological components were the only ones the Park was going to seriously address. He stressed the importance of the whole Park: "Archeology, at the virtual exclusion of all else, has been emphasized for many years in Mesa Verde. Yet, biology, geology, and scenery combine with archeology in giving the area significance as a national park."[31]

"The View Is Almost Repulsive"

Some things didn't change in the years immediately after World War II. Don Watson had been away for four years in the service and returned as the Park Naturalist to find Mesa Verde "in splendid condition except for the unbelievable porcupine damage to the piñon trees." He was amazed that this "totally destructive animal" was still not eradicated. He found the setting of Cliff Palace particularly in peril: "The talus slopes are so littered with dead and dying trees that the view is almost repulsive." Consequently, porcupines found in the immediate vicinity of the alcove sites were killed. Some other habitual thinking persevered into the mid-50s, with complaints about the threat to the Park's aesthetics due to the severe defoliation of serviceberry, mountain mahogany, and bitterbrush by tent caterpillars.[32]

Under the Master Plan being developed, fire management continued to sacrifice natural conditions to the protection of both the archeological resources and perceived aesthetics. Fires were extinguished as soon as possible, in part because it was feared major fires would so deplete the soil that "complete natural recovery within a reasonable time cannot be expected." Detection and immediate suppression of fires—regardless of cause—was to take precedence over all activities except protecting human life.[33]

On the other hand, as noted above, the increasing awareness of the ecological condition of the Park as a whole manifested itself in several ways.

In 1952 the Park started fleshing out a checklist of species present: 39 mammals, 153 birds, and 16 reptiles were included in a total of 365 species. New species were constantly added.[34]

There was continued interest in reestablishing the complete complement of species present with the Ancestral Puebloans. The initial turkey reintroduction failed, so the Park tried again, releasing six birds near the Chapin Mesa campground, and they appeared to stay in that area. Beaver activity was noted in the Mancos River along the east boundary of the park. The bighorn sheep transplants of 1946 were deemed a success, and by 1954 were proclaimed to have become permanently established.[35]

There was a concomitant concern over invasive cheatgrass, believed to be a result from the over-grazing prior to 1928. It was feared that the exotic invasion would be exacerbated by ongoing trespass grazing by sheep, cattle, and horses in the canyon bottoms along the southern and eastern boundaries. However, in his comments on this section of the Master Plan, the Superintendent took exception to the amount of livestock trespass implied in the document. He admitted that along the southern boundary there had been considerable trespass of Ute Indian stock in past years but that it had been practically eliminated. He believed the impacts to the Park's natural vegetation may have been more due to the ongoing grazing of the concessioner's horses. While grazing in Navajo and Wickiup Canyons had been discontinued, the concessioner's stock still had about 2,400 acres of pasture elsewhere in the Park. The twenty to thirty head usually spent April and May in Morefield or Prater Canyon, then were moved onto Chapin Mesa for the outfitting season (where they received supplemental feed), and then back down into the canyons for September and October—and sometimes even as late as December, dependent on the weather.[36]

"All Archeological Features Are Included"

Scientific collection of artifacts continued. Sherds from over 600 sites on lower Chapin Mesa were placed in numbered boxes stored in the museum's basement. This amounted to a huge collection: one site yielded "several thousand sherds and a large number of bone and stone artifacts."[37]

But collection was no longer an end in itself. As part of this emphasis on the holistic management of Mesa Verde, systematic archeological research was increased starting in 1951. A complete survey was expected to take many years, resulting in a comprehensive picture of the prehistoric occupation of the Mesa Verde. The overarching directive: "all archeological features are included"—cliff dwellings, mesa-top and canyon-head sites, dams, reservoirs, shrines, and rock art. Sherd collections would be made, all pertinent data recorded, each site marked and mapped. On Chapin Mesa south of the Park headquarters alone, in an area of approximately four square miles, 472 sites were surveyed.[38]

"A Worthy Expansion"

One of the most important aspects of managing Mesa Verde as a whole was the ongoing effort to expand the Park southward through more of the Ute Mountain Ute lands to the Mancos River. The Park had long directed visitors to cliff dwellings on the Reservation, but now it became more important for Mesa Verde to actually include those lands within the Park.

There were biological, administrative, and archeological reasons for this expansion. The Mancos made a logical southern boundary for wildlife management, the Mesa Verde cuesta comprising an entire biological unit. In addition, there were livestock watering tanks near the park boundary, with numerous signs of domestic sheep grazing within the Park. George Wright had long argued that the wildlife present at the time of the cliff dwellers were integral to what the Park should be preserving and that it would be impossible with the present boundary. Torres-Reyes quoted Superintendent McLaughlin, writing to the Director in 1941, that if the Park couldn't get the rest of the mesa, an extensive—and expensive—fence was needed. "We cannot expect the cattle to know when they are in the park and apparently the Indians cannot or will not comprehend what the boundary means." It was obvious McLaughlin had little regard for the Utes and wanted to get the remainder of the mesa.[39]

But the primary reason for the expansion was the perception by the Park Service that the sites to their south were either so magnificent or so abused that they should fall under the management of the NPS. As early as 1939, Park Naturalist Watson commented on the condition of the ruins in Mancos Canyon south of the Park. Many sites had been pot-hunted, and the new road up the canyon had unnecessarily damaged many others. Besides, the Park thinking went, the Ute land adjoining the Park was of little commercial value, while holding additional excellent examples of the prehistoric culture found within the Park. Extending to the south had been discussed for years as "a worthy expansion," but had been stymied by the inability to solve the problem of a land exchange with the Utes.[40]

What to offer in exchange? In 1941, Nusbaum had suggested that the Park might offer a small strip of "remote park lands" situated below the rim of the East Escarpment down to the Mancos River.[41]

After the war, the drive for expansion resurfaced. Chief Ranger Jack Wade resurrected the Wright/McLaughlin/Nusbaum trade idea in a memo that not only recognized how much an exchange would be of value to the Park, but to the Utes as well. He argued that the Mancos Canyon on the east side of the Park did not contain any special features that made it important to the Park. In fact, he believed it would be preferable to move the boundary west to the mesa top and exclude the entire Canyon. Doing so would eliminate the management difficulties in this area, so remote from the remainder of the Park. Plus, it would create good will among the inhabitants of the local region—always a boon. He then went one step further, suggesting to exchange not only the Mancos Canyon lands, but also the adjacent mesa-top lands which contained "no features of importance." In return, the Park would get an equal tract of land on Chapin Mesa south of the present park boundaries. This, he claimed, would be good for both the Utes and the Park Service. The Utes needed grazing areas—there is little water on Chapin Mesa, but there was plenty in the east. Wade believed the Utes could run as many cattle on a few acres in Whites Canyon as on the same number of sections on southern Chapin Mesa. In the exchange, Mesa Verde would get Inaccessible House and all the cliff dwellings in Pool Canyon.[42]

The Director wrote Assistant Secretary of the Interior Lewis in support of the exchange. The NPS had, for many years, thought the Mancos River should be the southern boundary of the Park in order to protect outstanding and unique cliff dwellings and other archeological resources.[43]

Nothing happened.

The reasons for the failed negotiations were, in part, rooted in longstanding grievances, which Park officials blamed on the Utes. "Bill Gunn grazed cattle and horses on Ute Reservation lands south of the Park Boundary, and within bordering park lands, whenever possible. . . . Old Nathan [Wing] constantly claimed hereditary rights to graze his stock in the Wickiup Canyon region. . . . [He] and Bill Gunn were Ute leaders in claiming that the Park gypped the Utes under the land exchange negotiations of 1911." Rather than give up lands, the Utes wanted to have part of the present park.[44]

Another problem arose. The southern boundary of the Park had been improperly surveyed, and the Cliff Palace/Balcony House loop trespassed onto the Ute lands at Soda Point. Ute Mountain Ute Council Chairman Jack House came to the Park with other tribal members to discuss the possibility of the Park's proposed land exchange—the Ute lands on Chapin Mesa for the Park lands to the east. Then the tribal representatives bought up their land on Soda Point, indicating that it "could well be developed with a lodge, lunch stand, or similar business." Sensing the strength of their bargaining position, the Utes offered to include Soda Point in the exchange as well, and perhaps some of Moccasin Mesa. To Superintendent Carlson, the exchange sounded favorable.[45]

Seeing an opening by way of the Park's eagerness, it appears the Utes drove a harder bargain in late 1954, saying they wanted all the land east of Soda Canyon but were willing to settle for less, in three parallel transactions: 1) the East Escarpment in exchange for the Ute land on Soda Point; 2) land east of Morefield Canyon to the East Escarpment, in exchange for Ute land on Chapin and Moccasin Mesas (with the NPS retaining the right to survey, study, and excavate any ruins on the land going to the Utes); and 3) Prater Mesa and, in the west, the canyon bottom in the east fork of Rock Canyon and the part of Wildhorse Mesa in the Park, in exchange for the Ute portions of Wetherill and Long Mesas south of the current boundary.[46]

To make sure they weren't giving up too much, the Park conducted the first systematic survey of the surface sites in the Whites Canyon/Big Mesa area on the east side of the park and compared them with surface sites on Chapin Mesa. The Park archeologist concluded the area which would be received had greater archeological values than the area which would be given up.[47]

In 1955, Superintendent Carlson wrote an extensive report on the advantages to trading most of the current Park east of Morefield Canyon in exchange for the prime mesa tops, incorporating many of the ideas of his predecessors.[48]

From an administrative point of view, the exchange would make for more logical management blocks: the Park already had most of Chapin, Moccasin, and Wetherill Mesas—and would get the

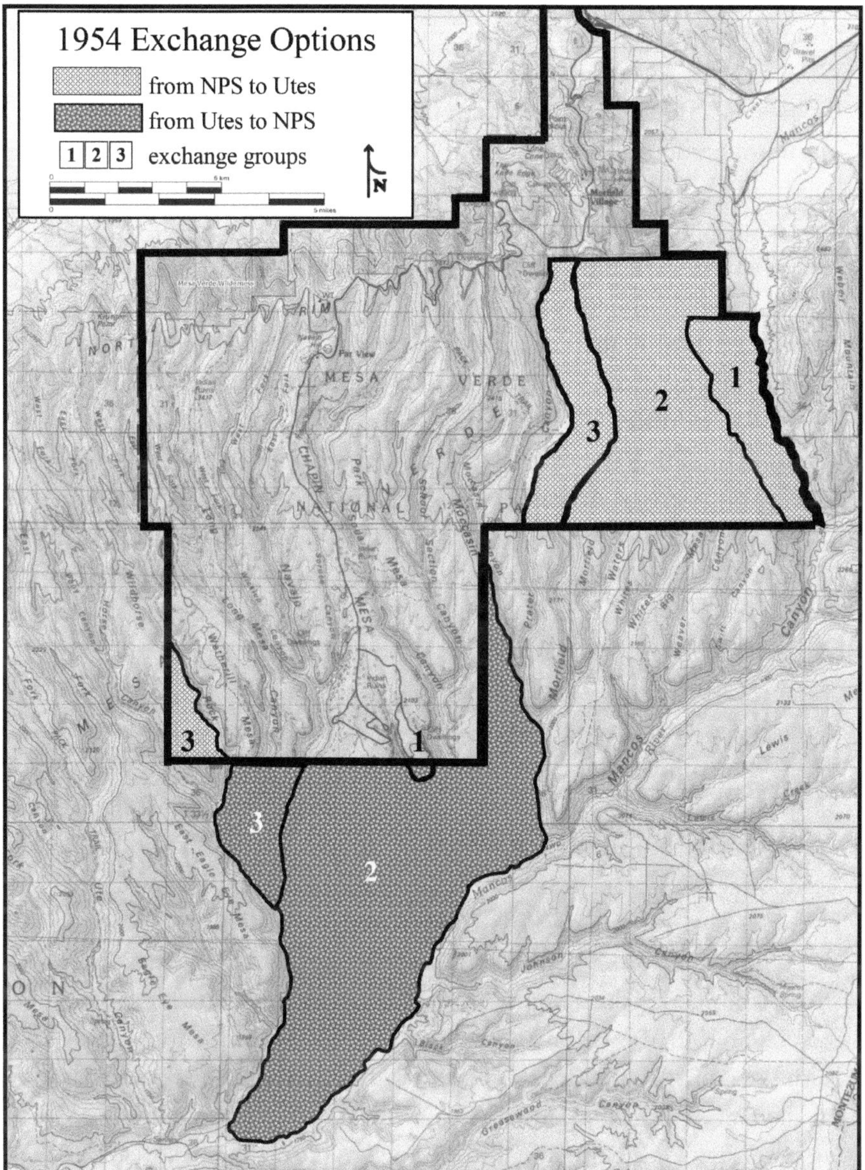

Figure 10. Proposed 1954 exchange between Mesa Verde National Park and Ute Mountain Ute Tribe.

remainder through the exchange; the Utes already had most of Whites and Big Mesas—and through the exchange would have all.

Besides, the Park's land along the Mancos River was a long-standing management nightmare due to its relative inaccessibility from headquarters and that it contained the only remaining inholding—315.75 acres owned by rancher Lee Sheek. Among other headaches for the Park staff, Sheek placed drift fences in each end of the Mancos River valley between the Park and Weber Mountain, and used the entire length (including the Park's land) for grazing his cattle, refusing to acknowledge that the Park had any jurisdiction.[49]

As for wildlife, Carlson figured the Park wasn't giving up too much. True, mink, beaver, and muskrat would be lost if the Mancos River valley were traded away, but they were not known to have been of material importance to the Ancestral Puebloans. On the other hand, no bighorns—important to the prehistoric inhabitants—had been seen on the lands the Park proposed to give the Utes, while many lived on the lands the Park would acquire.[50]

But for Carlson, as it had been for McLaughlin, Nusbaum, and Wade before him, the greatest boon was the increase in important cultural resources. First, there were no known cliff dwellings (always of most importance) on the land the park would give up, while there were over one hundred such structures on the Ute land that the Park would receive. These included the first cliff dwelling discovered by W. H. Jackson in 1874, Two Story Cliff House.[51]

What was more, Carlson envisioned infrastructure development with enhanced visitor opportunities. A loop road on the southern part of Chapin Mesa along Navajo and Soda Canyons could be added to the present "Ruins Road" system, with an interpretive center built on the rim of Mancos Canyon. From there, a short trail could lead to views of Jackson's campsite and Sixteen-Window House, discovered by W. H. Holmes in 1875. The interpretive center would also overlook part of the Ute Reservation. In Carlson's words, "Indians and their camps would often be visible. Connecting the history of the modern Utes with the prehistoric Indians . . . should help ameliorate their feelings toward the Park and white people in general."[52]

The Superintendent's Annual Report of 1955 officially proclaimed the Park's intent to pursue the exchange.[53]

Mesa Verde, like many other parks in the mid-1950s, had great plans—but insufficient money. And there was no overall, coordinated vision throughout the System on how to achieve those plans. That was about to change.

CHAPTER SIX

Mission 66 and the Wilderness Bill

1956–1964

IN THE MID-1950S, TWO major land-use initiatives started to play out in the National Park Service, with varying impacts on Mesa Verde.

The first of these was a result of the growth of visitor use in the Park System at a rate far in excess of the capability of the facilities, which in turn was due to a number of societal factors: a post-WWII population boom, the relative peace following the Korean War armistice, normalization of a five-day work week accompanied by a growth of income, plus a rapid increase in the number of cars, all fueling the demand for outdoor recreation.[1]

In response, the Service embarked on an ambitious ten-year plan to deal with the expected continuing increase in visitation. The plan was called "Mission 66"—usually written in all capital letters in Park Service documents, dramatizing visionary zeal in preparation for the NPS 50th anniversary in 1966. The intent of the program was to develop the parks so they could properly accommodate the visitors expected, with use of the parks generally intended to be spread over a greater portion of each park. The program was designed by NPS Director Conrad Wirth, a skilled politician as well as one of the most dynamic leaders of the Park Service, to mirror the ten-year plan for the interstate highway system, which shared a similar genesis. Wirth saw that money was available for big projects like the highway system, so the NPS ask would be big as well, involving every Congressional District, assuring its popularity and insuring its funding.[2]

In a March 1955 memo to the Mission 66 planning team, Wirth

outlined the twin objectives of the program: protection and optimum use. If he knew maximizing both was impossible and that one had to take precedence, it wasn't mentioned at the time. Rather, as long as protection served the public's enjoyment, further development would be required to accommodate the larger and more affluent automotive public that was on its way, and protection could be achieved by developing less-sensitive areas. As Lon Garrison, chair of the Mission 66 planning team explained, "visitor enjoyment" was the best means of protecting parks from the pressures of extractive industries. But visitors had to be "channeled" to avoid overuse of sensitive areas, and channeling required "proper development." Therefore, use and development would realize the preservation objectives.[3]

"We Simply Cannot Have Our Cake and Eat It Too"

At Mesa Verde, Mission 66 created an overwhelming impetus to push frontcountry development. Primary among these was moving overnight accommodations from Spruce Tree Point to Navajo Hill (for lodging) and the head of Morefield Canyon (for camping). Both were thought to satisfy the objective of increasing capacity while doing so in archeologically less-sensitive areas. When television finally came to Montezuma County, the one station's transmitter was placed on archeologically barren Park Point.[4]

Navajo Hill (now called Far View) would get a visitor center as well, and it would serve as the gateway to Wetherill Mesa, where development identical to Chapin Mesa eventually was planned in order to distribute visitation. The Wetherill Mesa Project had evolved into a two-phase operation. First came the excavation and investigation of the cliff and mesa-top dwellings, and stabilization of those that would be used by the public—a massive interdisciplinary effort that started in 1958. In the second phase, roads, trails, overlooks, a museum, indoor and outdoor exhibits, picnic areas, concession-operated lunch facilities, and utilities to support all that infrastructure would be built. Though most of them never materialized, these planned developments—in essence—turned backcountry into frontcountry and are not discussed further in *Mesa Verde's Secret Garden* except for when these impact other backcountry resources or experiences.[5]

However, access to Wetherill was tied up in needed boundary modifications, and Mission 66 created an opportunity for continuing to pursue the changes the Park had so long desired. The Regional Director used Mission 66 to raise the profile of the desired exchange, claiming it was just such an opportunity envisioned by the program. If the exchange wasn't consummated, he warned, the Park would lose the opportunity of spreading out visitor impact, since the land east of Morefield Canyon proposed for exchange to the Utes was useless for that purpose. And there was no way to get the desired additions to the Park except by exchange for the grazing lands now within the boundaries. "In other words, we simply cannot have our cake and eat it too."[6]

"I Do Not Feel That This Would Be Acceptable"

In August of 1956 it looked like an exchange with the Ute Mountain Utes would be worked out. The official recommendation was contained in a Boundary Status Report, incorporating many of Carlson's ideas. The report called for an exchange of approximately 9,600 acres from each of the parties. As for what the Park Service would give up, it was firmly believed that the land east of Morefield Canyon held less archeological value than southern Chapin Mesa. Biologically, the lands the Utes would get were more valuable for grazing, which would serve as a powerful incentive for the tribe to complete the exchange.

On the other side of the equation, the Park would still gain the land to the south, from which another fifty cliff dwellings could be viewed. Importantly, Carlson's vision of an interpretive center built on Chapin Mesa at the rim of Mancos Canyon was adopted. The Service was already contemplating reducing access to frontcountry sites, which could be ameliorated by the exchange. "These added features would encourage visitors to spend much less time on ruins trips and would partially compensate for the loss of the privilege of being able to enter cliff dwellings, trips to which, in time, it undoubtedly will be necessary to eliminate."[7]

Alternatively, an interpretive area could be developed at the south end of Moccasin Mesa, with a rim drive providing views of cliff dwellings in School Section and Moccasin Canyons. As late as 1963, developing visitor services on Moccasin Mesa was seen as essential to the future interpretation of the Park.[8]

However, oil and gas—in possibly commercial quantities—had been discovered on the Ute land. The USGS Regional Oil and Gas Supervisor wrote the Ute Agency Superintendent that due to these deposits the Ute land involved in the proposed exchange now had a greater value than the land they would get from the Park. He suggested that perhaps an equitable exchange could work if the Utes retained mineral rights with safeguards to protect the National Park's interests in the cultural and biological resources. When this idea was floated to Mesa Verde Superintendent Carlson, his response was simple: "I do not feel that this would be acceptable." The Director was informed that due to the conclusions of the Geological Survey, the chances of consummating a land exchange were "practically nil," though if the reserves failed to pan out, negotiations might resume.[9]

Being thwarted to expand the Park to the south placed new emphasis for development on areas to the west that were already within Park boundaries, and Mission 66 funding would make feasible opening Wetherill Mesa, rather than South Chapin, to the public. That meant, however, some form of negotiation with the Utes was still necessary. At the time, access along the mesa top in the vicinity of Rock Springs crossed Ute land. Consequently, the Superintendent went so far as to request that "all members of the Park family take every available opportunity to promote good relations with the Ute Indians."[10]

"Trespassing on Reservation Lands for Years"

By 1960, as the Park was committed to opening Wetherill Mesa, there was increasing urgency in at least trading for the Wetherill access. In

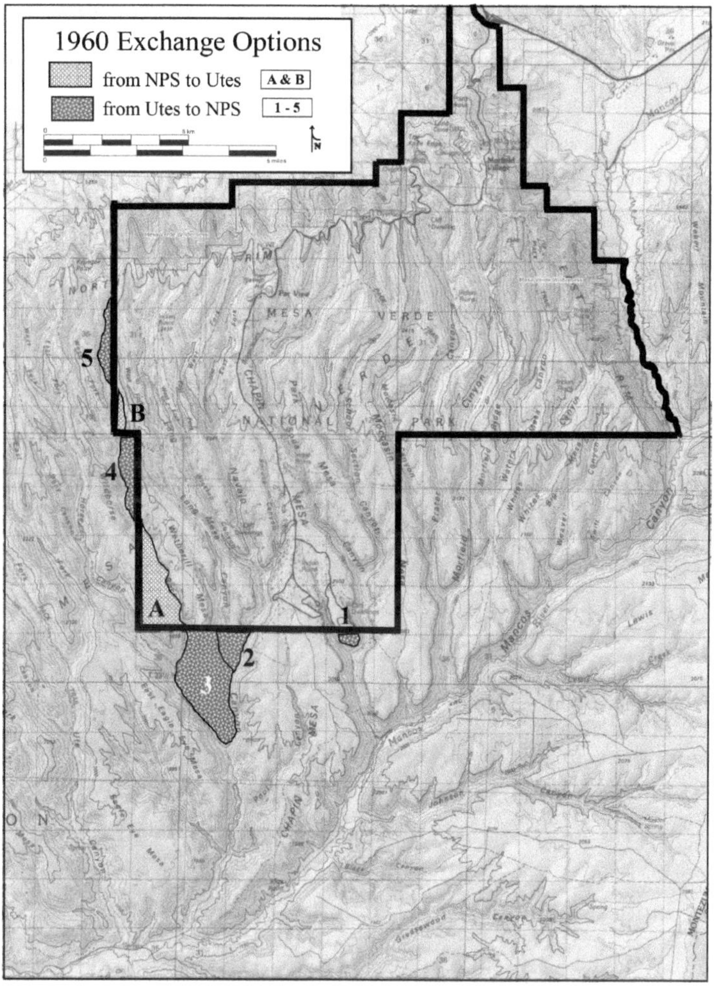

Figure 11. Proposed exchange, scaled down in 1960.

July, the Park Service issued a scaled-down Boundary Status Report, which called out tracts needed for legal, unrestricted access to the most important areas to be brought to the Park.[11]

Five parcels were targeted for acquisition in the 1960 Report:

1) Soda Point. The Service recognized they had been in trespass on the Ute Reservation since 1930–31 when the loop road

> was constructed. The Utes were aware of this and had plans for commercial development on this land, deterred only by the lack of water.
> 2 & 3) The southern end of Long and Wetherill Mesas—in keeping with the Park's objective of acquiring all of the "fingers" of the Mesa Verde.
> 4 & 5) The portion of Wetherill Mesa on Ute land necessary for public access (the top priority) and the remainder of Wetherill east of the East Fork Rock Canyon and currently outside the Park boundary.

In exchange, the Utes would get the southwestern corner of the Park (A) and a sliver of land west of the East Fork Rock Canyon currently inside the Park boundary (B).

The proposal was tweaked over the next several months. These included changes alternating between using geologic strata as boundaries and using the drainage channels in the bottoms of the canyons.[12]

By late 1962, the Park was under increasing pressure to facilitate development on Wetherill as part of Mission 66, and gaining access to Ute lands went from urgent to critical.

Superintendent Thomas tried to keep alive the dream of a Greater Mesa Verde by advocating a long-term view that would add all the land west and north of the Mancos River, and possibly even the area south of the Mancos to include the cliff dwellings in Johnson Canyon. Realistically, however, he noted that fantasy would likely go unfulfilled, given what he considered the obstinacy of Jack House, the current Ute leader, who did not want to release any Ute land, payback for how he had been "abused and kicked around" by the Park Service for decades. In addition, "Chief House is also an ardent wilderness supporter. He sincerely advocates that some of the Reservation be left totally undisturbed and resents the efforts of some of the younger men to 'develop' the land for economic uses."[13]

Nevertheless, Superintendent Thomas continued working directly with the Utes on the Park's two most pressing realty needs. He jettisoned the idea of an exchange and proposed either purchase or easement to facilitate access to Wetherill Mesa. Then he broached the touchy subject of the Park's trespass at Soda Point. He offered to solve both problems at the same time—two easements at first, then two eventual exchanges: Wildhorse Mesa to the Utes, for Soda Point and the Wetherill Access; and then he resurrected the idea of swapping the other lands the Park wanted in exchange for public land adjacent to existing Ute holdings, including north and west of Ute Mountain (land that is now within Canyons of the Ancients National Monument).[14]

Internally, the Park continued to press the Service for expansion, with Superintendent Thomas erroneously pointing out to the Regional Director that the Park "does not contain anywhere within its boundaries all of any one of the larger finger-like mesas complete with its bordering canyons."[15]

In March of 1964, the Ute Mountain Ute Tribal Council passed Resolution 1278, granting temporary permission to cross Reservation lands at the Wetherill Access. The wording praises the Park Service for developing and staffing "these priceless possessions of the American people" as well as providing "maximum protection of the scenic, scientific, wilderness, and historic resources that give them distinction." The resolution goes on to affirm what was obvious to all: "The Mesa Verde National Park Service has been trespassing on reservation lands for years, without consulting the Tribal Council for permission which has not been conducive to fostering good relations."[16]

Then, another twist. The Utes stated they were willing to talk about trading all the archeologically important lands that the Park desired—the southern portions of Wetherill, Chapin, and Moccasin Mesas, Soda Point, the Wetherill Access, and even Johnson Canyon on the south side of the Mancos River. All they wanted in return was to retain rights to the oil and gas minerals . . . plus, "the Utes want a share of the receipts from the Park."[17]

Superintendent Thomas recognized time was of the essence to secure Mission 66 funding. To expedite negotiations, he met with Ute Tribal Council members to discuss the outlines of an agreement that would not require an actual transfer of land but satisfy the desires of the Utes as well as the Park's desire to expand their archeological and recreational reach.

Thomas described the agreement to the Regional Director. The Tribe would keep ownership but transfer management of all what they called their "wilderness area"—all of the Mesa Verde landform south of the Park and north of the Mancos River. The Park Service would assume responsibility for: the excavation, stabilization and scientific research of all archeological resources on the Ute land; all fire prevention and law enforcement; and would construct and maintain roads, trails, and any other visitor facilities the Park deemed appropriate for public use. In exchange, the Utes could continue to hunt, graze, and prospect their lands for oil and gas.[18]

One lingering sticking point would require legislation: the Utes still wanted half the money from the Park's entrance fee as well as a percentage of the profits from facilities operated by the Park's concessioner.[19]

In selling this proposal to the Regional Director, Thomas noted the great flexibility this would give the Park in planning future visitor use development, especially on Lower Chapin Mesa and Pool Canyon. He acknowledged that there would be some risk involved if important mineral discoveries were made, but he thought the chances of that were slight. He also indulged in hyperbole: "It could be the largest undisturbed biological unit remaining in the Southwest," and "If this splendid collection of archeological remains is not preserved for park purposes, it will be lost within the next 10 years or less" due to Ute plans to denude the mesa "and seed the land to grass for leasing to white men for grazing purposes."[20]

All that was needed, Thomas summarized, was for a legal, "solid agreement" to be reached with the Tribe and then to be submitted to the Department for approval.

"Fire-Ways"

At the same time as exchanges were contemplated, development projects were completed in case the more ambitious exchange proposals fell through. The Ute Mountain Utes got permission to build a road from the Whites Mesa fire tower south to the boundary to facilitate construction of new reservoirs in their lands on that mesa. Consequently, a fence across Big and Whites Mesas became necessary to control the trespass of Ute animals. Similarly, to the west, almost six miles of the boundary with the Utes was fenced to prevent grazing trespass on Wetherill Mesa and in Long and Rock Canyons. Furthermore, the Utes informed the Park that they intended to fence the Park/Reservation boundary on Chapin Mesa, build a reservoir in Pool Canyon, and run livestock in the area.[21]

In addition, the Park continued creating infrastructure to combat fire by improving the Utes' road down Whites Mesa and blading a new route down the mesa between the east and west forks of Navajo Canyon (today variously called Gant or Navajo Mesa). Three years later, the Park proposed construction of over thirteen miles of "fireways," almost two miles of firebreaks, and a heliport.[22]

"A Natural Area on Park Mesa"

In the face of all this development, natural conditions—and the science to study and protect them—suffered across the entire National Park System. Much of this was due to the distrust of the biological sciences by Director Wirth, a landscape architect. In 1956 he wrote to former Director Horace Albright, a fellow traveler, "You can get too scientific on these things and cause a lot of harm." Albright embraced this attitude, and two years later, at a meeting of the National Parks Advisory Board, he said, "There should not be too much emphasis laid on biology." After all people, not the animals, were "the ones who are going to enjoy the parks," and "ninety-nine percent . . . are not interested in biological research." Eventually, even usually supportive *National Parks Magazine* countered these sentiments and questioned what were seen as the Service's misplaced priorities.[23]

The Mesa Verde staff did the best they could, given the scant resources passed down along with the lip service to biological integrity.

Efforts continued to reestablish the fauna present at the time of the Ancestral Puebloans presence on the mesa. Prairie dogs were reintroduced, and ten more turkeys were released (though success may have been due to putting corn out every evening near the CCC area on Chapin Mesa). The bighorn sheep were monitored; some were sighted *in* the House of Many Windows on the West Rim of Cliff Canyon near the Park boundary. By 1962, the Superintendent's Annual Report declared that bighorns "roam throughout the park. The reestablishment of wild turkey seems assured."[24]

New or unusual sightings were noted, though some are suspect. Raccoons were seen for the first time in 1959. Abert's squirrels, previously common, reappeared in 1960. Someone reported a marmot in Morefield Canyon. A lioness with *five* cubs was reported in 1961. In 1962, "Two separate reports of a wolf were received this month [from] a seasonal ranger and a concessioner employee at different locations near the Headquarters area."[25]

There was an increasing concern with exotic animals as well. Colyer's history of grazing in the Park summarizes conditions at the time, with over 150 head of feral cattle and 140 head of feral horses grazing in the Park.[26]

Perhaps the most impressive change in stewardship was the Park's decision to manage a portion of the Park as a whole ecosystem. In October 1956, a report was completed "designating a natural area on Park Mesa to preserve a typical sample of Piñon Pine-Juniper forest type." There was, of course, no money to implement such a plan.[27]

The lip service given to the increasing importance of the natural conditions at Mesa Verde was also reflected in the Park's 1963 Master Plan. Not only would the natural environment be protected, but it would be interpreted as an integral part in the development of the Mesa Verde Story.[28]

This new emphasis on the whole ecosystem in some parts of the Park did not mean an end to planned trammeling. Porcupines were finally given a reprieve, though only because there was no more aesthetic damage. Thirty pounds of piñon nuts were planted in a one-acre permanent plot on the Morefield burn to assess once again the efficacy of such post-fire remediation. In the late 1950s, spraying for sawflies and tent caterpillars was common, though dependent on the severity of infestation. By the mid-60s, the Park's inclination to garden was thwarted by a higher power: "There will be no spraying for the control of forest insects next spring. . . . [The] projects were disapproved by Region."[29]

"Vignette of Primitive America"

In 1963, two reports from outside the Park Service initiated a profound change in the way parks were managed. The National Academy of Sciences issued a report in August, clarifying that parks were "dynamic biological complexes" that encompassed far more than the charismatic megafauna that had dominated park management. It also levied considerable criticism at the NPS for its failure to properly support science within the agency.[30]

Five months earlier, the more famous so-called "Leopold Report" (after its principal author, A. Starker Leopold—Aldo's eldest child), was released. It, too, recognized the complexity of ecosystems and called for science-based park management under the "full jurisdiction of biologically trained personnel." What Leopold's report is best known for, however, is his call for the parks to be managed as a "vignette of primitive America."[31]

There were several problems with this "vignette" approach that surfaced over time. First, it was an artificial benchmark that ignored the effects of Native Americans on the land and ecology. In many places, the effect was substantial, yet Leopold et al. were saying the parks should re-create "the condition that prevailed when the area was first visited by the white man" without considering the impact on those conditions by the now-displaced Indigenous people.[32]

Second, the team made little mention of existing exotic species that were not present at the time of the benchmark; summarizing the report to employees at the Yosemite Conference of Challenges in October, he made no mention of them at all. Fifty years later, however, wilderness managers cited exotics as the number two issue facing them.[33]

Finally, it implied a sense of stasis after the benchmark was met, even though the authors realized natural biology was dynamic. What was being proposed was largely a matter of massive reductions of ungulates, which would then likely need to be replicated year after year in the absence of their predators, who would not be reintroduced due to political pressure. The Leopold team, and Leopold himself at the Yosemite Conference, harped on the knowledge necessary to undertake what by their own account would be this extensive gardening of the parks—knowledge that the parks currently did not have: "With the limited knowledge that we have now, there are very few steps on management . . . that I personally would want to endorse or see you undertake." Yet Leopold believed "If we are trying to show a natural scene typical of an area, we can build it—if we have to." It is difficult to comprehend just how massive any proposed manipulation would have to be, given their self-admitted ignorance. The focus would be on the areas seen by the public, so visitors could appreciate this "vignette." But they believed with enough time, money, and personnel they could learn enough to appropriately rearrange the biota. Such wholesale trammeling would run up against the observation of the ecologist Frank Egler: "With respect to science, we must never forget that nature is not only more complex than we think, but more complex than we can think."[34]

Enter Howard Zahniser, Executive Director of The Wilderness Society and (as noted in the introduction) principal author of the Wilderness Act. While generally praising the work of the Leopold team, he cautioned: "The Board's report poses a serious threat to the wilderness within the National Park System and indeed to the wilderness concept itself. . . . We urge that the general goals of the report on 'Wildlife Management in the National Parks' be carefully scrutinized in the light of this ideal. With regard to areas of wilderness we should be guardians not gardeners."[35]

How far managers should go to "correct" "unnatural" conditions has been a point of controversy—and hubris—ever since.

"Subordinate Preservation of Wilderness"

Any new awareness of the natural ecosystem did not diminish the primacy of archeology at Mesa Verde, where "preservation" categorically implied "of the archeology." The 1963 Master Plan may have pointed out the importance of the biophysical environment, but only with caveats. "Preserve the wild lands that existed at the time of the occupation, but subordinate preservation of wilderness on the prehistoric sites to preservation of the ruins themselves." The Park would interpret the natural history story at Mesa Verde only to the extent that it strengthens the prehistoric story and would not interpret the geology or biology independent of that prehistory.[36]

Superintendent Thomas staked out Mesa Verde's position in even stronger terms. He thought it impractical to manage natural resources in archeological areas as they would be in natural areas, or to allow public use in the same manner or degree. "Archeological areas . . . must be managed as museums. The field features are as much museum pieces as are the objects exhibited behind glass in formal museums."[37]

The attitude that Mesa Verde needed to be managed with the tightly controlled access of a museum was not Thomas's alone and was consistent with the Mission 66 guiding precept of channeling visitors to avoid damaging sensitive areas. "The entire ruins area of the Park should be considered as sacred and displayed to the public only when and if such action will not destroy any important irreplaceable features. In general, this would apply to all areas beyond Navajo Hill" [i.e., west to, and including, Wetherill Mesa]. Coupled with increased visitation, it is no wonder that greater constraints were imposed on visitors. At least some of this was warranted. The Park suffered an "outbreak of vandalism" attributed to "lawless elements and drifters brought into the country by the oil and gas boom near the Park."[38]

But as Nusbaum had stated years before, the greatest danger was not from intentional vandalism, but from the inadvertent (and, to some extent, unavoidable) impacts of more and more people. Visitation increased rapidly—from 1956 through 1959 by a total of 16 percent—with no end to the increases in sight. Superintendent Thomas told his staff, "If visitation continues and Congress can't be awakened to our needs, then the Parks will be destroyed by human erosion." He exhorted them to plan for an increase in visitors without having to restrict them through some sort of predetermined limit, concluding, "If we don't control these things, then we will lose irreplaceable values here on the Mesa."[39]

"There Is Some Demand for Hiking as an Activity"

With that sensibility, Mesa Verde started changing the recreational opportunities in the backcountry. The 1954 brochure and map provided to visitors (*Figure 9*) shows several trails throughout the Park and "because of the danger of getting lost, hikers must obtain maps and a permit before leaving the headquarters area" (emphasis in original).[40]

The map in the 1958 brochure is limited to the area around headquarters and the Ruins Road. Trails shown are limited to Petroglyph Point Trail, Spruce Canyon Trail, and the trail down Spruce toward Navajo (though the junction with Navajo is outside the area depicted by the map).[41]

Three years later, the Mesa Verde Company brochure includes only a simplistic map with trails to Pictograph [*sic*] Point and the Navajo Canyon Trail, yet still offers saddle horse excursions for mesa-top trails, and longer half- and full-day trips "to remote unexcavated ruins."[42]

There was a recognition that if the backcountry was going to be closed off, other opportunities needed to be provided in its place. The old trail to the "Cliff Dweller Dams" near Cedar Tree Tower was brushed out for hiking.[43]

Yet, as the 1958 Master Plan Development Outline notes: "There is some demand for hiking as an activity. At present the Park has two short hiking trails but nothing to meet the need for all-day hiking.

. . . Long and short hiking trails could well be developed in scenic, non-critical areas of the Park," such as "along the north rim of the Park and in the Prater-Morefield Canyon area." The cliff sites, even those stabilized, were seen as "too fragile, too dangerous, and too valuable" to allow visitors entry without a ranger. "Hiking, riding, etc. must be restricted to areas where there are no cliff ruins." When addressing the "Preservation of Surface Ruins," visitor use is not identified as a problem. In April of 1959, the Superintendent authorized a study to determine the best use of the Park's trails.[44]

By 1961, the staff was developing another Master Plan. These plans were developed at what today would be considered lightning speed when compared with government planning in the twenty-first century. Secrecy—not legal today—made the work easier, but also engendered complaints from conservation organizations.[45]

In the 1961 Draft Plan, most of the trail ideas developed three years earlier were abandoned. Instead, a scenic hiking trail was proposed for the old Knife Edge road segment from the Montezuma Valley Overlook to "the entrance road below Park Point [*sic*]." In addition, "Western tradition as well as the necessity of letting visitors ride some of the trails requires that we make saddle horse service available."[46]

"A Great Awakening"

The election of 1960 brought in a new administration with a new outlook, a shift from Eisenhower's modernization to Kennedy's conservation, implemented under the direction of the new Secretary of the Interior, Stewart Udall.

At a staff meeting in March of 1962, the Park's management team discussed President Kennedy's message to Congress in February 1961 on natural resource policy. The meeting minutes reflect "a great deal of interest now and we should be encouraged by what appears to be a final culmination of a great awakening to the need for our recreation and conservation of resources." If earlier ideas of trails along the North Rim and in the Prater-Morefield area were dropped, questions remained for Park staff as to just what kind of opportunities would be sufficient to provide the public in the coming years.[47]

Park Ranger Tom Hobbs once led a two-day horseback trip for members of the local 4-H club to Spring House and Pool Canyon.[48] *Were guided special trips for special groups to special places (including outside the Park) sufficient?*

The Park records at the time are replete with reports including variations on "All ruins visited by the public were cleaned and inspected each week during the travel season."[49] *A sanitized experience may be easier on the resource, but was it sufficient?*

As discussed earlier, in May of 1957 the Park started talking about initiating a comprehensive development program on Wetherill Mesa "to alleviate [crowding] and to achieve dispersal of visitors."[50] *Dispersal would certainly improve visitor experiences, but was duplicating Chapin development on Wetherill sufficient?*

By 1960, Superintendent Thomas regretted there were not enough employees to staff all the surface sites excavated on the Mesa Top Loop, since "these ruins really tell the story of the Mesa Verde rather than the spectacular cliff dwellings which represent only the final phase of prehistoric occupation."[51] *More rangers may have improved interpretive capabilities, but would that experience be sufficient?*

It simply was not fiscally feasible to staff the Mesa Top Loop with hot-and-cold-running rangers. Otherwise, it seemed the Park was answering these questions of sufficiency with "yes."

"87.8 Miles"

In 1958, Congress established an Outdoor Recreation Resources Review Commission (ORRRC) to study the recreational "crisis" of insufficient opportunities and facilities in the country. The Park Service took this as a direct affront to their expertise and mission, and cooperated at the bare minimum possible, given the Department of the Interior's support for the fledgling bureaucracy. Two years later, ORRRC sent a questionnaire on recreational opportunities to parks and other providers across the country. In response, Superintendent

Figure 12. Remnants of the APW trail built in 1963, climbing the unnamed mesa between Moccasin and Prater Canyons. The APW trails have not weathered as well as the Navajo or CCC trails, because of either a greater lack of maintenance, or simply inferior construction. Compare with Figures 4 and 6. November 2020.

Thomas reported there were "87.8 miles of trails open to hiking" in the Park. There is no documentation to support that number, and it exceeds the total mileage of trails that ever existed in Mesa Verde. It is not known why the Superintendent would submit such a demonstrable exaggeration. Could this be another example of reputation burnishing? Was he including all the trails on the Ute Mountain Ute Reservation that had formerly been used by Park visitors? Or was it just a conscious effort to give a competing organization bogus data?[52]

What *is* known is that most of whatever mileage was open would eventually be closed.

In 1963, Accelerated Public Works (APW) projects—the '60s short-lived program corresponding to the '30s CCC—developed routes in the Mesa Verde backcountry. The plans included a horse trail from Chapin Mesa near the quarry across Soda, School Section, and Moccasin Canyons to tie in with the Old Tourist Trail in Prater

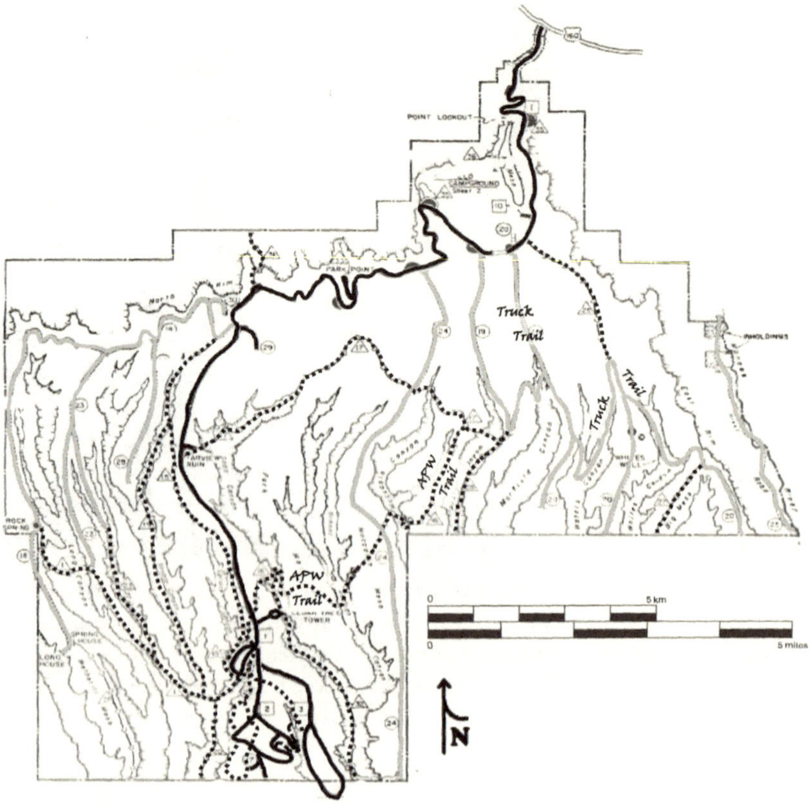

Figure 13. 1963 road and trail inventory. For comparison with other maps, primary roads are black; secondary (administrative) roads are overlaid in gray; and trails are shown as dotted lines. The APW Trail is an added annotation, as is the route across the eastern third of the Park sometimes referred to as the "Truck Trail." Compare with Figures 3, 8, 9, 17, and 43.

Canyon. The crew of about sixty-five men finished the six-mile route in under two months. The crew also built the Soda Canyon Overlook Trail and started a "Forest Protection Trail, Morefield Canyon to Point Lookout."[53] The Soda Canyon Overlook Trail was always intended to be for public use, and the Point Lookout Trail was converted to public use after the Morefield Campground was built.

The map accompanying the Park's 1963 inventory of maintained trails shows many of the same routes on the 1941 and 1949 maps.[54] The contemporaneous version of the Park's Master Plan sums up what was the latest policy on backcountry visitor use: "Permit visitors to go into cliff dwellings only when accompanied by a ranger. . . . Hiking, riding, etc., must be restricted to areas where there are no important accessible cliff ruins." Camping is considered "a legitimate and desirable use," though by "camping" it is clear the document meant car camping. Park planners thought there should be a "greater opportunity for use," met by "development, where needed and appropriate, of lunching, picnicking, horseback riding and camping facilities, and archeological and nature trails."[55]

In May of 1963, three lost hikers took the wrong trail at the bottom of Spruce Canyon and walked an extra fifteen miles beyond their destination.[56] This was just the kind of "adventure" that Everett Ruess would have loved—but by this time the Park had already determined no one else would have this "opportunity."

"For the Permanent Good of the Whole People"

By the end of Mission 66, almost one billion dollars had been spent across the National Park System on thousands of miles of roads and hundreds of miles of trails; water, sewer, and electric lines; employee housing and administrative buildings; training centers for an expanded professional staff; and more than one hundred visitor centers. The buildings reflected contemporary trends in design, from ranch houses to shopping centers. The whole program "was imbued with the 'new spirit' of mid-century modernism," all to serve more people more efficiently.[57]

However, a second major land use initiative was unveiled in Washington, DC, that in many ways served as a counterpoint to Mission 66. The idea of protecting wilderness by law had been an ideal held by the Wilderness Society for almost twenty years, but the potential assault on wilderness by the development program of Mission 66 made it an imperative.

In early June 1956, Minnesota Senator Hubert Humphrey

introduced "A Bill to establish on public lands of the United States a National Wilderness Preservation System for the permanent good of the whole people." Drafted by Howard Zahniser, the first Wilderness Bill contained many of the provisions found in the final version of the Law passed by Congress in 1964. The purpose was made clear early in the Bill: "The Congress recognizes that an increasing population, accompanied by expanding settlement and growing mechanization, is destined to occupy and modify all areas within the United States . . . except those that are set apart for preservation and protection in their natural condition. Such preservation of areas of wilderness is recognized as a desirable policy of the Government of the United States of America for the health, welfare, and happiness of its citizens of present and future generations." To that end, the Bill called for the protection of areas "where the earth and its community of life are untrammeled by man." In addition, among other prohibitions, the Bill stated, "Within such areas . . . there shall be no road, nor any use of motor vehicles . . . or other provision for mechanized transportation, nor any structure or installation in excess of the minimum required for the administration of the area for the purpose of this Act."[58]

The Bill also included a list of the areas to be designated as Wilderness, a provision dropped in subsequent versions of the legislation and from the final Act. Among the places listed, "Mesa Verde National Park, Colorado." The Bill named forty-six other units managed by the National Park Service to be immediately included in the National Wilderness Preservation System, with the opportunity for other units to be added later. (Scores of portions of national forests, wildlife refuges, and Indian reservations—if tribal councils consented—were also identified by name.) As for the extent of the wilderness, the Bill proposed that the entirety of each named Park would be designated as wilderness "except those portions set aside . . . for roads and accommodations for visitors."[59]

In other words, if this bill were to become law, almost all of Mesa Verde National Park would be designated as wilderness.

"Wilderness of a Special Kind"

Park Service opposition to the Wilderness Bill has been well-documented.[60] This was not so much a matter of conflict with extractive uses, as would have been expected from the Forest Service and various industry organizations, but rather the Park Service simply claimed it was unnecessary. However, underlying this position was the threat wilderness restrictions posed to the agency's bureaucratic autonomy. Wilderness prohibitions included building roads and—unless necessary for wilderness management—the use of motorized equipment, motorized and mechanical transport, or structures. This clearly restricted the Park Service's discretion in managing its back-country. Wilderness designation would also forfeit any future potential for using at least some of those areas to accommodate increasing numbers of visitors. That in turn, concerned many concessioners—an influential body in determining national park policy. Wilderness historian Craig Allin quoted NPS Director Wirth's testimony to the Senate Interior Committee in late June of 1957: "The inclusion of the National Parks in a general system of wilderness areas . . . will have the effect of placing National Parks on a less firm foundation of protection than has already been provided by Federal Law" (Allin's ellipsis). As an example of Wirth's failure to understand the underlying basis for wilderness preservation, conflating wilderness with scenery, Allin again cited the Director: "As we build a road into Wonder Lake in Mt. McKinley National Park, that does not mean that the park is no longer a wilderness. The road is a wilderness road, to bring people into the wilderness." Perhaps Wirth's lack of understanding stems from the fact, as historian John Miles put it, he "had never seen duty in the field at any level" and "nowhere in his writings and speeches can *passion* for nature, for wilderness, or even park beauty be found" (emphasis added).[61]

But preventing ever-increasing development in the National Parks was exactly one of the purposes of the bill. Wilderness researcher James Gilligan's testimony to Congress in July 1956, put it succinctly: the Park Service "is subject to the unrelenting pressures of mass use, and retreats gradually behind the cold logic that more areas must be developed to care properly for the public to which the land belongs." David Brower, in his typical fashion, was more blunt: "They build too many things for their own convenience—for rangers who have forgotten how to range." Howard Zahniser pointed out the problem with Wirth's testimony: "Under the existing legislation all the roads and buildings now in the national parks have been constructed, and more and more could be built. There is nothing [in existing law] to protect future administrators from pressures to use more and more of the backcountry for developments that would destroy them as wilderness."[62]

In an attempt to drum up public support for leaving the Park Service out of the Wilderness System, Wirth had a thirty-six-page, full-color glossy booklet developed: *The National Park Wilderness.*[63] Published in the year after the Wilderness Bill was introduced, it had text written by Howard R. Stagner and photos of stunning vistas in the National Park System accompanied by captions such as "The Nation's most treasured wilderness lands are set apart and dedicated as National Parks and Monuments"; and "Man is a part of the scene—wilderness has little human value without him." To set the scene, "The fundamental concept of National Park wilderness has never been more clearly defined than in this publication."[64]

The document was an obvious salvo in the war to maintain complete NPS autonomy. With content structured around Wirth's antipathy toward the Wilderness Bill, the booklet made four main arguments against including the NPS in that legislation.

First, the booklet made a case that the National Park Service already protected wilderness. Part of Mission 66 was to review the National Park laws, and the text claimed, "All of these laws emphasize the preservation of wilderness values." In fact, it argued, the men who established the first National Park, Yellowstone, "were thinking in wilderness terms," and subsequent designations came from those "who were inspired by their experiences in the wilderness they sought to preserve." The booklet asserted that anyone can find wilderness in the national parks. This is not an accident, as it "reflects discrimination in the selection of superlative scenic, scientific, wilderness areas for inclusion in the System." The booklet claimed the Service "began to pull back on new road construction before it was generally recognized outside the Service that roads—too many of them, or in the wrong places—could impair park and wilderness values." At the same time, it noted, "Even those who never venture far from roads, experience the quality of wilderness, [and] visitors see, sense, and react to wilderness, often without leaving the roadside."[65]

Second, the booklet pointed out a successful history of resistance to commercial threats, reinforcing the idea that the NPS could, in fact, protect wilderness areas better than other agencies: "This booklet is about wilderness of a special kind—the superlative wilderness areas and wilderness qualities preserved in the National Parks." With echoes of Stephen Mather's 1921 attempt to block recreation funding for the Forest Service (covered in chapter 2), the booklet implied that the NPS was much better positioned than other agencies to preserve real wilderness. This was due to both historical mission and expertise. The National Parks were identified as a national resource, and "like minerals, water, timber and soil, it has value to man only when it is made useful to man." The Organic Act of 1916 was a clear recognition of preserving this resource "undamaged and unimpaired." For proof of the NPS preservation dedication, the booklet references "numerous attempts, well organized and powerfully supported, to despoil the National Parks" that were "vigorously" defeated. Without naming the Forest Service, the booklet cites other agencies that "give good protection to commercially valuable forests," but only the NPS preserves "a complete fauna, in a natural habitat, with minimum disturbance and control."[66]

Third, the brochure pointed out that Mission 66 gave ample direction on planning for wilderness protection, and asserted it was inappropriate to force a one-size-fits-all set of management proscriptions on the NPS in contradiction with the agency's original mandate. Wilderness designation might mean "discarding the tradition of National Park hospitality and require rationing of visitors, elimination of lodges and campgrounds, or other radical changes. . . . The National Park Service seeks a sane and practical middle ground." The purpose of the National Parks "inseparably combines use with preservation." To emphasize one over the other would "imperil the validity of the whole National Park concept."[67]

Finally, within the pages lie informal guidelines for development under the Mission 66 initiative and how those would affect wilderness. Among the principles was defining what would be the appropriate park use. In determining what developments should be provided, proposals should be guided by these sideboards: "(1) that the activity result in no impairment of significant natural or scenic values, (2) that it does not itself become a primary attraction, and (3) that it does not lessen the opportunity for others to enjoy the park for what it is."[68]

Summarizing, the booklet concludes:

> It is now 85 years since the idea of National Parks became a reality, and was clearly defined by law. Today, it is fair to claim that nine-tenths of the area within the National Parks can be included under a reasonable definition of wilderness, that the admonition to preserve for the benefit of the people and to pass on unimpaired to future generations has been faithfully carried out.[69]

The last page features a picture of the confluence of the Green and Yampa Rivers in Dinosaur National Monument, where the Bureau of Reclamation had planned to place a dam that had recently been defeated. In large type above the picture are the words: "The laws of the Nation require preservation of wilderness in National Parks and Monuments."

It is ironic that the defeat of the dam at Echo Park was largely due not to the efforts of the Park Service, but to the very people who purposefully included the NPS in the Wilderness Bill.[70]

"Like Horatius at the Bridge"

It is not known how wide a distribution this booklet received beyond copies being sent to each unit in the NPS. On reading his, Mesa Verde's Superintendent Carlson was so impressed he ordered a copy be given to every seasonal ranger.[71]

Mesa Verde changed Superintendents in 1959, and Chester Thomas replaced Carlson. He returned from that year's national Visitor Services Conference quoting Director Wirth: "The wilderness is in our blood," and "the National Parks highlight America's determination to preserve our tie with the wilderness and the land, and thus to preserve one source of our strength of national spirit." Wirth had apparently criticized so-called "multiple use," management. Thomas related that Wirth opined "Land which should be used primarily for watershed protection should not be used for logging, and wildlife refuges should not be used for hunting." The implication was clear: wilderness areas should be managed by the Park Service, and any Wilderness Bill therefore would be unnecessary. Thomas went so far as to assert—without further explanation—that wilderness designation "could go a long way toward destroying Mesa Verde National Park."[72]

Interior Secretary Udall's so-called New Conservation was at odds with Director Wirth's Mission 66 vision. Ronald Foresta wrote, "Mission 66 reflected a great faith in progress rather than a healthy distrust of it. Its building program reflected assumptions about the harmony of development and wilderness which were no longer in fashion." He went on to quote Udall's reference to a Roman general, all alone, defending his city from the barbaric Etruscan hordes: Wirth was standing "like Horatius at the bridge," in opposition to Udall's direction for the agency. Wirth was forced to resign as Director of the National Park Service without seeing Mission 66 to its conclusion.[73]

The Director may have changed, but the institution he cultivated had not. Many of the newly powerful environmental groups believed that long after Mission 66 officially ended, it still reflected the basic inclinations of the Park Service, and if given a chance, the agency would resurrect Mission 66-style policies.[74]

For a while, the New Conservation movement bypassed Mesa

Verde—hidden in a corner of Colorado, small in size, and known almost exclusively for its archeology. Park management was content to continue working on the development of the frontcountry while keeping the backcountry what had become a forbidden secret. All-in-all, the Wilderness Bill had little effect on the stewardship of Mesa Verde. Park management returned to "normal." For now.

CHAPTER SEVEN

Mesa Verde Meets the Wilderness Act

Business as Usual

1964–1976

ON SEPTEMBER 3, 1964, President Lyndon Johnson signed into law The Wilderness Act, Public Law 88–577. The ramifications of the law's passage would eventually catch up with Mesa Verde—but that would take a few years. Initially, it was business as usual, and the staff carried on, confident that the new law would have no bearing on their management.

"It Humbles Our Citizens"

In 1966, Chief Archeologist Jean Pinkley wrote an interpretive prospective for the Park:

> Though Mesa Verde was set aside primarily to preserve and use wisely the prehistoric manifestations, the scenery is unique, and spectacular, the animal and plant life varied and interesting, and the geology presents a good example of certain phases of earth history. . . . This national park commemorates and reminds us of the debt we owe to those who have gone before. It gives pause to the brash citizen who proclaims that our good way of life is the invention and attainment of one particularly ingenious generation

of Americans. It humbles our citizens into the realization that we owe so very much to all of the people of all lands and all times.[1]

This touched on the idea of managing Mesa Verde as a whole and emphasized our humility on the land. Would this be possible in the Park that had, understandably, put its cultural resources first, last, and always? In one way, Mesa Verde was more advanced than many of the other units in the System, where leadership gave "lip service" to science initiatives. Wirth had made it clear that scientists were only "advisory," and that scientific decisions were reserved for Superintendents—an attitude that persisted long after Wirth was gone. In 1964, the Chair of the House Interior Department Appropriations Subcommittee, Michael Kirwan (D-OH), declared that research was not any business of the National Park Service. At the time in Mesa Verde, there were no biologists, but the science of archeology was respected and valued.[2]

Despite Pinkley's moving narrative, elevating biological resources beyond their aesthetic impact on the visitor would take a major realignment of the Park's direction and the sensibilities of many of the staff.

"Open the Parks in the State to Hunting"

The gardening/trammeling of the Park continued. Deer appeared to have "seriously over-browsed" the vegetation. In keeping with Leopold's "vignette," the Park decided it needed to "manage" the species "so that it assumes its natural place in our native fauna and so that it will balance out with its environment and other species in the Park." Consequently, in 1965 the Park tried to get approval from the Washington Office to have Colorado Game, Fish, and Parks trap seventy-five deer in the Park during the upcoming winter.[3]

The next year the Park staff decided that live trapping would be too difficult and that euphemistic "direct measures" would have to be taken. Word leaked out that the Park intended to reduce the summer herd by killing 200 deer. The expected controversy seemed to have cooled when Harry Woodward, Director of the Colorado Game, Fish, and Parks Department, riled the public by claiming that since "the State owns all the game," then the logical course of action would be to "open the [national] parks in the State to hunting." In his history of Mesa Verde, Smith states that eventually the deer were killed despite the State of Colorado's claim of ownership as well as the objections of "emotional protesters [who] saw the plan as a plot to kill the lovable 'Bambi.'" However, internal Park documents indicate the plan for the Park staff to kill deer was deferred because of Woodward's opposition to having the Park Service take matters into their own hands.[4]

Whether or not reduction was a good idea in policy or biology, the Park could have proceeded without State consent. In discussing this episode, Smith continues, "Colorado might think [the State owns all game], but the question has never been decided in court."[5] Smith is wrong on this point. Federal "ownership" of animals on federal land has been affirmed by several courts, most fundamentally in 1928 by the US Supreme Court in *Hunt v. U.S.*[6] However, it appears that instead of immediate "direct reduction," the Park opted for more research. They contracted with Colorado State University for a two-year deer study to determine movement and distribution; physiological condition; population dynamics; and range utilization, condition, trend, and carrying capacity.[7]

In his administrative history, Torres-Reyes makes no mention of significant numbers of deer being killed by Park personnel. Instead, in 1967 deer were tagged as part of the study, with one tagged near headquarters eventually seen near the highway between Cortez and Shiprock. In addition, exclosures were placed around bitterbrush and serviceberry—bushes favored as browse by deer—on Long, Wetherill, Chapin, Whites, and Big Mesas, some of which are still in place over fifty years later. Three years later, the Park conducted several overflights trying to locate the tagged deer; very few were spotted.[8]

On the other hand, the populations of Abert's squirrels and Gunnison's prairie dogs were supplemented to bolster their dwindling populations. These attempts at gardening the Park proved futile.[9]

In keeping with national priorities, the Park continued its battle against native insect and fungal diseases "to prevent serious destruction of forest values." Fire suppression continued—the Park averaged 6.6 fires per year between 1938 and 1968—and added a policy that all fires must be extinguished in what was then called the Park's "protection zone"—that part of the Ute Mountain Ute Reservation south of the Park and north of the Mancos River.[10]

"We Currently Do Not Have a Naturalist on Our Staff"

This must have been a difficult time to manage the natural condition of Mesa Verde. The Park's 1965 Master Plan notes that they needed at least one park naturalist on the staff.[11] Three years later, in response to a forestry professor's letter desiring information about a particular insect genus in the Park, the Superintendent replied that Mesa Verde "was basically set aside to preserve the best collection of outstanding prehistoric Indian dwellings in America and as such emphasis of research has been on man and his use and adaptation to his environment. . . . We currently do not have a naturalist on our staff."[12]

It was easy enough to notice the charismatic fauna, and sometimes Park references reveal a rare and welcome sense of humor. One Superintendent's "Monthly Narrative Report" for November mentions "The turkey population has not been seen in the headquarters area for the past three weeks. This may, in part, be due to their knowledge of modern man's holidays."[13]

However, simple occasional observations were insufficient. Following the Leopold Report's lead, the Superintendent announced, "Wildlife populations will be managed in such a way as to maintain the health of the species and attain optimum relationship between them and their environment."[14] It is not clear how that would have been accomplished in the absence of a naturalist.

The Park's staffing inadequacies are even more apparent in uninformed statements made concerning the Mesa Verde flora: "Nonnative flora, such as Canadian thistle and Mexican whorled milkweed, will be eliminated insofar as possible." The milkweed is native. Exotic cheatgrass was so widely spread that management action to eliminate it "would be impractical," but, contrary to cheatgrass biology, the 1965 Master Plan claimed, "natural grasses and forbs will probably eliminate it through competition." To make matters worse, the Park intentionally planted the exotic grasses smooth brome and crested wheatgrass to stabilize soil in construction areas. After the Morefield Fire of 1959, the park seeded the burned area with smooth brome. Forty years later the Park realized, "After planting a non-native grass, and a rhizomatous grass at that, this piece of park land may never have plant succession beyond this exotic grass monoculture stage." (See Figure 30).[15]

"Scenes of Indian Corn and Wild Turkeys"

The comprehensive, interdisciplinary Wetherill Mesa Studies brought biological expertise to the Park, but they were focused on the bigger picture of how natural conditions differed between the present day and when Ancestral Puebloans populated the mesa. A heavily forested Mesa Verde, as now existed, was thought likely to resemble conditions prior to Indigenous people living on the mesa. Native Americans may have burned the mesas to maintain shrub vegetation, which in turn would support more game animals than a piñon-juniper forest. "Actually, if we wished to recreate the prehistoric scene, we would denude the area of vegetative cover and plant the mesa tops and canyon draws and terraces with fields of corn, squash, and beans."[16]

For a few years, the Park considered just that: manipulating "sizeable portions" of the mesa tops to restore the conditions of "agricultural openness" that were believed to have been present at the end of the occupation by the Ancestral Puebloans. It is not clear how far the Park was prepared to go in this manipulation. After many generations of living on the mesa, firewood cutting and clearing vegetation for cultivating crops "must have resulted in denuded and eroded ground." This "restoration" would go beyond the Leopold Report's "vignette of primitive America" (previously examined in chapter 6) by replicating what the mesa looked like—not when seen by the first white men, as was Leopold's benchmark, but what it must have looked like six centuries earlier. For Mesa Verde, it was suggested to clear some of the piñon-juniper forest and replace it "with scenes of Indian corn and wild turkeys." The experience of visitors could be enriched by watching demonstrators as they "coiled pottery, ground corn, repaired roofs and masonry of the ruin replica, chopped wood with a stone ax, used an atlatl, or worked with a crude digging stick," and would be invited to try these activities.[17]

Aside from the complications of such a living history interpretive program, the many problems associated with such large-scale manipulation of the mesa-top ecosystem were quickly realized. The 1974 Management Objectives for the Park includes "Consider plant manipulation for enhancement of ruins settings, but not to a condition of prehistoric openness, which could damage the natural environment irreparably." In other words, perhaps a little light gardening, rather than whole landscape conversion.[18]

"The Ravages of Man's Occupation"

By the early 1970s, natural resource management at Mesa Verde followed—to some degree—the changed practices at the national level. The Service had started moving away from Starker Leopold's active management to one of "natural regulation," where populations were controlled by food availability in winter, severe weather, predation, and naturally occurring diseases. Only the acceptance of fire lagged. Though its natural role was acknowledged, and there was a growing awareness of the part Native Americans had played in fire ecology, the risks of fire were feared in a landscape where it had not been allowed its natural function for decades.[19]

At Mesa Verde, in preparation for the next round of Park master planning, the Regional Director wrote that the Park should give more attention to setting standards and guidelines for "the restoration and maintenance of the park's biological resource." The new Superintendent, Ron Switzer, agreed, writing with more than a touch of exaggeration to make his point: "Although the prehistoric story of Mesa Verde is without question the primary resource of the park, the piñon-juniper forest contained therein is one of the few remaining undisturbed forests of its kind in the nation. Consequently, it deserves greater attention in the interpretation of park resources." The 1974 Statement for Management and Planning includes a task to research piñon-juniper forest ecology, and "initiate control programs necessary to preserve the ecosystems that have survived the ravages of man's occupation." It is not clear which "man's occupation" the document is referencing.[20]

There are hints of managing to allow a process, as opposed to the snapshot "vignette," but always with a deference to visitor use: "Maintain areas not used for interpretation and visitor services in as natural a state as possible through the use of a fire management plan, elimination and/or control of the exotic flora and fauna, and continued ecological research." A fire management plan would identify areas where fire might be used as a management tool and define conditions under which its use would be appropriate. Two years later, the Superintendent lamented the absence of any progress on such a plan.[21]

In 1976, the Park undertook an extensive monitoring study of horse herds in the Wetherill Mesa area.[22] There were daily observations of horse locations, movements, and interactions. Andrea Sharon found thirty-eight horses in eight herds. All animals were described by distinguishing features and given names, varying from descriptive ("Blaze") to whimsical ("Sluggo"). Interestingly, Rock Springs, the most reliable natural water source on the Mesa, was rarely used by the horses. Instead, they seemed to rely on water sources created by developments (road culverts and leaking water pipes). The horses acted wild, and there were no signs of horseshoes, branding, or gelding, unlike observations during the 1930s. And yet, when it came to these feral horses, the concept of a Mesa Verde garden had not yet completely disappeared: "During summer months when visitors are bussed on the thirteen mile road to Wetherill Mesa, a sighting of these horses often enhances the visit and adds to the understanding of the park and Ute Indians. . . . It is the observer's opinion that these horses should not be totally eliminated but that the Park Service should attempt to control the population."[23]

"The Tramway Could Be Located so as to Be Mostly Inconspicuous"

In keeping with the spirit of Mission 66, development in Mesa Verde followed several fronts.

Meredith Guillet had come to the Park as Superintendent in 1966. He saw recreational potential in the eastern acreage that his predecessors had missed. If the inholdings could be acquired, the Mancos River floodplain would be "an ideal location for large groups that wish to camp in an isolated area for extended periods of time." Eventually, the Park might acquire lands to make this area accessible from the Park entrance. However, the Acting Regional Director opposed acquisition because "it was not considered during the field study." His opposition was to the recreational development, not the ownership itself.[24]

The Acting Regional Director was replaced by Frank Kowski in the permanent position. He saw that on both the east and north sides of the Park ownership issues could be addressed through congressional appropriations. Private land at the Park entrance, used for sheep grazing in spring and fall, was an obvious need for acquisition. And two parcels along the Mancos River were being severely overgrazed. In addition, private ownership effectively blocked entrance to downstream Park lands, and hunting by the owner and his guests was problematic since the boundary there was not fenced. Acquisition of this land became a top priority. (Over fifteen years later, the inholdings had still not been acquired, and it was almost thirty years before grazing was terminated.)[25]

On the other side of the Park, the archeological work on Wetherill Mesa had been finished in 1963, and the Park started planning for developments to turn what had been backcountry into a front-country experience to complement that on Chapin Mesa, including another archeological museum and an elevator to Long

House—both to be built "next year," according to the Park's Annual Report to the Director for Fiscal Year 1966.[26]

Public access to this development was a problem. The route taken by researchers—the truck trail used to fight the 1934 fire—could be re-constructed for passenger vehicles, but if additional sites on other mesas were to be made available to Park visitors, even more roads would be required. Expanding to another mesa had long been considered by the Park, and the mesa most frequently mentioned was Moccasin. But opening Wetherill Mesa created an opportunity for development of Long Mesa and the unnamed mesa to its east. After much study, NPS planners suggested access could be better achieved by use of an aerial tram starting near Park headquarters. "The tramway could be located so as to be mostly inconspicuous by keeping the cables and gondolas below the elevation of the mesa rims. Such a location would provide the visitor with the opportunity for viewing unexcavated cliff dwellings." Stops could be added if the Park decided to make the sites available to the public.[27]

How close to Disneyland could the Park get?

The answer came the next year in a report by an engineering firm the Park Service had asked to look at Wetherill Mesa access options.[28] The company estimated it would take four years and more than four million dollars to construct a road to Wetherill capable of handling the volume predicted by the Park. Once there, the visitor would have to park his car and "climb up and down the face of the cliffs where the major attractions exist," an impediment to "elderly persons." The company recommended the aerial tram along a route starting about a half mile north of the Headquarters/Mesa Top Loops intersection on Chapin Mesa and going below the canyon rims on its way to Wetherill Mesa near Two Raven House. The route would go past several cliff dwellings, including Little Long House, Square Tower House, Echo House, Navajo Watchtower, Double House, Buzzard House, and Thomas House.

A cynic could be excused for noticing there was no mention of adding animatronic mountain lions stalking animatronic bighorn sheep. Even without these additions, nothing else could so certainly

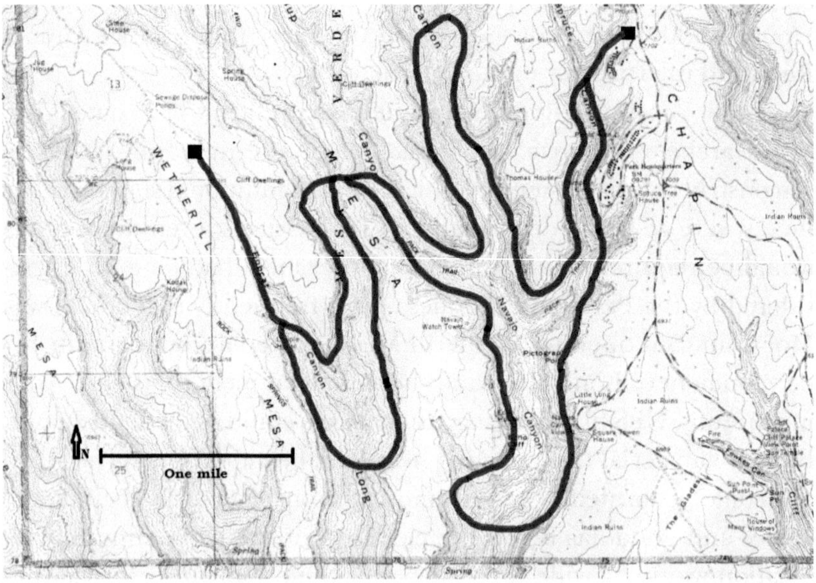

Figure 14. Proposed 1968 route of a tram connecting Chapin and Wetherill Mesas.

Figure 15. Artist's rendering of the proposed tram passing a cliff dwelling (Clarkson Engineering 1968).

impose modern development—what the Wilderness Act in Section 2(a) refers to as "growing mechanization"—on any remaining semblance of wild country on the western side of the Park.

Instead of the aerial tram from Chapin, the next year the Park opted for visitors to drive out to Wetherill where they would pick up a "mini-train" system that would go south to Nordenskiöld 12 and 13 on the west and Double House on the east. Then, a change of plans: to avoid "astronomical" congestion: buses were to take visitors from the Far View Visitor Center to the planned Wetherill Mesa Visitor Center. There, people would pick up the mini-train, which would retain "that Disneyland-ish dimension" favored by some long-time staff.[29]

"An Efficient Gondola Lift System"

Access problems went beyond Wetherill Mesa to the entire Park itself. Most of the alternatives examined would have serious impacts on the "undeveloped" quality of the existing backcountry.

After a major slide on the Point Lookout grade, there was renewed discussion of additional access from the south. Superintendent Guillet offered one possibility: making a road out of the old trail from the Mancos River up Navajo, Rock, and Horse Canyons to Krueger Point on the Ute Reservation, and then east along the North Rim to the Wetherill Mesa Road. Or, if not a road, how about a different aerial tram? The Superintendent of the Consolidated Ute Agency suggested a tram to the rim of Chapin Mesa from the bottom of Mancos Canyon. The Utes could develop visitor facilities, get the proceeds from the tramway operation, and the Park could expand its mini-train concept.[30]

Options expanded. If not an aerial tram from the south, perhaps one from the north? A businessman from Cortez proposed one as "a ride of immense grandeur" that would be both fast and able to accommodate the expected increase in visitation. Superintendent Guillet, looking for guidance from the Regional Director, expressed his opinion that the tram from the south would be preferable because the lower elevation at the Park's terminus meant the possibility of year-round operational capabilities. And as a bonus, it would be an incentive "should we ever negotiate a joint management agreement for Ute lands on Chapin Mesa."[31]

These access proposals were bolstered by a Park planner from Denver who deemed the twenty-mile, narrow, winding entrance road as difficult, distracting, and "an unproductive prolongation of the time it takes to get to the ruins." Perhaps the automobile had no place at all in the future of Mesa Verde; perhaps the Park should be looking at a tram not as additional access, but perhaps as the only access.[32]

That opened the door for a proposal from the Wankanta Lift Company of Boulder, Colorado, to replace the entrance road with "an efficient gondola lift system, operated in conjunction with a mesa-top public transportation system."[33] The tram would leave from an area managed by the Bureau of Land Management at the base of the North Escarpment, arriving at a point north of the Far View Visitor Center. Since there would be no private vehicle access, the company suggested a system of double-decker buses across all the mesas. They would also construct and operate a campground near the lower terminal.

Five months later, the new Superintendent, Ron Switzer, wrote the Regional Director in opposition to the aerial tram and mass transportation system. He took exception to the denigration of the entrance road by someone insufficiently familiar with the Park, instead calling it "an interpretive experience in itself."[34]

Enter politics. In September, Colorado's Senator Peter H. Dominick wrote Interior Secretary Rogers C. B. Morton, pressuring the Park Service to take favorable action on the Wankanta proposal. To his credit, the NPS Associate Director pushed back, writing the Senator, that this would be a "drastic change" from traditional park developments and concession operations. It would necessitate an Environmental Impact Statement to address why the Park Service would consider making obsolete the existing road after spending "several million dollars" so far on its construction. He concluded with condescension: "If we are successful in finding a park where such a concept can be used, the company will have an opportunity to bid. We appreciate your interest in this matter."[35]

There would be no aerial tram accessing Mesa Verde.

"Several New Trails"

Part of the Park's infrastructure that the aerial tram would have bypassed was the large campground at the head of Morefield Canyon built as part of Mission 66 to replace the campground on Spruce Tree Point. Concurrent with this development was the recognition that, with a backcountry now closed to visitors, there were few amenities other than guided or interpreted visits to the cliff dwellings. Using the campground as a trail hub made perfect sense.

In 1964, a new trail was proposed to follow the Knife Edge portion of the old entrance road west and then south from the north side of the new campground to Montezuma Valley Overlook—a portion of which is a foot trail today. Another was to go north from the campground down to Windy Point (below Point Lookout) on an even older section of road. Park staff and the concessioner also planned a horseback trip to scout out the feasibility of a horse trail between Morefield and Prater Canyons.[36]

Almost two years later, a decision was made. "Several new trails" and facilities would be constructed for the horse concessioner in the Morefield Canyon Campground area. Eventually, a seven-mile trail from the Morefield Campground to Prater Ridge and around the perimeter of the mesa top was begun in 1966, to be finished the next year. "This project will open up a most interesting area for the visitor. . . . Several small ruins are along the route."[37]

The Prater Ridge Loops make for interesting hikes, but one would be hard-pressed to say "several small ruins" contribute to that interest in any meaningful way. William Winkler, Mesa Verde lodging and campground concessioner and the son-in-law of Ansell Hall (who was the Service's first "chief naturalist" in the Division of Education and later became one of the Park System's first conservationist-concessioners) pined for the old half-day and full-day trips that had been offered out of the Spruce Tree area, south on Chapin Mesa to sites including Casa Colorado and Two Story House. But then Mesa Verde moved the concessioner to Morefield, adjacent to the new campground. Of the Prater Ridge Loops, he wrote, "It was a good

Figure 16. Site 5MV4659, the most obvious "ruin" on Prater Ridge, about twenty-five yards off the trail.

ride for people who had been in the car all day, but it was never a replacement for the great trips on Chapin Mesa."[38]

Both the Park and the horse concessioners, Emmett and Frances Koppenhafer, could see what was coming. They wrote the Superintendent, trying to stave off the inevitable by reminding him how important they had been as part of the team. The couple had been operating in the Park since 1948, and were relocated twice in that time, moving at the Park's request to Morefield. "We have always and will continue to support the N.P.S."[39]

Nevertheless, "the Park Service decided horseback tours were inappropriate," and the concession was officially terminated.[40] Another recreational opportunity in Mesa Verde was foreclosed.

"Experience Some of the Same Thrill"

The trams were defeated; new trails serviced the new campground. But what kinds of experiences were in the mind of Park planners?

Duane Smith quoted archeologist Alden Hayes: "Those of us who were privileged to take part in the exploration of Wetherill Mesa devoutly hope that each visitor in the future, who looks down at the sightless windows of Double House from a rock ledge or who rounds the bend in the cliff to set foot in Long House, will experience some of the same thrill of discovery that was ours."[41] How many visitors get to look down at the sightless windows of Double House? None. People do get to round the bend approaching Long House, but only in a tightly regulated tour group.

Experiences were becoming increasingly constrained. More of the Park was being kept secret.

By 1966 the Park brochure no longer showed the trail down Spruce Canyon to Navajo Canyon. Registration became required for the two trails in the headquarters area still open for public use (Spruce Canyon and Petroglyph Point). The 1970 Park brochure explained, "Hiking is restricted because Mesa Verde's fragile, irreplaceable ruins must have maximum protection."

As the 1965 Master Plan stated, "Controlled use is mandatory." The Plan continued by asserting that "People wandering into the canyons and backcountry without restraint" threaten the archeology and cannot "be given unrestricted movement and action." Interpretation of the natural values must be limited to "roads, and some trails located out of high ruins concentration such as along the North Rim. Hiking, riding, etc., must be restricted to *areas where there are no cliff dwellings*" (emphasis added). However, there was some realization that, "With visitor use increasing constantly we must consider ways of allowing the visitor to enjoy part of the area on his own."[42]

For all the writing about allowing visitor discovery in areas where there are no cliff dwellings, the Park's 1965 Master Plan emphasized experiences that were not self-directed. Additional visitation meant needing to prepare additional sites to spread use and lighten the inevitable impacts from visitors to the existing interpreted sites. "It may be that in the future we shall have to allow seeing the ruins to consist of viewing them from the cliff across the canyon." Or "a reconstructed cliff dwelling, or dwellings, could be erected in unused caves. . . . If this is ever done, then a series of reconstructed mesa-top sites will be needed to give the entire picture."[43]

Why not just send them to the pseudo-cliff dwelling at Manitou Springs?[44]

The Chief Park Archeologist believed the Wetherill Mesa development would be able to mitigate the impacts on Chapin Mesa for many years to come, but if necessary, she felt other areas could be developed for visitation and interpretation. In an attitude unusual in the Park Service at the time, she added, "There is a distinct reluctance and aversion to continuous development in the great natural areas, and this is as it should be." Nonetheless, in addition to the long-held belief that Moccasin Mesa would make the logical choice for the next development, she suggested the entire complex of the reservoir, ditch system, and multiple great kivas, referred to as the Morefield Canyon Village, "is another area we should think of as eventually opening to the public."[45]

The idea that Mesa Verde had to be "exhibited" like a formal garden, and interpreted for the visitor came from two distinct influences. First, this was in the period of increasing appreciation of the brilliant theoretical work of Freeman Tilden, *Interpreting Our Heritage.*[46] In that vein, Chief Archeologist Jean Pinkley wrote in a 1966 interpretive prospectus:

> The "old, busted houses" are not particularly beautiful nor attractive within themselves. It is only when we "put people back into them" through interpretation that they become alive and can make their valuable contribution to our culture and human enjoyment. Thus, unlike the situation in other parks, *visitors could get practically nothing from their visit to Mesa Verde National Park did we not literally take them by the hand and guide them through the features* (emphasis added).[47]

Though this may be true for many visitors, it is spectacularly wrong for some. Kenneth Nyberg quoted one researcher on the topic as saying, "Not having an interpreter in a park is like inviting a guest to your house, opening the door, and then disappearing." To which Nyberg responded, "I rather suspect that not having an interpreter in a park is more like returning to your own home and not having a salesman there waiting for you." While understanding and appreciation is often enhanced through quality interpretation, there are some experiences where anything other than self-discovery is an impediment.[48]

Perceptions of visitor experiences aside, the other reason for making sure that visitors were not left on their own in Mesa Verde was the legitimate fear of vandalism, though there is considerable disagreement on just how prevalent that was at the time. Pinkley admitted there was some purposefully destructive behavior but did not consider vandalism a significant problem. At the same time, former Superintendent Thomas had a different view shortly after the end of his tenure. He believed there were many more crimes committed because the ranger force was too small to keep all visitors under surveillance at all times. He asserted that the primary reason the Park conducted guided trips was for protection, not interpretation. "I decry the tendency of our present administrators in Region to encourage area superintendents to do away with guided trips and let the public roam at will through prehistoric ruins." While Thomas admitted "the average visitor today is much better behaved than his counterpart of 20 years ago, the sum total of crime is greater because we have so many more potential criminals to deal with."[49]

Violations occurred across a spectrum of damage. Some involved theft: "November 15 a search was initiated for the owner of a car which had been left in the Headquarters Parking lot for several days. . . . A young man and woman were found and apprehended, after it was learned that they had been hiking and camping in the back country. . . . They were cited for entering a closed area, abandonment of property, and possession of artifacts. They received fines totaling $125." Some violations were simple sightseeing: "Written warning citations were issued to two California students for entering Little Long House." Some were purely "experiential": "Four beatniks [*sic*]—including three boys and a girl—were located in the canyon near

Spruce Tree House. . . . They stated they wanted to experience, on their own, the feelings of their ancestors who had once lived in the cliff dwelling. . . . They were reprimanded by the Chief Ranger."[50]

Interestingly, in a memo from the Superintendent to the Regional Director, the degree to which the backcountry was legally closed was phrased somewhat differently: "Backcountry use is *not encouraged* to provide maximum protection of archeological sites" (emphasis added). There also seemed to be confusion over whether the concern was the cliff dwellings or the entire backcountry. The 1969 Master Plan conflates these: "Due to the fragile nature of the cliff dwellings, the ruins must be protected from unauthorized use during off hours. Hence, much of the Park may be considered closed to visitation except on guided tours." Note the choice of the phrase "may be considered closed," rather than "is closed."[51]

"Television and Other Devices Could Be Substituted for Tours"

Whatever would or would not happen with the backcountry, the frontcountry was getting crowded. The opening of Wetherill Mesa was delayed year after year. The Park was considering several alternatives, some of which have already been described, but are touched on here not necessarily because of their impact on the backcountry, but because of what they say about the type of experience the Park staff thought they should be providing.

One obvious—if unpopular—option that came up from time to time was to limit visitation. As expected, the Cortez Chamber of Commerce objected to limiting the number of private vehicles allowed to enter the Park. Instead, they suggested limiting visitation to any given ruin "at some future date."[52]

It wasn't that Park staff didn't recognize the problem of limited experiential opportunities.[53] The question was, what should be done about it? Due to ever-increasing visitation, by 1972 the consensus of the Interpretation Division was, "The chance of ever getting visitors into the ruins with a very 'personal' experience is over." The new Chief Archeologist proposed a solution for still providing "a good visitor experience." He suggested the Park build an interpretive center northeast of Sun Temple, where the Park would show "a ten-minute color film on the Cliff Palace. . . . Good interpretation could be afforded the visitor. Those visitors wishing to go through the ruin (for a few more years), could proceed to Cliff Palace and have the opportunity. Many people would be totally satisfied. Eventually, it might be necessary to combine this movie with one of Indian life and eliminate visits within the ruins entirely when crowd use becomes unmanageable."[54]

When Superintendent Switzer passed this proposal on the to the Regional Director, he appended, "When visitor use here becomes unmanageable, television and other devices could be substituted for tours."[55]

Why even bother coming to the Park? It is difficult to imagine a more oblivious opinion on visitor needs. But when the decision is set in stone to keep most of the garden a secret, perhaps the only way to preserve the remainder is to film it for viewing in the comfort of . . . somewhere else.

Some Park Service employees were aware of the dangerous ground Mesa Verde was treading. "Currently, interpretive services offered at Mesa Verde National Park are not of a sufficient number and variety to satisfy the needs of all park visitors." One partial solution: "Make more archeological sites and other remains available for public viewing and interpretation" including "water control devises and farm terraces" at the Far View complex, Spring House, Square Tower House, and Swallow's Nest. In addition, "Study backcountry use in light of Wilderness Proposal."[56]

In fact, these ideas were largely swept aside in the Park's wilderness planning, as covered in the next chapter.

"He Dislikes the Government Intensely"

Other than the process of wilderness designation, the issue creating the most difficulty for Mesa Verde during the late 1960s and early '70s was the multifaceted and interconnected set of problems posed by the Park's relationship with the neighboring Ute Mountain Ute Tribe. These included: the Park's continuing desire to expand operations south into the Ute's lands; the need to settle access questions over the Park's trespasses at Soda Point and to the development on Wetherill Mesa; and the threat of oil and gas mineral development south of the Park's boundary on the mesa.

Outright exchange seemed permanently off the table, but negotiations continued throughout 1965 by which the Park would manage approximately 100,000 acres of Ute land—all of the Mesa Verde landform not already within the Park.[57]

However, Chief Jack House was adamant that no collecting, survey, or study would be conducted on the Ute Mountain Ute lands, and Park staff were careful not to propose any activity that could further anger House and "ruin our negotiations for an easement on the Wetherill approach road. . . . He dislikes the government intensely."[58]

NPS Director George Hartzog became involved, bypassing Chief House and going directly to Scott Jacket, Chairman of the Ute Mountain Tribal Council. He proposed a cooperative agreement for the management and interpretation of these "nationally significant resources" on the Ute Reservation and suggested it might be possible to have "a joint admission charge for the combined areas" of the Park and the Reservation.[59]

There was a sticking point in that the Utes, as noted in the previous chapter, had opened their land south and west of the Park for oil exploration. Superintendent Thomas offered Park staff to help assure optimal location of roads and seismograph lines, with archeologists accompanying exploration crews. Then he countered with yet another exchange idea: the Utes would get to use Park roads for transporting seismograph crews and equipment; in return, there would be discussion about the administration by the Park Service of a portion of the Reservation.[60]

But the Tribe turned the tables on the Park. Rather than continuing discussion on whether the Park would manage part of the Ute lands for Park purposes, they announced their intention to construct a concessioner facility on Soda Point. The Park informed the Utes that "this development was not compatible with our aims for Chapin Mesa and that the National Park Service was definitely against the proposal." The Park must have realized their "aims" for land that belonged to the Utes were immaterial; perhaps they could trade access to potential mineral development for an undeveloped Soda Point.[61]

In January 1967, the Utes went ahead with an invitation to bid on oil and gas leases, but the response to the lease sale must have been a disappointment. In late September, the Tribal Council met to discuss other ways in which money might be generated, and a transcript was provided in confidence to Superintendent Guillet by Charles Traylor, a lawyer hired by the Tribe. At the Council meeting, the Park's proposal from two years earlier was again raised, trading permission for archeological study on the Ute lands for part of the entrance receipts. Traylor said, "We [the Tribe] can't lose anything by letting them make their survey, and we could gain access to roads and valuable information"; the Tribe's principal attorney, Wade Dillon, said, "I think it's a good deal." After what the transcript refers to as "Discussion in Ute," the decision was announced: "The council says no." The influence of Chief House remained strong.[62]

Superintendent Guillet did not give up on his two-pronged negotiations with the Tribe, and the Park's trespass at Soda Point and Wetherill Mesa needed urgent attention. In October, he wrote the Tribe proposing short rights-of-way on Wetherill and Soda Point in exchange for allowing the Utes to graze livestock in Rock and Horse Canyons and on Wildhorse Mesa. However, the Assistant Regional Director wrote the Park Service Director to recommend against this deal. His position was that the problem would simply be perpetuated and suggested the Park "first construct our new roads on our land, and thereby eliminate dependence upon the Utes. If there is need for negotiating with Utes after that for boundary adjustments or other considerations, our position at the bargaining table will be greatly improved."[63]

Eventually, there was no trade, and the Park did indeed construct bypasses. Or so they thought. It turns out the BLM erred in surveying the boundary on Soda Point, and the new route built by the NPS was still on Ute land. Ute food and souvenir concessions are now a permanent fixture in Mesa Verde frontcountry.

That left the question of what to do with the archeological resources south of the Park on the cuesta, and Superintendent Guillet was gently persistent. He wrote the Regional Director, "Although progress here will probably be slow, there would be certain advantages that would accrue to the Service in scientific research and joint management of areas on Chapin and Wetherill Mesas as well as other Ute lands bordering the Park."[64]

Progress was indeed slow. A year later, in March of 1969, the Park's Master Plan still contemplated getting lower portions of Chapin and Moccasin Mesas, with "significant archeological and ecological resources," in exchange for the grazing lands in the southeastern portions of the Park, "*areas with nominal archeological resources*" (emphasis added). But soon the Park's attitude went from trying to acquire or manage the sites on the Ute land to helping the Utes develop their own park. In September of 1969, Guillet wrote the Ute Mountain Ute Indian Agency Superintendent, informing him that the Park may have to limit visitation because of resource impacts. He suggested the Utes develop access roads in Mancos Canyon and the side canyons in which the cliff dwellings are located. It would give visitors a different point of view to the cliff dwellings. In addition, "I believe that there are great possibilities in developing this section as a tourist attraction and could result in a sizeable contribution to the economy and social development of the Ute Mountain Ute Tribe." In support of this, the Park's Chief Archeologist wrote the Superintendent that the cliff dwellings on the Ute portion of the cuesta were especially valuable because few researchers have investigated them.[65]

"Splendid Cooperation"

The Mesa Verde Master Plan draft of 1969 concisely describes the state of archeology in the backcountry at the time. Wetherill was the only mesa that had been completely surveyed, though Chapin had been surveyed within Park boundaries. Intensive inventories had been completed in advance of developments at the Park entrance, in Morefield Canyon at the area of the new campground, and along the entrance road realignment in Morefield and Prater Canyons. Finally, the southeastern area of the park had been "spot" surveyed in 1954 in connection with a proposed land trade with the Ute Mountain Utes outlined in the previous chapter.[66]

Most of the pertinent archeological work to address the lack of adequate inventory at this time was in connection with the wilderness investigations discussed in the next chapter. But two items are worth note here.

First, there was a leap in what is termed "temporal development" by employing modern machinery. In 1966, a helicopter was used for the first time to support stabilization work in the Park. All materials and supplies for work on Navajo Watchtower and Echo House, on the east side of Long Mesa above Navajo Canyon, were airlifted to preselected spots near each. The cost of helicopter rental was more than offset by savings in time transporting materials and personnel.[67]

Second, there was a change in the leadership at the University of Colorado's Archaeological Research Center at Mesa Verde National Park. Robert Lister wrote Superintendent Guillet to say he was being replaced by David Breternitz, and in an attached personal note, Lister wrote, "Any success that we have had at Mesa Verde has been due to a large degree to the splendid cooperation we have had from you and your staff, and from many others in the N.P.S."[68]

The relationship between the researchers at Colorado and the Park continued to be productive—and supportive—for years to come.

CHAPTER EIGHT

Mesa Verde Meets the Wilderness Act

The Fight over Wilderness Designation

1964–1976

THE NATIONAL PARK SERVICE was strongly opposed to being included in the Wilderness Act, as introduced in chapter 6. But wilderness advocates included the Park Service in the legislation on purpose. "The National Park Service responded to the postwar tourism boom with seemingly boundless enthusiasm for more park development. Conservationists had long viewed national parks as reservoirs of wilderness, but the agency adamantly refused to define any specific lands as permanently off-limits to development."[1]

The change of administrations in 1961, with Stuart Udall becoming Secretary of the Interior, brought a marked decrease in the official opposition to the Act. That did not, however, eliminate the antipathy toward the Act among some NPS staffs. The Act was a threat to each unit's bureaucratic autonomy. Wilderness prohibitions on the use of motorized equipment, not to mention roads, clearly restricted the Park Service's discretion in managing its backcountry zones. Formal wilderness designations would also forfeit the potential for using at least some of those areas to accommodate overflows of visitors in the future.

Nowhere was local Park Service opposition more apparent than at Mesa Verde.

"Forever Prevent Its Use by People"

Section 3(c) of the Wilderness Act of 1964 gave direction to the Park Service to inventory for wilderness characteristics, giving the agency ten years to review every roadless area of five thousand contiguous acres or more, and then report to the President (through the Secretary of the Interior) the recommendation as to the suitability or nonsuitability of each such area for wilderness preservation.[2]

External advocates expressed early interest in the wilderness possibilities of Mesa Verde. In August of 1965 members of the Park staff met briefly with representatives of the Wilderness Society. The Park also arranged for the advocates to meet with officials of the Ute Mountain Ute Tribe. There is no record of what was said in either of the meetings.[3]

But Mesa Verde soon undertook distancing itself from the Wilderness Act. The 1965 Master Plan, released in November, clearly stated: "The land itself will be administered in its natural state and constitutes a modest wilderness area. However, the primary values in the park will forever prevent its use by people in the same manner and to the same extent that wilderness areas will be used in the great natural parks." The Plan did not address the idea that some use of the wilderness in some area of the Park might be possible short of that all-or-nothing approach. The Plan continued that it is "evident" that "antiquities" drive visitors with "an irresistible urge to explore with shovel and appropriate souvenirs," so that use of the backcountry "could not be permitted." Therefore, "We must forbid our visitors to travel into the wilderness," though they could make available to the public "a wealth of scenic grandeur, and abundance of wildlife interests, and a fascinating environment of forest and plant associations."[4]

Again, it was an all-or-nothing attitude, without addressing the feasibility of reducing that "irresistible urge." It was simply assumed to be an impossible task. In addition, it seems that the planners believed what the Park would make available to the public might serve as an adequate substitute for a wilderness experience. It is obvious today that it does not, but it isn't clear if the Park's position was due to lack of awareness, or willful blindness. Perhaps one reinforced the other, heralding Mesa Verde into a non-Wilderness future—a permanent secret. There certainly was misunderstanding of wilderness parameters for conditions at the time of inventory: "Mesa Verde . . . was totally utilized by prehistoric man, and no part of it may be strictly termed a natural area."[5]

"We Have No Areas"

The Park looked at other designations that might forestall wilderness designation. Perhaps the resurrected idea of a Natural Area on Park Mesa would suffice? Some hope came from the Washington Office: "In response to growing national recognition of the need to preserve natural environments and ecosystems" the NPS would identify, classify, and establish "Federal Natural Areas." However, "The Director has not yet determined the full role of the Service in the designation, management, and protection of natural areas under this program."[6]

Any such administrative designation would not be sufficient to supersede the congressional direction to inventory for wilderness suitability. A little more than three years after the passage of the Wilderness Act, in December of 1967, the NPS Washington Office started to issue guidance, starting with boundary identification. The boundary should, in order of preference, use: 1) Lines connecting prominent topographic features, or following ridges, valleys, or streams; 2) If #1 was not feasible, use section lines or subsection lines; 3) Finally, if other methods of boundary identification were not feasible, elevation contour lines could be used. Most importantly, if possible, "The boundary selected should be readily identifiable on the ground so as to facilitate management," though only the first enumerated preference would satisfy that prescription. This common-sense approach to boundaries was expressed decades earlier by USGS Chief Geographer R. B. Marshall: "I want to urge in the strongest possible way that all park boundaries be made to conform to natural lines wherever practicable."[7]

Obviously, boundaries alone were not enough. Further direction came in a memo to the Regional Directors on the progress in making wilderness recommendations to Congress: "One of the major shortcomings has been the lack of a thorough searching out of facts. . . . We cannot afford to do anything less than a complete and thorough job." What was termed a wilderness "research report" would have to be completed and should include: examination of original legislation designating the unit; any impinging Valid Existing Rights or Rights-of-Way; private land within or adjacent to roadless areas; and current land uses and facilities. Three other items in the memo's list have penciled check marks on the copy in the MEVE archives: agreements with other federal agencies, states, or counties that would affect the roadless areas; existing research contracts within the roadless areas; and direction that all "management roads" (administrative roads not open to the public) were to be accurately delineated on a topographic map, including frequency and purpose of use, and condition.[8]

A week later, at the end of December, the Regional Director followed up: "Please note that the [wilderness] research must be accomplished without delay."[9]

Superintendent Guillet would have none of it. On January 12 he sent a one-sentence report to the Regional Director: "We have no areas that would necessitate wilderness proposal studies or research."[10]

Twelve days later, the Regional Director's response was almost as terse: "Unfortunately, your brief statement to the effect that you have no areas necessitating wilderness studies is not enough." Then, to be clear, "Determination of Wilderness versus No Wilderness will not be made at the field nor regional levels, hence the need for advanced research. We suggest a careful review of the December 19 memorandum."[11]

"We Recommend Approval of the Negative Report on Wilderness"

The minutes of the Park Staff Meeting on March 5, 1968, include: "Work has begun on the wilderness proposal for Mesa Verde. We are defining three areas, each exceeding 5,000 acres. Only two will be recommended by us for inclusion in wilderness areas." There is no record of what three areas were defined, nor which two would be recommended. But by the time the Park was finished with the inventory, significant changes were made. These were consistent with the usual Park Service suitability reviews at the time which emphasized the agency's use of master planning to identify areas as suitable for development, rather than identifying places suitable for wilderness designation.[12]

In August, Mesa Verde submitted a wilderness proposal. Apparently, only the accompanying map has survived in the Mesa Verde Research Center. However, the response from the Office of Resource Planning indicates that the Park found only one roadless area, and the Office agreed with the Park's justifications against its designation as Wilderness. Multiple excuses were offered: "archeological research, management, and ruins stabilization should have priority over any other use." Moccasin Mesa has "an interpretive potential equal to Chapin and Wetherill. The area between Chapin and Wetherill Mesas "might qualify" but it was dropped "because of the tramway proposal. . . . Sometime in the future, it may be desirable to utilize this form of transportation between the two major mesas."[13]

In other words, the Long Canyon-and-Mesa area would be left out because the aerial tram might go through there someday—even though the Park was on the verge of vetoing that idea, as detailed in the previous chapter. On the east side of the Park, the map shows the Whites Trail from the East Rim down to the Mancos River as a road, thereby fragmenting that portion of the Park into areas the staff felt were too small to be considered. All that remained was Park Mesa, including the adjacent canyons up to the vaguely defined rims of the mesas on either side, down to the Park's southern boundary. The northern boundary was arbitrarily drawn along the section line separating sections 23 and 24 from 26 and 25. This Roadless Area was deemed inappropriate for wilderness designation because of the needs of "archeological research, management, and ruins stabilization."[14] It was a rationale against wilderness designation that would be developed and used repeatedly over the next several years.

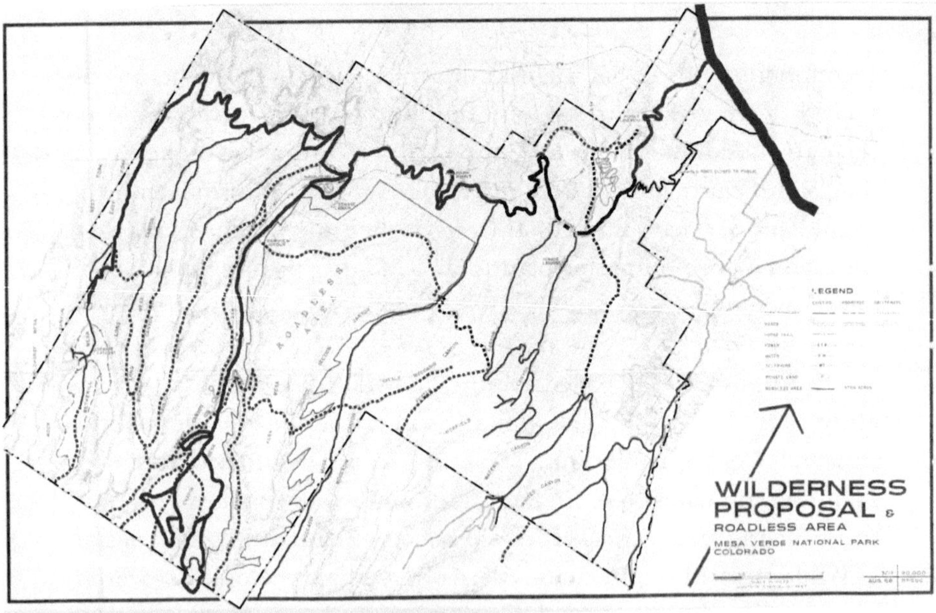

Figure 17. Roads (solid) and trails (dotted) emphasized on the map used to justify the first Mesa Verde wilderness proposal (Figure 18). Compare with Figures 3, 8, 9, 13, and 43.

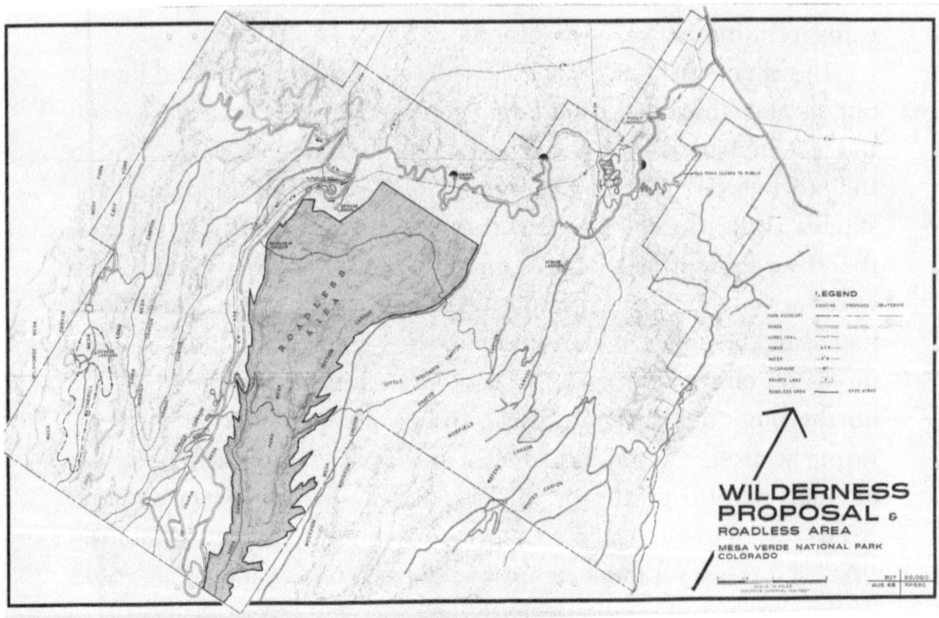

Figure 18. The first Mesa Verde wilderness proposal, August 1968. [RG03-01.05-001]

The Acting Regional Director approved of this approach, writing the Director: "We recommend approval of the negative report on wilderness."[15]

A polished draft still needed to be presented to the public during open hearings, which had been postponed until the spring of 1969. In the meantime, Superintendent Guillet followed up on the persistent idea that Park Mesa would be designated a Natural Area, thought to make wilderness designation an unnecessary redundancy. He received a letter from the Society of American Foresters requesting clarification that Park Mesa was indeed receiving the protection they required and that the purpose of such areas was research—recreational use was discouraged. This perfectly fit the Park's needs. Guillet wrote back that Park Mesa was indeed receiving the protection required. However, eight years later Superintendent Switzer noted that there was no Park Mesa Natural Area. "There have been little or no natural history studies done [on Park Mesa]. This is generally because Park Mesa is roadless and other comparable and more accessible mesas have served equally well for past research studies."[16]

In addition to possibly making wilderness designation redundant with the "Natural Area" designation for Park Mesa, Guillet oversaw a Proposed Rule in the Federal Register that would legally close visitor access to the Mesa Verde backcountry: "Hiking is permitted only on trails designated for that purpose by the Superintendent." The Proposed Rule appeared in the Register in April of 1969, giving the public thirty days to comment. Someone dropped the ball, however, for the Final Rule was not published until October of 1971—two-and-a-half years later. This extraordinary delay appears to have created confusion in Park management in subsequent years, as explained below.[17]

In summing up through the end of 1968, "The work on the Wilderness Study took a lot of man-hours."[18] They had hardly begun.

"Cement Mixers and Trucks of Sand and Cement"

The Mesa Verde Wilderness Hearing did not take place in the spring of 1969 as originally scheduled—it didn't occur until December of

1970—but in February of 1969 the Park did revise its "Wilderness Study (No Wilderness Area Proposed) Roadless Areas" map. This new edition was based on a schematic map, rather than a topographic one as had been used previously.

The new map addressed some of the more glaring shortcomings of the first map. Three areas were identified. Area 1, approximately 10,300 acres, was the country surrounding Long and Navajo Canyons, bordered by the Wetherill Mesa road and development on the west, and the Chapin Mesa developments on the east. Area 2, approximately 11,500 acres, was the Park Mesa and Soda Canyon territory, bordered by the Park developments on Chapin Mesa on the west, and the Moccasin Mesa road and Park boundary on the east. Area 3, approximately 16,400 acres, was most of the Park east of the Moccasin Mesa road, with an exclusion of the Morefield sewage ponds. The map included the Morefield-Whites truck trail as well as the fire trails in the western portion of the Park as part of the wilderness units.

The Park also finished the third draft of its updated Management Plan, still without recommending wilderness. There were two basic

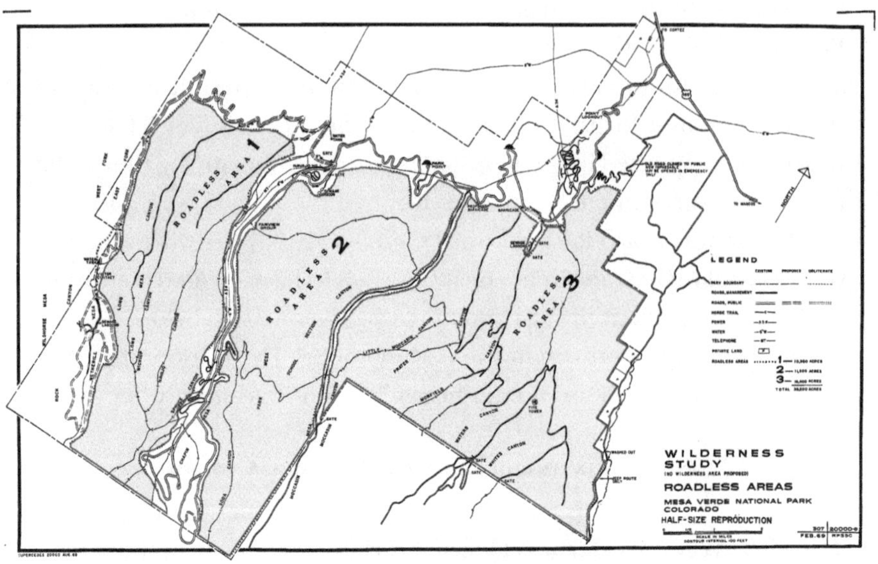

Figure 19. Mesa Verde "Roadless Areas," February 1969. [RG03-01.05-001]

reasons given for the "No Wilderness" recommendation. The first reason cited was owing to "the constant need to patrol remote areas" to prevent "pot-hunting." The second was the needs of research. Excavation would require "importation of mechanical equipment and semi-permanent camps, since some excavations require more than one season. Many of the ruins are then stabilized, which requires cement mixers and trucks of sand and cement." Therefore, the land classification should remain archeological or natural, rather than primitive. In addition, there was an "urgent need" to complete archeological surveys, with the implication that this could not be done in a wilderness.[19]

These barriers to wilderness designation were overblown and misleading at best. Excavations may be permitted in a wilderness, including with the use of motor vehicles and motorized equipment if they are deemed the minimum that are necessary; a second season of field work does not make a camp "semi-permanent," and even so it may be permitted; using cement mixers with "trucks" of sand and cement is not the usual method for stabilizing backcountry sites.

As for the "classification" barrier, there is no reason archeological surveys can't be done in a designated wilderness.

In short, either the staff at Mesa Verde didn't understand wilderness management, or they constructed straw men to justify the Park's "No Wilderness" position. This proclaimed inability to conduct research was one of three objections to wilderness designation to be repeated in later years, when staff certainly should have known better.

At the time, the Park Service saw no problem with this rationale. (Nor, apparently, with their conclusion that management directions in archeological and primitive land classification areas are mutually exclusive.) Looking at the new map, the Chief of the Office of Resource Planning discussed the possibilities of "wilderness escrow"—that is, land that has biophysical or (in the case of Mesa Verde) managerial constraints that preclude immediate wilderness designation, but that, when the constraint is no longer present, the land would become Wilderness without further congressional action.

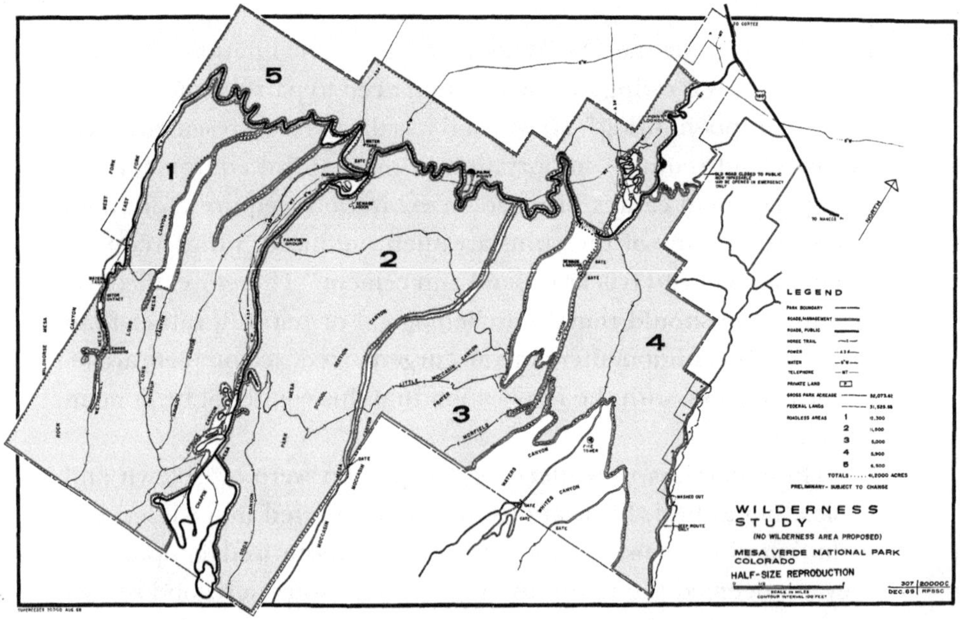

Figure 20. Mesa Verde "Wilderness Study," December 1969. [RG03-01.05-001]

He concluded that "The need for archeological preservation and research activities which precludes the management of the roadless areas as wilderness is of a permanent nature. . . . Therefore, no lands within Mesa Verde are suitable for 'wilderness escrow.'"[20]

Nevertheless, in August the Superintendent wrote that the upcoming management objectives for Mesa Verde included completing the wilderness studies and managing "the three roadless areas according to their final designation," whatever the final designation might be.[21]

In preparation for issuing the preliminary Wilderness Suitability Study Report, the map was refined once more. Now, instead of three roadless areas, the Park identified five. Area 1, now 12,300 acres, was essentially the same except it included the southwest corner of the park, and the fire roads were cherry-stemmed.[22] Area 2 (11,500 acres) remained the same. What had been the third area was now split in two. Area 3, 5,000 acres, now had for its eastern boundary the patrol road in Prater Canyon, the old (1914 to 1923) entrance road over the ridge between Prater and Morefield Canyons, and down the route on Morefield Ridge, with the spur to the Morefield Spring cherry-stemmed. Area 4, 5,900 acres, now had for its western boundary the main backcountry route down Morefield Canyon all the way over to Big Mesa, where it followed the route on top of the East Rim. Area 5, 6,900 acres, was new: the North Escarpment, north of the main Park road and wrapping all the way around the Morefield Campground development, down the entrance road as far as the road to the water line's pump station near the current entry booth. The map shows every evidence of being carelessly drawn, as the wilderness units included telephone, power, and water lines, the Far View sewage lagoons, and even the Park Point fire lookout and road. But at least the truck trails were cherry-stemmed.

"It May Be Necessary to Patrol by Motor Vehicle"

Mesa Verde was caught in the Park Service dichotomy of natural areas versus historic areas, with precious little room for overlap. In 1970, The Secretary of the Interior's Advisory Board on National Parks, Historic Sites, Buildings and Monuments approved a study of the themes that should be covered in the stewardship of every unit in the National Park System. Not surprisingly, Mesa Verde's "prime theme" was centered on the "earliest Americans." When looking at natural history themes, Mesa Verde was only briefly mentioned, and was entirely omitted from the map depicting parks and monuments that represent natural regions across the country.[23]

The separation of historical and natural parks was explained a few years later by Ross Holland, Assistant Director for Cultural Resources. He asserted there was "a fundamental difference between a natural park, which is dynamic, and a historical one, which is static [and] normally must be frozen in time."[24] Managing for an unchanging condition may be the obvious choice for a historic homestead or battlefield, but it is considerably more complicated when the cultural and natural resources are entwined, as at

Mesa Verde. This management tension is discussed in more detail later in this book's conclusion.

In May of 1970, the Park Service released a draft Preliminary Wilderness Suitability Study Report for Mesa Verde National Park, and its reasoning was rooted in this artificial natural/historical dichotomy. The purpose of the National Wilderness Preservation System, the Report summarized, "is to preserve areas 'where the earth and its community of life are untrammeled by man . . . with the imprint of man's work substantially unnoticeable,'" whereas the purpose of Mesa Verde National Park is to "'provide specifically for the preservation from injury or spoilation of the ruins and other works and relics of prehistoric or primitive man within said park.' Since the park is essentially a concentrated area of ruins and relics of primitive man, it has a basically different purpose, use, and management concept than wilderness. Therefore, it is concluded that none of the lands in the five roadless areas studied is suitable for wilderness designation."[25]

Superintendent Guillet's copy has penciled notes on page 1: "The whole park and its community of life were changed by prehistoric man." "It will be managed as wilderness except it could not be opened as such to the public because of [archeological] sites and it would have to be fenced to prevent visitors from trespassing on Ute lands." It isn't clear if Guillet did not know that the "untrammeled" quality was forward-looking, not historical; or that wilderness boundaries can be fenced (and that portions of the boundary with the Utes already had been)—or if he was using this as additional support, however flimsy, for the real reason the Park management didn't want wilderness designation: they didn't want these areas opened to the public.

Page 5 of the draft Preliminary Report described the roadless areas, generally in terms of their archeological resources. The Report offered detailed Findings on page 6, which elaborated on the previous reasons why wilderness designation would be inappropriate at Mesa Verde:

> Unescorted visits to isolated ruins are retracted as a means of preserving unexcavated sites. . . . As park visitation increases, it may be necessary to patrol by motor vehicle the management roads in the isolated areas to prevent depredations.
>
> Research and stabilization of archeological features often use mechanical equipment. . . . Complex land management measures may be necessary or highly desirable in selected sections within roadless areas. This could involve . . . recreating [the Ancestral Puebloan] farming environment by eliminating existing vegetation.
>
> Retention, and possibly, extension of the management roads, is necessary for the research, stabilization, plant control work, and for surveillance patrols to protect the ruins and relics.
>
> At present there is a research and archeological salvage contract with the University of Colorado. . . . As the salvage work is extended to the more isolated parts of the park, semi-permanent camps may be set up within the roadless areas to conserve travel time."

These objections were, for the most part, developed reiterations of the 1969 Master Plan. Once again, the rationales were either erroneous or fabricated. Since the patrol roads were excluded from wilderness consideration on the latest map, there is no prohibition about patrolling on them. Research and stabilization are permitted in Wilderness. Re-creating farming landscapes of the Ancestral Puebloans would be highly unlikely in the roadless areas—the Park had a demonstration garden adjacent to the Mesa Top road. The management roads, excluded from the wilderness proposal, could be maintained, and there was no reason to think they needed to be extended—in fact, they have been contracted over the intervening decades. And as mentioned above, there is no absolute prohibition on overnight camps, even ones that might be used for more than one field season. Once again, it is not known whether these objections were raised out of ignorance or out of a perceived necessity to further stack the anti-Wilderness deck.

Of the many reasons for opposing wilderness designation in these Findings, only one was legitimate: the fear of pot-hunting or other vandalism resulting from unescorted visits to remote sites.

"The Wilderness Act of 1964 Does Not Establish Any New Standard"

The draft Preliminary Wilderness Suitability Study Report was revised in August. There was some minor wordsmithing that did not change the intent of the sections quoted above, but there was a change in the map in Areas 3 & 4 to more accurately reflect the actual conditions of the routes in these areas. The Far View sewage lagoons and the developments at Park Point were now omitted—though water, power, and telephone lines were still within the wilderness areas being considered.

In September, in preparation for the public comment period, the draft report was changed once again, with inserted sections on general NPS Policy for Historical Areas as well as Wilderness Use and Management Policy. These appear to have been tailored specifically for Mesa Verde. One insertion: "In making the Wilderness Act applicable to the National Park System, however, Congress clearly did not intend to change the basic purpose of such areas." This is an incomplete interpretation of the Wilderness Act: "The purposes of this Act are hereby declared to be within *and supplemental* to the purposes for which . . . units of the national park . . . systems are established and administered" (emphasis added). In other words, the "basic purpose" of the area would not change, but that purpose would have to be administered in conformance with the Wilderness Act, which may be in a different manner than it was carried out prior to wilderness designation.[26]

The report continued, "Importantly, however, the Wilderness Act of 1964 does not establish any new standard or criteria for national park wilderness use and management."[27] This is an astonishing statement. To support this interpretation, the report cited Section 4(a)(3)

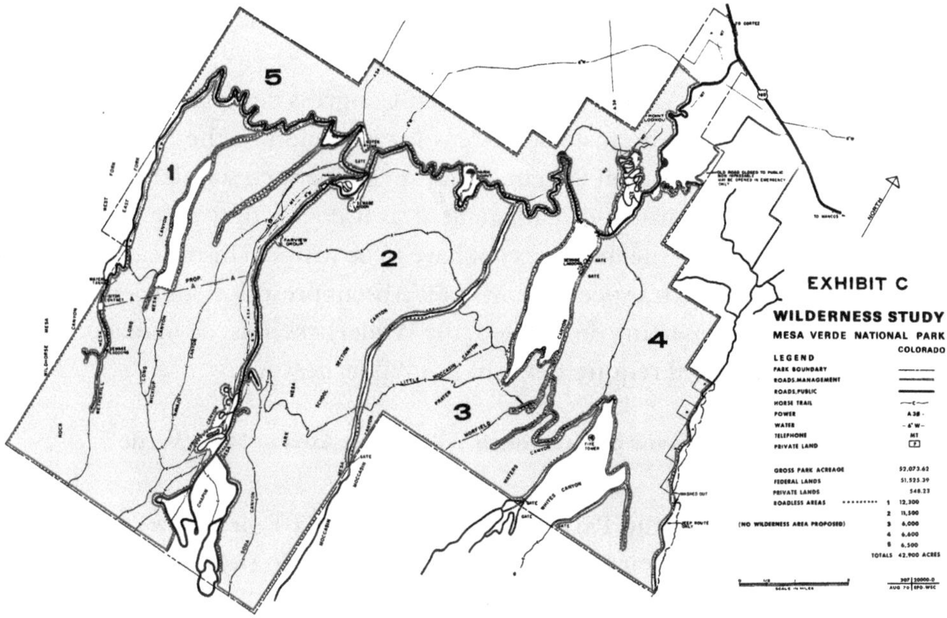

Figure 21. The final "Wilderness Study" map used for public comments, August 1970. [RG03-01.05-002]

of the Wilderness Act: "Nothing in this Act shall modify the statutory authority under which units of the national park system are created. Further, the designation of any area of any park . . . as a wilderness . . . shall in no manner lower the standards evolved for the use and preservation of such park." The NPS was correct in citing there would be no lowering of standards—this language in the Wilderness Act was included to assuage the fear that NPS Wilderness areas would have to be managed similarly to Forest Service Wilderness areas (e.g., allowing grazing or new mineral exploration).[28] To suggest that allowing public use lowers management standards is not an assertion that conforms to the NPS Organic Act. In addition, the report ignored the salient language from Section 4(b) of the Wilderness Act: "Each agency . . . shall so administer such area for such other purposes for which it may have been established *as also to preserve its wilderness character*" (emphasis added). This error of omission was repeated in subsequent planning documents.

The report added, "Of course, when Congress designates wilderness units within the historical areas for inclusion in the National Wilderness Preservation System, it may prescribe such standards and criteria for their use and management as it deems desirable."[29] Of course it may, and the unit does not have to be within a historical area for inclusion of extra special provisions. Absent prescriptions specific to the wilderness being designated, the Wilderness must be managed under the general requirements of the Wilderness Act.

"I Am Not in Favor of Creating a Wilderness Area at Mesa Verde"

In October 1970, the Park Planner met with staff members of the Senate Committee on Insular Affairs, the Colorado Delegation, and the staff of Colorado Congressman Wayne Aspinall, Chairman of the House Committee with jurisdiction over the Park Service. They all agreed that the Service's reasoning in not proposing wilderness in Mesa Verde was sound. A Federal Register Notice announced the "Nonsuitability as Wilderness Hearing" would be held December 16th in Cortez.[30]

Near the end of the month, David Breternitz, who had taken over leadership of the University of Colorado's Mesa Verde archeological research project (and was to lead research archeologists' opposition to the Mesa Verde wilderness), wrote John McComb, the southwest representative of the Sierra Club, outlining his objections to a Mesa Verde Wilderness.[31] "First of all, nowhere in the proposed area [of Park Mesa] is it more than 10 miles from a current paved road. This isn't very 'wildernessy' to begin with." In fact, no point on Park Mesa is more than 2 miles from a paved road—but topography influences "wildernessy" feelings.

Breternitz continued: "Actually, protection of the many Indian ruins in the proposed area is probably better now than it would be if it were to become a Wilderness Area." There is little question that archeological sites in areas closed to the public have greater protection than those open to the public. The questions are, for whom are they protected? What is actually at risk? And to what degree?

Breternitz: "Also, one of the problems at Mesa Verde is the inability to handle summer visitors who flock to the area in excess of 6000 a day. Additional areas in MVNP will have to be opened in the future. How many persons would be in the Park Mesa area each day?? 20, 50, 100?? I seriously doubt that the public, who owns Mesa Verde, will agree to set aside an area for the benefit of a few people when it has the potential of serving several thousand visitors a day." Breternitz made two fundamental errors here: one was that Park Mesa was being considered as the site of yet another visitor center. More importantly, he completely misjudged "the public" and their appetite for setting aside Wilderness Areas. The law was enacted as an antidote to the country's "increasing population, accompanied by expanding settlement and growing mechanization" only six years earlier, and was passed in Congress by votes of 73 to 12 in the Senate and 374 to 1 in the House.[32]

Breternitz: "Most of the existing roads in the Park Mesa Area [*sic*] are fire roads and in wet weather are four-wheel drive tracks." There are no roads at all on Park Mesa. Perhaps Breternitz was confusing Park with Moccasin Mesa and its lone two-track, which would make sense because of Mesa Verde's old proposal for a third visitor center on Moccasin.

Breternitz concluded with: "As you can see, I am not in favor of creating a Wilderness Area at Mesa Verde, and I have not even considered future archaeological research." At the very least, Breternitz argued, an archeological inventory "should be undertaken. It should be intensive, and comprehensive. . . . It is particularly crucial to know where the ruins are in light of . . . the Park Mesa Wilderness Area proposal." In a separate letter[33] he estimated it would take ten years to complete the inventory.

"Units in the Wilderness System Contain Areas of Archeological Significance"

The testimony at the Nonsuitability as Wilderness Hearing opened with a statement from Regional Director Frank Kowski. He briefly described the five roadless areas and noted that there had yet to be a thorough archeological survey of the entire Park. Though a survey was planned to start in 1972, until it was completed it was not possible to know precisely the extent of archeological resources in Mesa Verde, and so the NPS could not be in favor of wilderness designation at this time. In addition, he repeated the necessity of patrolling the management roads to deter pot-hunting. He then brought up the cultural resource needs that he believed would preclude wilderness designation and which had been raised in previous reports: mechanical equipment is needed for archeological work; visitor use may dictate opening more sites to public visitation; semi-permanent camps may be needed, as might an expansion of the road system; and the legislation designating Mesa Verde was at fundamental odds with the Wilderness Act.[34]

Of the activities cited by Kowski, only the expansion of a permanent "management road system" would be illegal in a Wilderness. In over fifty years since this hearing, the Park has never identified where such an expansion might be considered.

It is surprising that in his conclusion, Kowski did not mention the threat to sites from visitors. Rather, he overstated the needs for motor vehicles and motorized equipment (which, as noted above, are not absolutely banned), and resurrected the possibility of future development for visitors. Ultimately, he described the differences between the demands of the Wilderness Act and the law creating Mesa Verde without addressing how they both might be satisfied.

No statements from the governor, members of Congress, or members of the State Legislature were recorded.

The Southwest District Commissioner of Colorado's Department of Game, Fish, and Parks agreed that there should be no Wilderness. He then suggested hunting should be prohibited only "where ruins have been identified and marked, but supervised public hunting by Park Service approved hunters should be allowed in adjacent areas." Mesa Verde had been largely exempt from the controversy over using public hunting in the parks as a gardening tool to meet ungulate carrying capacity—unlike Rocky Mountain National Park.[35] Hunting was never approved in Mesa Verde.

The District Commissioner from the Colorado Department of Highways testified against wilderness designation, claiming it would not be in the public interest. "The Department, like most of the general public [believes] the preservation of the environment would actually be defeated by the creation of a wilderness area."[36] This appears to be a personal objection by the Commissioner having nothing to do with his official position in the Highway Department, which logically would have no position on the designation, nor would he be qualified to say what the general public wanted, nor assess the environmental ramifications of designation.

Then a representative of Ute Mountain Ute Tribal Council spoke against wilderness designation. "As you know, our reservation borders Mesa Verde on three [*sic*] sides. The only way to get to about 90,000 acres of our land is through Mesa Verde and if it was wilderness area it could hurt the tribe very bad as far as developing our land [or for] fire protection."[37] These legitimate concerns could have been assuaged by making it clear that all the access roads through the Park to the Ute lands would be excluded from the Wilderness. The map used at the hearing shows these routes excluded. But no such assurances were made by the Park Service at the time.

Then came testimony offered by nongovernmental organizations and individuals. William C. Winkler, President of the Mesa Verde Company, and Emmett Koppenhafer of the Mesa Verde Pack and Saddle Outfit agreed with the Park Service's non-suitable determination.[38]

Everyone else who spoke favored at least some Wilderness in Mesa Verde. The representative of the National Parks and Conservation Association (NPCA) pointed out that study and excavation of archeological sites can be "accomplished effectively within a wilderness setting." He then argued for what had been the original proposal in the 1956 bill: the entire Park should be wilderness with the exception of the roads and already developed areas and urged that no more visitor accommodations should be established within the park. "Only existing roads should be retained; all other roads should be allowed to revert to wilderness. Scenic foot trails leading to the various sites can provide man both with recreation and an opportunity to view and explore the relics at his leisure."[39] It is difficult to understand what he meant by retaining existing roads and letting other roads "revert to wilderness." Perhaps he meant existing *paved* roads and letting other *dirt* roads "revert"? In any event, he ignored visitor impacts, though it is impossible to know where and how many of the "various sites" would have "scenic foot trail" access.

Representatives from The Wilderness Society, the Sierra Club, the Colorado Mountain Club, Colorado Open Space Council, and People United to Reclaim the Environment (PURE) all favored a somewhat more modest proposal for Wilderness: three units, roughly corresponding with the Park's Areas 2, 3, and 4.[40]

Several noted that wilderness and archeology are not incompatible. Cultural resources "in no way conflict with the legal or aesthetic definition of wilderness," and would, in fact, "enhance classification of these areas as wilderness." "Since stabilization is a valid archeological objective, it is scientific in nature and thereby permitted in wilderness areas." "There are many existing and proposed units in the Wilderness System that contain areas of archeological significance. If the existence of early man's work, no matter how primitive, were to be used as a rationale for exclusion from the Wilderness System, then very few areas would qualify for wilderness classification."[41]

"Access Is Rightfully Denied to the General Public"

Most interesting in the testimony of the pro-Wilderness organizations is their acceptance of visitor restrictions. The Southwest Representative of the Sierra Club testified, "To much of the public, wilderness is primarily a recreational resource. There is, however, no legal requirement in the Act for unrestricted recreational use to be permitted in wilderness. The National Park Service feels that severe restrictions must be placed on unsupervised travel in the park in order to protect the archeological resource. The Sierra Club recognizes the need for and supports these restrictions." "Should the Park Service deem it necessary, [The Wilderness Society] would be more than willing to go along with continued limitation on backcountry use." The representative of the Rocky Mountain Chapter of the Sierra Club went even farther by supporting total closure: "Here, in an area of a park where access is rightfully denied to the general public, is a unique opportunity to have a wilderness for the sake of the land."[42]

Strictly speaking, the Southwest Representative of the Sierra Club was correct in saying there is "no legal requirement in the Act for *unrestricted* recreational use." But there is a requirement for *some* recreational use in the Wilderness Act: "A wilderness . . . has outstanding opportunities for solitude or a primitive and unconfined type of recreation."[43] There is a continuum of degrees of access, and there may be a range across locations and over seasons. What would be appropriate in a Mesa Verde Wilderness? The legal requirements and some alternatives are addressed in this book's conclusion.

Seven private citizens spoke up, all in favor of wilderness designation, with two of them having especially well-considered comments. From George Kelly, who guided visitors into what is now Canyons of the Ancients National Monument: "An informal approach [to inconspicuous sites] supplements and adds much to their experience under the necessarily regimented tours at Mesa Verde. Leaving some of the park area in its primitive nature will allow this sort of experience to many." Nancy Colbert, having been on all the Park's trails and tours: "I would like to have a part of the park where I could go . . . to have a more wilderness-type experience and . . . to come upon a ruin unexpectedly."[44]

"Search Them as They Go In And Out?"

Then there followed a question-and-answer period. Superintendent Guillet said, "If we open up these trails to the people, I suppose we could make them take a Boy Scout oath that they wouldn't pothunt. . . . We could propose a few [trails] in spots where we do not have a great many real valuable archeological remains. But I doubt if anyone going by a ruin, seeing a bunch of potsherds, regardless of his good intentions, wouldn't stop and pick one up and stick it in his pocket."

In response to a further question about whether some controlled, limited access might be afforded, Guillet responded, "What would you do, search them as they go in and out?"[45]

At this point, Regional Director Kowski broke in:

> If I ever see an arrowhead lying on the ground, I don't care whether it's at Mesa Verde National Park or where it is, I'm going to pick it up and I am going to take it home because that's going to be the first one I'll ever have found! I say this facetiously, but I make a point. . . . We don't even know what our archeological resources are back in there. When the day comes (and this survey is programmed to begin in 1972) and we have a better idea of what our resources are, we will be in a position to adopt different management controls with regard to letting people just roam all over the park; at least we'll have an idea where these more priceless archeological sites are.[46]

The idea of visitor-as-vandal is a leitmotif in areas with significant archeological resources—and not without reason. But might there be a management direction somewhere between complete closure and "letting people just roam all over the park"? At that time, the Park Service could not contemplate one for Mesa Verde.

The Mesa Verde staff then tallied the written responses of both opposition and support for wilderness. The Park received letters opposing wilderness from both Cortez and Durango Chambers of Commerce and the *Cortez-Durango Herald*, as well as such non-germane organizations as the Department of the Army and a group referred to as the National Federation of Rodeo Associations. On the other hand, the Kappa Sigma Fraternity in Boulder wanted to go on the record for wilderness. Letters from individuals were tabulated as fourteen letters against wilderness, and ninety letters for wilderness. But it appeared that "Citizens of Cortez, Dolores, & Mancos CO" and "Citizens of Durango, CO" had a coordinated letter campaign with their letters for wilderness signed by 147 and 34 people, respectively. So, as has become commonplace in federal land management agencies decades later, the Park Service decided those letters should not be given equal weight with individually crafted letters. In the end, Mesa Verde opaquely reported the total individual responses had changed somehow to 203 opposed to wilderness designation and 107 in favor. By the time of the official Wilderness Recommendation the following September, the numbers had inexplicably changed again to 233 against Wilderness in Mesa Verde, and 114 for Wilderness.[47]

"The Report Is to Be Revised"

In mid-July of 1971, the Regional Director met with the Director and staff to go over the wilderness recommendation for Mesa Verde. Kowski recommended against wilderness for the usual straw-man disqualifiers: there was evidence of "aboriginal man"; mechanical equipment might be needed for future archeological work; and the Park might need to develop areas and access. Then . . .

> After considerable discussion, it was determined that most of the extensive archeological work in the park had been accomplished, particularly regarding standing wall ruins. Since prior partial surveys indicated less extensive archeological resources in certain areas of the park, it was decided that these areas could accommodate future survey work without the use of mechanical equipment. Therefore, the report is to be revised to recommend wilderness designation for most of the roadless area #4, and in portions of roadless area #5, east and west of the existing utility lines. (The area between the utility lines is to be considered for a possible tramway route.)[48]

What had happened? The Park and the Regional Office had everything organized to block wilderness designation in Mesa Verde. As Guillet wrote Robert Lister, "I received a good resume of your recent meeting in Washington on the Wilderness Proposal from Frank Kowski, and gathered that pressure from somewhere had been put on the Director. Thanks for trying to help us."[49]

"Three Units of Wilderness Totaling 7100 Acres"

The Park Service issued the official Wilderness Recommendation in September 1971. It had an extensive portion dealing with management plan policy for historical areas, noting the necessity for a "historical base map and/or archeological base map" that "rests on comprehensive research and is thoroughly documented."[50] At that time, Mesa Verde had no such map for most of the areas in the Wilderness Study.

Using a slight rewording of the text from the Preliminary Wilderness Suitability Study Report, the Recommendation explained once again why the Park Service's initial Report found none of the Park suitable for wilderness designation. Then, switching gears with little warning, the Recommendation concluded:

> As a result of careful study of the oral and written statements received as a result of the public hearing, and after further consideration of the management needs, it was recommended that three units of wilderness totaling 7100 acres be established. . . . There are lesser concentrations of archeological ruins, both in numbers and significance, in these sections of Mesa Verde, which permits placement of the recommended lands into the wilderness category. Any archeological work necessary in the proposed wilderness units could be done without mechanical equipment. These lands are also not necessary for future visitor development needs. It is felt that on the balance of the roadless area lands that no wilderness should be established because of the continuing need for archeological preservation, with its associated research programs, involving excavations and investigations requiring the use of motorized equipment.[51]

Once again, the necessary use of motorized equipment for research activities was raised as a reason for precluding wilderness designation. As the archeological resources clearly would be a component of the area's wilderness character, the use of motorized

Figure 22. Wilderness Recommendation, August 1971.

equipment *could* be authorized as "necessary to meet minimum requirements for the administration of the area for the purposes of [the Wilderness] Act."[52]

The Wilderness Recommendation included a map labeled Exhibit A of the recommended Wilderness Areas that—with one exception—appears to be the boundaries that eventually were designated by Congress. The exception is that here, the wilderness boundary was pulled back from any external Park boundary or edgeholding by 1/8 mile. This was the setback found in the first two NPS Wilderness Areas designated by Congress (Petrified Forest and Craters of the Moon) and was created to allow simple use of motor vehicles and motorized equipment in tasks such as boundary patrol and fence building.

"The Public Response for Wilderness"

The next task was to write an Environmental Impact Statement (EIS) disclosing potential impacts from wilderness designation and any appropriate mitigation. The Draft EIS (DEIS) is a confused and confusing document, starting with the error that "The park is bounded by the Ute Mountain Ute Reservation [only] on the south."[53] The DEIS repeatedly perpetuated the ongoing misinterpretation of the Wilderness Act, claiming designation would preclude the use of motorized equipment, when in fact it could be used if determined to be necessary.[54]

More unusual, the DEIS recognized that "The criteria of a wilderness experience include . . . outstanding opportunities for solitude or a primitive and unconfined recreation," but it also stated, "Hikers are not permitted to use this area now, nor would they under the proposed wilderness designation." There was no rationale given for excluding visitors from use of the wilderness. Presumably it was because of the fear of vandalism and theft, but that was never mentioned. Instead, the impact to wilderness experiential criteria was plainly stated: "Since public backcountry use of these areas is not presently contemplated, the opportunities for solitude and primitive recreation will not be realized here."[55]

In totality, the DEIS seemed to support the No Wilderness alternative, rather than what it identified as the Preferred Alternative of 7,100 acres in three units. It was quite up front that the NPS had proposed no wilderness, explaining that this was "based on the premise that Mesa Verde had been established primarily for the preservation of the ruins, not the wilderness or natural values." The Preferred Alternative grew out of "the public response for wilderness," and so the NPS agreed that perhaps these three units could be established as wilderness because they have "what is believed to be lesser concentrations of ruins."[56]

In tabulating the public response from the December 16, 1970, public hearing, the DEIS stated "249, supported the NPS proposal, 129 advocated wilderness designation." Once again, it is not clear how these numbers were derived, since they match neither the minutes of the hearing nor the 1971 Recommendation report, as noted above. In addition, the DEIS slanted the positions of governmental agencies: "None of the Federal, State, or local governmental organizations who voiced an opinion supported the wilderness designation."[57] Technically this is true, but most—10 out of 13—registered no opinion.[58] Moreover, if such a great majority of respondents actually favored No Wilderness, why was the NPS claiming to change their position due to public response?

The Draft EIS listed impacts from wilderness designation, including: "Exclusion of future visitor facility developments, such as roads, improved trails, developed campgrounds, hotels, electronic devices, and similar facilities." Perhaps there is no greater example of the systematic bias of the DEIS than in the labeling of these exclusions as "adverse environmental impacts which cannot be avoided."[59]

It certainly seems as though the Park Service was still hoping that the next comment period might produce enough public opinion to overcome what Guillet had identified as "pressure from somewhere."

"Areas the Archeologists 'Could Live With'"

Mesa Verde was not the only Park Service unit confused about the process of determining wilderness suitability, so the Assistant Secretary for Fish and Wildlife and Parks issued guidance in the form of Secretarial Order 2920 in June of 1972. The order stated that areas should not be excluded solely because management practices require the use of tools generally prohibited by Section 4(c) of the Wilderness Act. In addition, facilities do not automatically disqualify an area if they are the minimum necessary for the safety of the wilderness traveler or the protection of wilderness resources. However, areas which might qualify at the present time but would be needed in the future for some sort of development not consistent with wilderness designation should not be considered suitable. And, importantly for Mesa Verde, "Areas that otherwise qualify need not be excluded from wilderness designation because the area is being used as a site for research unless that use necessitates permanent structures or facilities in addition to those necessary for management purposes."[60]

In March of 1972, the NPS had forwarded to the Department the official Wilderness Recommendation for 7,100 acres, unchanged. On the other hand, the May 1972 Planning Directive to update the 1969 Mesa Verde Master Plan contains nothing on wilderness. In September, the Park released a map that removed the 1/8-mile buffer and therefore increased the size to 8,100 acres. No explanation was given for this change, but there were no buffers in the NPS Wilderness Areas designated that year (Lassen Volcanic and Lava Beds), nor in subsequent NPS Areas.[61]

In January of 1973, a draft bill with transmittal letters and the DEIS were sent to the Legislative Council. The draft bill has no language addressing additional special provisions for archeological research. The Regional Director and Environmental Specialist had "unresolved legal questions" to which the NPS Associate Director of Legislation clarified that wilderness designation does not preclude research. He did, however, repeat another frequent inaccurate interpretation of the Wilderness Act, confusing the *minimum* tool with

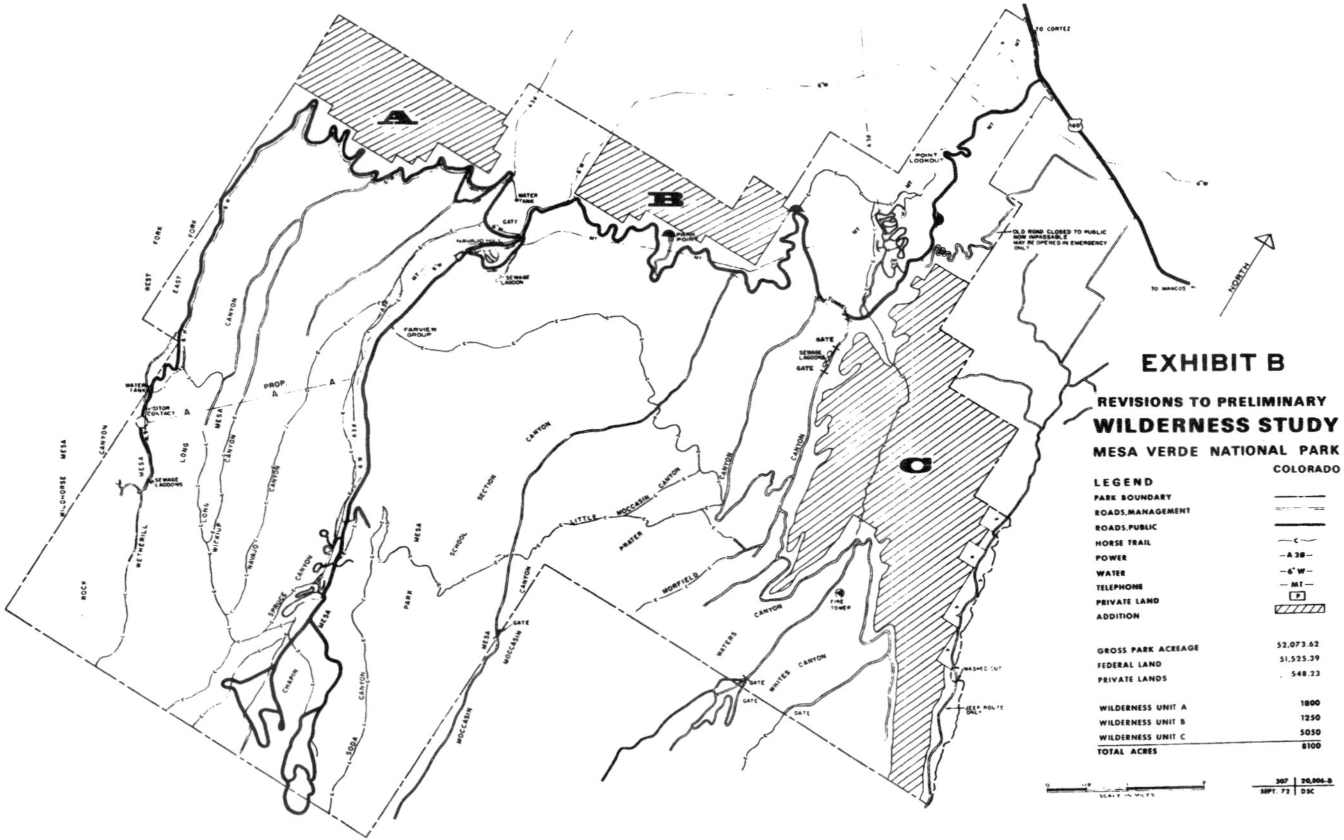

Figure 23. Final Mesa Verde wilderness proposal, September 1972. This is the map referenced in the 1976 legislation designating the Mesa Verde Wilderness, Public Law 94-567(h).

necessarily a *primitive* tool: "Archeological research, salvage, and stabilization . . . would have to be accomplished using *pioneer* tools" (emphasis added). After conferring with agency archeologists, the Associate Director continued, "These units of recommended wilderness were the segments of Mesa Verde which these persons stated would have the least impact on continuing archeological work. . . . [They] were the areas the archeologists 'could live with.'"[62]

Not all archeologists "could live with" the Wilderness Proposal. Breternitz once again refuted a claim that wilderness designation would increase security. "I doubt that, as there is no access now. I would say there will be less security for archaeological remains if the area is opened up to wilderness seekers." He mocked the idea of "'Solitude in virgin wilderness.' The two areas on the north escarpment present great views of Cortez, Highway 160, and the plywood smoke stack near Dolores."[63]

He was not alone. Colorado's State Historic Preservation Officer, Stephen Hart, wrote that he, too, was concerned about possible loss of "prehistoric materials" through reduced fire suppression and unauthorized visitation. He recommended "a systematic survey of the areas prior to designation" to determine what was at risk from "indiscriminate collection or destruction if control is lessened."[64]

Then Breternitz wrote Hart, informing him that just such a survey was underway. So far, his team had documented 108 sites in about 75 percent of Unit C. "Predominantly surface ruins," Breternitz wrote, and most were "in an undamaged condition." Furthermore, "As an archaeological resource, it would be a disaster to open up Area C of MVNP to Wilderness Area visitors. . . . The archaeological resources within MVNP become scientifically more valuable with the passage of time and the loss of archaeological resources in nearby areas." Breternitz forwarded the wilderness portion of the inventory to the Park Service in November.[65]

The survey to which Breternitz referred was part of a multiyear project under the direction of Jack E. Smith, described in *Mesas, Cliffs, and Canyons.* It was intended to cover all previously unsurveyed portions of the Park. Beginning in June 1971, survey activities continued through the following summers until completion in July 1977. Approximately 38,693 acres (about 74 percent of the park) were surveyed; 1,897 archeological sites were recorded—96 historic and 1,801 prehistoric. The original plan had been to move eastward season by season until the east park boundary was reached at the Mancos River, but in 1973, the survey jumped ahead to the portions of the park that were under wilderness consideration. At that time, of greatest concern to Smith was his belief that designation would make access for archeological survey more difficult at the same time that the area would be opened to greater visitation.[66]

Smith surveyed approximately eight square miles including the proposed wilderness and most of the park east and north of the Morefield-Whites Mesa Truck Road, and another eight square miles south of the Truck Road, finding a total of 317 sites. His results were more precise than in the letter from Breternitz to Hart. "Very large pueblos seem to have been limited to the open portion of Whites Canyon near Whites Well [the Whites Canyon Pueblo Community, south of the Wilderness]. . . . No comparable sites were located in the remainder of the survey area, and the pattern seems to have been one of small surface pueblos widely scattered throughout the area." The wide canyons in this portion of the Park have water relatively near the surface, attracting early homesteaders to sites that could be reasonably assumed to have been used for farming in the prehistoric era as well, and evidence of that may have been lost to subsequent development by the homesteaders.[67]

The number of reported sites is certainly an undercount of what is actually present. Smith wrote, "No doubt we walked over many La Plata Phase [roughly Basketmaker III, ca. 450–700 CE] pithouses, but there was no way to positively identify any of them solely from the evidence on the surface." Evidence of dwellings from the Piedra Phase (roughly Pueblo I, ca. 700–900 CE) "is often sparse even in open areas, and in areas of heavy scrub it may be quite invisible." Most of the sites found by the survey date to the Ackman and Mancos Phases (roughly Pueblo II, ca. 900–1075 CE), with little later occupation. The relative scarcity of Pueblo III architecture, coupled with the absence of alcoves necessary for the eye-catching cliff dwellings found elsewhere in the Park, led to the undervaluing of this eastern portion earlier in the Park's administration.[68]

In September 1973, the Regional Director solicited comments on wilderness designation from the Advisory Council on Historic Preservation, reassuring the Executive Secretary that no sites within the proposed wilderness areas had been identified as eligible for National Register listing. Mitigation to address potential effects to the sites present included "limiting potential for public visitation to archeological sites and backcountry natural areas."[69]

In November the draft legislation was finally transmitted from the Secretary of the Interior to the President. It included: "Section 4: Within the wilderness area designated by this Act the Secretary may undertake minimum activity necessary in order to investigate and stabilize sites of archeological interest."[70] This section was unnecessary, as that authority was already granted by the 1964 Wilderness Act. (Such redundant additions have become increasingly popular over the decades.[71])

In December, the NPS Regional Director finally heard back from the Advisory Council on Historic Preservation. They objected to wilderness designation because—once again—it would "severely handicap archeological research, stabilization and preservation." The Acting Regional Director responded that the proposal had already been sent by the President to Congress. "We understand that the Wilderness Act is being restudied in order to resolve the apparent conflicts between historic and wilderness objectives."[72]

The Council responded that they were "most interested" to find out the Park Service was working to resolve the apparent conflicts between historic and wilderness preservation. However, they warned, they would consider any proposal inadequate without demonstrating compliance with Section 106 of the National Historic Preservation Act, which requires consultation with the State Historic Preservation Officer (SHPO) to determine the effect of a federal agency's action.[73]

"Consider Ranger-Guided Trips"

As the legislation was being prepared for transmittal from the President to Congress, it seemed the Park Service was beginning to finally interpret Section 4(c) of the Wilderness Act correctly, now understanding that the Act could allow motorized equipment if necessary for the protection and preservation of a wilderness area's archeological resources.[74]

However, the Park Service continued to be alarmed by the prospect of wilderness recreation. The Management Objectives from early 1974 stated that "Backcountry use is *discouraged* to provide maximum protection for archeological resources" (emphasis added). By not calling the use *prohibited,* the Objectives pointed out what the new Superintendent, Ron Switzer, thought was a weakness in Park regulations that he would address after wilderness designation. The Objectives committed the Park to "Study backcountry use in light of the current Wilderness Proposal, and consider ranger-guided trips on a limited basis of one or more days duration."[75] The fiscal impracticality of such an activity was not considered. Nor was the fact that such a trip would not constitute a *wilderness* experience but would differ from other Park interpretive events only in its location.

Two weeks after signing the Management Objectives, Superintendent Switzer wrote the Mesa Verde Division Chiefs on the status of programs at the Park. In three pages, wilderness was not mentioned. But he did include the erroneous statement that "Mesa Verde, unlike other historical areas, lives under the dual mandate of managing both cultural and natural resources."[76]

"Permit Designation of Natural Areas Devoid of Man-Made Objects"

Though Switzer may not have appreciated the dual stewardship responsibilities in other NPS units, he understood—at least from a visitor's point of view—that wilderness was different. During the Park Service process of writing a Final EIS to disclose to the public (and

Congress) the effects wilderness designation, he wrote a lengthy memo to the NPS Wilderness Studies Chief: "Wilderness must be viewed from a standpoint other than that encompassed by physical characteristics. Wilderness is a quality defined by human experience and feeling, the exact attributes of which may not satisfy the sensibilities of all people."[77]

He then went on to list reasons why there should be no Wilderness in Mesa Verde. His legitimate concerns tend to get lost in all his errors.

First, public opinion: "The summary of responses received indicated that public opinion was more than 2 to 1 against the designation."[78] Problems with the accounting of public opinion are addressed above.

Then he noted conflicting legislation, repeating the habitual, erroneous claim that the 1906 Act establishing the Park conflicts with Section 2(c)(1) of the Wilderness Act because the Park's archeological features are substantially noticeable and human control by the original inhabitants over the environment are well known. In addition, he claimed that the Wilderness Act's Section 4(a)(3) supports excluding the public by claiming existing policies are thereby allowed to supersede the Act.[79] The fallacies underlying these beliefs are also addressed above.

Switzer argued that Units A and B were certainly unsuitable. They were too small, with "predominantly shrub vegetation and radical climate"; with views of Cortez, highways, "daily flights between Durango and Cortez at 1,000 to 4,000 feet above ground level," and emissions from power plants; and where visitors could never get more than one mile from a paved road.[80] Plus, he argued, there was no source of water in any of the Units—as if, somehow, absence of water makes an area less suitable. There is no question that views from the higher elevations of Units A and B are overwhelmingly dominated by modern civilization. The feeling of remoteness returns at the lower elevations, currently inaccessible to the public.

Switzer noted there was sufficient wilderness nearby: "It appears that the US Forest Service will recommend for wilderness

Figure 24. Remnants of the old Frink Trail on the north side of Mesa Verde Wilderness, Unit B. August 2019.

classification 80,150 acres of the [nearby] National Forests."[81] It is unknown how Switzer derived this number; within the year, Congress designated the Weminuche Wilderness at (then) over 405,000 acres, with about 320,000 of that in the San Juan Primitive Area.[82] If Switzer was suggesting that the Forest Service would supply sufficient wilderness for southwest Colorado, it brings to mind wilderness champion Bob Marshall. When asked how many wilderness areas were needed, he is said to have replied, "How many Brahms symphonies do we need?"[83]

Switzer's memo went on to include several other errors. He stated Wilderness designation would create conflict with the Utes: "Trespass grazing by Ute Mountain Ute livestock from reservation lands is common occurrence. However, an impasse and possibly hostile relationships would result from any attempt of the Service to compel the Ute Mountain Tribe to fence approximately 21 miles of boundary." Much of the boundary was already fenced (see chapter 6). Besides, Colorado is a "fence out" state. That is, by default the range is open, and if a landowner doesn't want livestock on his property, he must "fence out" the animals. Though Colorado State grazing regulations could not bind federal land bordering an Indian Reservation, the NPS ended up fencing the boundary. In addition, Switzer claimed, "Wilderness designation will effectively prohibit the Ute Mountain Tribe access by motor vehicle to certain areas of the reservation . . . over traditional routes through park lands." There were no such routes in the proposed Wilderness, and in the rest of the Park, all such routes were excluded from Wilderness consideration.[84]

Switzer noted that Secretarial Order 2920 allowed research in wilderness. But, he argued, "Research costs . . . already staggering in size cannot help but increase with . . . higher transportation costs and the use of 'minimum tools.'"[85]

Switzer concluded with a determination on how areas should be considered for designation. He advocated designation as "Potential Wilderness Additions," formerly known as "wilderness escrow," that would become Wilderness only if certain circumstances were met: "Portions of these areas not containing archeological resources would be subject to designation as wilderness by the Secretary of the Interior after they have been surveyed. . . . [This] would eventually permit designation of natural areas devoid of man-made objects as wilderness.[86]

In other words, let us do all the research we need, and afterwards, if we find any part of the Park "devoid of man-made objects," it will automatically become Wilderness and open to the public. This work-around found its way into the Final EIS.

The substance of this memo was not, however, Switzer's testimony before Congress less than a month later, on March 22nd. He recommended the 8,100 acres of Wilderness: "The recommended wilderness consists of areas which are predominantly natural in appearance and do not contain the extensive archeological resources found elsewhere in the park. Nonetheless, Mr. Chairman, we believe that legislation designating this wilderness should expressly authorize minimum activity necessary to the investigation and stabilization of archeological resources located in it."[87]

At the same hearing, the NPS Director made comments about wilderness in general, and then spoke specifically about Mesa Verde—supporting the recommendation and adding that other areas of the Park "were studied, but because they contain ruins and we may have to provide access to them, we did not recommend these areas for wilderness." Ironically, Bandelier National Monument was discussed next at the hearing, with Superintendent Linwood E. Jackson testifying: "Mr. Chairman, there are many important archeological sites within the Bandelier National Monument. The administration proposal would, therefore, authorize minimum activity necessary to investigate and stabilize those sites as necessary within the wilderness," while recommending wilderness designation for 22,030 acres out of the Monument's 29,661 acres.[88]

"Designate All Roadless Areas as Potential Wilderness Addition"

The Final EIS (FEIS) for the proposed Mesa Verde National Park Wilderness was released in May 1974.[89] Much of it contradicts the NPS testimony. It is internally inconsistent, filled with false statements and other errors.

As such, given the importance of the document in the management of the Mesa Verde Wilderness, it is examined in detail here.

Relatively early in the document appeared this shocking declaration: "Backcountry hiking and public use of the roadless areas have not been permitted since the Park was established."[90] This statement, obviously untrue, is a precursor of everything that follows.

The Recommended Action stated that, "Public use of the proposed wilderness will not be permitted until all archeological resources have been surveyed and those which are deemed to have special significance have been thoroughly investigated or salvaged from destruction." In addition, "No public use . . . will be permitted until human carrying capacity can be determined." This implies that at some point public use will be permitted. The FEIS continued: "Once permitted, public use of wilderness will be restricted to visiting significant ruins . . . in the company of a uniformed ranger." If a uniformed ranger were to be present, certainly tours to any site could be conducted prior to complete investigation. More importantly, once again what was described is not a wilderness experience (as noted by the Forest Service in their comments on the Draft EIS, attached to the Final at page 44). It is no different than the experience offered at any of the cliff dwellings, simply with a longer hike. And this restriction was completely contradicted in the FEIS Purpose of Action: "Wilderness areas will be preserved for primitive types of recreation. Solitude in virgin wilderness will permit modern Americans to sense the wild character of early America. It should be recognized that opportunities for solitude and isolation from human activities in these small wilderness areas is somewhat limited." The Park Service intended to make such opportunities impossible by guiding every visitor. The FEIS later admitted "If public visitation is eventually permitted [only] in the presence of a Park Ranger, solitude in a primitive area will be adversely affected."[91]

The boundary descriptions of the three Units did not correspond to the map, which is a duplicate of the one accompanying the 1972 Revisions to Wilderness Preliminary Study (*Figure 23*). The text talked of boundaries delineated by roads and utility corridors as well as the Park boundary itself. This was generally in keeping with Park Service national policies sent to the parks in 1967, as discussed above. The map, however, showed the boundaries in Units A and B along the surveyed lines of aliquot parts (subdivided sections), and Unit C bounded by a free-form line of undetermined (in the FEIS) origin. (In fact, the 1976 post-designation official boundary description follows this 1972 map, not the FEIS text.[92]) This was not the only occurrence of sloppy inconsistency. In discussing Unit C, the FEIS stated, "Archeological surveys have not been made in this area."[93] They were completed the previous year.

While covering the archeological potential, the FEIS made an important point, quoting without attribution the phrasing of David Breternitz, cited above: "These archeological resources in the Park become scientifically more valuable with the passage of time and the loss of archeological resources in nearby areas." But then the FEIS grossly overstated the abundance of those resources in the proposed Units. While Breternitz believed Units A and B to have "very few" sites,[94] the FEIS stated "a large number of small multi-component sites are likely to be found" in the North Escarpment Units.[95] Given the topography, this really was a nonsensical claim, and indeed, the University of Colorado's survey in 1977 found a total of one prehistoric and five historic sites in the vicinity of these Units.[96] Unit C, of course, would have more sites. The FEIS variously claimed, "perhaps 100 or more per square mile" and "80 per square mile," and predicted "many pithouse villages dating between A.D. 550 and A.D. 600, [and] numerous large multi-component pueblos of the late eleventh to late thirteenth centuries and associated ceremonial structures will be found by survey."[97] As noted above, the survey was already completed, though the reporting was only in its preliminary phase. What was known at the time of the FEIS was that the early pithouses were almost impossible to identify from surface expression, and Smith had already found no evidence of large PIII pueblos in the proposed wilderness areas.[98] As for density, it is difficult to tell from Smith's 1987 public report, but Breternitz's estimate of 108 sites in 75 percent of the unit would yield a density of slightly less than 20 sites per square mile.[99] The Park Service knew this, yet overestimated the density by four or five times. Later in the document, without explanation, the FEIS again contradicted itself: "Although it is now apparent that Unit C contains more prehistoric archeological resources than when the unit was first proposed for wilderness designation it is concluded that, overall, the unit meets the criteria and should be recommended."[100]

The FEIS mentioned the "prehistoric agricultural environment" for "the visitor's understanding and enjoyment of the park," which would require a non-natural "vegetation control plan." Since the plot under consideration was not in any of the areas discussed in the FEIS Alternatives, there was no reason for it to be raised here. This is not an isolated example of fabricating impacts. The document repeatedly uses frontcountry examples to warn of effects to the backcountry.[101]

The FEIS could be excused for stating "Natural environments in wilderness units A, B, and C have reached a fairly stable ecological balance,"[102] since it was not universally recognized at the time that natural ecology is dynamic, not stable. But the remainder of the Environmental Impacts section was a puzzling muddle, sometimes internally inconsistent, at other times homogenizing impacts from the proposed alternative with impacts from the other alternatives.

Once again, the document raised the canard of how onerous it would be to conduct research in a Wilderness: "Archeological research will proceed with primitive tools. . . . Most access will be on foot or horseback."[103] The FEIS made no mention of all the access roads that were cherry-stemmed out of the wilderness alternatives. "Wilderness designation will preclude or very seriously impede certain forms of research due to the limitation on the use of motorized equipment and vehicles, and the use of permanent or semi-permanent research camps and facilities."[104] In actuality, only a permanent research camp would necessarily be prohibited—and then only if inside the boundaries of the wilderness. The FEIS mentioned, in contrast to all its claims of prohibitions, that "When motorized equipment is needed to preserve Park resources, the minimum tool will be used,"[105] but this one sentence is outweighed by the many implications of absolute prohibition. The discussion of cost included exaggerations such as the extra "man days of labor" it would take "if the site is several miles from camp."[106] There is no place in Mesa Verde that is several miles from a road (as many in opposition to wilderness designation have pointed out, deeming the areas offer little opportunity for solitude). And there is no reason a temporary camp couldn't be relatively close to a site.

The FEIS stated "Some people will derive benefits by visiting the wilderness, while others will have peace of mind from knowing it is there to be visited." However, "Potential for public visitation to archeological sites and backcountry natural areas will be *limited*" (emphasis added). The FEIS then argued that wilderness designation would preclude visitation by the "physically handicapped and elderly," and that only a small fraction of Mesa Verde's visitors would be willing to use "trails extending farther than two miles into the proposed areas."[107] Of course, no one at all was currently visiting these areas.

Once again, the FEIS claimed, "Wilderness designation does not take precedence over either the Mesa Verde or NPS Organic Acts."[108] The statement is true, but so is the reverse. Wilderness law is "within and supplemental"[109]—that is, all laws must be satisfied to the degree each law explicitly demands and the other laws allow.

Under the sensational heading "Potential catastrophic effects of uncontrolled forest fires," the FEIS noted that masonry and pottery would be degraded "as a result of letting a natural forest fire burn."[110] It went on to a less dramatic conclusion that fires could be controlled, including by using motorized equipment. Almost as alarming, "Watershed management will be hindered." The FEIS warned that access would be restricted or limitations placed on installed equipment, but, curiously, this "would not adversely affect the park."[111]

The FEIS maintained that removing trespass livestock would be more difficult in the wilderness, because "motorized vehicles will not be permitted."[112] There is no record of motor vehicles being driven cross-country to gather trespass animals. Even more outlandish, "Wilderness designation will effectively prohibit Ute access, through park lands, to certain areas of the reservation by motorized vehicle."[113] Once again, only one small portion of Unit C was adjacent to Ute lands, and none of the roads that continued on to the Utes' property were to be within designated Wilderness in any of the alternatives.

The FEIS offered to mitigate the worst of fears by proposing the special provision in the legislation that had been inserted in the draft bill: "Within the wilderness area designated by this Act, the Secretary may undertake minimum activity in order to investigate and stabilize sites of archeological interest."[114] As noted above, this provision would have been superfluous, as the Wilderness Act of 1964 already allows such uses "as necessary to meet minimum requirements for the administration of the area for the purpose of this Act," which includes the area's "historical value."[115]

The FEIS then turned around and flatly stated: "Archeological research, salvage, and stabilization will be impeded by wilderness management practices, thus delaying the gathering of knowledge about any significant archeological features that may exist within designated lands."[116] And then the FEIS turned around again and said that since Congress could undesignate the Wilderness if proscriptions proved onerous, designation would create "no irreversible and irretrievable commitment of resources."[117]

Next, the FEIS detailed alternatives that had been considered, but rejected.

"The original Park Service recommendation was for no wilderness." What changed? "[Those] favoring a wilderness designation stressed their opinion that the roadless areas do have wilderness character *despite* the presence of cliff dwellings, mesa-top ruins, and other archeological sites" (emphasis added).[118] Perhaps this was an allusion to the mistaken interpretation of the Wilderness Act that these ancient structures meant that the Wilderness was not "untrammeled" and "undeveloped" as referenced in the Wilderness Act's definition of Wilderness.[119] Or perhaps it was to emphasize the increase in workload since some of the wilderness advocates, apparently unfamiliar with the law, had wrongly claimed modern tools could not meet the "necessary" requirement since "any archeological work . . . could be done without motorized equipment, as was done before modern . . . techniques evolved."[120] Ultimately, the No Wilderness alternative was not selected due to "a result of careful study of the oral and written statements received as a result of the public hearing"[121]—exactly the opposite of what the NPS had, with dubious calculations, maintained earlier in the FEIS.

The next alternative examined was the three units with the external buffer. Among the benefits, this would "permit the construction of a ranger station near the boundary of the park in the future if public use should increase to a point that management personnel would be required." However, "Public feelings, expressed at public hearings, were overwhelming toward inclusion of this management zone in the wilderness."[122]

The FEIS then looked at alternatives for designating other areas within the Park. Commonalities included that research, stabilization, and salvage would be more difficult and more costly; public access would be limited to a few people, though they would have better opportunities for solitude "when, and if, public access is permitted in the future"; and that wilderness designation would preclude building more visitor infrastructure.[123]

The Park Service—at least at Mesa Verde—preferred there be no wilderness. This was clear from staff prior comments as well as communications that followed. The FEIS appears to be written to undermine the so-called Preferred Alternative of the DEIS. The Forest Service, the Bureau of Mines, and the Bureau of Indian Affairs, in their comments on the Draft that were appended to the Final, all picked up on this.[124] It is difficult to ascribe the errors and slant of the document to ignorance or incompetence. Clearly, someone "above" Mesa Verde was calling the shots for wilderness designation, exactly as Regional Director Kowski had informed Superintendent Guillet six years before.

If the No Wilderness alternative was off the table, the FEIS described what is clearly the next best thing, giving lip service to wilderness without actually designating any: "Designate all Roadless Areas as Potential Wilderness Addition."[125] By this measure, as noted previously in Switzer's memo to the Wilderness Studies Chief, areas without archeological resources could be designated as wilderness by the Secretary of the Interior without further action by Congress. Furthermore, "In developing the [Proposed Alternative] it was assumed that there were fewer and less important archeological resources in these areas than elsewhere in the park." Calling this assumption "unsupported," this new alternative would allow survey without "undue restrictions on archeological research and interpretation." If wilderness were designated now, and sites worthy of public interpretation were found, then neither roads to those sites—or, possibly, actions to protect them—would be permitted.

No, this alternative concluded, "Designation as Potential Wilderness Addition would permit orderly accomplishment of the original purpose of the park . . . and would eventually permit designation of natural areas devoid of man-made objects as wilderness." Unstated is the obvious fact that no area in Mesa Verde large enough to qualify as Wilderness is so devoid.

The last half of the FEIS consisted of comment letters from various agencies on the Draft EIS and the NPS responses. Some of these have already been noted, and in some of the cases the proposed changes were incorporated into the Final and are not addressed here separately.

The Bureau of Outdoor Recreation had the most perceptive new comment: "Can the Park Service preserve, explore, and adequately interpret for the public the archeological sites if they are administered as wilderness? If the answer is yes, then wilderness study units 2 and 3 should also qualify for wilderness classification. If indeed the archeological values for which the park was established are compromised by wilderness status, then even the token wilderness areas A and B considered in the proposal should not be classified as wilderness."[126]

The Park Service's response: "[This] has succinctly reduced the issue of wilderness designation . . . to a single question." Then the FEIS listed the criteria used to answer that question: "Areas selected should have . . . lesser concentration of ruins and those ruins are of lesser size and importance than in other areas; and areas selected are not appropriate for development of visitor facilities to interpret ruins found."[127] In other words, the Park Service was not looking at what qualified as Wilderness, but rather what they thought could acceptably be lost to Wilderness.

"It Is a Farce to Create It as an Area of Wilderness"

The fight was far from over. Stephen Hart, the Colorado State Historic Preservation Officer, reiterated his problems with wilderness designation to the Regional Director, asserting that visitors would "carry away portions of the site every season." He feared that the legislation would not carry any regulatory mechanisms to prevent these depredations. And, once more, he complained about the limitations on archeological research under wilderness designation. Finally, he pleaded, "It would be hoped that a site of the significance of Mesa Verde would warrant special considerations as exceptional to the wilderness designation."[128]

Hart got a response from Regional Director Lynn Thompson in a week, assuring him that the legislation would include the special provision allowing archeological work mentioned in the FEIS, while acknowledging that research, stabilization, and protection is somewhat more difficult and costly. She went on to say, "With reference to apprehension you have expressed that increased public use will result from wilderness designation, we doubt this will occur. . . . There will be no change in administrative . . . practices. As stated on page 3 [of the FEIS]: 'Public use of the proposed wilderness will not be permitted until all archaeological resources have been surveyed and those which are deemed to have special significance have been thoroughly investigated.'"[129] The Regional Director's reassurance is misleading. Allowing public use—no matter the preconditions—would be a change in administrative practice. Unless, of course, she was implying that a *thorough* investigation would never be completed.

Others weighed in. The Director of the Colorado Division of Planning, Philip Schmuck, wrote the Regional Director, asserting that visitors would be unable to experience solitude in a Mesa Verde Wilderness, and that designation would not provide better protection for the archeology. Further, "Why does the Park Service seek wilderness designation which is intended to preserve areas of spectacular national scenery from the intrusions of man (excluding, I presume, those of prehistoric Indians)?"[130] Putting aside his snarky equating of modern intrusions with the impacts of "prehistoric Indians," Schmuck repeated the common misconception that wilderness designation is about preserving scenery. Yet the underlying question remains valid. Why did the Park Service "seek wilderness designation"?

Breternitz had some idea of what was going on. In a letter to the Colorado State Archeologist, he wrote: "It seems by granting Wilderness Status the NPS is trying to serve not only two or three, but all available masters. Since Area C contains a significant number of archaeological sites, under the present program it will not be made available to the public until 'all archaeological resources have been surveyed and those which are deemed to have special significance have been thoroughly investigated' [emphasis by Breternitz]. . . . The current policy is to avoid any and all unnecessary excavation. Consequently, there are no plans to 'thoroughly investigate' within Area C. So it is a farce to create it as an area of wilderness."[131]

A farce indeed.

The State Archeologist, James Hester, wrote the Regional Director, summarizing his opposition to wilderness designation along with that of Breternitz, Hart, and Schmuck. "Those Colorado agencies and individuals having an assigned responsibility to protect and study cultural resources believe that a wilderness designation will result in a direct threat to those resources."[132]

The national Advisory Council on Historic Preservation became involved, and Regional Director Thompson assigned a staff member to assuage the Council's fears, at the same time acknowledging the objections of Breternitz, Hart, and Hester. "We recognize that it may be necessary . . . to invoke the consultation process [following Section 106 of the National Historic Preservation Act of 1966 for actions which may affect historic properties]. However, hopefully, it may develop that there is a misunderstanding that can be eliminated. In the interest of all concerned, it is imperative to reach a decision in the near future. Your assistance will be greatly appreciated."[133]

By January of 1975, The Regional Director was working with the Chief of the NPS Regional Archeology Center and the Superintendent to flesh out a Memorandum of Agreement (MoA) with the Advisory Council on the MEVE wilderness proposal.[134] The Draft MoA in the Park files contains annotated comments from an unidentified staffer. The Draft started out: "It was agreed that the wilderness designation will, in fact, increase the protection of all cultural resources within the designated wilderness areas and ensure the preservation of such archeological and natural resources for the benefit of future generations. It was agreed further that if the [NPS] continued to manage the wilderness areas in the following manner, any adverse effects of the wilderness designation will be satisfactorily mitigated."

The Draft MoA then outlined a management framework: "The [NPS] will conduct a research program to determine human carrying capacity in designated wilderness areas." An annotated comment reads: "I hope not!!" The Draft went on to say: "Potential for public visitation to archeological sites and backcountry natural areas will continue to be limited, as it has been since the park was established, under restrictive management policies." In annotation, "Potential for" is crossed out, and "limited" is replaced by "prohibited." The Draft MoA continued: "Human use of the designated wilderness areas will be limited and managed so that the areas so designated will provide a wilderness experience without destroying the conditions that originally made it desirable as wilderness." In the annotation, the phrase "wilderness experience" is circled, and written next to it is "No!!"

These annotations indicate the growing animosity between some of the Mesa Verde staff and the direction from higher levels of the NPS. Despite these comments, which must have been shared with Superintendent Switzer, the Superintendent's official reply to the Regional Director reported "We have reviewed the proposed agreement and find it adequate and acceptable in all respects."[135]

By the end of February 1975, the final language of the MoA was being hammered out with the Colorado SHPO.[136] It was essentially the same as the Draft, except for specifically allowing limited use of motorized equipment for "research, stabilization, and preservation of archeological resources" and "to acquire archeological data" supporting scientific knowledge and park interpretation "when considered necessary" as per Reed's Secretarial Order 2920.

"Human Use of the Designated Wilderness Areas Will Be Limited"

In March, Superintendent Switzer sent a memo to the Regional Planning Team on the status of the wilderness legislation. He reminded the team that Mesa Verde "is the only national park . . . established for the protection of archeological resources." He then stated that in recognition of this, he expected the legislation would include "the following additional authority: 'Within the wilderness area designated by this Act, the Secretary may undertake minimum activity necessary in order to investigate and stabilize sites of archeological interest.'"[137]

He then discussed the cultural resources. "There are believed to be 2,500 archeological sites within the park boundaries located in Units A and B proposed for wilderness designation and on other lands not proposed for wilderness designation."[138] This statement is both misleading and meaningless. There are almost no sites in Units A and B, and far more than 2,500 in areas not proposed for designation.

Switzer went through the language of the MoA. Two items in particular are worth mentioning as reflecting how the Park Service expected the Wilderness to be managed post-designation, despite the vigorous objection to this wording by some on his staff as noted above:

> Potential for public visitation to archeological sites and backcountry natural areas will continue to be limited, as it has been since the park was established, under restrictive management policies.
>
> Human use of the designated wilderness areas will be limited and managed so that the areas so designated will provide a wilderness experience without destroying the conditions that originally made it desirable as wilderness.[139]

This language begs the question, how limited is "limited"? And how restrictive were the "restrictive management policies"? The policies for visitation of the Mesa Verde backcountry varied over the years, becoming increasingly restrictive over time. So which policy was going to be "continued"? However secret the Mesa Verde wilderness was to be kept, it appears the Superintendent expected some "wilderness experience" to be provided.

In December 1975, the Park produced a twelve-page Statement for Management (although it wasn't approved by the Regional Director until the following July). In discussing the significance of the

Park's resources, the Statement devoted three pages to the cultural resources, as would be expected. Breternitz's observation is repeated: "These non-renewable resources become scientifically more valuable with the passage of time, and the loss of archeological resources in nearby areas."[140]

"Second only to the archeological resources of the Park are the natural resources." These were given one-half page. "Climax" vegetation is described, calling it both "Typical of the piñon-juniper zone" and "unique for the general area because livestock grazing has been effectively prevented in most areas of the park for nearly 40 years" (emphasis in original).[141]

Among the "miscellaneous" influences on management, the Statement mentioned House Resolution 7192 and Senate Resolution 1089 calling for "a statutory wilderness area of 8,100 acres."[142] The only other mention of wilderness was the ongoing separation of zones in the Park's "land classification" description: the "natural zone" was equated with wilderness, and separate from the "historical zones" which included the remainder of the backcountry.[143] This artificial dichotomy perpetuated and reinforced the idea of incompatibility.

In June 1976, Mesa Verde conducted public workshops in preparation for a new General Management Plan (GMP), generating comments from sixty-eight individuals and groups.[144] Though the GMP concerned the entire Park, there were several comments specifically regarding wilderness, emphasizing variations in some sort of backcountry use program. The Wilderness Society was still advocating for 28,900 acres of wilderness in Mesa Verde and wanted to make sure none of those lands were proposed for development by the GMP.[145]

The next month, a revised Statement for Management for Mesa Verde was released and distributed to the Colorado congressional delegation.[146] It made no reference to wilderness.

"Make Further Recommendations for Wilderness Designation"

Mesa Verde was included in a package of NPS wilderness proposals that appeared in House Report 94–1427 and Senate Report 94–1357.

In these, Congress was clear that "National Park wilderness designation . . . does not change the earlier designation of a park, monument, or related area but rather superimposes another classification, providing the highest order of Federal resource protection, and a near absolute curtailment of development." Furthermore, "When the imprint of man himself becomes too severe, limitations on his numbers and methods of use may be imposed, to assure wilderness character of the area." Some of the other NPS units in the legislation identified "Potential Wilderness Additions" that had been an alternative in the Mesa Verde Wilderness FEIS, but Mesa Verde was not among them.[147]

It was never the intent of Congress that wilderness designation in Mesa Verde would necessarily stop with this 1976 bill. Regarding Mesa Verde specifically, the House Report stated: "The Committee adopted the acreage figure recommended by the National Park Service, although it was recognized that there are other areas within the park which would qualify for wilderness designation." The Senate Report "recognizes that substantial additional acreage within the park qualifies as wilderness." The House Report continues, "It is understood that there is additional archeological work to be undertaken on these lands, and the Committee anticipates that *at some future time* when these resources are more fully understood, the National Park Service should *make further recommendations for wilderness designation*" (emphasis added). The Senate Report also concludes with an expectation of further recommendations. Preliminary recommendations were completed—almost forty-five years later.[148]

On October 20, 1976, Congress enacted Public Law 94–567. Section 1(h) designates 8,100 acres in Mesa Verde National Park as the Mesa Verde Wilderness. It references the 1972 Wilderness Plan map. There is no special provision language concerning the use of motorized equipment for archeological research.

Is this an example, as wilderness historian Doug Scott has written, of Congress being "a more responsive agent for designating wilderness than were the agencies when designation decisions were in their hands"?[149] Or is it an example of national interests running roughshod over local expertise? The answer depends on whom you ask.

CHAPTER NINE

The Mesa Verde Wilderness

Initial Management

1976–2006

DESIGNATION OF THE MESA Verde Wilderness immediately brought two problems.

"To Locate These Lines on the Ground Is Difficult If Not Impossible"

The first problem, stemming from previous, inattentive work, was identifying just where the wilderness boundaries were. Superintendent Switzer wanted the Washington Office to provide an official map at a larger scale, since the boundary of Unit C was difficult to ascertain at the small scale that used, in part, contour lines and "changes in vegetation." Changes in vegetation were not in the legal description; nevertheless, it was practically impossible to know where the wilderness boundary was on the ground. In December of 1979, on reviewing previous instructions on boundary identification (and even those were not followed by Mesa Verde), the Associate Director realized a revised set of guidelines for wilderness boundary descriptions and maps was necessary. At the top of the list was using natural features easily located on map and ground (streams, mountain peaks, well-defined ridges). Next were man-made features (using offsets from roads, utility lines, or trails). Then came section and subdivision lines; contour lines were down the prioritized list, second-to-last.[1]

Park management appreciated the improved boundary direction, acknowledging that for Unit C, "to locate these [contour] lines on the ground is difficult if not impossible."[2]

As of 2024, the Mesa Verde Wilderness boundary has not changed.

"Other Options Need to Be Considered"

The far greater problem was how to manage a wilderness the Park did not want. The archeology/wilderness dichotomy was largely a result of an "agency culture and organization that segregated management of 'natural' and 'historic' parks," even though Congress passed the General Authorities Act in 1970 directing the NPS to manage all units as part of one system, with no policy-level distinction between natural, historic, or recreation areas. Despite this, agency inertia continued the practice of giving serious consideration to cultural resources only in "historic" zones. Apparently, the converse was also true—a lack of consideration for natural resources (including the broader category of "wilderness resources") in "historic" areas such as Mesa Verde.[3]

So perhaps it is no surprise that Mesa Verde's 1977 Statement for Management referred to the recently-designated wilderness only once in eleven pages—as an "Administrative Constraint." It is not mentioned in the Park's Management Objectives.[4]

In 1979, the Park issued a General Management Plan (GMP), which claimed to be "based upon legislative and administrative constraints, management objectives, resource capabilities and limitations established in the approved Resources Management Plan and Wilderness Recommendation, and the public's desires."[5] The Plan had a map of the Wilderness on page 11, and said the management direction for the "Wilderness Subzone" was "Preservation of undeveloped areas of primitive character and influence." This ignored 3 of the 5 qualities of wilderness character. It might be considered that the "other features of value" quality—here, cultural—was a given; and perhaps the writers considered the "untrammeled" quality included in primitive character or influence. But there is no mistaking the glaring absence of anything to do with the "recreation" quality, which is understandable when discussing direction for an area where no recreational use was to be permitted. The document was otherwise silent on how the Mesa Verde Wilderness would be managed, and the list of pertinent reference materials in the document included the September 1972 Wilderness Recommendation, but neither the law designating the Mesa Verde Wilderness nor the Wilderness Act.

However, the GMP did point out:

> The best way of attaining . . . empathy with the Anasazi is by spending time in the ruins—listening in a quiet, uncrowded atmosphere to stories of the people in concert with the wind, the ravens, or the sound of rain, feeling the warmth of the sun, and the cold of the night. Unfortunately, increased visitation and the fragile nature of the dwellings and their limited visitor capacity have precluded most opportunities for such in-depth personal exploration. Consequently, a more shallow exposure to the resources has resulted, with a corresponding reduction in feeling for what the ruins represent. . . . Other options need to be considered for those who seek a more intimate involvement with the resource.[6]

The document then went on about how to maximize visitors per hour, rather than exploring possibilities for that intimate involvement.

Two years later, the Park's next Statement for Management contained three paragraphs on MEVE being made a World Heritage Site—a great honor with no specific management requirements—while two sentences are devoted to the fact that a Wilderness had been designated. Again, the document was silent on its management. There was an opaque notice that "Activity at Mesa Verde has been designed to prevent any attrition to the remnants of the prehistoric culture." Presumably, this was a reference to continuing to prohibit the public in the Wilderness or other backcountry, but perhaps saying so directly might have raised alarms. The document continued,

"Legislation establishing the park is based on the sanction [*sic*] of preservation." The Park's organic legislation, however, is not the only law that must be applied in the management of Mesa Verde.[7]

To be fair, Mesa Verde was not alone in wanting to ignore its wilderness. The so-called "Vail Agenda" meeting in 1991 highlighted the seventy-fifth anniversary of the NPS. What was originally billed as an opportunity for self-examination, constructive criticism, and renewed commitment, ended in mixed messages. Historian Richard Sellars summed up the NPS attitude: "Legislation such as the Wilderness Act or the National Environmental Policy Act should not interfere unduly with traditional management and operations of the Service." He noted the Vail Agenda's call for "a strong ecosystem management culture," yet concluded, "Such changes are not impossible—but they are improbable."[8]

"The Back Country of the Park Is Legislatively Closed"

For the public, the Mesa Verde Wilderness was either ignored or dismissed.

Robert Lucas, one of the country's early wilderness research experts, wrote the Park inquiring about use of the Wilderness. He received a lie in response: "Backcountry hiking and public use of all roadless areas including the wilderness have not been permitted since the park was established."[9]

Mesa Verde Archeologist and Interpreter Gilbert Wenger wrote *The Story of Mesa Verde* in 1980.[10] At 79 pages long, the book doesn't mention the Wilderness designated just a few years earlier.

Louisa Willcox, from the Center of Environmental Studies at Williams College, was conducting research on rationing or limiting wilderness use across the National Wilderness Preservation System. She asked about balancing the conflict in the Wilderness Act between providing for recreational use and the preservation of the ecosystem.[11] The response from Superintendent Heyder was deceptive at best: "We are very limited in the management alternatives allowable, due to Congressional mandates in the enabling legislation for the park and by other legislation." There is nothing in any legislation that prohibits wilderness visitation by the public. In addition, the Superintendent referenced the MoA: "This memorandum insured that, in order to protect all cultural resources within the wilderness areas, those lands designated as a wilderness would continue to be managed under the same policies as the rest of Mesa Verde National Park had been since establishment."[12] This clearly misrepresents the content of the Memorandum, as detailed above, in two ways. First, management policies at Mesa Verde concerning visitation to the backcountry (except for cliff dwellings) changed greatly over time. Second, the Memorandum explicitly states that visitation will be limited, not prohibited, while still allowing for a wilderness experience.

In response to another inquiry about access to the Wilderness, the Superintendent offered another misleading answer: "Due to the steepness of the north and east escarpments, access is limited." While the two Wilderness units on the north side of the Park are little more than the escarpment, most of the eastern unit would be physically accessible rather easily.[13]

Evasion continued for over a decade. Responding to one inquiry from would-be visitors, Heyder wrote, "We are sorry that we cannot accommodate your request to hike in the backcountry of Mesa Verde National Park. The backcountry of the park is legislatively closed so as to protect the archeological ruins for which the park was established."[14] It is not clear why he would make up an excuse so demonstrably false as a legislative closure, when a simple statement of policy would have been more honest.

"Why Not Enlarge the Park"

Objections over wilderness use extended to adjacent lands.

As the BLM looked at management alternatives for Weber Mountain, directly east of the Park, Superintendent Heyder was concerned that the BLM might designate Weber a Wilderness Study Area (WSA). He wrote the Regional Director that if the BLM did so, it would present an "interesting P.R. problem" since someone hiking in the WSA could not continue on into the (almost) adjacent NPS Wilderness. Heyder suggested the NPS might propose that, rather than designating a WSA, the BLM should designate it as an Area of Critical Environmental Concern. But he also offered an ingenious alternative: "If Weber Mountain is of Wilderness character . . . then why not enlarge the park to include it?" The idea of annexing adjacent land to the Mesa Verde Wilderness received support from the National Parks Conservation Association Boundary Study, which called it "meritorious of wilderness status."[15]

This was not the first time that Mesa Verde contemplated expansion to include Weber Mountain. In 1935, one idea suggested extending the MEVE boundary to the rim of Weber Mountain on the east side of the Mancos River for a "faunal boundary" and to "obviate having undesirable neighbors on the east bank of the river."[16] Fifty years later, the Park's concern had changed from protections *for* wildlife to protections *from* visitors.

Ultimately, Weber Mountain was not transferred to Mesa Verde, and was formally designated as a BLM Wilderness Study Area in 1991.

"Visitor and Employee Use of the Mesa Verde Wilderness Will Be Allowed"

If the wilderness and backcountry were to remain closed to the public, would restrictions also be placed on researchers and employees? In July of 1977, Superintendent Switzer issued operating procedures for use of the wilderness and backcountry, limiting use of the Wilderness to research by "qualified professionals" with his approval. "These restrictions are based on legislation, regulation, policy, and on [the] MoA." His memo did not explain how any of these served as the basis for the restrictions. Use of non-wilderness backcountry was somewhat less restricted, needing only to be "mission supportive and in the line of duty." In both wilderness and backcountry, solo visits were not allowed, with a minimum group size of three, and limited to day use.[17]

It soon became obvious that Mesa Verde needed a more

thoughtful and comprehensive plan to manage its backcountry in light of the Wilderness designation. Thus began the conflicted process of internally planning for backcountry use while publicly ignoring the resource.

In August of 1979, Superintendent Heyder issued a directive to the Chief Park Ranger on visitor use in the backcountry, noting that it had been closed for years. "There are many questions in my mind as to the legality of this closing." He seems to have been unaware of the 1971 Final Rule closing the backcountry, but was he concerned over the Wilderness Act's prescription that a Wilderness "has outstanding opportunities for solitude or a primitive and unconfined type of recreation"? He asked for three specific alternatives for management of the backcountry. The first was continued closure, with a rationale and estimate of patrolling requirements. The secod alternative was limited use under a permit system. Here, too, he wanted staffing requirements as part of the description of this alternative. Finally, he wanted an alternative for unlimited use, again including staffing requirements and potential problems associated with this alternative. He wanted a draft plan by January 15—four-and-a-half months away.[18]

This planning framework was relayed to the Regional Director in November as part of the Park's annual objectives for 1980. The Superintendent went so far as to go into the field "to evaluate some possible back-country visit areas."[19]

The resulting document in the Mesa Verde National Park files[20] is not dated or paginated, nor does it clearly decide among the alternatives. There is no location for a signature of approval, which would indicate the document is likely a draft, though it is not so marked. It does, however, capture the tension between wilderness experience and archeological preservation. Naturally, the understanding of the Park's cultural resources is stronger than that of its wilderness resource.

The Plan relied in part on the tenuous Proposed Rule Making from 1969, apparently unaware (as noted above) that the rule had eventually been finalized two-and-a-half years later. But perhaps the most surprising omission is in the Appendix of applicable laws, regulations, policies, and memoranda: the Wilderness Act of 1964 was not listed.

The Plan did, however, refer to this Act in formulating policy: "The Wilderness Act specifies that designation . . . as wilderness shall in no manner lower the standards evolved for the use [and] preservation of such park." In addition, "Wilderness areas shall be administered for the use and enjoyment of the American people in such manner as will leave them unimpaired for future use and enjoyment as wilderness, including 'outstanding opportunities for solitude or a primitive and unconfined type of recreation.'"

In these phrases, the Plan defined the conflict. The Wilderness Act directs that there shall be recreational use, but also that there shall be no lowering of the standards of management. The Plan made no formal decision on whether recreational use lowers that standard, but it's clear that it leaned heavily in that direction. Indeed, that had been the guiding principle in the management of the Mesa Verde backcountry for at least two decades.

The Plan stated that most Park visitors would appreciate wilderness "as part of the park scene, viewed from park roads and developments." It is not clear if the authors expected scenic views to completely satisfy the Wilderness Act's "outstanding opportunities." It would seem not, as the Plan immediately referenced "the visitor who hikes into the wilderness." Yet, no visitor has been allowed a wilderness experience in the decades since this Plan was written.

Was keeping it secret the only way to preserve the garden? The Plan expanded Heyder's requested alternatives for public use: maintaining the current action (complete closure); unlimited use; limited use of trails with an NPS guide; use of trails by issued permit; and use of trails by self-registration.

In describing the current situation, the Plan made errors in both fact and judgment. "Traditionally visitors have *always* been accompanied on most trails by National Park Service guides or trails guides provided by a horse concessioner" (emphasis added). As already repeatedly detailed in *Mesa Verde's Secret Garden*, this was not true—the Park

Service had actively promoted personal exploration. The Plan continued, "No overnight hiking has been allowed." This statement, while literally true, is misleading, as multiple-night horse trips were advertised for decades. The Plan also claimed that going into stabilized cliff dwellings with a trained interpretive ranger and reading interpretive signs at overlooks or protected surface ruins is an experience "superior to a visit without such an interpreter." For many visitors this may be true, but for some, being in the Mesa Verde cultural and biological landscape with a horde of others is not "superior." Is there an obligation to provide an experience for those visitors?

To be fair, the Plan's discussion of the current situation did mention some of the "meaningful experiences enjoyed by early park visitors" that were now off limits. Tellingly, the Plan noted recreational experiences have been "limited . . . even in areas where little risk to cultural resources exists."

The listed impacts of the unlimited use alternative included the rehabilitation of old trails, construction of new trails, and that "interpretive devices would be needed for installation at some backcountry sites." There was no explanation of why any of these developments would be needed. This alternative assumed there would be an increase in vandalism, excavation, and theft of artifacts. To minimize such damage, only an intensive backcountry patrol program was mentioned.

The impacts of a visit with an NPS guide alternative mentioned the Spring House Trail as an example (though none of this trail is within the Wilderness). Illegal activities would be greatly reduced, as would the need for the intensive backcountry patrol program, but the costs of providing the interpretive guide would be high. The Plan claimed, "This type of use would provide high quality visitor experience." The Plan failed to note hiking with a ranger and (presumably) several strangers would not be a wilderness experience.

The impacts of allowing use under a permit were determined to be a mix of the previous two. Only a few trails would be opened; patrol costs would be moderate, with no cost for an interpretive guide. The Plan mentioned that some trails might have interpretive stations—a decidedly un-wilderness development—but claimed the quality of visitor experience would be "high." The advantages of this system over the next alternative included the "opportunity to provide visitor contact and orientation."

Allowing use under a self-registration system would have similar impacts to use under a permit system except for the important loss of opportunity for visitor contact prior to entering the wilderness. As with the permit alternative, there would have to be increased backcountry patrols to prevent damage to the cultural resources, though not to the extent necessary if unlimited use were allowed.

There is a glaring omission in the Plan: each of the alternatives was addressed on a park-wide basis. There was no thought of zoning visitor use—that is, allowing some sort of use where, as the Plan stated, "little risk to cultural resources exists," and prohibiting it elsewhere. It was no coincidence that the Mesa Verde Wilderness was designated in just such low-risk areas.

A section of the Plan outlined procedures for employee use, prohibiting solo trips, a permit to a specific destination, and day use only.

In making some sort of determination on use of the wilderness by the public, the Plan summarized: "The above policies allow for public use of the Mesa Verde Wilderness but also emphasizes control and direction of use in the interest of protection of resources." The Plan noted that the MoA with the Advisory Council on Historic Preservation included the statement, "Human use of the designated wilderness will be limited and managed [to] provide a wilderness experience without destroying the conditions that originally made it desirable as wilderness."

The Plan concluded with, "Visitor and employee use of the Mesa Verde Wilderness will be allowed under the same conditions as stated in Alternative 2." The problem with this declaration is that "Alternative 2" was three alternatives of limited use: with a ranger-guide, by permit, and by registration. Which was the intent?

Perhaps the question of intent was moot. Mesa Verde continued to prohibit all public use of the wilderness.

"A Feeling of Overprotection"

Superintendent Heyder reiterated restrictions on backcountry use for Park staff in a memo to all employees in June of 1981, reminding employees that it was illegal to enter cliff dwellings without authorization. Acknowledging the temptation, he pleaded, "The enjoyment you may gain is really not worth the damage you may do. Bear in mind that . . . once a part of these ruins is lost, it is lost forever. It can never be the same again; the copy is not the original."[21]

Less than two weeks later, another memo was sent to the employees:

> A recent check of Painted Kiva House ruin has revealed clear and unmistakable evidence of destruction of elements of the prehistoric features of that site. This destruction was caused very recently and is presumably ascribable to members of the park staff who are known to have entered the ruin illegally and to have spent the night there. . . . The integrity of the park as well as that of the entire National Park Service has been jeopardized, the rights of Native Americans to a proper respect for their ancestral sites has been violated, and a pall of mistrust has been cast over the present corps of employees. . . . This is not the only instance of illegal entry into backcountry ruins. . . . It is unfortunate that the situation has reached its present state, for it has been only within the past few months that the supervisory staff of the park, in considering a revision of the plan for management of the backcountry, has sought ways in which more access could be provided for park employees.[22]

Personnel records are kept private, so there is no record of consequences for the offending members of the staff, but clearly there were "issues" in the management of the backcountry. Perhaps what was needed was some sort of analysis—an intervention—from outside the Mesa Verde family. In May 1982, the Superintendent wrote the Regional Director, asking for a "management appraisal" to be conducted by the Regional Office.[23]

The review was conducted in August. The section on backcountry use contained recommendations for a vast departure from the practices at Mesa Verde, and more in keeping with other NPS units with significant archeological resources. It called for allowing "a little more feeling of freedom" for visitors and employees. Not only should hiking be permitted on some of the old primitive routes, but the Park should consider limited backcountry camping permits along existing fire roads under "very restrictive conditions," to protect natural and cultural values—which also would require a check-out process with a ranger. Overall, a change in management tone was warranted. "We were told that in years past there was always a feeling of overprotection and super-sensitivity for vandalism."[24]

The Mesa Verde Chief Ranger concurred with most of this recommendation (except overnight use) within the limits of certain constraints which included adequate patrolling, requiring registration, and using only trails built to NPS safety standards in areas "not containing fragile ruins or easily removed artifacts."[25]

The Chief of the Research and Cultural Resource Management Division emphasized the Park's archeological responsibilities:

> Whoever told the team that "in past years there was always a feeling of overprotection and super-sensitivity for vandalism" was speaking, in my opinion, for themselves and certainly not for this division. In past years there has been a considerable amount of damage from . . . both visitors and park personnel, who have made unauthorized visits to the prehistoric remains in this park. This damage is documented and unquestionable, and it is not consistent with the primary responsibility of this park, which is to protect the prehistoric ruins. I have no argument with the recommendation for greater access to the backcountry so long as measures are taken to guarantee the protection of those ruins.[26]

Superintendent Heyder's official response to the Region's management review was sent in January. "The park is moving toward some expanded use of the backcountry," but the Superintendent balked at the idea of permitting camping because there was insufficient staff to properly monitor such use. At the end of the day, that was the issue that prompted "deep philosophical discussions of why the park was established and the conflict of preservation versus use." Nowhere does Heyder's memo mention wilderness. There is no attempt to differentiate it from backcountry or to address the additional managerial direction required by law.[27]

During this time, the Park's trail crew rebuilt four miles of the Old Tourist Trail from Chapin Mesa at Far View, across Park Mesa to Moccasin Mesa, with a Boy Scout group from Durango rehabilitating another mile. It is not clear if this was part of a plan to prepare some trails for public use, but if so, that plan never came to fruition.[28]

"There Is Currently No Wilderness Management Plan for Mesa Verde"

The Mesa Verde Wilderness slipped into obscurity. As mentioned in the introduction, even some employees who worked at the Park had no idea there was a designated wilderness in Mesa Verde. The Park's Annual Goals for Fiscal Year 1985 made no mention of the Wilderness. The next year's Statement for Management mentioned wilderness only in passing, with nothing about actual management. When the NPS Draft Policy on Wilderness Preservation & Management was sent out to all the units for review, Superintendent Heyder forwarded it to the division chiefs for their input, with a note saying that the Park needed "a draft reply—more than just 'no comment.'" Presumably, Heyder wanted to explain why the Mesa Verde Wilderness should be managed differently. His official response to the Regional Director consisted of one sentence: "Mesa Verde National Park has no comments on the draft policy."[29]

In 1989, The Wilderness Society inquired about the Mesa Verde Wilderness, wanting to know: 1) if the Park had gotten around to the inventory as Congress directed back in 1976; 2) if there was any de facto wilderness; and 3) the status of the Park's Wilderness Management Plan. The response referenced Units A, B, and C as designated "in September 1972"—more than four years in error. It made no mention of de facto wilderness, and simply stated, "There is currently no Wilderness Management Plan for Mesa Verde." Thirteen years after designation and still with no Wilderness Management Plan, the Park was out of conformance with the most recent direction from the Washington Office requiring every wilderness to have a wilderness management plan containing "specific, measurable management objectives that address the preservation of wilderness-dependent cultural and natural resources and values."[30]

Later that year the Park was contacted by Stephen McCool from the School of Forestry at the University of Montana. In preparation for the conference celebrating the twenty-fifth anniversary of the Wilderness Act, McCool wanted to know where wilderness management progress had been made in the last five years, which problems remained unresolved, if new problems had arisen, and what stewardship concept had been the most helpful. Heyder's reply listed fencing the boundaries as the progress. New problems included predators getting killed outside Park boundaries and difficulty in the preservation of niche environments for endemic species or for relic species from older climate regimes. Interestingly, he referenced "Recognition of the value of wilderness" as an unresolved problem. His answer to what stewardship concept had been most helpful was even more illuminating: "Non-access and non-development of the wilderness areas have made them special areas in terms of studying natural environments."[31]

The Park's next Statement for Management, in 1991, again mentions wilderness only in passing, with nothing concerning actual management.[32] If such a broad document might be excused from mentioning a less-than-important facet of the Park, surely that year's more specific Resource Management Plan would give a clearer picture of what was important and what was not important to Park management. This Plan was well-written, with strong statements on the purpose and significance of the Park; the significance of the Park's cultural resources and natural resources; the purpose of the Plan; and the Management Objectives of the Park. There is no mention of the Mesa Verde Wilderness.[33]

Figure 25. Off-duty Park employees climbing into a cliff dwelling, July 1991. Such activities were not only potentially damaging, but disrespectful, and led to further restrictions on employee use of the backcountry.

In 1993, the staff started another draft Backcountry Management Plan. Any consideration of use by the public was strictly pro forma. The real issue was how to manage employee use in light of persistent abuse by some of the staff, and there was a push to severely limit—or close entirely—backcountry use by employees.

In the meantime, the Park purchased two trail counters for backcountry trail problem areas and installed "Intrusion Detection Systems" at remote closed sites where illegal activities were occurring. Spring House, Double House, and Hemenway House joined Painted Kiva as cliff dwellings closed to employees to visit on their own, though backcountry hikes were led by permanent staff for seasonal employee development.[34]

In October of 1996, the Mesa Verde National Park Backcountry

Use and Access Plan was approved by Superintendent Larry Wiese. All employees were required to take "backcountry etiquette training" and, except for official duties, employees were allowed to go only to sites that were open to the public, after receiving written permission, and were permitted to be "accompanied by immediate family members or no more than 2 guests." Employees could hike only on trails open to the public. As for public use, "In summary, the backcountry of MEVE is closed to public visitation." The only reference to wilderness appears in the discussion of employee vehicle use: "Vehicles will not be used in the park's designated wilderness areas."[35]

In March 2000, Superintendent Wiese signed the Mesa Verde Strategic Plan for Fiscal Years 2001–2005, seen as an opportunity "to reexamine the Park's fundamental mission and the results or outcomes needed to more effectively accomplish that mission." The Wilderness designation in 1976 was interpreted as adding to the Park's mission the duty to "manage and protect the pristine character of [the] designated wilderness." Since no wilderness areas are managed to preserve "pristine" character, the choice of this word indicates a lack of understanding the wilderness character as defined in the Act and as discussed in the introduction. The Plan lists 41 long-term goals. Thirteen of these could be relevant to wilderness management, but there is no specific reference to wilderness anywhere in these goals.[36]

"This Is a Major Problem that We Cannot Allow"

If the backcountry was to be kept closed to the public, the horse concession became increasingly irrelevant. For decades, horseback trips had been available for those visitors who wanted to see some of the outlying sites. But the concession was moved from the Chapin Museum area to the Morefield Campground, and the available trails were hardly memorable when compared to what had been offered previously. Then, when the concessioner's contract expired, it was not renewed by the government: "The Service has determined that a pack and saddle operation is no longer necessary or essential to serve visitors."[37]

Elsewhere, the recreational sense of discovery was given short shrift, even in areas moving out of backcountry and into frontcountry status. In looking at Wetherill Mesa Development alternatives, the planning document stated, "The opportunity for the visitor to 'find' Mug House is unique and should be preserved." However, that sentiment follows the immediately preceding sentence: "Mug House will be made available to the visitor on a limited basis, by reservation tours." This can hardly be considered a 'find.' When the next plan was drafted, there were trails to overlooks of Spring House, Ruin 20 ½, and Double House. None of these were built, and they were the closest to a backcountry experience that would have been offered. During the Pony Fire in 2000, much of the infrastructure on Wetherill Mesa was destroyed. The subsequent plan presented three alternatives for redevelopment, ranging from "permanent facilities" to a "primitive backcountry experience." There was to be no primitive backcountry experience.[38]

Figure 26. Near the lower (eastern) end of Whites Trail, showing lack of maintenance (and use) since shortly after the Bircher Fire. August 2019.

Volunteers continued to do trail work. The Youth Conservation Corps (YCC) worked on several projects, including constructing the D-cut trail (following the old road bed west of Park Point) and some trail work in Soda Canyon. Operation Raleigh, based in the United Kingdom, worked for a few days on the Old Tourist Trail. The Park's trails crew brushed out the Old Tourist Trail from Moccasin Mesa to Prater Canyon, rebuilt Spring House Trail from Long Mesa to Long Canyon, and inspected the entire system of historical trails in the Park, noting trail alignment, condition, accessibility, and maintenance needs. Working on the Whites Trail off the East Escarpment after the Bircher Fire in 2000, Park staff and Colorado Outdoors volunteers installed rock cairns, and cleared burned snags. In 2005, Park staff supervised a group of Sierra Club volunteers on projects to clear and mark the Accelerated Public Works (APW) trails, originally built in the early '60s, "for access for park personnel" (see Figure 12).[39]

It is unlikely that any of this work, with the possible exception of the D-cut trail, was done to facilitate public use.

The Ute Mountain Utes requested to conduct horseback tours into the southeast portion of the Park. The proposal was denied. "The use of the back country by this operation would open up the question of use of the backcountry by all park visitors. This is a major problem that we cannot allow under the stipulations of enabling legislation and by existing park policy."[40] Once again, Heyder was fabricating—the prohibition was solely a matter of policy, not law.

"The Power Line Is a Violation of the Wilderness Act"

Although the Park managers resisted providing any recreational opportunities in the Wilderness, they were cognizant of keeping the three units undeveloped. In 1980, it was noted that an old power line passed through Unit B to Park Point. "We feel that our mandate is clear. The power line is a violation of the Wilderness Act of 1965 [*sic*] and must eventually be removed." Eight years later the Superintendent's Annual Report included, "Overhead lines . . . pass through a designated wilderness area and will have to be removed." Twelve years after the intrusion was first noted, the line was removed by Empire Electric Association at the park's expense. "With the removal of the line, there are no longer any encumbrances within any of the three units of wilderness." That, however, was not quite correct. The northern overlook at Park Point, which had been repaired by the Park in 1981, extends approximately fifty feet into the Wilderness.[41]

Also in 1980, a trip was made to the Waters Cabin in Unit C of the Mesa Verde Wilderness to evaluate its condition and to determine what action should be taken to recover historic artifacts remaining on site. Since this sheepherder's cabin was of historic value, it was not considered an "encumbrance."[42] It was destroyed by the Bircher Fire of 2000, but some artifacts that survived the blaze still mark the cabin's location.

Other developments in the non-Wilderness backcountry included the ongoing effort to adequately fence the boundary to prevent livestock intrusions, and periodic maintenance of the existing fence and patrol roads. After the Chapin 5 Fire of 1996, a series of installations, including terraces and waterbars made from logs of Excelsior (netting filled with aspen mulch), were placed to reduce erosion. Eighteen alcove sites had silicone driplines installed to divert rainwater so that further damage would not occur.[43]

And the idea of a tram was resuscitated by the Cortez Tramway Commission. The group raised $45,000 for an economic feasibility analysis of a tram from Cortez into the Park. It was still not feasible.[44]

"The Propensity for Visitors to Remove Artifacts"

In 1976, the University of Colorado's Survey of Mesa Verde National Park continued on Park Mesa, where the relative lack of easy access made work more difficult. The following year they finished the survey with the North Escarpment and the area around the Park entrance.[45]

Since the backcountry was closed to the public, it was rarely patrolled. Yet illegal use was occurring, sometimes discovered by helicopter crews on reconnaissance flights. Occasionally, perpetrators were caught: "The U.S. Magistrate . . . sentenced Mark S. Rubenstein to one year's probation, 160 hours of public service in a national park, and $452.00 in restitution for stealing . . . a large, corrugated jar of the classic Pueblo III period that still had remnants of a yucca fiber carrying strap attached to its mouth. [This was] one of only three in the park's extensive pottery collection still bearing traces of a fiber carrying device." At Square Tower House, "Floors were damaged by heavy boots in contact with fragile floors and plaster knocked off of walls as the 'visitors' climbed out of kivas. . . . The individuals were prosecuted for entering a cliff dwelling without a ranger."[46]

For every thief caught, many more were not, and frontcountry sites were far from immune. Park staff grappled with the ongoing impacts of visitation on archeological sites and what countermeasures might be taken. Occasionally larger items were stolen, but the clearest example of continued problems was seen in the lack of sherds on trails open to the public as opposed to those closed to the public. This provided "evidence of the propensity for visitors to remove artifacts from the park. Countermeasures are law enforcement and public education," though how to structure the education was not included in the written report. Today, the middens at sites closed to the public have far more cultural resources remaining on the surface than those that are open, though collection by researchers has also greatly denuded many sites—the difference being, of course, that collections made by researchers usually still belong to the public somewhere, even if not in their original and natural home.[47]

"Far from Park Roads and Trails"

Cultural resource management turned to overseeing numerous smaller-scale research projects from various institutions and addressing the ongoing schedule of maintenance and stabilization. In a 1987 interview with Duane Smith, Chief Park Archaeologist Jack Smith noted the perceived difficulty with this task: "The big problem is getting to the places, not only the people, but water, tools, stabilization supplies, etc. We have been very lucky. There has been a helicopter available to us. . . . That way we can do this work in ruins that would virtually be impossible if we had to go on foot. It is almost prohibitive the old way; now we can fly in and out in a few minutes." The difficulty was similarly exaggerated in the Superintendent's Annual Report following the 1989 Long Mesa Fire: "All of these ruins [to be stabilized] are far from park roads and trails; and in order to get stabilization materials to them, a helicopter stationed in the park for fire control was employed."[48] No part of that burn was more than one mile from a road. The Mesa Verde backcountry is small and heavily roaded north to south, with two main trails and another road running east to west (though the condition of the trails has deteriorated significantly since 2000). Getting people to sites should have been relatively simple, with the somewhat more difficult portion of the stabilization task being transporting the necessary materials.

Work intensified following the large fires in this era: the Long Mesa Fire of 1989; Chapin 5 in 1996; the Bircher and Pony Fires in 2000; the Long Mesa Fire of 2002; and the Moccasin Fire in 2003. The fires uncovered new sites, and efforts to control erosion over thousands of acres were complicated far more by their density and complexity, than by any perceived remoteness. Some sites were destroyed, among them the petroglyphs at Battleship Rock. "Consultation was held with representatives from the affiliated tribes. The representatives from the tribes felt the fire was a natural occurrence and that the destruction of the panel was 'meant to be.' Based on the tribes' input and the fact that there was no assurance that treatment could prevent further deterioration, park management determined that treatment was not advisable." Bell shows dramatic before-and-after the fire pictures.[49]

Other cultural resources, however, were not going to be allowed to deteriorate. An Archeological Site Preservation and Conservation Program was initiated, selecting three hundred sites as top priority, with a clear major emphasis on the alcove sites.[50]

"A Backcountry Ranger Position Was Hired"

"For the first time in the history of Mesa Verde National Park a Backcountry Ranger position was hired through the funding assistance of the Archeological Resources Protection Act [ARPA]." Superintendent Heyder complained to the Regional Director: "The Park received $9,000 for this program. This represents 3/10 of 1% of the Park's operating budget. Considering that Mesa Verde National Park is the premier park in the nation for the preservation of archeological resources, this amount is a mere pittance."[51]

During the next several years, the so-called ARPA Ranger provided at least some of the backcountry presence that the Staff had argued would have been necessary to open this part of the Park to the public. Analysis of the ARPA Ranger's reports shows both trends and utility of this position. (Some patrols in some years were at other NPS sites, including Goodman Point, Hovenweep National Monument, and Yucca House National Monument. For the first three years, data for those sites have been filtered out of the following analysis).[52]

The ARPA Rangers made between thirty-two and sixty-seven patrols each year between 1991 and 1999, and claimed to have visited between 500 and 750 sites each year. Roughly half were made by horse, slightly less on foot, and the remaining few by helicopter. The first year the ranger stayed overnight in the backcountry twenty-four times, though this diminished to seven nights within two years. The ranger found two remains of Ancestral Puebloans, and an average of ten new sites per year. There were one or two instances of digging discovered each year, along with an average of seven instances of graffiti or vandalism. Other evidence of trespassing in closed areas—both tracks and items left behind—averaged around twenty instances. It is not clear who was responsible, but several of the incursions were along the southern border with the Ute Mountain Ute lands, and a few bore the hallmarks of employees: among the items left behind in 1993 in Double House were "4 marijuana joints and a flower offering."

From 1997 on, the Superintendent's Annual Reports have little detail, but the ARPA Ranger program was invaluable, not only for the archeological resources in Mesa Verde, but for monitoring wildlife, reporting trespass horses and cattle, repairing fence, and even for "maintaining relations with local ranchers and the Ute Mountain Ute Tribe."[53]

In 2000, backcountry patrols started to decrease, and by 2004 the ARPA Ranger made only three patrols.

In 2005, the backcountry patrol was considered "revitalized." It appears much of the patrol ranger's time was spent on an intensive inventory of over fifty miles of trails and roads and of associated features such as culverts, waterbars, steps, and retaining walls. There was never consideration of this work being done as preparation to open up the backcountry to visitors, except as possible ranger-led hikes during the next year's Park Centennial. By now, extraordinary authorization had to be considered even to allow staff archeologists to camp overnight (eating only cold food!) in the backcountry to reasonably accomplish essential work.[54]

"A Skilled/Motivated Resource Management Specialist"

The 1982 Management Review noted the Park's recognition in the area of cultural resource management and called for a similar effort toward Natural Resources. The review team believed that such a program would not work "without a strong commitment from all divisions, top management, and a skilled/motivated Resource Management Specialist."[55]

The battle to have a more natural garden in the Mesa Verde backcountry and wilderness developed on two fronts. One was to inventory, protect, and (where necessary) re-introduce native species and then allow natural processes to operate. The other was to eradicate nonnative species, both plant and animal. This battle was complicated by the tension created by ever-present critical archeological values, further muddied by the recognition that the Ancestral Puebloans had substantially manipulated their environment—perhaps not as drastically nor as easily as people today, but archeological research was pointing out the ways in which Mesa Verde was both similar and different to the mesa of 700 years ago. Discussing the Wetherill Mesa studies conducted before the large fires of the early twenty-first century, archeologist George Cattanach noted that the mesa-top vegetation at the time of his writing in 1980 was probably very similar to conditions before the Basketmaker era began. However, he argued that during the seven-century occupation of the mesa, the forest cover must have been drastically reduced by clearing the land for farming, fuel, and building materials. Further evidence of these changes was found in the stratigraphy of pollen deposition, with a post-occupation decrease in maize pollen and corresponding increase of juniper and pine pollen. Populations of Douglas-fir had steadily decreased on the mesa from centuries of building with these desirable trees. The portions of the park that were burned by major forest fires in the recent past may more closely resemble the land when it was occupied by prehistoric farmers than do the unburned, forested portions.[56]

If there was now an intent to allow natural process to regulate the vegetation, except for a small frontcountry site where the Ancestral Puebloan environment would be re-created, then a decision needed to be made concerning how far to allow those natural processes to operate while protecting the archeological resources.

Research showed a less clear-cut path forward in determining which animal species existed in the area prior to and during the occupation of the mesa by the Ancestral Puebloans. It seems turkey had supplanted deer as the major animal food by the time people moved into the cliff dwellings, though it is not known if the change was a result of people having over-hunted the available wild animals, hunters finding it more dangerous to travel far after game, or simply a reflection of "further sophistication of culture." Some sites on Wetherill Mesa revealed few remains of bighorn sheep, while unworked bone recovered in the refuse at Long House had roughly equal proportions of bighorn and deer bone, and the excavations in the Badger House Community indicated that there seemed to be more bighorn than deer in PII dwellings while the reverse was true in PIII cliff houses. Interestingly, researchers found no bear bones.[57]

Perhaps more surprisingly, elk are largely absent from lists of utilized animals. As part of the comprehensive Wetherill Mesa Archeological Project, Rohn cited only one elk bone out of almost 3,000 bones recovered at Mug House, and elk are not mentioned as a food source in his summary, with speculation that the bone was a possible trade item. This is in keeping with the results reported by Swannack at Big Juniper House, where one elk bone tool was found but no unworked elk bone, and elk were omitted from his summary. In Badger House, Hayes and Lancaster reported a scapula and one bone from an elk's foot in the refuse. While they speculated that elk may have lived within ten miles in the Montezuma Valley, Cattanach said they were not native to the Mesa Verde and that no elk bones were found among the 3,000 studied from Long House. Colyer summarized their presence by writing that "Fewer than a dozen elk bones have been identified in [the entire] prehistoric cultural context at Mesa Verde National Park." In all likelihood, there were no elk on the mesa, and it is fairly clear they were of minimal importance to the Ancestral Puebloans of Mesa Verde.[58]

In the end, it seems that the Park Service considered animals "native" if they were utilized by the Ancestral Puebloans or subsequently migrated onto the mesa without the conscious manipulation of modern humans. Included by that latter exception are elk, which (as noted immediately above) seem not to have been present in the area until introduced in the La Plata Mountains by the State of Colorado in the early twentieth century, and not seen in the Park until 1921 (as noted in chapter 3). In 1979, there were five sightings of elk in the Park. By the next year, elk sightings had increased substantially, and it appeared an elk herd had been established. By the late 1980s, elk were so common that they were rarely mentioned, and by 2002 it was estimated up to 200 were living in the Park.[59]

Likewise, bear became more common. There was only one sighting during 1980. In 1984, a bear expert from Arizona Fish and Wildlife Service believed there was no evidence of a resident black bear population in the Park, even though he found bear scat and clawed trees. By 2001 they were considered established, year-round residents.[60]

On the other hand, mountain lions became rarer over the years. Twelve to twenty-four sightings were recorded each year in the early 1980s. In 1987, "One hundred and eighteen actual sightings of mountain lions (one to three animals per sighting) were made from April through October by park staff, residents and visitors. These were thought to represent at least twelve animals, most of which range on and off of the park on all sides." By 1990 there were still more sightings of lions than bears. Then the population began to drop, correlated to reduced deer herds due to persistent deep snow. There were ongoing conflicts between local ranchers and federal agencies—including Mesa Verde—about the local lion population, and "predator control" on adjacent lands was another likely contributor to the drop in the number of lions. In 2000, major fires reduced forage and cover for the lions' prey base, and they have not returned to those 1987 levels.[61]

"The Last Remaining Bighorn Sheep"

Some of the species of concern in the Park needed a helping management hand over the decades. This trammeling eventually tapered off, largely as a matter of practicality.

Turkeys had failed in the past (see chapter 7), but Mesa Verde tried again. In January 1990, the Park released fourteen turkeys in Prater Canyon, three miles south of the tunnel. This time the transplant seemed successful. In just two years the birds were believed to be distributed throughout the Park, with a population in 1993 estimated to exceed 120 birds.[62]

Bighorn sheep proved more problematic. The Park had thought the transplant in the late 1940s had been successful, but throughout the 1980s the sheep appeared to have trouble sustaining their numbers in the habitat available to them. By 1991, the Park staff believed that as few as three sheep remained. Mesa Verde started discussions with Colorado Division of Wildlife to evaluate the potential for bighorns to be transplanted once again. A Joint Work Statement was drawn up whereby Colorado would translocate twenty-five bighorns, and the Park would allow the State to use Mesa Verde as a source for transplants elsewhere once the herd reached seventy-five animals. The release was postponed in 1992 and again in 1993 because of deep snow at the release site on Long Mesa. It was feared the Park simply had marginal habitat due to the absence of large fires that would reduce overstory vegetation.[63]

In 1997, a multi-agency task force looked at the feasibility of restoring bighorn sheep in fifteen National Park units. The conclusion for Mesa Verde was that there existed too little habitat for the maintenance of viable population. However, fire might thin dense vegetation, improving bighorn habitat and perhaps making it possible for a transplant.[64]

In 2000, one adult ewe was seen on May 17, wandering along the cliff base below Hemenway House Overlook. "It is possible that this is the last remaining bighorn sheep in the park area."[65]

But fires that summer and again in 2002 opened up habitat, so Mesa Verde's dream of having bighorns return was not dead. In 2006 the Park looked once again at the feasibility of reestablishing bighorn sheep in the park, aiming for two releases of at least 25 animals.[66] They never happened.

"Added to the Park's Checklist"

During this period, attention to the natural fauna expanded beyond the iconic turkey and mammalian megafauna.

A pair of peregrines nested on Lone Cone, adjacent to Point Lookout. Their two eggs were replaced with dummy eggs, and then three nestlings were placed in the eyrie. All three later successfully fledged. Three years later the birds moved their eyrie to the cliffs at the north end of Prater Mesa above the Knife Edge Trail.[67]

Spotted owls were noted in House of Many Windows in 1986. Almost twenty years later, the owls were less noticeable, if present, and the Park briefly considered establishing Protected Activity Centers. No spotted owls have been detected since 2008.[68]

There had been no established prairie dogs in the Park since

1965 when the colonies died out due to plague. An established colony of sixty mounds was noticed in Mancos Canyon in 1988. It periodically revived and died down through 1999, as did a small prairie dog town in Morefield Canyon. Plague was the presumed cause of the die-offs.[69]

Yellow-bellied marmots were reported from Morefield Canyon and the Prater Grade in 1998, but after the Bircher Fire in 2000 they seem to have disappeared.[70] The marmots must have been at the periphery of their range. Sightings of other animals are considerably more dubious. The "mink" reported by a visitor was probably a long-tailed weasel. There was a report of "possible wolverine tracks," which would have been highly unlikely, and the whooping crane that was reported in 1983 almost surely must have been a sandhill crane.[71]

As the concept of a complex ecosystem became more important, other classes of animals were seen as equally valuable. In 2002, Marilyn Colyer developed a comprehensive, eighteen-page list on the status of "Faunal Species of Concern" in Mesa Verde.[72]

The interest in specific plants, too, increased. Ponderosa pines were considered "Pleistocene relics," so they were numbered and recorded.[73] But this new-found attention went far beyond "charismatic megaflora" of the Park's trees.

In 1980, nine research plots were established to monitor the status of three designated rare and endangered species. These plots were purposefully located in areas which received moderate visitor or development impacts. In three years, the population of one of these rare plants—Chapin Mesa milkvetch—was found to have more than doubled. This was welcome news; it is believed to be endemic only to Chapin Mesa and a small area on Moccasin Mesa. Another of the park's endemic plants, Cliff Palace milkvetch, was found at three new sites on Wetherill Mesa, extending its known range. In addition to these rare species, "Two hundred and thirty new [plant] species have been added to the Park's checklist since 1980."[74]

The vegetation at Mesa Verde became a marker for environmental change. Citing a paper on regional drought, the 2006 Superintendent's Annual Report noted the recent insect-induced die-off of conifers was much greater than during previous outbreaks in the twentieth century. The success of the insects was believed to be caused by the severe drought the region had been undergoing, coupled with unusually mild winter temperatures. "The implication is that our piñon mortality was exacerbated by global climate change very likely being triggered by anthropogenic factors."[75]

"Musk Thistle, Canada Thistle, Smooth Brome, and Cheatgrass"

The major concern for plants, however, became the non-native species. Some of these had been noted in previous decades but were now recognized as threats to the biotic integrity of the Park.

In 1986, a helicopter and ground survey of the entire Park was conducted. Approximately 2,000 acres of vegetation dominated by musk thistle were found, the largest single area being the 1972 burn on Moccasin Mesa. Other areas of concentrated musk thistle were found in canyon bottoms (particularly those subject to grazing by trespass cattle and horses), mesa rims where the tree canopy had opened up, and in development areas where the ground had been disturbed.[76]

The following year, Colyer developed a plan to control this plant, first recorded in Mesa Verde in 1978 and found to be quickly increasing. But control was no simple matter. A seed-eating weevil had been introduced by the Department of Agriculture on private lands north of the park, but the weevil, also non-native, was known to attack a native thistle. After looking at a wide range of alternatives, in 1987 Colyer proposed a combination of mechanical control (cutting out tap roots), revegetating disturbed areas with vigorous native plants, monitoring for the exotic seed-eating weevil, and researching other biocontrols. The use of chemical herbicides was examined and rejected.[77]

By 1991, the Natural Resource Management staff continued mechanical control of musk thistle in developed areas and attempted to reduce the stands in Prater and Morefield Canyons, which had spread to forty acres.[78]

In 1997, the list of non-native plant species was updated. Many of the 107 species on the list were noninvasive and estimated to have limited distribution, but eight were chosen for specific attention: Canada thistle, spreading pepperweed, houndstongue, diffuse knapweed, Russian knapweed, cheatgrass, smooth brome, and tamarisk. A year later, the most serious were believed to be "musk thistle, Canada thistle, smooth brome, and cheatgrass." And yet, in 2002 the Park reported that "The only [non-native plant] species that have become a major problem in undisturbed backcountry are Canada thistle and musk thistle," despite the widespread presence of both smooth brome and cheatgrass.[79]

Biocontrol seemed to have some success in limiting, though not eradicating, non-natives. Chemical control appears to have been used only in the frontcountry prior to the Bircher Fire in 2000, after which the post-fire infestation of Canada and musk thistles in Morefield and Prater Canyons was so bad that a tractor-mounted boom-sprayer was needed to apply herbicide. New non-native species continued to appear, with a population of leafy spurge found about 1,000 feet northwest of the tunnel in Prater Canyon in 2000.[80]

In 2004, George San Miguel, the Park's Natural Resource Manager, wrote a brief report on the spread and attempted control of invasive species.[81] One of the prime vectors of weeds in the backcountry was wildfire. Sometimes the introduction of non-natives was intentional, as after the Moccasin Mesa Fire of 1972, but more recently it was the result of the fire itself opening up new habitat, compounded by weeds inadvertently being introduced during suppression efforts. An intensive inventory was conducted on areas that had burned in the Long Mesa Fire of 2002. Fifteen non-native species were identified. As expected, musk thistle was the most common, infesting over 200 acres.[82]

San Miguel summed up the status of the invasive plants in Mesa Verde, arguing that large parts of the Park were still weed-free, and that the key to keeping them so was to reduce ground disturbance. Fire was the greatest problem, but other management actions (such as past seeding of exotics) set the stage for post-fire infestations. Lack of funding and staff exacerbated the problem.[83]

"An Ambitious Plan"

The primary non-native species of concern to the Park remained trespass livestock. These were mainly horses, with some cattle, though there were occasional reports of goats, and even an emu.[84]

The specific origin of some of these trespass animals was known. Sheek & Company legally grazed about 190 acres of inholdings remaining along the Mancos River. The Park's 1985 Draft Land Protection Plan noted that these private tracts presented a livestock trespass problem: "Some damage to archeological sites has occurred in areas adjacent to the tracts." Contradicting itself, the Plan continued, "Grazing is probably the highest and best use of these lands" and "Current level of use is not having significant adverse impacts on park resources to the point that immediate acquisition is required." Contradicting itself once again, the Plan concluded, "However, fee acquisition meets long-term needs of Mesa Verde National Park."[85]

Most of the time, however, the provenance of trespass animals was not so easily determined. Almost every year for three decades, the Superintendent's Annual Report or the Chief Ranger's report included a count and location of cattle and horses, and the efforts taken to remove them and prevent future encroachment. Of particular note were the following:

In 1977, eighty trespass cattle were removed with help of the Bureau of Indian Affairs (BIA) and the Ute Mountain Utes; boundary fences were erected in Morefield and Prater Canyons and boundary gates were installed on the Moccasin and Chapin Mesa management roads. No cattle were observed in Morefield or Prater Canyons the next year, but their presence continued near the Far View Visitor Center, in east Navajo and Soda Canyons. Fourteen were rounded up and removed. Trespass of Ute Mountain Ute horses in the Wetherill Mesa and Far View areas continued, with foals being born in the Park.[86]

In 1979, another interagency roundup of cattle took place in School Section Canyon with the BIA paying for a helicopter and the Ute Mountain Utes providing personnel in addition to Park staff. Seventeen head were removed from the park. However, horses were seen during the winter months at Sun Temple and Cedar Tree Tower. In addition, the horses on Wetherill Mesa appeared to be increasing, with as many as eighteen being seen at one time.[87]

Easy access to the park by Ute horses and cattle had been a continuing problem for many years, but now the Park staff realized boundary fencing projects were inadequate at best—and useless in controlling resident herds. Animals living year-round in the park appeared to be dramatically growing, estimated at forty-five to sixty head of horses and approximately twenty-five head of cattle. Impacts included damage to archeological sites, destroying native vegetation, danger to motorists, and "sanitation problems" around public-use buildings. In 1981, more robust fence construction was undertaken with the cooperation of the Bureau of Indian Affairs.[88]

Two years later, one report claimed "25 to 35 horses lived year-round" in the Park, and "between 20 and 100 head of cattle lived seasonally" in various canyons. Colyer called this a gross underestimation of the number of horses. She believed there were approximately 120 feral horses running in the Park, coming from the west and south through the new fences that had been broken down by the horses—or occasionally, as she relates, supposedly cut by members of a Ute family "who begrudged their exclusion from the Park." She also reported ongoing issues with an outfitter in Weber Canyon who deliberately opened gates to let his animals into the Park.[89]

Among the Annual Goals for Fiscal Year 1988, the Acting Superintendent listed "Finish boundary fence project" and "Remove trespass stock from park upon completion of fence project."[90]

In 1989, the new Superintendent took a different tack. He wrote to the Ute Mountain Ute Tribe, proposing that the Utes remove their livestock by a negotiated deadline. If they failed to do so, then MEVE would hire a contractor to do the work and any remaining animals would be "disposed of."[91] The Mesa Verde files do not contain a response.

In 1990, apparently receiving no satisfaction from the Utes, Superintendent Heyder went to the Colorado Brand Inspector requesting the State remove the trespass horses. He sent an identical letter six months later, and one almost identical a year after that.[92] The Mesa Verde files do not contain a response to any of Heyder's letters.

The Park continued to remove trespass cattle and horses. Twenty-six head of cattle and fifty-one horses were removed in 1991. In 1992, six head of cattle and two horses were removed. Five years later: "An ambitious plan to remove [trespass cattle] is being initiated."[93]

Progress on removing these animals was set back by the fires in 2000. During suppression efforts, sections of fence were cut and gates left open to facilitate movement of fire-fighting equipment. These breaches of the boundary were not remembered for over three months, and the staff had no idea how many horses and cows entered the Park.[94]

By the time of the Park's centennial in 2006, it was believed that the feral horses numbered fewer than 30, compared to 150 to 200 in the mid-1990s. The animals were located in three main areas: Morefield Canyon in the vicinity of the Morefield Spring; Park Mesa and Upper Soda Canyon; and Wetherill Mesa and Upper Long Mesa. In addition, there were "occasional small herds of rejected young stallions or solitary old stallions scattered in marginal territory."[95]

"The Need for a Prescribed Fire Program"

Concern for the "natural" quality of the Mesa Verde backcountry and Wilderness went beyond specific plants and animals, expanding into concern for ecosystem health and processes. A first draft of an Air Quality Management Plan was completed in 1979. In 1984, the Park hosted a symposium on "Air Pollution Effects on Parks and Wilderness Areas," and Mesa Verde became an important data point in measuring regional acid precipitation, mercury deposition, and ozone pollution. The Park gathered data on water sources within the Park, growing the number from 186 to 263 in less than ten years. The Park even initiated monitoring of the night sky: The NPS Night Sky Team made three visits to Mesa Verde during 2004, recording visibility and light pollution, collecting baseline data for future comparisons.

Figures 27 and 28. Herds keep replenishing themselves. There are two foals with four adults in figure 27. Solitary stallions are scattered throughout the Park. November and September 2019.

However, "Because of cuts in funding for 2006, it simply has not been possible . . . to pursue air quality trends in Mesa Verde over and above generalizations and superficial, yet significant, observations."[96]

Understandably, wildfire had always been the natural process most constrained in Mesa Verde. But by the late 1970s, the ecosystem costs associated with fire exclusion were becoming apparent, and the policy of 100 percent suppression was beginning to be questioned. Perhaps some sort of modified fire suppression might be appropriate in some areas of the Park, with fires covering larger areas at reduced intensity a "tolerable trade-off" to rare, yet highly destructive fires. Of course, visitors and archeological features would be afforded protection, but "fire may [*sic*] play an important role in the Park ecosystems." The aim was for a gradual reintroduction of "carefully selected prescribed fires" (fires intentionally ignited by managers) to the Mesa Verde piñon-juniper ecosystem, as well as using ignited fires to create natural firebreaks and buffer zones for high-risk areas. It was recognized that such a plan would not be applicable every year. "Each fire and fire season is unique and presents its own decision-making problems and opportunities."[97]

The tension between the unnatural build-up of fuels as a result of putting out all fires versus the unknown impacts of "management burning" continued to grow and was called out by the 1982 Management Review. In response, Superintendent Heyder said the Park was "well aware of the buildup of fuels." On the possibility of a catastrophic fire, he added (with characteristic hubris) that, "with the quick response now provided by the helicopter, that potential is greatly reduced." The National Park System Advisory Board of the Secretary of the Interior had conducted its annual fall meeting at Mesa Verde. Among the resolutions passed that related to Mesa Verde was "the need for a prescribed fire program." Years passed without one, each delay providing fuel to damage archeological sites and native biota.[98]

The inevitable started with the Long Mesa Fire in 1989, burning almost 2,500 acres, and the Park staff realized a fire plan was urgently needed. Pressure was applied from the Washington Office to begin prescribed burns or allow some natural starts to be controlled, rather than immediately extinguished. Consequently, the Park approved a Wildland Fire Management Plan that would reduce the accumulation of forest fuels in and around the developed areas on Chapin and Wetherill Mesas, at Far View, and at the Morefield campground.[99]

The Plan had barely begun to be implemented when the Chapin 5 Fire started, burning over 4,700 acres and threatening Park infrastructure in the Far View area. The profound effect of this fire on cultural sites is discussed above. In addition, as mentioned earlier, intricate diversions often were constructed in what would have been natural runoff channels to avoid irreplaceable cultural sites.

Then, in 2000, the Bircher Fire burned most of the eastern one third of the Park, followed immediately by the Pony Fire, which burned over the developments on Wetherill Mesa. These were followed just two years later by another so-named Long Mesa Fire (though the fire was primarily on Chapin—not Long—Mesa), which posed even greater threats to Park infrastructure than had the Chapin 5. After the fires, several locations were seeded by helicopter with native grasses. On steep slopes, a polymer stabilizer was added to hold the soil in place and to retain moisture. The aerial seeding projects were unsuccessful; immediate seeding was deemed necessary, but evidently doomed to failure without adequate soil moisture.[100]

A post-fire phenomenon, concerning and much-debated as to cause, was the difference in tree regeneration between burned and unburned locations. In an unburned study plot, juniper was a healthy species replacing itself. Piñon was important, but less conspicuous, and may have been disappearing as elsewhere in the region. However, a burned study plot had no seedlings of piñon or juniper during the five-year study. There has been much speculation that this is a result of a warming and drying climate in southwest Colorado, but it may simply be an anomaly in an ecosystem with what has been hypothesized as "a minimum 300-year successional sequence." After the 2000 fires, Superintendent Larry Wiese is quoted in *Shadows of the Centuries*: "[The fires have] given us the opportunity, I think, to watch the development of a piñon/juniper forest. . . . We have a clean slate for a forest to begin developing, but yet, fifty percent of the park is still covered with a mature piñon/juniper forest. . . . All of us are excited about the rebirth of the natural ecosystem."[101]

The rebirth, to the extent there has been one, has not followed expectations. Surprisingly few seedlings have regenerated in those burned areas more than two decades into the twenty-first century.

"Return This Section of the River Corridor to Pre-Settlement Conditions"

Perhaps the most telling example of the growing importance of the natural environment in Mesa Verde during this period is the change in the management of the Mancos River corridor. An area that had, for decades, been considered "trade-bait" because of the lack of extant prehistoric cultural resources was now, for that very same reason, a focus of ecosystem inventory and restoration.

In 1987 the Park instituted an inventory of the cottonwood groves. Only fourteen trees over six inches in diameter at breast height were recorded, along with 1,351 saplings. This unbalanced age-class distribution was thought to be the result of heavy cattle browsing at the north end of the Park's river corridor, coupled with beaver use at the south end.[102]

Amphibians were monitored. The tiger salamander seemed to have declined, and there were no observations of leopard frogs, which had been plentiful in nearby ponds and streams until the early 1970s. Insects were monitored as well, with low numbers of aquatic insects blamed on turbid waters created by an upstream gravel mine.[103]

The Mancos River corridor was the main park habitat for lazuli buntings, yellow-breasted chats, blue grosbeaks, and indigo buntings. The big brown bat, a federal candidate for listing under the Endangered Species Act, was observed along the river. One researcher found suspected slides of the rare water shrew. The Park surveyed for the southwestern willow flycatcher, but none were found.[104]

Stream gauges were placed in the Mancos River at the north and south boundaries, and six transects were set up in the Mancos Canyon flood plain to determine effects of varying water levels.[105]

Livestock grazing continued along the Mancos River long after it had been stopped in the remainder of the Park. It was finally terminated in 1998, and the Park planned to "return this section of the river corridor to pre-settlement conditions." Vegetation was restored through seeding of native grasses, winterfat, and buffaloberry; musk thistles were subjected to biocontrol; and erosion control projects were undertaken.[106]

Grazing remained active upstream of the Park boundary, so the Park Service entered into an agreement with the BLM to fence across the river at the upstream point where the Park and the BLM share a common boundary. The fence ran approximately 200 feet east of the river into the Weber Mountain WSA, and the agreement included using herbicides for tamarisk control on both sides of the river. Unfortunately, the workers identified buffaloberry as Russian olive, and killed hundreds of the native shrubs, but tamarisk was successfully reduced. Musk thistle was dramatically reduced by the biological controls, and native grasses flourished. "Cattle trails are nearly completely healed."[107]

In addition, attempts were made to reestablish what were thought might be animals present in and along the river at the time of the Ancestral Puebloans. A pair of local beavers were transplanted. A fish survey found flannelmouth sucker, bluehead sucker, roundtail chub, and speckled dace. Non-native species occurring above and below the Park's length of the river were, surprisingly, not found. Native pikeminnows were absent, but the backwater areas of the Mancos River were judged to be suitable habitat, and oral history interviews indicated they may have been present until the 1950s.[108]

In all this restoration, the Park appears to have planned on reliable water in the Mancos River, spending considerable time and energy while ignoring evidence to the contrary. After the beavers were reintroduced in 1990, they seem to have inhabited the Park for a few years, but then disappeared. The Mancos went dry for part of

2002. Nonetheless, in early fall 2004, a family of five beavers were released in Mancos Canyon near the south boundary of the Park. In addition, Colyer continued her leopard frog surveys, with an eye toward restoring this species, but there appears to be no direct evidence that the six miles of the Mancos River within Mesa Verde ever supported a population of leopard frogs.[109]

Even after the Mancos went dry, the Park also planned to reintroduce roundtail chub. They never got around to it—fortunately, as it turned out. The Park reported sudden torrential flooding in September 2003 would have likely carried the fish far downstream. "The park called this a-hundred-year flood, but this actually has happened twice during the past twenty years."[110]

Floods notwithstanding, thinking the Mancos River in Mesa Verde could support species dependent on year-round water was well-intentioned fantasy. It seems the Park Service knew this at the time. "It must be emphasized that the drying of the Mancos River was no act of Nature. Even in this severe drought, the reason was the river diversions above the park." In the early 1990s, the Park Service had been trying to adjudicate reserved water rights for several parks, but the Department of Justice wanted to drop Mesa Verde's "right" to Mancos River water from the litigation because the "Mancos River does not originate in the park, and this may place other parks in jeopardy during their adjudication processes. The Mancos River issue will be treated separately sometime in the future."[111]

As of 2024, the Park has no reserved water right for the stretch of the Mancos River at the eastern edge of the Park, where it frequently runs dry. And no native fish, no leopard frogs, and no beavers. But there are plans—covered in chapter 10.

"These Resources Should Not Be Managed Separately"

During this period when the NPS grew more serious about protecting the natural resources in Mesa Verde, it is important to keep in mind that at no time was the primacy of the archeological program in doubt. In May 1992, the Division of Research & Cultural Resource

Figure 29. The Mancos "River." September 2018.

Management was expanded to include Natural Resource Management, which had been within the Division of Resource Management and Visitor Protection. This combination mirrored the Rocky Mountain Regional Office structure and reflected an increasing awareness within the National Park Service that "these resources should not be managed separately."[112] At Mesa Verde, Research was already in the Division of Cultural Resource Management, not in Natural Resource Management. And contrary to elsewhere, Cultural subsumed Natural, rather than vice versa.

In addition to the Mancos corridor, the idea of managing at least a portion of the Park as a whole was not concentrated on the Wilderness, but rather on Park Mesa because of its unique geography. In response to a research inquiry in 1993, the Park's Division Chief wrote that Park Mesa "was designated a Research Area" because it was the only roadless mesa of significant size in the Park that is entirely within the Park boundaries. She continued, "Because of the mesa's inaccessibility it has received very little use as a study area."[113] There are, however, two errors here: first, Park Mesa is hardly "inaccessible." It is less than eight miles in length, with simple access from the main Park road at the north end and a relatively easy hike from the quarry on a trail that crosses the Mesa less than two miles from its southern end. More importantly, as discussed above, the Mesa was never officially designated as a Research Area.

Yet there was continued interest in getting Park Mesa some sort of additional designation. Natural Resource Specialist San Miguel proposed trying to get it designated a Colorado Natural Area. He called such a designation "quite an honor" and assured the Park staff it would not change management in any way. He added, with more than a little embellishment, "It is a kind of honorary title similar to 'World Heritage Site.' Also, it could help us get research grants in the future. It could only add to the park's already distinguished reputation." But the method of determining the area's qualifications appeared to be a problem. San Miguel requested a three-day backpack to conduct a field review, to be completed "sensitively and safely under proper supervision."[114]

No evaluation was made, perhaps because the request for overnight use was not in conformance with the Park's policy. A year later, he tried again, without the request to camp overnight.[115]

That proposal died, too.

As the Park was about to enter its second century, it seems the designated Wilderness in Mesa Verde was held in the same regard as Olivia was reported to have had for Sir Andrew Aguecheek in Shakespeare's *Twelfth Night.* Sir Andrew was informed, "You are now sailed into the north of my lady's opinion, where you will hang like an icicle on a Dutchman's beard."

CHAPTER TEN

Wilderness in the Park's Second Century

2006–present

MESA VERDE NATIONAL PARK'S second century brought advances in the management of many of the Park's resources. What did not advance, however, was the management of the Park's wilderness as designated Wilderness, nor consideration of the wilderness resource in other areas of the Park.

"Develop and Maintain a Wilderness Management Plan"

In 2006, the NPS issued new Management Policies, moving the Service toward the "strong ecosystem management culture" envisioned by the Vail Agenda fifteen years earlier. The policies included *NPS-6: Wilderness Preservation and Management*: "All lands administered by the National Park Service . . . will be evaluated for their eligibility for inclusion in the National Wilderness Preservation System." In addition, "The superintendent of each park containing wilderness resources will develop and maintain a wilderness management plan or equivalent planning document to guide the preservation, management, and use of these resources." The bulk of the policy details the components and sideboards of a plan, including the direction to "encourage and facilitate those uses of wilderness that are in keeping with the definitions and purposes of wilderness and do not degrade wilderness resources and character."[1]

At Mesa Verde, no such evaluation of the portions of the Park that had not already been designated as Wilderness had been completed—even with the specific direction of Congress given in 1976. The Park had never developed a wilderness management plan for the portions that Congress had designated—though that was not all that unusual in the Park Service, despite the policy in *NPS-6.* The greatest deviation from the requirements of the Wilderness Act was the Park's refusal to allow (let alone encourage and facilitate) wilderness use by the public. The Park ignored much of NPS-6.[2]

Rather, in 2006 the staff of Mesa Verde was consumed by planning for the Park's centennial celebration, including discussions about providing Park visitors "special opportunities" to visit archeological sites not usually open to the public. Assessing the potential resource impacts of these trips was time-consuming, but backcountry tours to Oak Tree House, Mug House, and Spring House, plus twilight tours of Cliff Palace, accounted for "thousands of dollars of additional income."[3] The recreational benefits to the public are not mentioned in Superintendent's Annual Report. Perhaps they were taken for granted.

"It Was as if No Controls Had Been Applied"

After the centennial, Park management seems to have returned to its routine, though there was some additional effort dedicated to looking at the impacts from the visitors during the previous year, particularly the short-term consequences of hiking and horseback trips on the endemic Cliff Palace milkvetch. Researchers found more plants in 2007, attributed to favorable soil moisture, but noted that while bedrock protected roots from trampling, the plants were often killed when they grew in the open soil of the trail tread.[4]

The fight against invasive non-native plants continued, with limited success. As noted in the Superintendents Annual Report for 2007, cheatgrass was "winning the battle and also winning the war." The southern end of the 2000 Pony Fire burn on Wetherill Mesa had a 90 percent cover of cheatgrass. The bottom of Morefield Canyon appeared to be buried in non-native mustards through the spring, followed by dense stands of cheatgrass, followed by the solid purple blooms of five-foot tall musk thistle. The Superintendent's Annual Report noted, "It is hard to imagine that this bottom . . . grew 18-inch-tall bluegrass during the wet 1980s." Seedhead weevils and crown weevils were released, but they fared poorly. Herbicide was applied as a test to five acres in Mancos Canyon. Soon after, it was said to have "never looked better, at least not in the past hundred years. . . . It will be a showplace of restoration." But the next spring, the staff returned to Mancos Canyon to find that "solid mats of cheatgrass were overwhelming. It was as if no controls had been applied in much of the treatment area." Colyer previously had determined that some non-natives (smooth brome, crested wheatgrass, alfalfa) were deliberately planted by the NPS following fires in 1959 and 1972. She did not speculate about how other non-natives so prevalent now (including Russian knapweed, cheatgrass, Canada and musk thistles, alyssum, and tumble mustard) arrived in the Park.[5]

Figure 30. Non-native smooth brome now fills the channel of Waters Canyon. June 2018.

In 2015, the Park issued a comprehensive plan for managing invasive plants, stressing prevention, early detection, consistent monitoring, evaluation of various treatment options, and the restoration of native plant cover. Cheatgrass and smooth brome were so widespread and difficult to control that they rose only to a "medium" Park treatment priority. Another exotic species present, tumble mustard, though mentioned in the text, is not listed among the treatment priorities. The plan included a section on hypothetical impacts to wilderness, but since the detected populations had not yet reached "threshold levels for treatment," there were no plans to undertake control in the Wilderness. The plan did, however, outline the potential impacts to the various qualities of wilderness character should the need arise to take action.[6]

The most prevalent exotic animal species in the Park, the feral horse, continued to be a problem. In 2012, an aerial survey identified 100 horses in 32 groups (including lone individuals). A trapping plan was formulated in 2018. Though horses rarely use Unit C of the Mesa Verde Wilderness, they were expected to be lured to one of the baited pen trap sites. None of the traps are in the Wilderness, and those in the backcountry are along existing management roads. The extremely ambitious goal is to remove all livestock within five years. As of August 2023, twenty-nine horses had been removed using humane, low-stress techniques; it is estimated there are approximately fifty to sixty horses remaining, though reproduction will likely add to the Park's number each year.[7]

"The Effect of Fire Suppression"

The fires of 2000 and 2002 had made it clear that the Park needed a comprehensive fire management plan, with quantifiable goals and statistically valid measures. The overarching desire was to reintroduce natural fire on the mesa, but doing so would prove to be no simple decision. This dilemma, embracing fire as a natural event when fire in the disturbed environment might do greater ecological harm—not to mention risk archeological values—is a central

Figure 31. In addition to not being native to the Mesa Verde ecosystem, feral horses damage archeological sites (5MV2467). November 2019.

Figure 32. Pen in Morefield Canyon used to acclimatize feral horses for humane capture. August 2020.

conundrum to the long-term management of Mesa Verde National Park.[8]

Analysis of the trade-offs by the staff had to account for invasive weeds conducive to carrying fire and whether another fire might actually cross a threshold where recovery would no longer be possible. It had become clear that re-burning the same area over and over would merely stimulate weeds to the detriment of the native species. Any analysis also had to attempt to account for changing climatic conditions, "potentially the most serious threat of all." In the absence of this analysis, all fires were suppressed as immediately as possible—a total of thirty-six fires burned nineteen acres between 2007 and 2009.[9]

The Park finally drafted a Fire Management Plan in 2013, which included a detailed assessment on the effects to the Mesa Verde Wilderness. The plan correctly recognized that suppression adversely affects the "untrammeled" and "natural" qualities of wilderness. "The effect of fire suppression . . . would be to perpetuate an unnatural accumulation of fuels in wilderness that could lead to a catastrophic wildfire." In addition, Alternative B, which included fuel reduction plans, noted that the likely use of mechanized equipment would adversely affect the "undeveloped" quality. To prevent this additional assault on wilderness character, "The use of manual and mechanical thinning and prescribed fire would not occur in the wilderness areas."[10]

The Plan was revised in 2023, with a similar prohibition in the Mesa Verde Wilderness on fuel reduction through mechanical thinning or prescribed fire. Fires would be suppressed in the Wilderness, with acceptable tactics including aerial and ground operations using both "mechanical and non-mechanical tools" (presumably, motorized and non-motorized equipment). The section on wilderness is comprehensive, despite being found in "Appendix C: Resources considered but dismissed from further analysis." This section correctly identifies fire suppression as a form of trammeling and recognizes rehabilitation as necessary to decrease the impacts to temporary developments incurred during suppression tactics. Appendix D is a programmatic Minimum Requirements Analysis, referencing a System-wide policy obligation for actions proposed in wilderness that may impact the area's wilderness character. The Plan was approved with a Finding of No Significant Impact in 2024.[11]

"The Checkered History of Wilderness"

To a certain extent, the fires in Mesa Verde dictated the actions of the cultural resources staff, who continued condition assessments of nine alcove sites in the vicinity of the 2002 Long Mesa and 2003 Balcony House Complex fires while funds to do so lasted. In addition, a two-year project of architectural documentation of backcountry alcove sites was started in 2007 as part of a process to determine a stabilization priority list based on the severity of threats and current condition. Four sites were documented during the 2007 field season, and stabilization was completed on one site after partial repairs had been made in 2001, 2004, and 2006. Non-alcove sites received attention as well. Forty-two sites, mostly within the perimeter of the 1996 Chapin 5 fire, were monitored for condition status. One site was treated by the stabilization crew, with excelsior matting installed to retard severe erosion.[12]

As was the case every year, there was constant and ongoing stabilization and maintenance of frontcountry sites, especially those visited by the public.

Intermittent vandalism continued to be a problem. In one case, a person who stole a mano and metate and several pottery sherds from the Far View area was convicted and "banished" from the Park. Another was caught "with a shovel and other digging equipment," but the Superintendent's Annual Report does not mention the disposition of that case.[13] As far as enforcement in the backcountry was concerned, the Annual Reports are silent.

The Park Service stopped requiring Superintendent's Annual Reports following 2009. Over the last years, they increasingly read like transcribed dairies, rather than thoughtful distillations of each year's work. The 2007 Report was 129 pages; there was no mention of the Park's Wilderness. The 2008 and 2009 Reports, at 130 and 105 pages, respectively, each mention wilderness only once—in reference to one-day field trips by George San Miguel during which he talked about "the checkered history of wilderness at Mesa Verde."[14]

There are sufficient documents in the Park's files to determine that the work of the staff continued to follow predicable patterns: yearly chipping away at ongoing problems, occasionally addressing emerging issues, and supervising the work of researchers wanting to work in a National Park.

In 2011, the Senate Subcommittee on National Parks held a hearing at Mesa Verde on "issues affecting management of archaeological, cultural, and historic resources." In the hearing's transcript, reference was made to 106 backcountry sites identified and prioritized for preservation treatments. Indigenous representatives emphasized the need for consultation. No mention was made of wilderness.[15]

"Cuestas and Canyons"

Emphasis on cultivating a more-or-less natural garden—and the understanding to appreciate just what that was—led to a variety of research proposals and Park-initiated actions. Among them:

One group of researchers tackled the future of piñon-juniper woodlands in the Park. One group, Anderson et al., looked at past forest regimes to try to determine just what was "natural" in Mesa Verde. Interestingly, they postulated the MEVE woodlands are unusual in that they "may experience fire only every 400 years or so." Given this long fire rotation, they came to the startling conclusion that "there is little evidence that these woodlands have been impacted by 20th century fire suppression." It is possible this statement may have led Park managers to believe that current attempts at total suppression of wildfires simply would maintain the natural ecosystem. However, the lack of fire on the mesa for most of the past several centuries may well have been a function of two factors. First, removal of the trees by the Ancestral Puebloans, resulting in centuries of "discontinuous fuels"; and second, until recently, a "cooler and wetter climate."[16] This would be in keeping with a synthesis offered by paleontology researchers: "Fossils . . . show a transition from xeric-adapted flora in open settings to more mesic piñon–juniper woodlands over the past 1,500 years, with fluctuating fire frequency, [which peaked] about 740 years ago, close to the peak of the Ancestral Puebloan civilization on the mesa."[17]

Floyd-Hanna and Reed looked at the resiliency of the Park's forests in light of recent fires, beetle infestations, and increasing drought. These environmental stressors were, they noted, decreasing resistance to aggressive exotic plant species.[18]

George San Miguel outlined a long-term (and ultimately futile) attempt to justify reintroduction of bighorn sheep on the Mesa Verde cuesta. The project had the support of the Utes, who wanted the opportunity to offer trophy hunting. USGS ran a habitat suitability model with positive but less-than-ideal results. He also tried to get designated a "Cuestas and Canyons" Colorado Natural Area. This was unsuccessful, perhaps because "public access is expected" with such a designation.[19]

In an increasingly common pattern, the Mancos River went dry again in 2018 (Figure 29) and 2020. How could fish—and beavers—come back to the Mancos under such conditions? In 2023 and 2024, the Park undertook a significant alteration in the upstream section of the Mancos at the east boundary. The project included installing nine simulated beaver dams made of natural materials. These were intended to decrease the river's velocity and create pools upstream of the dams to provide habitat for fish during the late summer. Twenty-three other log structures were installed to "increase stream complexity"[20] Time will tell whether this extensive gardening will result in the Mancos River corridor that the Park staff desires. As it is, the project seems akin to Oscar Wilde's assessment of a second marriage: "the triumph of hope over experience."

"The Purpose of These Objects Is Uncertain"

Archeological contract work during this period included the

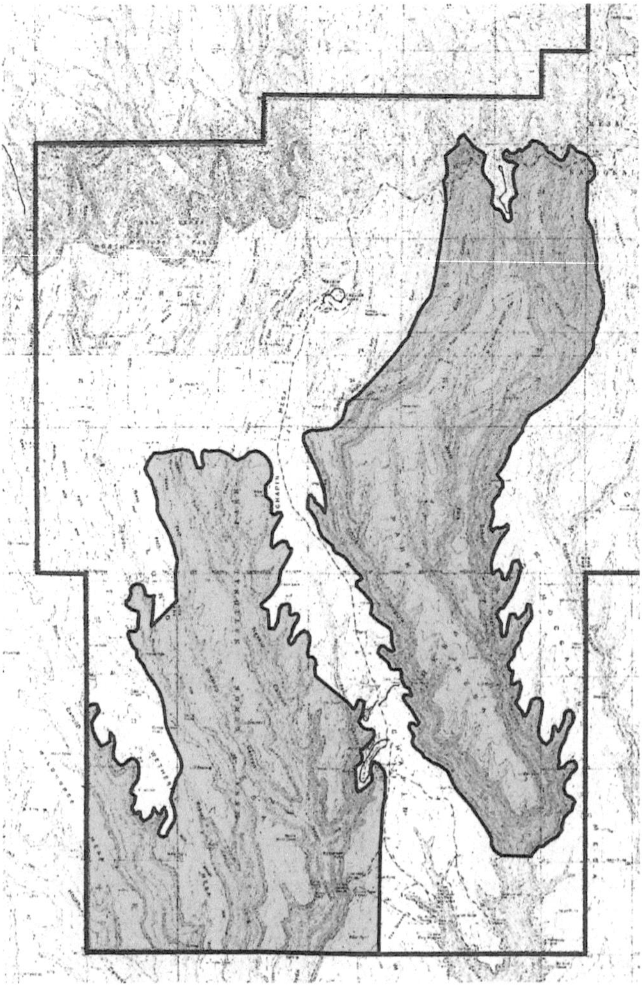

Figure 33. "Cuestas and Canyons" proposed Colorado Natural Area (shaded).

multi-year Mesa Verde Community Center Survey.[21] This project looked at thirteen clusters of Ancestral Puebloan dwellings in the Park, attempting to assess their relationship with each other and their environment. None of these community centers are within the Mesa Verde Wilderness, though two are just outside; all but one are in the backcountry.

Research on the "other features of value" was not restricted to

Figure 34. This piece of petrified wood, about 8 inches long, is unremarkable—except that it was found at an archeological site several miles from nearest source of petrified wood. Someone carried this home around 1,000 years ago. Such simple and direct experiences of Ancestral Puebloan life are largely unavailable to Park visitors in the Mesa Verde frontcountry.

the Park's archeology. An extensive analysis of paleontological resources was undertaken, including a synthesis of past investigations. The melding of paleontology with archeology is an intriguing aspect of Mesa Verde's cultural past. The Wetherill Mesa Project turned up petrified wood in Long House, both unworked and culturally modified into rods up to five inches in length. "The purpose of these objects . . . is uncertain." Other unworked pieces "may have been collected and saved because of their ritual value (inferred from the presence of the largest piece in the shrine of Kiva Q)." Petrified wood also appeared as a burial accompaniment in Mug House. There are 139 catalog numbers assigned to petrified wood in the archeological collections. The modifications of this mineral included awls, drills, hammerstones, knives, and a mano. [22]

"Interpreting Unexcavated Sites Is Good, But . . ."

In 2010, there appears to have been a reassessment of visitor experience opportunities, including in the backcountry.[23] Some of these (Oak Tree House, Spring House, Square Tower House) were eventually added in intermittent years as fee tours. There was no action taken on most of the possibilities mentioned (including Lower Morefield Canyon, School Section Canyon, and coordinating with the Utes for a trip from Square Tower to Casa Colorado). Only one of these—a new trail to an overlook of Little Long House—was planned to be unguided. Decisions on three (Little Long House Overlook, Far View West, and upper Navajo Canyon) were deferred until staff visits could be arranged. The possibility of a new trail to an overlook of Little Long House was, for the most part, deemed feasible and desirable. It was never built. The other two were scrapped early in the review because of concern over easy access increasing "the possibility of visitors returning to the area on their own and collecting surface artifacts. Interpreting unexcavated sites is good, but it might be better to consider other sites like Lower Morefield which would be more difficult to return to on their own."[24] The sites in question had been excavated but not developed to withstand regular visitation. In addition, the Park staff applied conditions of approval that would be impossible to meet: "There will not be any effect on threatened, endangered, or rare species and/or their critical habitat; [and there] will not be any effect on historical, cultural, or archeological resources."[25] Of course, *any* use would have *some* effect. Perhaps the document evidences merely a shorthand for the customary standard of "no *unacceptable* effects." Or perhaps it was an intentional screen to keep the backcountry a secret.

Other than the occasional, semi-annual hikes to Spring House, the only backcountry experience that was added was a planned yearly horse ride to the Whites Mesa fire tower along the Morefield-Whites Mesa Truck Road. The Mesa Verde Foundation touted this as having "opened more of the backcountry to hundreds of visitors," a statement of astounding exaggeration.[26]

The secret continued to be kept from employees as well. Another

Figure 35. Remnant of the Old Tourist Trail. After the Bircher Fire of 2000, parts of this trail were re-marked, but much of the trail has been lost to natural forces. November 2017.

Figure 36. In a few places trail infrastructure still exists, though in many places the trail itself has grown over. September 2018.

2010 document looked at the old backcountry trails that might be opened to them.[27] None were. The lack of maintenance after the 1996 Chapin 5 and 2000 Bircher Fires in particular created a notable problem, and the loss of trail "asset" has only gotten worse.

"Protecting These Sensitive Sites from Leases"

There continued to be adjacent land-use threats to the integrity of the Park. The Hindmarsh family asked the local BLM office to issue a right-of-way through BLM land to their private holdings north of the park's North Escarpment in order to facilitate the development of a residential subdivision. Apparently, the access was approved over objections from the Park. The Superintendent's Annual Report for 2006 noted, "Once constructed, the subdivision is expected to harm the park's viewshed, cultural landscape, and wilderness and ecosystem values."[28] (This is the only reference to "wilderness" in the 128 pages of the Report). As of 2024, the subdivision has not been built, but the Park had become increasingly worried about the intentions of the BLM, which manages much of the land adjacent to the North Escarpment and along the Park's east boundary.

At first, the concern with the BLM was over mineral development, when two sections on the north boundary were leased for oil exploration. Superintendent Wiese erroneously believed that "Local BLM management did not have a simple way of protecting these sensitive sites from leases, and an attempt to have the Department of Interior look into the matter was unsuccessful."[29] The wells drilled in the area to the north of the Park proved unproductive, and the land was subsequently closed to surface occupancy for mineral leasing.[30] But the Park was worried that the wells would have created a threat greater than simply a degraded viewshed. Opening lands next to the Park "would make enforcement in the Park virtually impossible."[31]

One possible solution would have been to transfer the BLM parcels adjacent to Mesa Verde to the NPS. Though there had been some pothunting, the BLM land had not been subject to the intensive collection

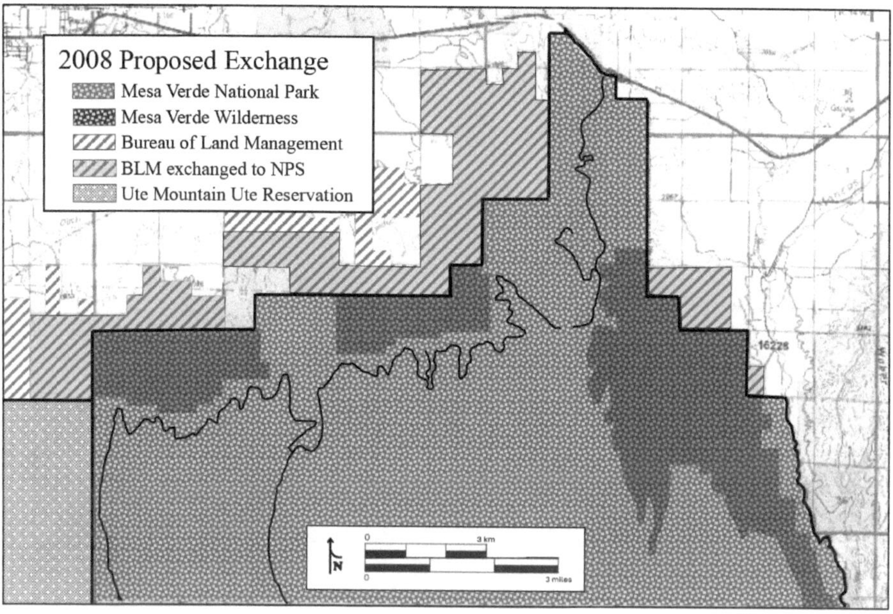

Figure 37. Proposed exchange in 2008. [RG03-01.01-018]

practices in the Park; to this day the middens of sites in this area are far richer than those of similar sites in the Park. There are historic resources as well. However, due to the inaccessibility of those lands from the remainder of Mesa Verde, resource protection would have been extremely difficult for Park staff. The transfer was not consummated.

"Mesa Verde National Park Supports Outstanding Wilderness Values"

In 2011, the Park issued another five-year Strategic Plan. On page 1, the plan stated the Park's mission: "We protect the world class resources of Mesa Verde National Park . . . for all people. This includes the cultural, natural, aesthetic and wilderness values." That is the last time the word "wilderness" appears in the document. Of the forty-nine management objectives listed, many pertain in part to

Figures 38 and 39. Most of the BLM land immediately north of the Park has no public access. October 2019.

Figure 40. Adjacent BLM lands also include historic sites. August 2019.

the Mesa Verde Wilderness, but only one specifically refers to use: "Maintain historic trails in good condition to allow access to park personnel and possible visitor usage to back country." As noted above, a preliminary accounting of these trails had been done in 2010, but apparently no further action was taken. The Strategic Plan's Appendix shows discarded objectives. One of them was "Create and implement park Backcountry Management Plan." There is no information on why this objective was dropped.[32]

In 2013, *Director's Order #41: Wilderness Stewardship* was approved as a supplement to NPS-6 to "provide accountability, consistency, and continuity in the . . . wilderness stewardship program." Once again, "For every designated wilderness, a Wilderness Stewardship Plan will guide management actions to preserve wilderness character. . . . Parks with lands determined to be eligible, proposed, or recommended should also develop plans to preserve wilderness character. Wilderness Stewardship Plans should be completed *within two years of designation*" (emphasis added). The bulk of DO41 gives guidance for management actions in Wilderness consistent with law and the policy in NPS-6.[33] While Mesa Verde still had no Wilderness Management Plan—at that point, thirty-seven years after designation—wilderness considerations started to be addressed in other activity plans concerning the management of fire, invasive plants, and feral livestock, as discussed earlier in this chapter.

In 2015, the Park issued what was called a Foundation Document[34] to provide guidance for planning and management decisions. It references the Mesa Verde Wilderness to a far greater extent than any earlier planning document.

The Mesa Verde Wilderness is mentioned in the Park's description, and its purpose states that the Park "protects, preserves, researches, and interprets an archeological landscape including more than 600 cliff dwellings, *wilderness values,* and remarkable scenic resources in southwest Colorado" (emphasis added). Park "significance statements" include "Mesa Verde National Park supports outstanding wilderness values." The Wilderness is listed as one of the Park's "fundamental resources and values," and is included as an interpretive theme.[35]

For the first time in a public Park-wide planning document, the Park acknowledged "Mesa Verde National Park must manage the Mesa Verde Wilderness . . . according to the 1964 Wilderness Act, as well as NPS *Management Policies 2006* and NPS *Director's Order 41: Wilderness Stewardship.*" The Appendix of pertinent legislation includes not only Public Law 94–567, which designated the Mesa Verde Wilderness, but also the congressional direction to make further wilderness recommendations, detailed in chapter 8.[36]

Two pages are devoted to an analysis of this "fundamental resource and value." The analysis starts with the assertion that "The overall condition of the wilderness is good"—a dubious claim since the wilderness was not monitored by any comprehensive method. It accurately identifies a number of threats, including trespass livestock, invasive plants, illegal hunting, and light pollution. It lists among the opportunities "potential trail and backcountry camping use." All of this is predicated on not-yet-obtained data and a nonexistent wilderness plan.[37]

From the point-of-view of wilderness stewardship at Mesa Verde, the most telling point of this Foundation Document is found in the section on Planning Needs. A Wilderness Stewardship Plan would "determine compatible experience or use opportunities while preserving the character of the Mesa Verde wilderness." On a scale of High, Medium, or Low Priority, writing this Plan is rated "Low."[38] Given the reality of day-to-day management, Low priority is No priority.

"Responsible for Preserving the Wilderness Character"

This era of management at Mesa Verde overlapped with arguably the greatest advancement in wilderness stewardship since the passage of the Act itself: a framework for monitoring trends in wilderness character.

The Wilderness Act directs that "each agency administering any area designated as wilderness shall be responsible for preserving the wilderness character of the area."[39] What constitutes wilderness character is apparent from the definition of wilderness in Section 2(c), as outlined in the introduction. But how was a manager to know if the agency was indeed preserving that character? Might it be degrading? Or even improving?

In 2002, Peter Landres (then a Research Ecologist at the Aldo Leopold Wilderness Research Institute) and Steve Boutcher (then the Forest Service Wilderness Information Manager) assembled a team of wilderness managers and researchers to devise a conceptual framework for how the Forest Service might select monitoring indicators related to wilderness character. They soon recognized that it would be valuable to have input from the Department of the Interior agencies that managed wilderness—BLM, NPS, and the U.S. Fish and Wildlife Service—and wilderness specialists from those agencies were added ad hoc to the team. The result was a General Technical Report, *Monitoring Selected Conditions Related to Wilderness Character: A National Framework.*[40]

It was immediately apparent that the informal participation of the DOI agencies was insufficient. Another team, again led by

Landres, refined the Forest Service 2005 document and offered possible implementation strategies for each of the four agencies. In general, agencies shared indicators, but the measures and data sources might vary from agency to agency, or even within one agency from wilderness to wilderness. The resulting 2008 document was titled *Keeping It Wild*,[41] which became the informal shorthand jargon for the monitoring strategy. This was updated and revised in 2015 as *Keeping It Wild* 2,[42] following observations and recommendations from implementing the previous version and included a section on the "other features of value" quality that had not been adequately addressed. The Interagency Wilderness Policy Council formally adopted the *Keeping It Wild* 2 strategy for use in all wilderness areas to monitor changes in wilderness character.[43]

In the meantime, the NPS tiered off a document of their own, *Keeping It Wild in the National Park Service.*[44] It was a comprehensive guide to integrating wilderness character into the planning, management, and monitoring at each NPS area with designated wilderness and other park lands that are, by policy, managed as wilderness. Rather than use a Mesa Verde employee to spearhead implementation of this direction, the Park was supplied with a "Wilderness Fellow"—a highly motivated college student—who produced an excellent narrative (following the direction of *Director's Order #41* at Section 6.2) and a list of wilderness character monitoring measures.[45]

As of 2024, the Park has taken no steps to monitor trends in the character of the Mesa Verde Wilderness.

"A Center of Excellence"

In October 2019, Garry Oye, retired Wilderness Division Chief for the NPS; Suzanne Stutzman, retired NPS Regional Wilderness Lead and Landscape Architect; and Peter Landres came to the Park to spend a day in the Mesa Verde Wilderness with Superintendent Cliff Spencer. Afterwards, Oye wrote the Superintendent:

> The total closure seems to assume that resuming public access

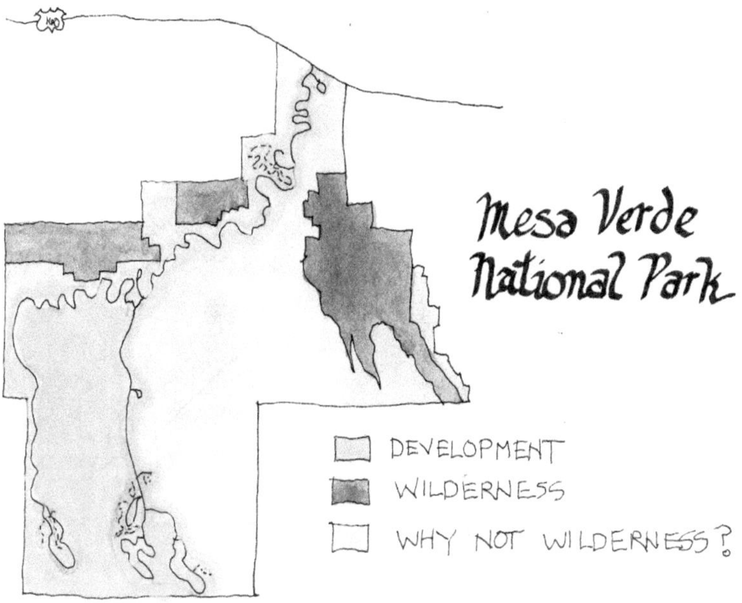

Figure 41. Stutzman's conceptual graphic of Mesa Verde National Park (originally painted in watercolor; adapted for black-and-white reproduction by the author). Rather than to be taken as a literal boundary, this illustrates the thinking behind the central question she expressed along with Oye, "Why not Wilderness?"

will cause us to lose our cultural heritage. I disagree. I think Mesa Verde offers a unique backcountry cultural landscape experience and the public should be given an opportunity to appreciate it. . . . I would suggest you continue with the assessment of all "historic" park roads and trails [and] consider resuming visitor travel (on foot) along these. . . . That in itself will be a unique experience. I would conduct this assessment with the perspective of Everything Open, then justify site-specific closures for highly sensitive sites. . . . [I suggest you] complete a new Wilderness Eligibility review for the park. . . . [Mesa Verde could] become a Center of Excellence for Backcountry Management and the Protection of Cultural Landscapes. . . . Future preservation efforts grow with

Figure 42. Wilderness suitability and eligibility adapted from Barns 2020, using the base map from the original designation process. Existing Wilderness is dark gray; suitable additions are medium gray; potentially eligible areas are light gray (the Moccasin Mesa Road separates two areas of eligibility). Compare with Figures 18–23.

> increased understanding and appreciation—not under secrecy, closure and darkness.[46]

Stutzman sketched a map, adding:

> The superintendent should set a goal of opening some public trail access in MEVE backcountry, . . . one in wilderness to meet the law, possibly another later in non-wilderness backcountry. Convene a staff task force that represents natural resources, cultural resources, interpretation, facilities, wilderness, compliance, and any other important perspectives. . . . [They] should think broadly about the visitor opportunities that are now being missed. Most visitors are concentrated at and tour the built environment at the cliff dwellings. The backcountry and wilderness offer much broader perspectives on the fluidity of people inhabiting the landscape over time through personal experience IN the landscape . . . Visitors should be offered an opportunity to forge a stronger connection with this cultural landscape.[47]

A first step meeting the 1976 Congressional mandate to "make further recommendations for wilderness designation," as cited above, was finally taken almost forty-five years later, and finished in 2020.[48] In August of 2023, Superintendent Kayci Cook Collins assembled staff leadership to begin looking at how to manage the existing Mesa Verde Wilderness. It is yet to be seen if the 2017–2020 Wilderness Eligibility inventory will lead to any formal recommendation.

CONCLUSION

The Path Forward

> Here is a thing so glorious that it threatens to be impossible. How can the secret beauty of the wilderness be opened to the public and remain unspoiled?[1]

THIS IS A CHAPTER of questions. The earlier questions in this book were mostly concerned with trying to ferret out what previous decision-makers and influencers were thinking. Their motivations. Their understanding of Wilderness purposes.

The questions in this chapter are more basic. The answers are necessary for proper stewardship of the Mesa Verde Wilderness and backcountry. Rather than offering answers here, the questions pose a framework for fundamental management decisions going forward.

"An Institutional Bias"

One of the fears archeologists working in Mesa Verde had at the time of the Park's wilderness legislation was the belief that designation would unreasonably impinge on their work. The perceived tension between archeology and wilderness preservation persists. In his regular column in *American Archaeology*, Mark Michel, President of The Archaeological Conservancy, wrote, "At Bandelier National Monument in New Mexico, regional wilderness managers totally disrupted important archaeological research. . . . [There is] an institutional bias in the NPS toward natural resources to the detriment of cultural resources." The Park Service has seemed to acknowledge this tension: "The ongoing controversy and debate about how stewardship of cultural resources fits in Wilderness seems to stem mainly from personal values and selective interpretation of parts of the Wilderness Act and National Park Service policies."[2]

However, when the Bandelier Chief Ranger was asked to comment on Michel's column, he wrote, "I do not know what he is referring to. I spoke to the current [and long-time] park archeologist, . . . and we cannot specifically identify a time when wilderness management disrupted archeology research. The management of all activity within a designated wilderness area usually requires additional attention by project planners to ensure wilderness character is considered and protected which usually requires compromise but I am not aware that this has disrupted any archeology research."[3]

When asked for clarification of his comment, Michel provided a memo from the retired Park Service Regional Archeologist Robert Powers, arguing against wilderness designation. In the memo, Powers made a variety of statements: "Archaeological research is rarely considered necessary by NPS." "The Minimum Tool may be slower and more expensive." "Archaeologists contemplating working in a wilderness area should probably begin with the assumption that they will not be allowed to use helicopters, motorized vehicles, backhoes, bobcats or power tools." "Even Park Service people may not agree on what is the acceptable minimal tool." And finally, he criticizes the idea that "Wilderness is Pristine" since so many of these landscapes were peopled many centuries ago.[4]

How can land managers come to a common understanding about the complementary roles of cultural and wilderness resources? How can they "develop a foundation for wilderness and cultural resources staffs to talk with each other and to make better decisions that respect all park values"[5]? Nowhere in the Act does the word "pristine" appear, and to believe that wilderness areas must be pristine misses the entire point of the designation.[6] There certainly must be a recognition that archeological research is likely to be necessary in a wilderness, rather than questioning whether wilderness designation is appropriate in an area where archeological research takes place. The so-called "minimum tool," derived from the uses prohibited by Section 4(c) of the Wilderness Act, may be slower and more expensive, but the prohibited uses may be allowed if they are necessary. This is apt to be less of a problem in Mesa Verde, with its network of administrative roads. It is not clear whether Powers's statements accurately reflect misunderstanding on the part of wilderness managers with whom he has had contact, or whether the misunderstanding is on his part. Either way, appropriate management of what Kirn calls "profoundly storied landscapes," described in more detail below, must be a joint venture with mutual understanding, if not identical goals. "The Wilderness Act and all of the cultural resource laws are part of the National Park Service's stewardship mandate and we must put our efforts into making them work in concert with one another, even when they appear to be in conflict."[7]

Once that hurdle is crossed, thornier questions remain.

"So Long as It Is Wild"

John Muir wrote: "God never made an ugly landscape. All that the sun shines on is beautiful, so long as it is wild." Sigurd Olson expanded this: "In nature, all things are beautiful. . . . Beauty . . . embodies the hopes and dreams of those who have gone before."[8] Sublime phenomena come in many flavors. Not just in scenic grandeur, but in the homes of Ancestral Native Americans. And not just in their homes, but in their changing landscapes—whether or not those landscapes are chosen as calendar art.

Over the last several decades, the management of the Mesa Verde's backcountry and wilderness "garden" has tilted increasingly toward the wild. This is not to say there haven't been interventions, but they have tended to be toward perpetuating natural conditions rather than a desired assemblage of species producing an attractive landscape. Instead of killing porcupines and tent caterpillars as in decades long ago, now the Park is more appropriately concerned with killing exotic plant species and removing feral horses.

What biophysical manipulations are appropriate in the Mesa Verde Wilderness? The Wilderness Act (Sec. 2(c)) recognizes a wilderness as "an area where the earth and its community of life is untrammeled by man." This unique legal mandate is a requirement only of areas designated as Wilderness by Congress, or in areas that are to be managed as Wilderness by agency policy. As noted in the introduction, the "untrammeled" quality of wilderness has long been recognized as an ideal which, in practice, must be tempered by the preferred state of a wilderness to be in its natural condition (i.e., before the intervention of modern, technological humans). To keep an area untrammeled (not manipulated) is not an absolute commandment but must be the default management option in Wilderness.[9]

Training is available[10] to assist wilderness managers in the essential question which, to paraphrase Glinda from *The Wizard of Oz*, might be asked: "Is this a good trammel or a bad trammel?" A serious difficulty arises if, out of ignorance, managers respond like Dorothy: "This isn't a trammel at all!"

In Mesa Verde, the most problematic trammeling is the response to a natural (i.e., lightning) fire start. The vast majority of these are immediately suppressed (or, at least, there is an attempt at immediate suppression). Given the archeological resources in the Park, this is an understandable reaction, though it must be realized that at some point, conditions will arise that make suppression impossible. Then the past years of suppression will actually create a greater fire danger, and burns such as those in 2000 will revisit the landscape. Fires large enough to show up in the stratigraphy of the Ancestral Puebloans' Morefield Reservoir occurred approximately every 25 years during the 350 years it was in operation.[11] Given current climate changes, large fires could occur even more frequently. Managing wildfire is a high-risk/high-reward program, and given the small size of Mesa Verde and the resources at risk, suppression rather than fire use is expected to be the ongoing policy.

"To Expose, Rather Than to Insulate"

If Mesa Verde's "garden" has become a little more wild—a little more unkempt—over the decades, its "secret" has only gotten darker.

Duane Smith condensed the writing found in a 1979 planning document by Park archeologist Don Watson: "To make these Anasazi [*sic*] and their culture come alive had always been a challenge to and a goal of the National Park Service." Even earlier, Park Service Planning Team leader Donald Purse had written, quoting Watson, "'Unfortunate, indeed, is he who views this ancient city and sees only the towering walls. Unfortunate because the stones are the least important part. Cliff Palace is really built of the hopes and desires, the joys and sorrows of an industrious people. It is not a cold empty city, for it is still warm with the emotion of its builders.'" Then Purse continued, "It <u>does</u> appear cold and empty, though, unless the visitor can be carried in spirit seven centuries into the past" (emphasis in original).[12]

In praising the system of rim drives in the Park, Jesse Nusbaum said, "Looking at the cliff dwellings never deteriorates them, so it enhanced the entire attractiveness of the area and saved more of the archaeology." There is no question that restricting visitors to views from their cars saves sites from wear and tear. For many, and perhaps even for most visitors to Mesa Verde, this is a wonderful experience. Duane Smith quoted a piece in the October 1999 *National Geographic* in which that article's author wrote: "Except for ancient stone-and-mortar cliff houses stuck to precipitous canyon walls, there is scarcely a building in site [*sic*]. What prevails throughout the national park is a feeling that one must be near the rim of the world."[13]

But that sentiment is not universally held. "The feeling of the ruins and life of the Old Ones can not be experienced from a modern vehicle or in a crowd of tourists." The tours at Mesa Verde reduce the Park to an outdoor museum; for some, "wilderness landscapes [offer] touchstones for learning about and appreciating human history [in a way that is] more profound and meaningful than any museum."[14]

"The purpose of reserving natural areas, however, is not to keep people in their cars, but to lure them out; to encourage a close look at the infinite detail and variety that the natural scene provides; to expose, rather than to insulate."[15]

Are not the cultural and natural "scenes" inseparable? Alden Hayes wrote, "The archeologist [should] view his anthropological core-interest as a core only; . . . view the past and present . . . as simply aspects of a continuum; and, further, . . . view human and other life in the area . . . as a sort of superecology. . . . [W]e must blur the divisions of many of the life and physical sciences."[16]

If this is true for the archeologist, it certainly holds true for some visitors where "there can be an immersion in the . . . scene, [and where one can] submit fully to the rhythm of the place."[17] **Does Mesa Verde owe a wilderness experience to visitors who desire such an immersion? S**igurd Olson wrote, "Many times after camp is made and chores are finished, there is a moment of quiet when reality comes and the outside world seems like a mirage."[18]

Currently in Mesa Verde there is little opportunity for immersion, that moment of quiet. Rather, the rhythm of the place is one of modern dashing from place to place in a car, on a timetable dictated by the start and duration of tours before hurrying off to the next point on the visitor's itinerary. Sax wrote, "To the extent that the Park Service has allowed urbanizing influences to dominate park management . . . a quite different lesson has emerged. . . . The managerial principle seems to be that the parks become whatever the parks are permitted to be."[19] Even without the Wetherill tram, it seems only a slight exaggeration to say the visitor experience at Mesa Verde has been permitted to become an outdoor version of a ride at Disneyland. You wait in line (or, since 2022, "online") to buy your ticket for a tour at a certain time, and on that tour you are shuttled along at a predetermined rate and given predetermined "interpretation." For an additional fee, you can even purchase an "E ticket" for a smaller group and longer appointment to a site less frequently visited—but

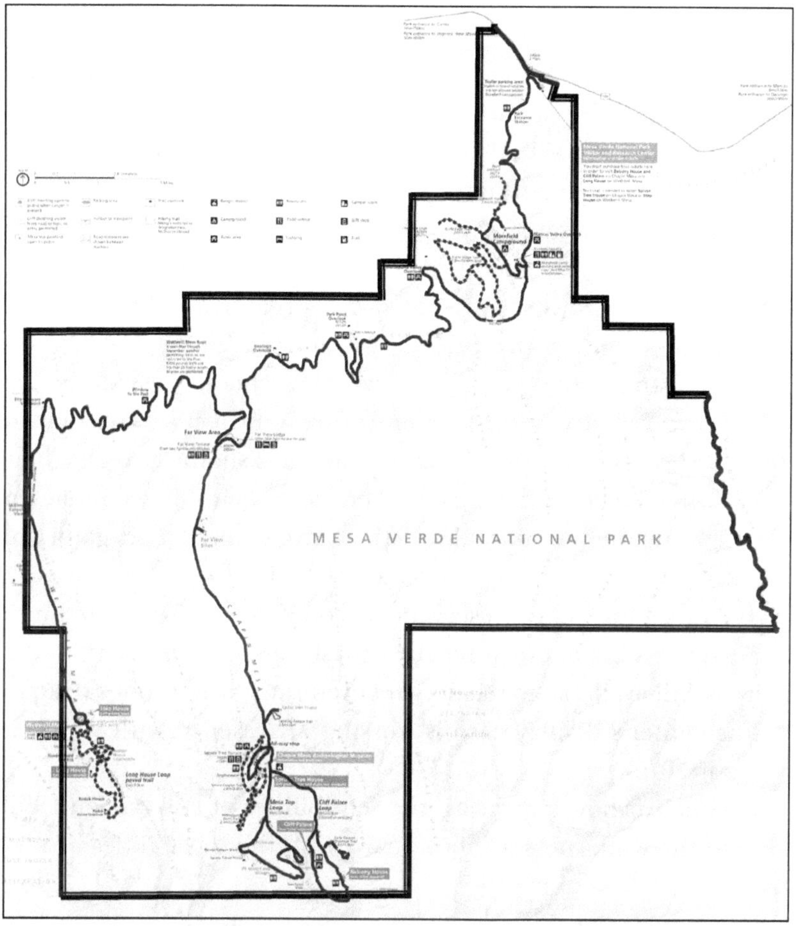

Figure 43. The Park brochure given to visitors in 2023, duplicated in black-and-white. The heavy black lines are roads open to the public. Trails open to the public are dotted lines. Compare with Figures 3, 8, 9, 13, and 17.

just as rehabilitated and cleaned as tours to the "major" sites. For some, this is not "immersion."

"Pick Me Up and Take Me Home and Love Me"

If an opportunity for "immersion" is to be provided, what cost to the resource is acceptable? Craig Childs has quoted the private collector and treasure-hider Forrest Fenn as saying that cultural remnants speak to him: "If you don't pick me up and take me home and love me, Joe Smith is going to find me tomorrow and sell me for twenty-five bucks.'"[20] While it is unlikely that a wilderness visitor in Mesa Verde will find anything of monetary value, the underlying sentiment remains the same. And while the known sites in the Mesa Verde Wilderness have been heavily collected by researchers, there are still remnant potsherds in somewhat greater numbers than in sites easily accessible to the public.

On the other hand, Childs quoted the archeologist Will Tsosie: "'In order to be alive, all things must die,'" and Childs went on to explain, "He was stating his belief that objects should live out their lives and then be gone."[21] Objects taken from their natural home do not die, but neither are they alive—they have entered a purgatory of things.

Of course, the item "preserved" on someone's coffee table is not only dead but is lost to everyone; the item sitting in a box in a museum archive is still available to science. Yet even the glorious pot sitting in a visitor center's display case is missing an essence with which it vibrates in situ.

It is unclear how many with the sensibilities of Forrest Fenn will hike into the wilderness. Or how many with the sensibilities of Will Tsosie.

For whom is the Mesa Verde Wilderness protected? Is it possible for a Forrest Fenn to be transformed into a Will Tsosie? This has long been a subject of interest in the Mesa Verde frontcountry. Over forty years ago, at a meeting in 1987 to discuss threats to the archeological resources, topics included the negative impacts of visitation on the park's archeological sites and what countermeasures might be taken to ameliorate them. As noted above in chapter 9, the lack of potsherds on trails open to the public as opposed to those closed to the public is obvious evidence of the tendency for some visitors to remove artifacts from the park, a feature certainly not unique to Mesa Verde.[22] It has long been believed at the Park that appropriate countermeasures are a combination of law enforcement and public education.[23] Yet even with the most successful educational campaigns and cutting-edge interpretation, including required meetings between NPS staff and wilderness visitors, eventually some items will be removed to coffee tables. There are at least five times the visitors to the Park today as the last time backcountry use was encouraged.[24] Still, the question remains: should the Mesa Verde Wilderness be protected from the Fenns or experienced by the Tsosies?

"Each Structure Has a Life and Has an End of Life"

This debate is echoed in the larger context of the buildings themselves. There is a palpable sterility in the structures open to public tours such as Cliff Palace, Long House, Balcony House, etc. There is an essence present in wild, "untrammeled" dwellings that is absent in the Mesa Verde structures destined for the limbo generated by the Park Service. Perhaps sites such as Cliff Palace might be rationalized as captured and tamed to provide wonder and "provoke" visitors, engendering an interest to protect all other cliff dwellings so they may live out their natural lives, and honor the culture that produced them.[25]

Naturally, sites open to constant public visitation need some degree of stabilization, but what of the scores of sites in the Park that are not now—nor are likely ever to be—visited by the public? In her fascinating mix of history and memoir, the former lead of the Mesa Verde stabilization crew, Kathleen Fiero, stated that these sites had to be physically maintained to make them "stable and safe for the resource." "The goal is to make the wall or feature stable with minimal impact to the scientific information contained in the site." She even takes issue with the thought of not examining the human remains of the Ancestral Puebloans found in the Park: "Although I sympathize with the Native American consultants . . . I sincerely believe that ignoring evidence and removing it from study, is not the appropriate response."[26]

On the other hand, there is the desire of many of the indigenous peoples associated with Mesa Verde to have the Park stop "repairing" their ancestors' dwellings. As explained by Zuni cultural specialist Dan Simplicio, "Each structure has a life and has an end of life, just like human bodies. There are consequences when we interrupt the natural process of returning to the Mother's flesh. This is a universal Pueblo belief." It is echoed by Rina Swentzell of Santa Clara Pueblo: "The place never forgets us. Even more, the structures that we build also have breath. They are alive and participate in their own cycles of life and death."[27]

The Fieros see it as heresy not to put scientific value first. The Simplicios and Swentzells see a different heresy, one fundamental to their worldview. As the Talmud says in Berakhot 55b:21, "A person is shown in his dream only the thoughts of his heart when he is awake." Or, as Lloyd Burton wrote in *Worship and Wilderness,* "We see things not as *they* are, but as *we* are."[28]

Is there a middle way? How much is enough to be protected—if "protected" means collected or stabilized by a professional? Is it reasonable to believe a thorough investigation of designated access routes would go a long way to further mitigate possible negative consequences of public access? Hayes quoted A. L. Kroeber's 1916 paper for the American Museum of Natural History: "Five thousand sherds can tell us more than one hundred whole vessels, and the bare knowledge of the average size of a room in a dozen contiguous ruins may be more indicative than the most laborious survey of two or three extensive sites." In the past, the Park has tried to make collection complete. For example, this memo from the Park Archeologist to the Superintendent: "All artifacts acquired during the year were cleaned, repaired, catalogued and placed in storage or used in exhibits." However, the copy of the memo in the Mesa Verde Research Center has a handwritten comment of unknown authorship: "Taint So."[29]

The answer to the question of how much should be collected or stabilized certainly can't be "everything." Known backcountry sites still have many remnants that were left behind in their "live" context by researchers. But the key word in the previous sentence may be "known." Archeologist Arthur Rohn estimated that perhaps only

80 percent of the sites on Chapin Mesa had been found, intensively as that area has been searched. Even an extensive survey, such as conducted in the Mesa Verde Wilderness during the 1970s, might be insufficient to discover many types of sites. While a survey is certainly adequate for PIII cliff dwellings, of which there are none in the Wilderness, Basketmaker III pithouse sites may escape detection: "The surface indications of such a structure may be nonexistent or so indistinct as to be unrecognizable from the natural ground surface." This problem extends even to Pueblo I dwellings. In the Chapin Mesa surveys "a number of slabhouse sites were too obscure to command attention during the survey."[30] It is entirely reasonable to expect that the Wilderness, with so many documented PII sites in and nearby, has many undetected sites of earlier periods. This presents a mixed problem in opening these areas to the public. On the one hand, the scientific potential of the area is possibly great, and may be compromised by public access. On the other hand, the sites are so obscure that they are likely to remain undetected even by a trained archeologist passing through the landscape.

If Mesa Verde is going to manage for a wilderness experience, how much time and money should be devoted to these "fewer opportunities for access" when the budget is constrained? "A compromise is called for: a willingness to trade quantity for quality of experience. . . . We need a willingness to value a certain kind of experience highly enough that we are prepared to have fewer opportunities for access in exchange for a different sort of experience when we do get access."[31]

Three Options

Most of the Mesa Verde staff—and perhaps the readers of this history—already have their own answers to many of the questions raised above. But there should be a transparent and publicly disclosed consensus on these answers for the Park as Mesa Verde charts the future for its *Secret Garden*. There are three options.

OPTION 1: KEEP THE *Garden* A *Secret*—THE STATUS QUO

This would be the easiest path for the NPS to follow. After all, this is how the Mesa Verde Wilderness has been managed since 1976. Who is going to object if the status quo continues? So far, the Park hasn't been taken to court over this—the NGOs (Non-Governmental Organizations) that would care have more pressing problems, as can be seen in every issue of *Wilderness Watcher.* The Park could send visitors elsewhere for a wilderness experience in an archeologically rich location: across Montezuma County to Canyons of the Ancients National Monument, with its Wilderness Study Areas, and ample opportunities for solitude; or, if limiting recommendations to areas managed by the Park Service, visitors could be sent to Chaco Culture National Historical Park where there is an opportunity to day-hike at will to a variety of cultural sites; or a little farther to Bandelier National Monument, with its opportunity not only to hike but camp overnight in the designated Wilderness.

There are at least two problems with this option. The first is that Park staff should have to come to some sort of rationalization why the Wilderness in the Park is closed, while such areas in other wildernesses are open. Of the 806 wilderness areas designated by Congress, only ten are closed to the public.[32] The other nine are inaccessible or tiny islands managed by the U.S. Fish & Wildlife Service, the largest of which is a Pacific archipelago totaling less than 600 acres. Together those nine areas are approximately equal in size to Mesa Verde Wilderness Unit B—the smallest of the Mesa Verde units. The Park Service would be hard pressed to offer a coherent rationale for sending visitors to the areas listed in the previous paragraph but denying access in Mesa Verde. Bandelier is just as important to some modern Puebloan people; Chaco has archeological resources every bit as impressive as Mesa Verde's; and Canyons of the Ancients was likely home to far more people, living in much greater densities, than the Park.[33]

The more important problem, however, is that keeping the Mesa Verde Wilderness closed to the public does not conform to the law.

The Wilderness Act says, in part, "A wilderness . . . has outstanding opportunities for solitude or a primitive and unconfined type of recreation."[34] It does not say "may have outstanding opportunities . . . ," which would imply the characteristic is optional. It does not say "would have outstanding opportunities if people were allowed in the Wilderness." The area does not have to provide both solitude and primitive, unconfined recreation. But it must provide at least one of these. Nor does the area have to provide one of these opportunities everywhere within the wilderness. The NPS often "confines" wilderness recreation to specific areas or trails, and one could certainly expect that to be the case in a Wilderness with the resources of Mesa Verde. But, by law, there must be some opportunity for recreational use. Mesa Verde National Park currently does not allow such use.

As noted in chapter 8, arguments that the Park is not required to allow public use of the Wilderness have stemmed from a misapplication of the Wilderness Act Section 4(a)(3): "The designation of any . . . unit of the national park system as a wilderness pursuant to this Act shall in no manner lower the standards evolved for use of such . . . unit." This might seem to imply that allowing visitors into the Mesa Verde Wilderness would somehow "lower the standards" of management that were made by policy, and that the Wilderness Act does not supersede that.

First of all, as noted earlier, the idea that allowing use somehow lowers management standards is mistaken. Moreover, Section 4(a)(3) continues to say that the referenced standards are "in accordance with" a series of laws, which includes the NPS Organic Act of 1916, the law that designated the park unit in question, and the Antiquities Act. Specific regulations were promulgated in response to the general direction to protect the Mesa Verde cultural resources found in the legislation creating the Park: "Such regulations shall provide specifically for the preservation from injury or spoliation of the ruins and other works and relics of prehistoric and primitive man."[35] However, no law closes the Mesa Verde Wilderness to the public; the Wilderness Act says there shall be public use of the Wilderness, and neither policy nor regulation can override a law. What

Section 4(a)(3) of the Wilderness Act actually does is protect the NPS from having to allow the "Special Provisions" listed in the subsequent Section 4(d) which are otherwise prohibited by law in particular units of the National Park System.[36]

OPTION 2: MAKE THE *Garden's Secret* IRRELEVANT—UNDESIGNATE THE WILDERNESS

This might be the preferred choice of some, including some on the Mesa Verde staff. As demonstrated in the previous chapters, there was no intention of managing the Mesa Verde Wilderness according to the Wilderness Act at the time of its designation, nor since.

The problem with this option is that undesignating an entire wilderness has never been done. Parts of wilderness areas have been undesignated but, with one exception, always in the context of elsewhere adding more acreage to the wilderness. Revoking the designation of a wilderness in its entirety would be a precedent that, while embraced by some in Congress, would be bitterly opposed by others. There simply is neither sufficient political nor societal will to start unravelling the National Wilderness Preservation System.[37]

OPTION 3: OPEN THE *Garden* AND SHARE THE *Secret*—ALLOW SOME RECREATIONAL USE

Is it possible for the Park to balance the general laws protecting cultural resources with the specific law mandating some sort of wilderness recreation? Laura Kirn, one of the leading NPS experts on the juncture of wilderness and cultural resources, phrased the question as how to "allow appropriate use in an area with highly sensitive cultural resources. Certainly some areas are not appropriate for the public, which should be limited to trails or other designated routes. In those cases it is reasonable to impinge upon 'unconfined' recreation because of that sensitivity. But a complete closure is not appropriate and it is probably not legally supported."[38]

Wilderness areas are not designated primarily for recreational use, but such use is one purpose of the Act. More than simply a matter of conforming to the law, direct experience in wilderness areas is a personal benefit to the individual and, therefore, to societal appreciation of both the wild land and the people that came before—because they are inseparable.

Kirn has argued, "Wild places and the cultural heritage resources within them are priceless and irreplaceable. . . . We can realistically and sustainably manage both, and indeed that it is crucial for the health of both that we do so. Understanding the human history of wild places is a vital part of addressing their complexity." The converse is also true: an appreciation for the wilderness is a vital part for understanding our human history. Wilderness Historian Doug Scott has cited both Aldo Leopold and Howard Zahniser from more than seventy years past—words that remain relevant and vibrant. Leopold: "Wilderness is the raw material out of which we have hammered the artifact called civilization"; Zahniser: "Out of the wilderness, we realize, has come the substance of our culture."[39] These sentiments hold true today across a wide range of civilizations and cultures—including ones that neither Leopold nor Zahniser had in mind when they crafted those sentences.

Kirn wrote extensively and persuasively on wilderness as a place of "many, varied, and important tangible and intangible heritage resources. These resources are visible aspects of the landscapes' intertwined and evolving natural and human histories and are worthy of some sort of deliberate management." Wilderness, through its cultural landscape, "harbors resources that reflect the stories and heritage of ordinary people," and "agencies must acknowledge the plain fact that many tangible heritage resources will cease to exist over time. Given this, the stories will, in many cases, be the only aspect of the heritage resources that remain." For some visitors, nowhere would this feeling be more profound than standing on the East Rim looking down Waters Canyon. Leslie Marmon Silko explained, "The relationship between the human being and his or her surroundings [cannot be correctly circumscribed in a 'viewshed']. This assumes the viewer is somehow outside or separate from the territory she or he surveys. Viewers are as much a part of the landscape as the boulders they stand on." Standing in such a place means "to be connected in both place and time to those who have gone before [and] between us and those who are yet to come." To paraphrase Edith Warner (known as "the woman at Otowi Crossing"), there are places in the Mesa Verde Wilderness and backcountry where one can experience a moment when life and the world seem to be standing still, with only time and the wind flowing over the mesa.[40]

How can the Park staff manage public use in the Mesa Verde Wilderness while protecting the cultural resources present? "How can we realistically and sustainably manage our tangible cultural heritage present in wilderness areas, recognizing the fundamentally irreplaceable nature of both wild places and heritage resources?"[41]

These are not simple questions and answering them on the ground would involve far more work than the other two options. In 2018, a dichotomous key was developed as a possible tool for determining appropriate recreational use in the Mesa Verde Wilderness.[42] The key was designed for the decision-maker to progress through a series of questions on public access through a variety of regulatory mechanisms and visitor restrictions. But deciding to allow visitor use would be only a beginning.

"The Reactionary Tribal Consultation Paradigm"

There is an important corollary to any of these three options. Historically, the peoples of the twenty-six tribes culturally affiliated with Mesa Verde had no voice in stewardship. This was not unique to Mesa Verde but was the case throughout the four federal land management agencies. "The Indians were generally relegated to the sidelines, while non-Indians determined the fate of the ancient ancestral places. The choices to be made—continued rampant extraction or some form of protection and preservation for the archeological sites—remained fundamentally a struggle between competing European-American factions." Consultation has become increasingly important over recent decades, but the term often means different things to different participants. "Some tribal governments view consultation as a seat at the decision-making table. The National Park Service views consultation as gathering information that will influence policy and decision-making." Mesa Verde has bridged this divide in the planned redesign of the Chapin Mesa Museum—now less about collected artifacts and more centered on indigenous lifeways—and a new introductory film, *Footprints of Our Ancestors*, from a Puebloan perspective. But there is a difference between creating interpretive materials and stewardship of the land. The Park evidenced this consultation over the post-fire decision to forego repairing Battleship Rock (covered in chapter 9). Will this level of cooperation be honored elsewhere in the backcountry?[43]

To what extent are culturally affiliated indigenous people to be more than simply "consulted" on questions of stewardship? This question formed the backbone of the recent work by Monte Mills and Martin Nie, which advocated for shifting "the reactionary tribal consultation paradigm to a more pro-active and sovereignty-affirming model in which Indian tribes envision their own approach and plans for managing their rights and interests on federal lands." A mechanism for answering this responsibility may be addressed through following the joint Secretarial Order 3403, which seeks to "Ensure that all decisions by the Departments [of Agriculture and Interior] relating to Federal stewardship of Federal lands, waters, and wildlife . . . include consideration of how to safeguard the interests of any [affected] Indian Tribes, [and to do so by making] agreements with Indian Tribes to collaborate in the co-stewardship of Federal lands." This direction, somewhat vague—as Secretarial Orders so often are by design—is made more explicit by Mills and Nie: "Efforts should aim to incorporate tribal consultation as an objective on an equal basis with existing federal land management priorities in order to integrate the process of consultation with the balancing of a multiple-use, wilderness, refuge, or other management framework." In addition, they argue that such consultation should be "a fundamental objective of federal public land management agencies that promotes long-term, ongoing, and co-equal federal-tribal relations."[44]

This objective has two inherent difficulties. The first is the precise mechanism of tribal consultation. Mesa Verde has twenty-six affiliated tribes,[45] encompassing many different histories, values, and worldviews. It would be naïve to suggest that they would automatically agree on all stewardship questions. This should *not* be taken as an argument against meaningful consultation, merely an acknowledgement that it will not be easy.

The second difficulty involves the inherent difference in the stewardship of wilderness as opposed to other federal land management. In wilderness stewardship, the result—defined by law—is more important than the process used to arrive at it. The court in the Eastern District of California put it succinctly: "The Wilderness Act is as close to an outcome-oriented piece of environmental legislation as exists. Unlike NEPA, or the Clean Air or Clean Water Acts, the Wilderness Act emphasizes outcome (wilderness preservation) over procedure. As such, it is as close to a 'purist manifesto' as may be found in the area of environmental law."[46]

This, too, does not necessarily mean consultation is of lesser value in wilderness management. But the reality of outcome-oriented stewardship in conformance with the Wilderness Act cannot be ignored. Recently, NPS Director Charles F. "Chuck" Sams III—the first Tribal citizen to be named Director—was interviewed by *The Washington Post.* He made an astonishing statement: "Wilderness as a concept really is a European concept, and it was used in a way—especially in children's fairy tales, if you look at the children's fairy tales that we have, to scare people from it. . . . Wilderness, by itself, still needs to be a managed landscape. We have to be able to protect the flora and fauna in it as Native people have done for thousands of years."[47]

There was certainly a "scary wilderness" dominating many European fairy tales. But that view of wild places started changing among the descendants of those Europeans on this continent in the mid-1800s. What has emerged is an American concept, embodied by The Wilderness Act of 1964, which has in common with the old European concept little more than root etymology. As Alaskan native Polly Napiryuk Andrews wrote in 2021, "It is true that my Cup'ik ancestors had no word for Wilderness. Nor did we have words for airplanes, computers, or the internet; or for climate change, endangered species, or biodiversity. But we've adopted these words and concepts for the modern, altered, and changing world we now live in." As defined in the introduction, congressionally designated wilderness is more than just native flora and fauna, and the manipulation of these areas by Native people for their physical sustenance is likely to be at odds with the stated purpose of wilderness designation. Director Sams is presumably aware of this, as the National Park Service manages almost 40 percent of the acreage in the National Wilderness Preservation System. It was, however, an on-the-spot question, and perhaps a more-considered answer might be given on reflection.[48]

Just such a thoughtful opinion was expressed by David Treuer's 2021 article in *The Atlantic*, "Return the National Parks to the Tribes."[49] In it, he cataloged the barest outline of the atrocities—physical, spiritual, and governmental—perpetrated by Americans of European ancestry on Native Americans. For those unaware of the history of White/Native relations in North America, his work is an appropriately appalling primer. He recommended that reparations should include giving the land of the National Parks back to the tribes, with management authority "turned over to a consortium of federally recognized tribes." As there are no details, perhaps his proposal was aspirational. If implemented, at some point decisions would have to be made: which of the over 500 tribes would have members in the management consortium; or, presumably, if "local" tribes would have a greater say in stewardship, how would local interests be determined, since many tribal "boundaries" greatly shifted over time through European aggression, inter-tribal conflict, and ecological stressors. Mesa Verde, as noted above, has twenty-six associated tribes. Such hypothetical problems would be difficult to satisfactorily resolve—but if nothing else, they serve as a goad to spur serious consideration of how the parks should be better managed, and the role of the First Nations in their stewardship.

This is not to say a tribe—or a consortium of tribes—couldn't manage a wilderness. Of course they could, and did, and some currently do in ways remarkably similar to the units of the National Wilderness Preservation System.[50] However, some may infer Treuer was suggesting National Park Wilderness areas (and, by extension, Wildernesses managed by other agencies) should be managed as Native peoples did when they lived there. As noted in the introduction, that would conflict with the basic purpose of legally defined Wilderness, which is not the way Native Americans managed these areas 700—or even 250—years ago. In terms of reparations, it may be more appropriate, rather than giving back the National Park Wilderness, to return selected non-Wilderness BLM and Forest Service lands. These "multiple use" lands could henceforth be managed for tribal benefits similarly to the Native Corporations in Alaska.[51]

"The Gardener Sees Only the Gardener's Garden"

So where does this leave the stewardship of the Mesa Verde Wilderness and backcountry? By NPS policy, the wilderness character of areas of parks eligible for preservation as wilderness is to be protected as rigorously as in areas designated as Wilderness by Congress.[52] And by law applicable throughout the National Wilderness Preservation System, stewardship of the Mesa Verde Wilderness must balance the essence of untrammeled land with an ecosystem that is natural. It should remain largely undeveloped, while protecting the area's cultural values—not just the physical remains, but the spiritual symbolism of the mesa. And it must offer opportunities for visitors to experience this place on their own, outside the confines of ranger-led tours in the frontcountry.

As Thoreau wrote shortly before his death, "The gardener sees only the gardener's garden."[53] In this Park, so focused on the frontcountry experience, managing the backcountry and wilderness as something other than the customary afterthought would be a significant shift. Yet just such a shift is required—a shift in personnel

Figure 44. Waters Canyon from the East Rim, Mesa Verde Wilderness Unit C. "Anybody can have that connection if they're open to that connection," Faith Gemmill.

and budget that to some may seem unreasonable given the reality that the vast majority of visitors to the Park will never avail themselves of a wilderness opportunity.

But it's not just the law. It's a good idea—for America's best idea.

Notes

Notes on Primary Sources

Most of the citations in this book come from the Mesa Verde National Park Historic Records and Central Files in the park's Research Center. They are referenced by a location in brackets, organized by the Record Group (RG), then a dash followed by the Series number, then a dash followed by the File Unit number, and then (where applicable) a period and the folder number (for example: RG01–001–001.1).

Some of the more recent unpublished documents in the references are stored in the employee office known as Barracks #4. They are referenced by a location in brackets, starting with the notation B4 and then organized by cabinet and drawer, all separated by dashes (for example: B4-1-1).

Dates for unpublished primary sources are as specific as possible, appearing in the format yyyy-mm-dd.

For ease in reading the notes, a series of abbreviations for frequently cited primary source persons and references are given. (See also "Abbreviations and Terminology.")

Carlson. O. W. Carlson in his official capacity as Mesa Verde Superintendent.

Guillet. Meredith M. Guillet in his official capacity as Mesa Verde Superintendent.

Heyder. Robert C. Heyder in his official capacity as Mesa Verde Superintendent.

MEVE. Variously documents produced by Mesa Verde National Park, or otherwise used as an abbreviation for Mesa Verde National Park.

MEVE-PB. The standard official MEVE Park Brochure given to visiting members of the public, regardless of its actual title, format, extent of content, or where or by whom it was published. Where a park "newspaper" is also distributed, that is referenced in the text, but considered part of the Brochure for bibliographic purposes.

MEVE-SAR. Mesa Verde Superintendent's Annual Report. The official yearly accounting of accomplishments; authorship is designated to MEVE regardless of which staff members wrote any given part of the report or at what level in the NPS (Park, Region, or National) these reports were submitted.

MEVE-SM. Mesa Verde Staff Meeting. The Staff Meeting (or Squad Meeting) of (usually) weekly meetings by the MEVE staff program leads. [RG01–002–029 & 032] (nomenclature explained above).

MEVE-SMR. Mesa Verde Superintendent's Monthly Report. The official monthly accounting of accomplishments, regardless of variations in title, generally unpublished but used for reporting purposes. [RG01–002–023].

Nusbaum. Jesse L. Nusbaum; his long association with MEVE extended beyond his official capacity as Mesa Verde Superintendent (1921–1931; 1936–1937; 1942–1946 (Acting)) and can be inferred by the date and/or subject of his communication.

Nusbaum interview. Nusbaum, transcript of interview by Herbert Evison, December 9, 1962. [RG19–001–030].

Smith, *Mesas.* Jack E. Smith, *Mesas, Cliffs, and Canyons: The University of Colorado Survey of Mesa Verde National Park 1971–1977,* Paper No. 3 (Mesa Verde National Park: Mesa Verde Museum Association, 1987).

Switzer. Ronald R. Switzer in his official capacity as Mesa Verde Superintendent.

Thomas. Chester A. Thomas in his official capacity as Mesa Verde Superintendent.

W Act. Public Law 88–577, The Wilderness Act of 1964.
WASO. The NPS headquarters office in Washington, DC.

Notes on Secondary Sources

Important secondary sources cited in multiple chapters are abbreviated in the notes as shown below. Other secondary sources are not abbreviated.

Allin. Craig W. Allin, *The Politics of Wilderness Preservation* (Westport, CT: Greenwood Press, 1982).

Carr, *M66.* Ethan Carr, *Mission 66: Modernism and the National Park Dilemma* (Amherst: University of Massachusetts Press, 2007).

Foresta. Ronald A. Foresta, *America's National Parks and Their Keepers* (Washington, DC: Resources for the Future, 1984).

Ise. John Ise, *Our National Park Policy: A Critical History* (Baltimore: Johns Hopkins University Press, 1961).

Nash. Roderick Nash, *Wilderness and the American Mind,* 3rd ed. (New Haven: Yale University Press, 1982).

Runte. Alfred Runte, *National Parks: The American Experience,* 2nd ed. (Lincoln: University of Nebraska Press, 1987).

Sellars, *Nature.* Richard W. Sellars, *Preserving Nature in the National Parks: A History* (New Haven: Yale University Press, 1997).

Smith, *Shadows.* Duane A. Smith, *Mesa Verde National Park: Shadows of the Centuries,* revised (Boulder: University of Colorado Press, 2002).

Sutter. Paul S. Sutter, *Driven Wild: How the Fight Against Automobiles Launched the Modern Wilderness Movement* (Seattle: University of Washington Press, 2002).

Torres-Reyes. Ricardo Torres-Reyes, *Mesa Verde National Park: An Administrative History 1906–1970* (Washington: USDI National Park Service, 1970), chapter: page, http://npshistory.com/publications/meve/adhi/index.htm (last accessed 2024-07-05).

Foreword

1. Mrs. Mae Belle Anderson, commenting on the diaries written during the Wrangel Island Expedition of 1921. In Jennifer Niven, *Ada Blackjack* (New York: Hyperion, 2002), 2.

2. Robert H. Keller and Michael F. Turek, *American Indians & National Parks* (Tucson: University of Arizona Press, 1998), chap. 3; Duane A. Smith, *Mesa Verde National Park: Shadows of the Centuries,* revised (Boulder: University of Colorado Press, 2002); Rose Houk and Faith Marcovecchio, eds., *Mesa Verde National Park: The First 100 Years* (Golden, CO: Mesa Verde Museum Association & Fulcrum Publishing, 2006).

3. Adam M. Sowards, *An Open Pit Visible From the Moon: The Wilderness Act and the Fight to Protect Miners Ridge and the Public Interest* (Norman: University of Oklahoma Press, 2020).

Introduction

1. Houk and Marcovecchio, *Mesa Verde National Park,* 22.

However, as the authors state, there have been many National Monuments created to preserve "pre-historic" archeology. The distinction between a National Park and Monument is somewhat arbitrary. For extreme examples, see the astonishing "upgrades" to National Park status of the Gateway Arch (Pub. L. No. 115-128) and Indiana Dunes National Lakeshore (Pub. L. No. 116-6, Div. E, Sec. 115). Seeking "Park" status to increase tourism is not a new phenomenon, having been identified by Robert Sterling Yard in the 1920s (Sutter, 130).

2. Ise, 165.

3. Robert Sterling Yard and Isabelle F. Story, *The National Parks Portfolio* (Washington, DC: U.S. Government Printing Office, 1931), 142.

4. Robert H. Lister and Florence C. Lister, *Mesa Verde National Park: Preserving the Past* (Mancos, CO: ARA Mesa Verde Company, 1987).

5. Smith, *Shadows,* 10.

Smith wrote, "The park's mission . . . now included 'protection of natural landscape, tribal and wilderness resources and values.'" Presumably this phrase came from the 1979 General Management Plan referenced in his next sentence, but it occurs in the chapter added for the revised edition, and that chapter is without the citations found in the rest of the book. His chapter on the 1970s (181–93) omits the passage of the Mesa Verde Wilderness bill, and the word "wilderness" does not appear in the index. He does, however, make a brief reference to Superintendent Jesse Nusbaum's foresight in recognizing the importance of the wilderness values of Mesa Verde in 1938. Nusbaum's writing on the subject is discussed in chapter 4.

6. George L. San Miguel, "Epilogue: Management Considerations for

Conserving Old-Growth Piñon-Juniper Woodlands," in *Ancient Piñon-Juniper Woodlands: A Natural History of Mesa Verde Country*, ed. M. Lisa Floyd (Boulder: University Press of Colorado, 2003), 361–74.

7. Houk and Marcovecchio, 82–83. To the editors' credit, this brief paragraph includes the recognition that "park administrators opposed any wilderness in the park, fearing it could interfere with future development plans or archaeological excavations."

8. James M Copeland, 2018-08-07 interview with author; Mark Harvey, 2018-02-22 e-mail correspondence with author.

Copeland, retired lead archeologist in the Farmington, New Mexico BLM office, is a leading expert on the archeology of Dinétah (the Navajo homeland). Harvey recently retired as Professor and Head of Department of History, Philosophy, and Religious Studies at North Dakota State University; among other writings, he is known for his biography of the original author of the Wilderness Act, *Wilderness Forever: Howard Zahniser and the path to the Wilderness Act* (Seattle: University of Washington Press, 2005).

9. For bibliographic information, see frequently cited "Secondary Sources."

10. NPS National Wilderness Steering Committee, "Guidance Paper No. 4: Embracing the Distinction between Wilderness and Backcountry in the National Park System" (May 6, 2005) http://npshistory.com/publications/wilderness/white-papers/4.pdf (last accessed 2024-07-05).

11. WAct, Sec. 4(b).

12. Peter Landres, Chris Barns, Steve Boutcher, Tim Devine, Peter Dratch, Adrienne Lindholm, Linda Merigliano, Nancy Roeper, and Emily Simpson, *Keeping It Wild 2: An updated interagency strategy to monitor trends in wilderness character across the National Wilderness Preservation System*, General Technical Report RMRS-GTR-340, USDA Forest Service (Fort Collins: Rocky Mountain Research Station, 2015), 7.

13. For "a point of view," see Sutter, 168. For "The real significance," see Sigurd Olson, "The Spiritual Aspects of Wilderness," 1961, in *The Meaning of Wilderness: Essential Articles and Speeches*, ed. David Backes (Minneapolis: University of Minnesota Press, 2001), 118. For "We cannot afford," see Leo McAvoy, "Majesty and Self-Reliance," in *Wilderness in America: personal perspectives*, ed. Daniel L. Dustin (San Diego: San Diego State University Institute for Leisure Behavior, 1988), 82. For "If there was no," see *American Values: American Wilderness*, High Plains Films, directed by Christopher Barns, Drury Gunn Carr, and Doug Hawes-Davis, featuring Christopher Reeve, aired 2004 and 2005 on PBS, https://www.youtube.com/watch?v=H7IS9ZCRZHo.

14. WAct, Sec. 2(c).

15. Landres et al., *Keeping It Wild 2*, 77. See also NPS, *Keeping It Wild in the National Park Service: A user guide to integrating wilderness character into park planning, management, and monitoring*, WASO 909/121797, (January 2014), iii.

16. Landres et al., *Keeping It Wild 2*, 10–12. The defining quotations of the

five qualities of wilderness character discussed in subsequent paragraphs come from this publication, which goes into greater detail on each of the qualities, how they may be monitored, and how they interact. It is essential reading for wilderness managers.

17. The Wilderness Act's definition in Section 2(c) includes, "3) has at least five thousand acres of land *or is of sufficient size as to make practicable its preservation and use in an unimpaired condition*" (emphasis added).

As of early 2024, 90 of the 806 wilderness areas designated by Congress are under 5,000 acres. See website "Wilderness Connect" (last accessed 2024-07-05): https://wilderness.net/practitioners/wilderness-areas/summary-reports/fact-sheet.php, and https://wilderness.net/practitioners/wilderness-areas/search.php where "Acreage" chosen is "Total acres <=" and "Acres" input is "4999."

18. Robert C. Lucas, "Wilderness: A management framework," *Journal of Soil and Water Conservation* 28, no. 4 (1973): 151.

19. Howard Zahniser, "Guardians Not Gardeners," *Living Wilderness* 83 (1963): 2.

20. Henry Beston, *The Outermost House* (1928) (New York: Viking Press, 1962), 25.

Beston's quote in context: "We need another and a wiser and perhaps more mystical concept of animals. Remote from universal nature, and living by complicated artifice, man in civilization surveys the creature through the glass of his knowledge and sees thereby a feather magnified and the whole image in distortion. We patronize them for their incompleteness, for their tragic fate of having taken form so far below ourselves. And therein we err, and greatly err. For the animal shall not be measured by man. In a world older and more complete than ours they move finished and complete, gifted with extensions of the senses we have lost or never attained, living by voices we shall never hear. They are not brethren, they are not underlings; they are other nations, caught with ourselves in the net of life and time, fellow prisoners of the splendor and travail of the earth."

21. A. S. Leopold (Chairman), S. A. Cain, C. M. Cottam, I. N. Gabrielson, T. L. Kimball, *Wildlife Management in the National Parks, 1963*. Reprint from Administrative Policies for Natural Areas of the National Park System, U.S. Department of the Interior National Park Service (Washington, D.C., U.S. Government Printing Office, 1969), 3. (http://npshistory.com/publications/leopold_report.pdf).

22. WAct, Sec. 4(c).

23. For "to make changes," see Aldo Leopold, "A Biotic View of the Land" (1939), in *The River of the Mother of God and Other Essays by Aldo Leopold*, eds. Susan L, Flader and J. Baird Callicott (Madison: University of Wisconsin Press, 1991), 269. For "areas of the earth," see Howard Zahniser, "The Need for Wilderness Areas," *Living Wilderness* 59 (1956): 38.

24. WAct, Sec. 4(c). For a more detailed legal interpretation of this critical phrase, see Martin Nie, Christopher Barns, Jonathan Haber, Julie Jolie, Kenneth Pitt, and Sandi Zellmer, "Fish and Wildlife Management on Federal Lands: debunking state supremacy," *Environmental Law* 47, no. 4 (2017): 885–886.

25. NPS, "NPS 6—Wilderness Preservation and Management," (2006): Sec. 6.3.1.

Chapter One

1. In addition, shortly before the designation of Mesa Verde, three "inferior" parks (Ise, 136) were designated: Wind Cave, Sully's Hill, and Platt. Wind Cave, originally one-fifth the size of Mesa Verde, was substantially increased in 1947. Platt was "demoted" in 1976 and incorporated into Chickasaw National Recreation Area. Sully's Hill is no longer in the National Park System. The tiny Mackinac Island National Park, designated in 1875, was transferred to the State of Michigan for a state park in 1895 (Ise, 49). For the decades-long battle to create Kings Canyon National Park, see Ise, 396–404.

2. Pub. L. No. 59-209. For proclamation targets, see §2; for permits, see §3.

The "smallest area" concept has long been controversial, from Theodore Roosevelt's 1908 proclamation (over intense regional opposition) of more than 800,000 acres as the Grand Canyon National Monument, to the recent fights over Grand Staircase-Escalante and Bears Ears National Monuments. Controversies over the use of the Antiquities Act are outside the scope of this work. For details on concern over impacts to Mesa Verde as precursor to the Antiquities Act, see Richard W. Sellars, "A Very Large Array: Early Federal Historic Preservation—The Antiquities Act, Mesa Verde, and the National Park Service Act." *Natural Resources Journal* 47, no. 2 (2007): 267.

3. For "the preservation," see §2; for penalties, see §4. For explicit protection of biota in 1928, see Pub. L. No. 70-317, §4.

4. Sellars, "A Very Large Array," 269.

5. For list of excavators, see John Wetherill, 1930-04-07 letter to Nusbaum [RG19-001-028]. For Charles Mason comment, see Don Watson, *Cliff Dwellings of Mesa Verde* (Mesa Verde: Mesa Verde Museum Association, n.d.) [RG19-001-058]. For "archeological loot," see Nusbaum, 1949-09-15 letter to Don Watson, MEVE Archeologist [RG19-001-066]. For Nusbaum excepting John Wetherill, see Nusbaum, 1930-03-26 letter to John Wetherill [RG1-001-028].

6. See J. Walter Fewkes, "Antiquities of the Mesa Verde National Park: Spruce Tree House," *Bulletin 41, Bureau of American Ethnology* (Washington, DC: Smithsonian Institution, 1909), 25; J. Walter Fewkes, "Antiquities of the Mesa Verde National Park: Cliff Palace," *Bulletin 51, Bureau of American Ethnology* (Washington: Smithsonian Institution, 1911), 64. For Randolph's observations, see Ise, 145–46; and James A. Lancaster, Jean M. Pinkley, Philip F. Van Cleave,

and Don Watson, *Archeological Excavations in Mesa Verde National Park, Colorado, 1950* (Washington, DC: USDI National Park Service, 1954), 1.

7. For Hewett's excavations, see Smith, *Mesas,* 7–8. For essential knowledge, see Lancaster et al., *Archeological Excavations in Mesa Verde,* 23. For other early archeologists, see J. Walter Fewkes, *Excavation and Repair of Sun Temple, Mesa Verde National Park* (Washington, DC: USDI, Office of the Secretary, 1916). For Randolph's recommendation, see MEVE-SAR 1908, 7.

8. Lancaster et al., *Archeological Excavations in Mesa Verde,* 29.

9. For placing signs, see Torres-Reyes, 2:1. For "no unlawful excavations," see MEVE-SAR 1910, 6. Randolph also claimed there were no violations of the game laws (MEVE-SAR 1909, 6; MEVE-SAR 1910, 6). Yet not long after, Superintendent Samuel Shoemaker proposed "In order to preserve the game from the depredations of the Ute Indians an 8- or 10-foot woven wire fence should be erected, practically enclosing the park" (MEVE-SAR 1913, 9). Subsequent claims can be found in MEVE-SAR 1911, 6; MEVE-SAR 1914, 6.

10. Nusbaum interview, 3.

Gustaf Nordenskiöld was a young Swedish amateur archeologist who came to the Mesa Verde region in 1891 with a letter of introduction to the Wetherills. He "worked" several sites and produced a record of his activities: *The Cliff Dwellers of the Mesa Verde* (1893), (Mesa Verde National Park: Mesa Verde Museum Association (1990)).

11. For "pony trails," see Torres-Reyes, 3:1. For Werner's report, see MEVE-SAR 1907. For Randolph's recommendations, see MEVE-SAR 1908, 6.

12. Runte, 158–59.

13. For Wright's report, see MEVE-SAR 1911, 7. For Shoemaker's promise, see MEVE-SAR 1912, 6.

14. "Light of Science Will Play on Old Ruins," *Daily News* (Denver), August 11, 1907, 10, https://www.coloradohistoricnewspapers.org/?a=d&d=RMD19070811-01.2.86&e=——en-20–1–img-txIN%7ctxCO%7ctxTA——0— (last accessed 2024-07-05).

15. For Department goals, see R. B. Marshall, "Park Administration," *Proceedings of the National Park Conference Held at the Yellowstone National Park, September 11 and 12, 1911* (Washington, DC: Government Printing Office, 1912). https://www.nps.gov/parkhistory/online_books/npc/proceedings-npc1/sec3.htm (last accessed 2024-07-05). For least visited, see Foresta, 12.

16. For horse trails, see MEVE-SAR 1908, 6–7. For roads, see MEVE-SAR 1915, 8.

17. For first regulations, see Torres-Reyes, 3:10. For Peabody House closure, see MEVE-SAR 1913, 7.

18. For "undisturbed majesty," see Sellars, *Nature,* 70; see also 11–25, 75–9; and Ise 47, 123–24, 178. At Mesa Verde, see especially MEVE-SAR 1908, 5.

19. Marshall, "Park Administration."

20. Sellars, *Nature,* 23, 37–38.

21. Nusbaum, 1942-09-04 memo to Director—re: Comprehensive Report of Grazing History from 1879 to present date [RG19-001-082].

22. For initial grazing prohibitions, see F. Frank Pierce, 1908-03-04 letter from Acting Interior Secretary to Superintendent [RG01-01.10-011]. For actual use, see Torres-Reyes, 7:2.

23. MEVE-SAR 1909, 8.

24. For windmills, see Torres-Reyes, 7:2. For grazing privileges, see Torres-Reyes, 2:3.

25. Marshall "Park Administration."

26. For grazing permits, see Richard Wright, 1911-07-01 letter from Acting Superintendent to Secretary of the Interior [RG01-01.10-011]. For coal lease, see MEVE-SAR 1911, 9.

27. For "locusts," see John Muir, The Mountains of California. (New York: Century, 1894, frontispiece); Ise, 59–60 and Allin, 37. For exclusion, see Torres-Reyes, 7:1–2.

28. For friends' fees, see Nusbaum, 1942-02-23 memo to Superintendent [RG19-001-082]. For Mummy Lake, see Torres-Reyes, 4:5.

29. Torres-Reyes, 1:1.

30. For "contains no ruins," see MEVE-SAR 1911, 9–10. For the five-mile strip, see MEVE-SAR 1910, 8.

31. For the Secretary's reasoning, see Ethan Carr, *Wilderness by Design: Landscape Architecture and the National Park Service* (Lincoln: University of Nebraska Press, 1998), 2–3.

32. For Glacier, see Ise, 171ff. For the National Monuments, see "National Monument Facts and Figures," NPS, https://www.nps.gov/subjects/archeology/national-monument-facts-and-figures.htm (last accessed 2024-07-05). Some of these monuments eventually became national parks; others were turned over to states to manage.

33. Marshall, "Park Administration."

34. Richard Wright, "The Mesa Verde National Park; Its Past, Present, and Future." *Proceedings of the National Park Conference Held at the Yellowstone National Park, September 11 and 12, 1911* (Washington, DC: Government Printing Office, 1912), https://www.nps.gov/parkhistory/online_books/npc/proceedings-npc1/sec4.htm (last accessed 2024-07-05).

35. Torres-Reyes, 3:10.

Chapter Two

1. Runte, 47. See also Sutter, 42, 113. Nash goes into detail on wilderness being seen in the nineteenth century as "uniquely American," 67–83.

2. For ambiguities, see Sellars, *Nature*, 38. For "perpetual tension" see Richard W. Sellars, "A Very Large Array: Early Federal Historic Preservation—The Antiquities Act, Mesa Verde, and the National Park Service Act." *Natural*

Resources Journal 47, no. 2 (2007): 323. For "sets forth," see Robert B. Keiter, "National Park Protection: Putting the Organic Act to Work," in *Our Common Lands: Defending the National Parks*, ed. David J. Simon (Washington, DC: Island Press, 1988), 81.

3. For Mather's "greatest good," see Sellars, *Nature*, 47.

This statement, borrowed from Forest Service Chief Gifford Pinchot (who added the qualifier "for the longest time"—further complicating the equation), was originally posited by the utilitarian philosopher Jeremy Bentham, though shown to be impossible by the French mathematician d'Alembert in the eighteenth century. See Garrett Hardin, "The Tragedy of the Commons" (1968), in *Managing the Commons*, eds. Garrett Hardin and John Baden (San Francisco: W.H. Freeman, 1977), 18. For an examination of Hardin's "Tragedy" applied to park planning, see Daniel L. Dustin, and Leo H. McAvoy, "*Hardin*ing National Parks," *Environmental Ethics* 2, no. 1 (Spring 1980): 39–44.

4. For "workable mandate," see Joseph L. Sax, *Mountains Without Handrails: Reflections on the National Parks* (Ann Arbor: The University of Michigan Press, 1980), 11. For protecting the scenery, see Sellars, *Nature*, 29, 38–45, 67, 69.

5. For Mather's fear of loss of support, see Runte, 103, 156. For one major road, see Sellars, *Nature*, 60–1. For "We want," see Sellars, *Nature*, 28. For golf courses, see Sellars, *Nature*, 63. For greater detail on Yard's life and contributions to the parks, see Sutter, 100ff.

6. For Mather's report, see Torres-Reyes, 3:7. For Rickner's proposal, see MEVE-SAR 1919, 5.

7. MEVE-SAR 1919, 5.

8. For Mather's recommendation, see Sellars, *Nature*, 61. For Square Tower, see MEVE-SAR 1919, 4. For other trails, see MEVE-SAR 1920, 6.

9. For only such feature, see MEVE-SAR 1921, 5. For trail, see MEVE-SAR 1917, 1. For tourist's description, see George L. Beam, *The Prehistoric Cliff Dwellings of Mesa Verde National Park, Colorado* (Denver: self-published, n.d.). For map, see MEVE-SAR 1920, 4.

10. Pub. L. 64-235 §3.

11. For "killed off," see MEVE-SAR 1916, 3. For introductions and winter feeding, see MEVE-SAR 1918, 4.

12. Nusbaum, 1942-02-23 memo to the Superintendent [RG19-01-082]. For "There is no one feature," see Thomas Rickner, 1919-01-31 letter to Director [RG01-01.10-011].

Leopold, discussing the idea of creating the Gila wilderness: "The entire area is grazed by cattle, but the cattle ranches would be an asset from the recreational standpoint because of the interest which attaches to cattle grazing operations under frontier conditions." Aldo Leopold, "The Wilderness and Its Place in Forest Recreation Policy" *J. Forestry* 19, no. 7 (November 1921): 721.

13. For typical Rickner report, see MEVE-SAR 1916, 1. In contrast, see Torres-Reyes, 5:2.

14. For Nusbaum's comments on Jeep, see Nusbaum interview, 13–14; and Nusbaum, transcript of talk to The Denver Posse of Westerners at Bent's Fort, Morrison, CO, August 16, 1964 [RG19-001-052]. For Daniels House, see Smith, *Mesas*, 9.

15. Torres-Reyes, 5:1–2.

16. MEVE-SAR 1918, 2.

17. Arthur Carhart, 1919-12-10 "Memorandum for Mr. Leopold, District 3," 2.

18. For "The first duty," see Runte, 70. For "The first principle," see Foresta, 14. For "disturbing agent," see George P. Marsh, 1864. *Man and Nature; or, Physical Geography as Modified by Human Action* (New York: Charles Scribner,1864; repr., Cambridge, MA: Belknap Press of Harvard University Press, 1965), 36. For Lacey, see Sellars, "A Very Large Array," 286–87.

19. Carhart "Memorandum" 2; 3–4.

20. Allin, 69. For details on the beginning of the long-standing rivalry between the Park Service and Forest Service, see Foresta, 13–21, 30–37.

Chapter Three

1. Sellars, *Nature*, 48, 55.

2. Nusbaum interview, 3–4.

3. For first job, see Nusbaum interview, 1. For Canyons of the Ancients and Hovenweep photographs, see RG19-001-047. For Fewkes approach to excavation, see Denise M. Meringolo, *Museums, Monuments, and National Parks.* (Amherst: University of Massachusetts Press, 2012), 68. For additional Nusbaum biographical information, see Meringolo, 60–61.

4. For "to replace," see Nusbaum interview, 5–6. For Mather's preferences in superintendents, see Sellars, *Nature*, 50–53.

5. For policy on scientific expertise, see Sellars, *Nature*, 57. For Step House, see Nusbaum, *The 1926 Re-Excavation of Step House Cave.* Mesa Verde Research Series Paper No. 1 (Mesa Verde National Park: Mesa Verde Museum Association, 1981). For Bone Awl House, see MEVE-SAR 1927, 8. For the Wetherill Mesa sites, see Smith, *Mesas*, 13.

6. For less pot-hunting, see MEVE-SAR 1921, 5. For 1929 survey, see Smith, *Mesas*, 13–14.

7. For "The first thing," see Nusbaum interview, 10. For "visitors," see Nusbaum, *Re-Excavation of Step House Cave*, 26.

8. MEVE-SAR 1921, 4; MEVE-SAR 1922, 2; MEVE-SAR 1923, 2.

9. Nusbaum interview, 21. In 1918, Secretary of the Interior Franklin Lane issued policy which permitted cattle grazing in areas of the parks "not frequented by visitors" (Sellars, *Nature*, 57, 84–5).

Nusbaum made no reference to this policy in discussing his decision to terminate grazing in Mesa Verde.

10. For inholdings, see Torres-Reyes, 7:2. For "I am going," see Nusbaum interview, 21–22.

11. Nusbaum interview, 24–25.

12. Nusbaum, 1942-02-23 memo to Superintendent [RG19-001-082].

13. R. A. Devlin, 1930-02-13 letter from Chief Clerk, MEVE—to Jesse L. Nusbaum, Laboratory of Anthropology, Santa Fe [RG01-01.07-050]. R. A. Devlin, 1930-02-13 letter from Chief Clerk, MEVE—to Director, NPS [RG01-01.07-050.

14. Nusbaum, 1930-02-15 letter to Director [RG01-01.07-050].

15. Horace M. Albright, 1930-02-24 letter from Director—to R. A. Devlin, Chief Clerk, MEVE [RG01-01.07-050].

16. Charles W. Quaintance, 1935-05-20 memo from Resident Wildlife Technician—to Superintendent Leavitt—re: Information requested for preliminary report [RG01-01.07-050].

17. For fear of humans, see MEVE-SAR 1925, 5. For stable population, see MEVE-SAR 1926, 6.

18. For "The first elk," see MEVE-SAR 1921, 4. For "Two small bears," see MEVE-SAR 1925, 5.

19. For "necessary," see Torres-Reyes, 9:1. For justification and Toll, see Sellars, *Nature*, 71, 119.

20. For "notwithstanding our efforts," see MEVE-SAR 1921, 4. For coyote reproduction, see for instance Dan Flores, *Coyote America: A natural and supernatural history* (New York: Basic Books, 2016), 7. For State of Colorado, see MEVE-SAR 1922, 3–4.

Nusbaum was wrong in believing the State owned the wildlife. For a detailed examination of management responsibility for wildlife on federal lands, *see* Martin Nie, Christopher Barns, Jonathan Haber, Julie Jolie, Kenneth Pitt, and Sandi Zellmer, "Fish and Wildlife Management on Federal Lands: debunking state supremacy," *Environmental Law* 47, no. 4 (2017): 797–932.

21. MEVE-SAR 1928, 10.

22. For "attractive features," see MEVE-SAR 1921, 6. For forestry policy, see Torres-Reyes, 10:1.

23. Nusbaum, Report: "A History of Porcupine in MEVE Prior to 1929," February 4, 1946. [RG19-001-029]

24. Franklin Lane, "Secretary Lane's Letter [to Stephen T. Mather, Director, NPS] on National Park Management, May 13, 1918," in *America's National Park System: The Critical Documents*, ed. Lary M. Dilsaver (1994). https://www.nps.gov/parkhistory/online_books/anps/anps_1j.htm (last accessed 2024-07-05). For Leopold's rant, see Aldo Leopold, "The River of the Mother of God" (1924), in *The River of the Mother of God and Other Essays by Aldo Leopold*, eds. Susan L, Flader and J. Baird Callicott (Madison: University of Wisconsin Press, 1991), 126–7.

Leopold's essay gives testament to just how quickly his ideas evolved. Only three years earlier he had written an essay in the *Journal of Forestry* on Forest Service wilderness. As for wilderness in the National Parks, he wrote: "The Parks are being networked with roads and trails as rapidly as possible. *This is right and proper*" (emphasis added). (Aldo Leopold, "The Wilderness and Its Place in Forest Recreation Policy" *J. Forestry* 19, no. 7 (November 1921): 720.

25. For "merely a wilderness," see Sellars, *Nature*, 63–4. For "first-class hotel," see MEVE-SAR 1926, 3. Details on Nusbaum's role in developing museums at Mesa Verde and throughout the Service are beyond the scope of this book. Interested readers are directed to Denise Meringolo's *Museums, Monuments, and National Parks*, 68–79, and the Nusbaum interview.

26. For "I planned," see Nusbaum interview, 20–21. For "If we think," see Aldo Leopold, "Conserving the Covered Wagon," *Sunset Magazine* 54, no. 3 (March 1925), 21.

27. MEVE-SAR 1921 (Natural Bridge, 4; Wetherill Mesa, 5).

28. MEVE-SAR 1922, 4.

29. The tribal land adjacent to MEVE, and from which the Park was carved, was part of the Southern Ute Reservation until 1940, when the Ute Mountain Utes organized their own government in response to the Indian Reorganization Act of 1934. See https://www.utemountainutetribe.com/ (last accessed 2024-07-05).

30. MEVE-SAR 1923, 5

31. J. B. Hamilton, 1934-12-29 letter from Assistant Engineer—to Branch of Engineering, San Francisco, 3 [RG01-01.03-063].

32. For the Rock Springs Trail through "Pictograph Point," see MEVE-SAR 1924, 5. For claiming credit, see MEVE, 1936-04 ECW Work Program Outline, Camp NP-5-C, for Period Beginning April 1, 1936, 6 [RG01-08-007]. For Williams, see MEVE-SAR 1941, 3.

33. For fifty miles, see MEVE-SAR 1927, 14. For "a trail district," see Nusbaum, 1927-02-28 memo to Director—re: Park Development Plan [RG01-01.07-002].

34. MEVE. "1927 Authorized rates, Mesa Verde Pack & Saddle Company" [RG01-01.10-001].

35. MEVE-PB 1930 ("experienced riders," 65; "only by trail," 13; "a week to 10 days," 66; "permanent camp sites," 55).

36. For "authorized," see MEVE-PB 1930, 55. For "present procedure," and "major ruins," see MEVE-SAR 1930, 3 and 7–8.

37. MEVE-PB 1930, 13.

38. MEVE-SAR 1929, 3.

Chapter Four

1. For national statistics, see Ise 326–28. For Mesa Verde statistics, see Smith, *Shadows*, App. B.

2. For Spring House popularity, see MEVE-SAR 1931, 20–21. For dimensions and purposes, see John D. William (Assistant Engineer, Field Headquarters, San Francisco), 1931-04-10 Trail Construction Account 512, 1 [RG01-01.03-063]. For "short enough," see Ira S. Stinson, (Assistant Engineer, Field Headquarters, San Francisco), 1932-02-10 Final Construction Report on Trails, 1931, 1–2 [RG01-01.03-063].

3. Jack Vandermayer, "Roads to Roam," *Mesa Verde Notes,* July 1931, http://npshistory.com/nature_notes/meve/vol2-1e.htm (last accessed 2024-07-05).

4. David Roberts, *Finding Everett Ruess* (New York: Broadway Books, 2011), 111–14. See also W. L. Rusho, 1983. *Everett Ruess, a Vagabond for Beauty* (Salt Lake City: Gibbs Smith, 1983), 84–89.

5. MEVE, 1932-06-07 Revised Six-Year Program of Employment Stabilization Projects for FYs 1934–1939, inclusive [RG01-01.07-003].

6. MEVE, 1935-05-09 Six Year Program, 1937–1942, inclusive, Sec. B-2, 7–8 [RG01-01.07-002].

7. Thomas E. Carpenter, 1936-01-27 letter for the Deputy Chief Architect—to Director [RG05-01.08-007].

8. For Mesa Verde visitation, see Smith, *Shadows,* App. B.

9. Pub. L. No. 73-5, §1. For manager preferences, see Sellars, *Nature,* 126.

10. For photographs and a more complete discussion of the CCC work at Mesa Verde, see Ronald C. Brown and Duane E. Smith, *New Deal Days: The CCC at Mesa Verde* (Durango, CO: Durango Herald Small Press, 2006).

11. For Painted Kiva and "tramp," see J. B. Hamilton, 1935-04-14 letter from Assistant Engineer, Branch of Engineering, San Francisco—Final Construction Report on Trails, 1933, 2 [RG01-01.03-063]. For "prolong the stay," see Charles W. Quaintance, 1935-02-20 Supplementary Report: National Park Additions on sub-marginal land, 5 [RG01-01.07-050].

12. For "certain areas," see Chester R. Markley, 1934-03-13 memo from Acting Chief Ranger—to Superintendent, 2–3 [RG05-01.08-001]. For quarry and additional grazing trails, see R. A. Devlin, 1934-12-04 Memo from Chief Clerk—to Superintendent [RG05-01.08-001]. For "enjoy the wonders," see *The Cliff Dweller* 1, no. 1 (1935), 5 [RG05-01.07-005].

13. For easier funding, see A. W. Burney, 1934-08-03 letter from Acting Chief Engineer—to Director [RG05-01.08-001]. For multi-purpose, see MEVE, 1934-06-11 Proposed Drought Relief Program for July 1 to November 15 [RG05-01.08-001]. For "old Ute Indian trails," see MEVE, 1935-05-09 Six Year Program, 1937–1942, 8 [RG01-01.07-002]. For horse trails v. truck trails, see MEVE, 1935-04-01 List of Projects for ECW Fifth Enrollment Period [RG05-01.08-003].

14. MEVE-PB 1935, 37.

15. MEVE-PB 1937.

16. NPS, "General Provisions #17: archeologic ruins and objects," v. 1, no. 76 Fed. Reg. 792–93 (June 27, 1936).

17. For "most disastrous," see J. Carlisle Crouch, 1934-08-28 Report: Fire Truck Trails, Fire Lookouts and Ranger Cabin, 1 [RG01-01.07-111]. For "normal conditions," see Hillory A. Tolson, 1934-08-07 letter from Acting Associate Director—to Superintendent [RG05-01.08-001].

18. J. Carlisle Crouch, 1934-08-28 ("eight-foot scar" 2; "not been patrolled" 6) [RG01-01.07-111].

19. L. F. Cook, 1934-12-23 letter from Associate Forester, NPS Western Division Branch of Forestry—to John B. Coffman, Chief Forester, NPS [RG0-01.07 111].

20. Nusbaum, 1935-01-04 letter to John B. Coffman, Chief Forester, NPS [RG01-01.07-111].

21. Hamilton, 1934-12-29, 1–2.

22. See Devlin, 1934-12-04; J. Carlisle Crouch, 1934-12-20 memo from the Chief Ranger re: Justification for (Horse) trails to East Side, 2 [RG05-01.08-001]; and Devlin, 1934-12-26 letter from Acting Superintendent—to Director; and Hamilton 1934-12-29 letter to Branch of Engineering, San Francisco [RG05-01.08-001].

23. For "What happened," see MEVE-SAR 1934, 33–34. For route comparison, see J. B. Hamilton, 1935-11-20 memo from Associate Engineer—to Paul Franke, Acting Superintendent [RG05-01.10-018].

24. Victor H. Cahalane, 1935-09-11 memo from Acting Assistant Chief—to Mr. Demaray [RG05-01.08-001].

25. For "lack of interest," see J. B. Hamilton, 1936-04-02 letter to Branch of Engineering, San Francisco [RG05-01.08-007]. For Work Program, see MEVE, 1936-04 ECW Work Program Outline, Camp NP-5-C, for Period Beginning April 1, 1936, 8–9 [RG05-01.08-007]. For final approval, see Charles H. Gerner, 1940-11-14 memo from Chief, Project Development Division—to Regional Director [RG05-01.10-007].

26. For number of fires, see Torres-Reyes, 10:3. For Murie and Cook, see Sellars, *Nature*, 128–31.

27. For first, see Robert W. Audretsch, *The Civilian Conservation Corps in Colorado, 1933–1942*. Vol. 2. (Indianapolis: Dog Ear Publishing, 2018), 40. For "seven days," see E. P. Leavitt, 1934-01-15 General Report on ECW for First Enrollment Period, 5 [RG05-01.04-029]. For "value," see *The Cliff Dweller* 1935, 7 [RG05-01.07-005].

28. Leavitt, 1934-01-15, 6 [RG05-01.04-029].

29. For "alarming proportions," see MEVE-SAR 1932, 10. For ten times, see Leavitt, 1934-01-15, 6. For "porcupine crew," see Brown and Smith, *New Deal Days*, 14.

30. MEVE, 1936-04 ECW Work Program Outline, Camp NP-6-C, for Period Beginning April 1, 1936 [RG05-01.08-007].

31. For NPS policy, see Chester R. Markley, 1934-03-13 memo from Acting Chief Ranger—to Superintendent Leavitt, 3 [RG05-01.08 001]. For proposal and trial, see MEVE-SAR 1937, 13–14.

32. For "park value," see Torres-Reyes, 10:2. For "take its course," see Cahalane 1935-09-11, 3. For "238,190," see MEVE-SAR 1943, 4.

33. For planting wheat, see Hillory A. Tolson, 1935-10-09 letter from Acting Associate Director—to Paul R. Franke, Acting Superintendent, 2 [RG05-01.08-005]. For Wetherill Mesa, see James W. Townsend and Paul R. Franke, 1935-04-01 to 1935-09-30 narrative report for E.C.W. Camp NP-6C, 25 [RG05-01.04-036].

34. For "tourist observation," see Markley 1934-03-13, 4. For "enthusiasm," see E. P. Leavitt, 1934-10-13 Quarterly Report for the ECW Camp D-NP-5C, Company 1843, 4–6 [RG05-01.04-028].

35. E. P. Leavitt, 1934-08-28 memo from Superintendent—to Messrs. Townsend, Richey, Bennett [RG05-01.08-001].

36. George M. Wright, "Report Regarding Wildlife Restoration Plan for Mesa Verde National Park, Submitted to the Director May 11, 1934," in *Fauna of the National Parks of the United States, Fauna Series No.* 2, George M. Wright and Ben H. Thompson (Washington, DC: USDI, NPS—Government Printing Office, 1935), 99–102.

Wright died in 1936, and by 1940 the Park Service biologists were all transferred to the Bureau of Biological Survey—soon to be renamed the Fish and Wildlife Service. Though field biologists were not relocated, their line of authority passed through an entirely different government bureau. On top of the loss of leadership with Wright's death, this move crippled biology in the Park Service for over a decade (Sellars, *Nature*, 91, 146, 312n1).

37. For other parks, see Denise M. Meringolo, *Museums, Monuments, and National Parks.* (Amherst: University of Massachusetts Press, 2012), 140–143. For Franke's proposal, see Paul R. Franke, "Premeditated Discovery." *Mesa Verde Notes* 6, no. 1 (August 1935): 3, http://npshistory.com/nature_notes/meve/vol6-1c.htm (last accessed 2024-07-05).

38. For plans, see Smith, *Mesas,* 15. For one worker, see Brown and Smith, *New Deal Days,* 12. For damage, see Don Watson, 1938-07-15 memo from Junior Park Naturalist—to Superintendent [RG01-01.08-075]. For Nusbaum's plan, see Brown and Smith, 100.

39. For "for the purpose," see Nash, 207. For "The modern metropolis," see Sutter, 169.

40. Robert Sterling Yard, "A Summons to Save the Wilderness," in *Living Wilderness* (The Wilderness Society) 1, no. 1 (1935): 1–2.

41. Nusbaum, "Wilderness Aspects of National Parks." *Mesa Verde Notes* 8, no. 1 (September 1938): 2, 6–7, http://npshistory.com/nature_notes/meve/vol8-1b.htm (last accessed 2024-07-05).

42. Ibid., 3–4.

43. Ibid., 7–8.

44. Ibid., 6.

45. Ibid., 4.

46. Thomas J. Williams, 1941-03-26 text for inclusion in MEVE Master Plan (summarizing, 11–13; "Tree Insect Pest," 22–26) [RG01-01.07-001.1].

47. Ibid., 16–21. The trail would have to continue farther east to Morefield Canyon to join the truck trail.

48. Ibid., 21.

49. For "lesser-known reaches," see Williams 1941-03-26 text, 21, 5. For map, see MEVE, 1941-01 Trail System and Fire Control Plan [RG01-01.07-001].

50. Nusbaum, 1941 notes for MEVE Master Plan [RG19-001-022].

51. Torres-Reyes, 12:2.

Chapter Five

1. For general impacts of the war, see Janet A. McDonnell, "World War II: Defending Park Values and Resources," *Public Historian*, 29, no. 4 (Fall 2007), 15–33. See also Ise, 447–53; and Sellars, *Nature*, 151–54. For Ickes, see Allin, 87–88. For MEVE visitation, see Smith, Shadows, App. B.

2. For entrance station, see Smith, *Shadows*, 146. For "freedom," see MEVE-SAR 1942, 5. For horse trips, see MEVE-SAR 1945, 3.

3. For vendetta, see MEVE-SAR 1943, 6. For authorization, blowtorches, and "noxious perennials," see MEVE-SAR 1945, 7, 8.

4. MEVE-SAR 1944, 1; MEVE-SAR 1945, 6; MEVE-SAR 1950, 5; MEVE 1952 Master Plan Development Outline, Interpretation, 5 [RG01-01.07-001.3].

5. MEVE-SAR 1945, 6; MEVE 1952, Interpretation, 5.

6. For First World War, see Ise, 301–302. For World War II throughout the NPS, see Sellars, *Nature*, 154–5. For Mesa Verde, see MEVE-SAR 1942, 6.

7. For "accept no organization," see Michael J. Ybarra, *Washington Gone Crazy: Senator Pat McCarran and the Great Communist Hunt* (Hanover, NH: Steerforth Press, 2004), 371. For "didn't like," see Ise, 436. For comments made at the Senate Hearing, see *Hearings Before a Subcommittee of the Committee on Public Lands and Surveys, pursuant to S. Res. 241*, 76th Cong. (November 19–20, 1942): "a little of the worst," 1981; Kelley testimony, 1973, 1975.

8. Senate Hearing, 1976–77.

While technically true, grazing was allowed to increase at national monuments and other non-park areas managed by the NPS (McDonnell, "World War II," 30). These were deemed "areas of lesser importance" (Sellars, *Nature*, 154). Drury had already gone on record in a memo to Ickes that the Park Service contribution to the war effort should not be measured in resources extracted but in benefit to the national spirit (McDonnell, 22).

9. Senate Hearing, 1986.

10. Nusbaum interview, 25.

11. Ibid., 25–26.

12. For Drury's directive, see Carr, *M66*, 31. For "I can only operate" and "the voice of the people," see Senate Hearing, 1886.

McCarran was spectacularly wrong in his prediction. Since the date of that hearing, fourteen new National Parks have been designated, eighteen previously existing units have been "upgraded" to National Park status, and well over 250 other units have been added to the National Park System. See https://www.nps.gov/subjects/npscelebrates/park-anniversaries.htm.

13. Senate Hearing, 1991–92.

14. For "protected range," see E. T. Scoyen, 1946-08-01 memo from Associate Regional Director—to Director [RG01-001.07-021]. For "range recovery," see MEVE-SAR 1946, 7–8.

15. Nusbaum, 1943-04-19 memo to Regional Director [RG03-05.05-001].

16. Carr, *M66*, 33. Visitor statistics from Sellars, *Nature*, 173.

17. For Drury, see Sellars, *Nature*, 174. For DeVoto, see Bernard DeVoto, "Let's Close the National Parks," *Harper's Magazine* 207 (October 1953), 52.

18. Smith, *Shadows*, App. B.

19. For proposed wording, see E. Jenkins, 1946-01-04 letter from AAA—to Jesse Nusbaum, Superintendent [RG01-01.06-017]. For Nusbaum response, see Nusbaum, 1946-01-18 letter to E. Jenkins, AAA [RG01-01.06-017].

20. Emerson Stringham, *Mesa Verde National Park* (Austin: self-published, 1946) [RG01-01.06-006].

21. MEVE-PB 1947 ("rigidly enforced," 3; "spectacular," and "Most trails," 14–15).

22. MEVE. 1949-11 map of Roads and Trails Systems [RG01-01.07-001].

Among the errors, the trail down Moccasin Mesa is shown entirely within the Park boundary, when geography dictates it would have crossed onto the Ute Mountain Ute Reservation, as the current road does today. In addition, it shows the route from that mesa down into Soda Canyon within the Park. The route is in the vicinity of Bone Awl House—almost 1/4 mile south of the Mesa Verde boundary.

23. MEVE-PB 1952, 2.

24. MEVE-PB 1954 ("Hiking," 13; "rented," 15).

25. MEVE, 1953 Master Plan Development Outline, 1–2 [RG01-01.07-001.3].

26. MEVE Chief Ranger, 1951-08-18 notes on Antiquities Violations occurring August 18, 1951 [RG01-02.01-073].

27. For "special effort," see MEVE Park Archeologist, 1954-05-23 memo to Superintendent re: Annual Report (with pencil notation) [RG01-02.01-001]. For "22 Boy Scouts," and "Local chambers," see Albert Rosenfeld, "Guardian of the Old West," *Empire Magazine*, April 25, 1954, 7, 42.

28. Nusbaum, "New Park Service Controls," *El Palacio*, 55, no. 3. (March 1948), 67–70.

29. MEVE Park Archeologist, 1954-05-23, 3 [RG01-02.01-001].

30. MEVE 1952 Master Plan Development Outline, Introduction, 1 [RG01-01.07-001.3].

31. Robert H. Rose, 1952-07-18 memo from Superintendent—to Regional Director—re: Introduction, Master Plan Development Outline [RG01-02.03-005].

32. For "splendid condition," see Don Watson, 1946-02-01 Report of the Park Naturalist for the month of January 1946, 3 [RG01-01.03-029]. For immediate vicinity, see MEVE-SAR 1947, 7. For tent caterpillars, see Jack Wade, 1954 Fiscal Year Chief Ranger's Annual Report, 12 [RG01-02.01-018].

33. For as soon as possible, see MEVE-SAR 1951, 8. For "complete natural recovery," see MEVE, 1953 Master Plan Development Outline, Soil & Moisture Conservation, 2 [RG01-01.07-001.3]. For precedence, see MEVE, 1952 Master Plan Development Outline, Forestry, 3 [RG01-01.07-001.3].

34. MEVE 1952 Master Plan Development Outline, Interpretation, 4 [RG01-01.07-001.3]; MEVE Park Archeologist, 1954-05-23 Memo to Superintendent; MEVE Park Archeologist [RG01-02.01-001].

35. For turkey, see MEVE Park Archeologist, 1955 Annual Report [RG01-02.01-001]. For beaver, see Carlson, 1953-11-09 memo to Director—re: Monthly Narrative Report for October 1953 [RG01-01.03-028.38]. For bighorn, see Wade, 1954 Chief Ranger's Annual Report, 10.

36. For prior to 1928, see MEVE, 1952 Master Plan Development Outline, Forestry, 7–8. For fear, see MEVE, 1953 Master Plan Development Outline, Soil & Moisture Conservation, 2. For trespass, see Carlson, 1953-12-04 memo to Regional Director—re: Master Plan, Soil and Moisture Conservation Section [RG01-02.03-005]. For concessioner's stock, see MEVE, 1952 Master Plan Development Outline, Forestry, 6–7. For twenty to thirty head, see MEVE, 1953–1963 Grazing Reports [RG01-02.07-040].

37. MEVE Park Archeologist, 1954-05-23 Memo to Superintendent [RG 01-02.01-001].

38. James A. Lancaster, Jean M. Pinkley, Philip F. Van Cleave, and Don Watson, *Archeological Excavations in Mesa Verde National Park, Colorado, 1950* (Washington: USDI National Park Service, 1954), 2.

39. For Mancos, see Torres-Reyes, 13:2. For impossible, see George M. Wright, "Report Concerning a Proposed Extension of Mesa Verde National Park, Submitted to the Director of the National Park Service October 24, 1933," in *Fauna of the National Parks of the United States, Fauna Series No. 2*, George M. Wright and Ben H. Thompson (Washington: USDI, NPS—Government Printing Office, 1935), 96–99. For "We cannot," see Torres-Reyes, 13:2.

40. For as early as 1939, see Torres-Reyes, 13:3. For Extension, see Williams, 1941-03-26 text for inclusion in Master Plan, 3–4 [RG01-01.07-001.1].

41. Nusbaum, 1941 notes for Master Plan, 1 [RG19-01-022].

42. Jack Wade, 1945-01-21 memo from Chief Ranger—to Superintendent [RG01-02.07-015].

43. Conrad L. Wirth, 1953-07-09 memo from Director, NPS—to Assistant Secretary Lewis—re: Desire of Southern Ute Indians to Obtain Lands in MEVE [RG01-02.07-015].

44. For "Bill Gunn," see Nusbaum, 1953-07-15 memo to Director—re: Desire of Southern Ute Indians to Obtain Lands in MEVE [RG01-02.07-015]. For Rather than give up, see Carlson, 1953-09-18 memo to Regional Director—re: Park Boundaries and Ute Indians [RG01-02.07-015].

45. Carlson, 1953-09-18 memo.

46. Fred C. Fagergren, 1954-11-08 Memo from Acting Superintendent—to Regional Director—re: Ute Indian Claims to MEVE [RG01-02.07-015].

47. For first systematic, see Smith, *Mesas,* 18. See also MEVE Park Archeologist, 1955 Fiscal Year Annual Report of Park Archeologist, 2 [RG01-02.01-001] and MEVE-SAR 1955, 2.

48. Carlson, 1955-08-22 memo to Regional Director—re: Ute Indian Claims and Potential Boundary Adjustments, 1–5 [RG01-02.07-015].

49. MEVE-SMR 1959, 6.

50. Carlson, 1955-08-22 memo, 3–5.

51. Ibid., 1.

52. Ibid., 2.

53. MEVE-SAR 1955, 10.

Chapter Six

1. For the drivers behind Mission 66, See Carr, *M66,* 46–7.

2. Ise, 547; Carr, *M66,* 54; Sellars, *Nature,* 183–87.

3. For the memo, see Carr, *M66,* 71. For the impossibility of maximizing both, see "Mesa Verde and the Birth of the National Park Service," note 3, above. For Garrison, see Carr, *M66,* 103. See also Sellars, *Nature,* 181.

Garrison's idea of developing a park in order to save it likely stemmed from the writings of Arno Cammerer, the third NPS Director. In 1936 he wrote the parks should build roads in a portion of a park as "an implement of wilderness conservation." With enough public use on those roads, the parks would have enough supporters to defeat those who would bear extractive economic pressures on park lands. The roads were seen as a "small price" to pay in order to gain the friends the parks needed to preserve the remaining wilderness (Sellars, *Nature,* 106). Twenty years later, conservationists would develop another view of roads.

"Necessary development" as a requirement of preservation is not an idea simply relegated to the mid-twentieth century. Ethan Carr, landscape architect and *Mission 66* author, wrote in 2007, "If the public is to enjoy parks without impairing them, then use must somehow be accommodated, controlled, channeled, choreographed, or otherwise designed. . . . To deny this is to evade the requirements and responsibilities of stewardship" (330). This is a landscape architect's response to the dilemma of the NPS "dual mandate." And it is not without merit. The problem, however, is one of balance, recognizing that developing to control use is unidirectional, requiring more development as use increases. An ecologist's response may be different. Richard Sellars (*Nature*, 105) quotes the early NPS biologist Lowell Sumner from 1936: roads were an "infection," bringing additional subsequent development until "the elusive wilderness flavor vanishes." True wilderness would vanish if the Service did not halt development.

4. MEVE-SAR 1957, 20.

5. For gateway, see MEVE-SMR 1959-11, 4. For Wetherill Mesa plans, see Torres-Reyes, 15:1. For a comprehensive summary of the archeological survey on Wetherill Mesa, see Alden C. Hayes, *The Archeological Survey of Wetherill Mesa, MEVE; Archeological Research Series No. 7-A* (Washington, DC: USDI, NPS, 1964).

6. Hugh M. Miller, 1955-08-26 memo from Regional Director—to Director—re: Ute Indian Claims and Potential Boundary Adjustments, MEVE [RG01-02.07-015].

7. NPS, 1956-11-16 Boundary Status Report, MEVE [RG01-02.07-017.1].

8. MEVE-SM 1959-11-17, 3; and MEVE, 1963-05 Master Plan for the Preservation and Use of MEVE, Objectives and Policies [draft?], 5 [RG01-02.03-005].

9. For oil and gas deposits, see John A. Anderson, 1957-01-25 memo from Regional Oil & Gas Supervisor, USGS—to Superintendent, Consolidated Ute Agency—re: Proposed Land Exchanges [RG01-02.07-017.1]. For "I do not feel," see Carlson, 1957-02-15 letter to James F. Canan, Superintendent, Consolidated Ute Agency [RG01-02.07-017.1]. For "practically nil," see David H. Canfield, 1957-03-01 (date received) memo from Acting Regional Director—to Director—re: Proposed Land Exchange-MEVE [RG01-02.07-017.1].

10. For opening Wetherill, see MEVE-SAR 1957, 6. For "all members," see MEVE-SM 1959-11-17, 3.

11. NPS, 1960-07-15 Boundary Status Report for MEVE [RG01-02.07-015].

12. MEVE-SMR 1960-07, 4.

13. Thomas, 1963-01-30 memo to Regional Director—re: Boundary Status Report, MEVE [RG01-02.07-015].

14. Thomas, 1963-02-01 letter to Jose Zuni, Superintendent, Consolidated Ute Agency [RG01-02.07-017.1].

15. Thomas, 1963-06-26 memo to Regional Director—re: Area Resources Outside Present Park Boundaries [RG01-02.07-017.7].

Thomas was wrong in this assertion. Park Mesa is entirely within the Park—and has been deemed especially important for that reason. He must have been aware of this, so it is unclear whether he didn't consider Park Mesa large enough to fit his parameters, or was simply exaggerating to influence his superior.

16. Ute Mountain Ute Tribal Council, 1964-03-11 Resolution 1278 [RG01-02.07-017.1].

17. Leslie P. Arnberger, 1964-04-30 memo from Assistant Regional Director, Cooperative Activities—to Regional Director—re: MEVE-Ute Land Situation [RG01-02.07-017.1].

18. Thomas, 1964-08-07 memo to Regional Director—re: Meeting with Ute Tribal Officials, MEVE, July 29, 1964 [RG01-02.07-027].

19. MEVE-SM 1964-08-04, 1.

20. Thomas, 1964-08-07 memo, 1.

21. MEVE-SMR 1959-11, 4; MEVE-SMR 1963-03, 4; MEVE-SMR 1960-02, 5; MEVE-SMR 1959-12, 5.

22. MEVE-SMR 1963-04, 5; MEVE-SM 1963-10-15; MEVE-SMR 1966-12, 5.

23. For Wirth and Albright, see Sellars, *Nature*, 168. See also Weldon F. Heald, "Urbanization of the National Parks," *National Parks Magazine* 35 (January 1961), 8.

24. For prairie dogs and turkeys, see MEVE-SAR 1957, 17; MEVE-SMR 1957-02, 5; MEVE-SMR 1957-03, 5. For bighorn dispersal, see MEVE-SMR 1959-02, 4; MEVE-SMR 1959-09, 6; MEVE-SMR 1960-07. For "roam," see MEVE-SAR 1962, 5.

25. For raccoons, see MEVE-SMR 1959-12, 3. For Abert's squirrels, see MEVE-SMR 1960-03, 5. For marmot, see MEVE-SMR 1960-07. For lioness, see MEVE-SAR 1962, 5. For "wolf," see MEVE-SMR 1962-09, 6.

26. Marilyn Colyer, "The Grazing History of MEVE (draft)" (February 26, 2004), 26 [B4-7-4].

Fencing began in earnest at this time, but Colyer claims it took improved fencing in the 1990s to reduce feral horses and cattle, with a corresponding significant improvement in the condition of the canyon bottoms and mesa meadows where the animals tended to congregate. However, she made it clear that it was likely not all horses within the Park came from the Ute tribal lands, since several pioneer families—and even the horse concessioner in the 1930s—left some of their stock to go feral.

27. MEVE-SMR 1956-10, 6.

28. MEVE. 1963-05 Master Plan [draft?], 5 [RG01-02.03-005].

29. For porcupines, see MEVE-SMR 1958-03, 3. For thirty pounds, see MEVE-SMR 1959-10, 8. For spraying, see MEVE-SMR 1959-05, 9 For "no spraying," see MEVE-SM 1964-01-21, 3.

30. National Academy of Sciences—National Research Council, *A Report by the Advisory Committee to the National Park Service on Research*, August 1963, 1, http://npshistory.com/publications/robbins.pdf (last accessed 2024-07-05).

The report was so harsh in its criticism that Director Wirth considered suppressing it. (Sellars, *Nature*, 216).

31. A. S. Leopold (Chairman), S. A. Cain, C. M. Cottam, I. N. Gabrielson, T. L. Kimball, *Wildlife Management in the National Parks*, March 4, 1963. Reprint from Administrative Policies for Natural Areas of the National Park System, U.S. Department of the Interior, National Park Service, Washington, DC: U.S.

Government Printing Office, 1969 ("full jurisdiction," 7; "vignette," 3), http://npshistory.com/publications/leopold_report.pdf (last accessed 2024-07-05).

32. For "the condition," see Leopold et al., *Wildlife Management in the National Parks*, 3. For more on ignoring Indigenous effects, see Sellars, *Nature*, 214.

33. For reference to exotics, see Leopold et al., *Wildlife Management in the National Parks*, 4–5. For Yosemite Conference, see A. Starker Leopold, "Wildlife Management in the Future," December 1963, http://npshistory.com/publications/wildlife/leopold-1963.pdf (last accessed 2024-07-05). For fifty years later, see Chad P. Dawson, Ken Cordell, Alan E. Watson, Ramesh Ghimire, and Gary T. Green, "The US Wilderness Managers Survey: Charting a Path for the Future," in *Journal of Forestry* 114, no. 3 (May 2016): 301.

34. For extent of manipulations, see Leopold et al., *Wildlife Management in the National Parks*, 9–13; and Leopold, "Wildlife Management in the Future," 2–10. For "limited knowledge," see Leopold, "Wildlife Management in the Future," 12. For "we can build it," see Leopold, "Wildlife Management in the Future," 5. For "With respect," see Frank E. Egler, *The Nature of Vegetation, Its Management and Mismanagement: An Introduction to Vegetation Science* (Norfolk, CT: Connecticut Conservation Association, 1977), 2.

35. Howard Zahniser, "Guardians Not Gardeners," *Living Wilderness* 83 (Spring / Summer 1963): 2.

36. MEVE. 1963-05 Master Plan [draft?], 16.

It is important to recognize that there were essentially no "wild lands" on the mesa at the time the Ancestral Puebloans left—circa 1300—as it had been extensively modified over centuries by the people living there. It is inconceivable that the plan's author thought the "vignette" at the time of Ancestral Puebloan occupation looked the same as the "vignette" that appeared to the Wetherill brothers. It is not clear from this plan whether the writer(s) did not understand the concept of "wildness," or somehow believed that manipulations by Native Americans didn't count since they weren't considered in Starker Leopold's "vignette of primitive America."

37. Thomas, 1964-06-15 memo to Regional Director—re: Statement of Management Principles, 2 [RG01-02.01-061].

38. For "entire," see MEVE. 1958-12 Master Plan Development Outline, 3 [RG01-02.03-005]. For "outbreak," see MEVE-SAR 1957, 15.

39. For visitation totals, see Smith, *Shadows*, App. B. For "If visitation continues," see MEVE-SM 1959-04-07.

40. MEVE-PB 1954, 13.

41. MEVE-PB 1958.

42. Mesa Verde Company, "Park Brochure" (1961).

43. MEVE Park Archeologist, 1957-05-24 memo to Superintendent—re: Information for Annual Report, 6 [RG01-02.01-001].

44. For "demand" and "Hiking, riding," see MEVE, 1958-12 Master Plan

Development Outline, 15, 20–21. For authorized, see MEVE-SM 1959-04-21, 2.

45. Carr, *M66*, 85–88.

46. MEVE, Draft Master Plan for the Preservation and Use of Mesa Verde National Park (1961), 2:4; 3:16 [RG01-02.03-005].
Presumably, the plan meant Point Lookout. Nevertheless, that would be an odd terminus without some sort of trailhead area, difficult to construct at that location (known as Windy Point). Ending the trail at the Morefield Campground would make more sense—once it was completed.

47. MEVE-SM 1962-03-06, 2.

The minutes offer no explanation of why it took thirteen months from the time of Kennedy's speech for the MEVE staff to discuss it. Nor do they make any mention of Kennedy's endorsement of a wilderness bill during that speech (Allin, 123).

48. MEVE-SMR 1964-07, 7.

49. MEVE Park Archeologist, 1957-05-24 Memo, 6.

50. MEVE Park Archeologist, 1957 Memo to Superintendent re: Material for ['1957' written by hand] Annual Report [RG01-02.01-001].

51. MEVE-SMR 1960-02, 4.

52. For more on ORRRC and its relationship with the NPS, see Foresta, 62–65. For "87.8 miles," MEVE, 1960 Outdoor Recreation Resources Review Commission Response [RG-01-02.07-084]. (For the 1962 ORRRC Report recommending a wilderness bill, see Allin, 3, 125, 129–30.)

53. MEVE-SMR 1963-09, 5; MEVE-SMR 1963-11, 7.

54. MEVE, 1963-07-29 Roads and Trails Systems As Maintained [RG01-02.03-079].

The inventory lists a total of 64.3 miles "graded" and 7.52 miles "surfaced." There are some apparent errors in classification—both the Petroglyph Point Trail and the Mummy House Trail (from Cliff Palace, across the head of Cliff Canyon, around Sun Temple's promontory, and up Fewkes Canyon) are listed in the "surfaced" category. The secondary route down Moccasin Mesa is shown entirely within the park, as is the trail at the end of that road into Soda Canyon, repeating the mistakes of the 1949 and 1954 maps, though Whites Trail down the East Rim to the Mancos River was not shown on the 1963 map.

55. For "Permit," see MEVE, 1963-05 Master Plan [draft?], 1:15. For "legitimate," see 1:13. For "greater opportunity," see MEVE, 1964-07 Master Plan, Area Objectives, 2:4 [RG01-02.03-005.3].

56. MEVE-SMR 1963-05, 5–6.

57. Carr, *M66*, 11–12, 123.

58. For "A Bill," see U.S. Senate, 1956. *S. 4013 (84th Congress, 2nd Sess.)*. For Zahniser, see Doug Scott, *The Enduring Wilderness: protecting our natural heritage* (Golden, CO: Fulcrum, 2004), 47–49. For "The Congress," see *S. 4013*, 2; for "untrammeled," see 3; for "Within," see 14–15.

59. For "Mesa Verde," see *S. 4013*, 7; for "except," 3.

60. See, for instance, Allin, 110–11; Foresta, 69; Ise, 650; Nash, 226; Runte, 241–43.

61. For wilderness as threat, see Sellars, *Nature*, 149. For concessioners, see Runte, 241. For "inclusion" and "a road," see Allin, 110–11. For "never," see John C. Miles, *Wilderness in National Parks: Playground or Preserve* (Seattle: University of Washington Press, 2009), 129.

62. For Gilligan, see Allin, 103. For Brower, see John McPhee, *Encounters with the Archdruid* (New York: Farrar, Straus, and Giroux, 1971), 71. For Zahniser, see Miles, *Wilderness in National Parks*, 143.

63. NPS, *The National Park Wilderness* (Washington, DC: National Park Service, 1957) [hereafter *NPW*].

64. NPW ("most treasured," 29; "Man," 33; "fundamental," 9).

65. NPW ("All," 9; "thinking" and "inspired," 12; "reflects," 22; "began," 21; "Even," 22).

66. NPW ("special kind," 10; "like minerals," 14; "undamaged," 15; "numerous," 18; "good protection" and "complete," 20).

67. NPW ("discarding," 10; "inseparably" and "imperil," 14).

68. NPW sideboards, 19.

69. NPW, 28.

70. Nash, 209–19. For the definitive treatment of the fight over the dam, see Mark Harvey, *A Symbol of Wilderness: Echo Park and the American Conservation Movement* (Albuquerque: University of New Mexico Press, 1994).

71. MEVE-SM 1959-04-21, 2.

72. MEVE-SM 1959-12-15, 1–2.

73. For "Mission 66," see Foresta, 67; for "Horatius," 68.

It seems John Carver, Udall's abrasive Assistant Secretary, was tasked with driving Wirth to resign. Wirth had been proud of the Tioga Road across Yosemite. It skirted the shore of Tenaya Lake, and so was particularly excoriated by conservationists, led by photographer Ansel Adams (who castigated the "bulldozers of bureaucracy") and David Brower (who argued for a "Mission *76*" to undo all the damage of Mission 66). Carver presided at the dedication ceremony in June 1961. With Wirth present, Carver noted "I am tempted to treat my delicate task as did the politician called to comment on the unlovely child. 'Say,' he exclaims, 'that <u>is</u> a baby.' For it is a fact, for good or ill, that here there <u>is</u> a road." (For Adams and Brower, see Sellars, *Nature*, 188–90. For Carver, see Carr, *M66*, 283).

74. Foresta, 71.

Chapter Seven

1. Smith, *Shadows*, 208. The ellipsis was made by Smith.
2. For subservience of NPS scientists, see Sellars, *Nature*, 219–235.

3. For "seriously over-browsed," see MEVE-SMR 1965-09, 5. For "so that it assumes," see MEVE, 1965-11 Master Plan, Chapter 3, Management Programs Narrative, 5 [RG01-02.03-005]. For trying to get approval, see MEVE-SMR 1965-12, 3.

4. For "direct measures" and claims by Woodward, see MEVE-SMR 1966-04, 5. For "emotional protesters," see Smith, *Shadows*, 177. For deferred, see MEVE-SAR 1966, 4.

5. Smith, *Shadows*, 177.

6. 278 U.S. 96.

In this case, the State of Arizona tried to claim ownership of deer that the U.S. Forest Service wanted to kill. The Court ruled that "The power of the United States to thus protect its lands and property does not admit of doubt, the game laws or any other statute of the state to the contrary notwithstanding" (278 U.S. 96, at 100; internal citations omitted). See also "The Nusbaum Decade," endnote 20.

7. MEVE-SM 1967-05-02, 4.

8. For tagging, see MEVE-SMR 1967-02, 4. For exclosures, see MEVE-SMR 1967-05. For overflights, see MEVE-SM 1970-02-24, 5.

9. Smith, *Shadows*, 177.

10. For national priorities, see Sellars, *Nature*, 223. For "to prevent serious," see MEVE, 1965-11 Master Plan, 41. For fire data and "protection zone," see MEVE, 1969-03 Master Plan, 3rd Draft, 18 [RG01-02.03-012].

11. MEVE, 1965-11 Master Plan, 41, 44.

12. Guillet, 1968-11-22 letter to Frank E. Kurczewski, Assistant Professor, College of Forestry, Syracuse University [RG01-02.08-044.1].

13. MEVE-SMR 1966-11, 5.

14. Guillet, 1969-08-14 memo to Regional Director—re: Management Objectives, MEVE, 6 [RG01-02.03-005.11].

15. For "non-native flora," see Guillet, 1969-08-14 memo, 6. For "would be impractical," see MEVE 1965-11 Master Plan, 3. For intentionally planted, see MEVE-SMR 1964-11, 5 and MEVE-SM 1967-10-04, 9. For "After planting," see MEVE-SAR 2005, 86.

16. For prior to Indigenous, see J. A. Erdman, C. L. Douglas, and J. W. Marr, *Environment of Mesa Verde, Colorado* (Washington, DC: USDI, NPS, 1969), 18. For "Actually," see Jean M. Pinkley (Mrs.), 1966-03-28 letter from Chief Park Archeologist—to Richard J. Hartesveldt, Assoc. Professor of Conservation, San Jose State College [RG01-02.01-073].

17. For "sizeable portions," see Donald A. Purse, 1972-05-23 Planning Directive for MEVE, 5 [RG01-02.03-005.13]. For "must have resulted," see Alden C. Hayes, *The Archeological Survey of Wetherill Mesa, MEVE; Archeological Research Series No. 7-A* (Washington, DC: USDI, NPS, 1964), 109. For "with scenes" and

"coiled pottery," see G. Douglas Nadean, 1973-12-21 memo on behalf of Donald A. Purse, Team Manager, Midwest Team, DSC—to Regional Director—re: MEVE Master Plan, 9 [RG01-02.03-011.1].

18. MEVE, 1974-01-24 Management Objectives—A Statement for Management and Planning, 11 [RG01-02.03-011.2].

19. Sellars, *Nature*, 255–261.

20. For "the restoration," see J. Leonard Volz, 1972-07-14 memo from Regional Director—to Director, Denver Service Center—re: Planning Directive, MEVE [RG01-02.03-005.13]. For "Although," see Switzer, 1974-01-15 memo to Regional Director—re: Concurrent Review of Document: Master Plan Concepts, MEVE [RG01-02.03-011.1]. For "initiate control," see MEVE, 1974-01-24 Management Objectives—A Statement for Management and Planning, 9 [RG01-02.03-011.2].

21. For "Maintain areas," see MEVE, 1974-01-24 Management Objectives, 11. For fire as a management tool, see Donald A. Purse, 1974-02-13 memo from Team Manager, Midwest and Rocky Mountain Teams, DSC—to Regional Director—re: Resource Basic Inventory Requirements [RG01-02.03-011.2]. For Two years later, see Switzer, 1976-02-11 memo to Regional Director—re: Planning Requirements [RG01-02.03-005].

22. Andrea J. Sharon, "Wetherill Mesa Horse Study" (December 30, 1976) [RG03-05.03-001].

23. Ibid., 59–60.

24. For "an ideal location," see Guillet, 1967-11-03 memo to Chief, Office of Resource and Planning, SSC—re: Master Plan, MEVE, 21 [RG01-02.03-005.11]. For opposition, see George W. Miller, 1967-11-13 memo from Acting Regional Director—to Chief, RP, SSC—re: Master Plan, MEVE [RG01-02.03-005.11].

25. Frank F. Kowski, 1969-01-16 Memo from Regional Director—to Director, through Chief, Division of Land and Water Rights—re: Legislative Program-91st Congress, First Session [RG01-02.10-006.1]. For over fifteen, see MEVE, 1985-02-25 Draft Land Protection Plan, 1 [RG01-02.07-013.1] For grazing termination, see MEVE-SAR 1998, 37.

26. MEVE-SAR 1966, 4.

27. Deputy Chief DCSSC, 1967-08-24 memo to Chief, Design & Construction, SSC—re: Mesa Verde Planning Study, 1–2 [RG01-02.03-005.13].

This was neither the earliest, nor most egregious, tram proposal in the National Parks. In the 1920s, Horace Albright, who was to become the second Director of the NPS, proposed one across the Grand Canyon to enhance public enjoyment (Sellars, *Nature*, 63).

28. Clarkson Engineering "Report on Wetherill Mesa Transportation Needs, MEVE, Colorado" (1968). [RG01-02.01-087.1]

29. For mini-train route, see MEVE, 1969 Master Plan, 3rd Draft, 28–29. For "astronomical," see Switzer, 1973-03-09 memo to Regional Director—re: Opening Wetherill Mesa for Visitation [RG01-02.03-011.1]. For "Disneyland-ish," see Kathleen Fiero, *Dirt, Water, Stone: a century of preserving Mesa Verde* (Durango: Durango Herald Small Press, 2006), 154.

Archaeologist Florence Lister went so far as to suggest the mini-train "would help maintain a welcome wilderness ambience." See Florence C. Lister, *Troweling Through Time: The First Century of Mesa Verdean Archaeology* (Albuquerque: University of New Mexico Press, 2004), 122.

30. For a road from the south, see Guillet, 1967-01-13 memo to Regional Director—re: South Approach to MEVE over Ute Lands [RG01-02.01-040]. For a tram from the south, see Guillet, 1968-09-17 memo to Regional Director—re: Report of Trip on Ute Reservation, August 26–27, 1968 [RG01-02.01-040].

31. For "a ride," see William E. Stroud, 1970-03-11 letter to Guillet [RG01-02.03-005.13]. For "should we ever," see Guillet, 1970-11-04 Memo to Regional Director—re: Proposed aerial tram [RG01-02.03-005.13].

32. Purse, 1972-05-23 Planning Directive, 2 [RG01-02.03-005.13].

33. John E. Goss, 1972-08-15 letter from President, Wankanta Lift Co.—to National Park Service [RG01-02.03-011.1].

34. Switzer, 1972-12-15 memo to Regional Director—re: Review of Master Planning Directive, MEVE, 1 [RG01-02.03-010.1].

35. For pressuring, see Peter H. Dominick, 1973-09-07 letter from U. S. Senator Dominick—to Rogers C.B. Morton, Secretary, USDI [RG01-02.03-011.1]. For "drastic change," see Ernest Allan Connally, 1973-09-20 letter from Associate Director, NPS—to Senator Peter H. Dominick [RG01-02.03-011.1].

36. For trail plans, see Thomas, 1964-01-28 memo to Chief, WODC—re: Advance Prints, Revised Roads and Trail, Part of the Master Plan, MEVE, 3 [RG01-02.03-037]. For scout out, see MEVE-SM 1964-09-15.

37. For "Several new trails," see MEVE-SMR 1966-06, 6. For "This project," see MEVE Interpretation Division, 1966 Calendar Year Highlight Briefing Statement [RG01-02.01-19].

38. William C. Winkler, in Duane A Smith and William C Winkler, *Travels and Travails: Tourism at Mesa Verde* (Durango, Colorado: Durango Herald Small Press, 2005), 160–61.

39. Emmett & Frances Koppenhafer, 1972-06-15 letter from MV Pack and Saddle—to Superintendent.

40. For "the Park Service decided," see Winkler, 161. For officially terminated, see Lynn H. Thompson, 1976-08-04 memo from Regional Director—to Associate Director, Legislation, WASO—re: Statement for Management, MEVE [RG01-02.02-013].

41. Smith, *Shadows*, 169.

42. MEVE, 1965-11 Master Plan, Chapter 3 ("Controlled use" 8; "people

wandering" through "must be restricted" 19–20; "With visitor use" 35) [RG01-02.03-005].

43. Ibid., additional sites 41; "It may be" 38; "reconstructed" 8.

44. Manitou Springs, a quasi-replica of a Mesa Verde-style cliff dwelling, was built near Pikes Peak in 1907. As of 2024, the tourist attraction still advertised itself as "cliff dwellings over 800 years old" (Visit Colorado Springs, website: visitcos.com/directory/manitou-cliff-dwellings/, last visited 2024-07-05).

45. For "distinct reluctance," see Jean M. Pinkley (Mrs.), 1966-03-28 letter to Richard J. Hartesveldt [RG01-21.01-073]. For "another area," see MEVE-SM 1967-06-20, 4.

46. Freeman Tilden, *Interpreting Our Heritage* (Chapel Hill: The University of North Carolina Press, 1957).

47. Kathleen Fine, 1988. "The Politics of 'Interpretation' at Mesa Verde National Park." *Anthropological Quarterly* 61 no.4 (October 1988):180.

48. Kenneth L. Nyberg, "Some Radical Comments on Interpretation: a little heresy is good for the soul," in *On Interpretation,* G. E. Machlis and D. R. Field, eds. (Corvallis: Oregon State University Press, 1984), 151.

49. For admitted, see Pinkley 1966-03-28 letter to Richard J. Hartesveldt. For Thomas's view, see Thomas, 1966-10-10 letter from Southwest Archeological Center—to Herb Evison [RG01-21.01-073].

50. For "November 15," see MEVE-SM 1971-12-01, 4. For "Written warning," see MEVE-SM 1968-02-01, 5. For "Four beatniks," see MEVE-SMR 1967-02, 3.

51. For "Backcountry use," see Guillet, 1969-08-14 memo to Regional Director—re: Management Objectives, MEVE, 4 [RG01-02.03-11]. For "fragile nature," see MEVE 1969-03 Master Plan, 3rd Draft, 13.

52. Paul Williamson, 1970-12-09 letter from President, Cortez Chamber of Commerce—to Superintendent [RG01-02.03-005.13].

53. See, for instance, Purse, 1972-05-23 Planning Directive, 3 [RG01-02.03-005.13].

54. For "The chance," see MEVE Interpretation Division. 1972-06-02 Comments on Design Directive [RG01-02.03-005.13]. For "a ten-minute color film," see Gilbert R. Wenger, 1972-12-14 memo from Chief Archeologist—to Superintendent—re: Review of Planning Directive, MEVE [RG01-02.03-010.1].

55. Switzer, 1972-12-15 memo re: Review of Master Planning Directive, 2 [RG01-02.03-010.1].

56. Frederick C. Babb, 1973-11-26 memo from Team Captain, MEVE Master Plan, DSC—to Superintendent—re: Management Objectives for MEVE. ("Currently" 1; "Make more" 2; "Study" 7) [RG01-02.03-010.1].

57. MEVE-SAR 1965, 4.

58. Jean M. Pinkley (Mrs.), 1965-06-10 letter from Chief Park Archeologist—to Estella B. Leopold, USGS Paleontology and Stratigraphy Branch [RG01-02.08-044.2].

59. George B. Hartzog, 1966-06-23 letter from Director, NPS—to Scott

Jacket, Chairman, Ute Mountain Tribal Council, 2–3 [RG01 02.01 041.1].

60. For Every effort, see MEVE-SMR 1965-09, 6. For Utes would get, see MEVE-SM 1965-11-16.

61. For announced their intention, see MEVE-SM 1965-12-07. For "this development," see MEVE-SM 1966-01-04.

62. For invitation to bid, see MEVE-SM 1967-01-10, 2. For minutes of the Ute Council meeting, see Charles J. Traylor, 1967-10-09 letter from Traylor, Kladder, Harshman & Palo, Attorneys at Law—to Meredith Guillet [RG01-02.01-040].

63. For proposing, see Guillet, 1967-10-20 letter to Wade Dillon, General Counsel, Ute Mountain Tribe [RG01-02.07-027]. For "Rather," see George W. Miller, 1967-11-24 memo from Assistant Regional Director—to Director, NPS [RG01-02.07-027].

64. Guillet, 1968-03-05 memo to Regional Director—re: Exploration and possible development of Ute lands [RG01-02.01-040].

65. For "nominal archeological resources," see MEVE 1969-03 Master Plan, 3rd Draft, 32. For Park Superintendent to Ute Agency Superintendent, see Guillet, 1969-09-16 letter to Espeedie Ruiz, Superintendent, Ute Mountain Ute Agency [RG01-02.07-017.7]. For especially valuable, see Gilbert R. Wenger, 1969-09-17 memo from Chief Park Archeologist—to Superintendent—re: Evaluation of Archeological Ruins on Ute Mountain Ute Lands [RG01-02.07-017.7.]

66. MEVE 1969-03 Master Plan, 3rd Draft.

67. MEVE-SMR 1966-06, 3.

68. Robert H. Lister, 1969-08-29 letter to Superintendent [RG01-02.01-040].

Chapter Eight

1. Doug Scott, "The Wilderness Act at Forty: Looking Back, Looking Ahead." *International Journal of Wilderness* 10, no. 1 (April 2004): 8–14.

2. WAct, Sec. 3(c).

3. MEVE-SMR 1965-08, 7.

4. MEVE, 1965-11 Master Plan, chapter 3 ("The land itself," 19; "evident," etc., 36–37).

5. Jean M. Pinkley (Mrs.), 1966-03-28 letter to Richard J. Hartesveldt [RG01-02.01-073].

6. Theodore R. Swem, 1966-11-22 memo from Assistant Director, Cooperative Activities—to Superintendent [RG03-01.05-001].

7. For guidance, see Theodore R. Swem, 1967-12-04 memo from Assistant Director, Cooperative Activities—to Chiefs, Office of Resource Planning [RG03-01.05-001]. For "I want to urge," see R. B. Marshall, "Park Administration," *Proceedings of the National Park Conference Held at the Yellowstone National Park,*

September 11 and 12, 1911 (Washington: Government Printing Office, 1912). https://www.nps.gov/parkhistory/online_books/npc/proceedings-npc1/sec3.htm (last accessed 2024-07-05).

8. Raymond L. Freeman, 1967-12-19 memo from Acting AD, CA—to Regional Directors [RG03-01.05-001].

9. Frank F. Kowski, 1967-12-27 memo from Regional Director—to Regional Superintendents [RG03-01.05-001].

10. Guillet, 1968-01-12 memo to Regional Director [RG03-01.05-001].

11. Frank F. Kowski, 1968-01-24 memo from Regional Director—to Superintendent [RG03-01.05-001].

12. For "Work has begun," see MEVE-SM 1968-03-05, 5. For use of master planning, see Laura A. Kirn, "A Case for Storied Landscapes: Wilderness and Historic Preservation" (master's thesis, Goucher College, 2013), 69.

13. Robert S. Luntey, 1968-08-27 memo from Chief, Office of Resource Planning, SSC—to Assistant Director, Cooperative Activities—re: Master Plan and Wilderness Proposal-MEVE, 2–3 [RG03-01.05-001].

14. Ibid.

15. James M. Eden, 1968-09-09 memo from Acting Regional Director—to Director—re: Master Plan and Wilderness Proposals, MEVE [RG01-02.03-005].

16. For postponement, see MEVE-SM 1968-10-29, 6. For receiving the protection, see John Lavin, 1968-10-31 letter from Chairman, Natural Area Committee, SAF—to Superintendent [RG03-01.05-001]. For MEVE response, see Guillet, 1968-11-08 letter to John Lavin, Chairman, Natural Area Committee, Society of American Foresters [RG03-01.05-001]. For "There have been little," see Switzer, 1976-06-07 letter to Nick Van Pelt, Department of Geography, University of Utah [RG01-02.07-086.2].

The idea of setting aside a portion of a national park for research and to be "unvisited and undisturbed" by visitors dated back over thirty years—to biologist Lowell Sumner's plan for Titus Canyon in Death Valley. It was a recommendation that apparently was ignored (Sellars, *Nature*, 103).

17. For "Hiking is permitted," see NPS, 1969-04-18 *Federal Register* Notice—34 Fed. Reg. 6660—"Protection of Prehistoric Ruins and Visitors—proposed revision to §7.39 of Title 36." For Final Rule, see NPS, 1971-10-23 *Federal Register* Notice—36 Fed. Reg. 20511—"Protection of Prehistoric Ruins and Visitors, Commercial Automobiles and Buses, and Hiking, Mesa Verde National Park."

18. MEVE-SM 1969-01-07.

19. MEVE, 1969-03 Master Plan, 3rd Draft ("constant," 4; "importation" and "urgent need," 20) [RG01-02.03-012].

20. Robert S. Luntey, 1969-04-16 memo from Chief, Office of Resource Planning—to Assistant Director, Cooperative Activities [RG03-01.05-001].

21. Guillet, 1969-08-14 memo to Regional Director—re: Management Objectives, MEVE, 6 [RG01-02.03-005.13].

22. "Cherry-stemmed" is a Wilderness boundary term-of-art. Since roads are illegal in Wilderness, if a road is a dead-end (i.e., does not go all the way through the Wilderness), the boundary may then be drawn up one side of the road, around the end, and down the other side. Frequently, what is at the end of the road (a helipad, stock tank, etc.) is the purpose of the road—the "cherry,"—and the road is the cherry's "stem."

23. For "prime theme," see USDI-NPS, *National Park Service Plan: Part One—History* (Washington, DC: U.S. Government Printing Office, 1972), 3. For natural history themes, see USDI-NPS, *National Park Service Plan: Part Two—Natural History* (Washington, DC: U.S. Government Printing Office, 1972), 13–14, 19, 46.

24. F. Ross Holland Jr., "The Park Service as Curator," (1979; repr. in *National Parks in Crisis*, ed. Eugenia Horstman Connally, Washington DC: National Parks & Conservation Association, 1982), 128–130.

25. NPS, 1970-05 Wilderness Suitability Report for MEVE (preliminary), 1 [RG03-01.05-003].

26. For "In making," see 1970-09 Wilderness Suitability Report for MEVE (preliminary), aa-bb [RG03-01.05-003]. For "The purposes," see WAct, Sec. 4(a).

27. 1970-09 Wilderness Suitability Report, bb.

28. Grazing is allowed only to "continue" (WAct, Sec. 4(d)(4)(2)); new mineral exploration was generally allowed only until December 31, 1983 (WAct Sec. 4(d)(3)).

29. 1970-09 Wilderness Suitability Report, cc.

30. For agreement, see Robert Kasparek, 1970-10-02 memo from Park Planner—to Deputy Director, Legislative & Cooperative Programs—re: Meeting with staff members of Senate Committee on Insular Affairs, and of Colorado Delegation [RG03-01.05-002]. For Federal Register, see NPS, 1970-10-17 FR Notice—"Nonsuitability as Wilderness; Hearing." *Federal Register*. 35 Fed. Reg. p. 16326.

In general, public hearings tend to be local, as was the case of the Mesa Verde Wilderness Hearing in Cortez. George Marshall (brother of Bob), who was serving as President of the Sierra Club as the Park Service wilderness hearings got underway, argued that local hearings are "symbolic of an essentially wrong approach to wilderness—that the opinion of those living close to it is more important [than the other Americans] to whom the wilderness areas belong." Quoted in Adam M. Sowards, *An Open Pit Visible from the Moon: The Wilderness Act and the Fight to Protect Miners Ridge and the Public Interest* (Norman: University of Oklahoma Press, 2020), 122.

31. David A. Breternitz, 1970-10-23 letter to John McComb [RG01-02.07-002].

32. For "increasing population," see WAct, Sec. 2(a). For votes, see Allin, 131, 135.

33. David A. Breternitz, 1970-10-27 letter from Director, CU-MEVE Research Center—to Gilbert R. Wenger, Chief Park Archeologist [RG06-01.01-003].

34. NPS, 1970-12-16 Nonsuitability as Wilderness Hearing transcript, 9–13 [RG03-01.05-002].

35. For Commissioner's comments, see transcript, 16. For pressure to hunt in other national parks, see Sellars, *Nature*, 195–201.

36. Transcript, 17–18.

37. Ibid., 18.

38. Ibid., 30–31.

39. Ibid., 21–23.

40. Ibid., 24.

41. Ibid., ("in no way," 29; "Since stabilization," 34; "There are many," 39).

42. Ibid., (To much of the public," 36; "Should the Park Service," 42–43; "Here, in an area," 33).

43. WAct, Sec. 2(c)(2).

44. NPS, 1970-12-16 Nonsuitability as Wilderness Hearing transcript ("An informal approach," 48; "I would like," 52).

45. Guillet, 1971-03-29 memo to Regional Director—re: MEVE Master Plan Hearing, December 16, 1970, Question and Answer Period, 11–12 [RG03-01.05-002].

46. Ibid., 12.

47. For the original count and then the count submitted by MEVE, see Guillet, 1971-01-19 memo to Regional Director—re: Wilderness Hearings, MEVE, December 16, 1970 [RG03-01.05-002]. For the "official" count, see NPS, 1971-09 Wilderness Recommendations for MEVE, 22 [RG03-01.05-003].

48. Division Chief, 1971-07-28 memo from WO Division Chief for Legislative Coordination & Support—to Director—through Deputy Director, Legislation [RG03-01.05-002].

49. Guillet, 1971-07-23 letter to Robert H. Lister, Chaco Canyon Research Center, University of New Mexico [RG03-01.05-002].

50. NPS, 1971-09 Wilderness Recommendations for MEVE, 4.

51. Ibid., 14.

52. WAct, Sec. 4(c).

53. MEVE, 1972-02-11 Draft Environmental Impact Statement MEVE Wilderness Proposal—forwarded to Regional Director by Superintendent, 4 [RG03-01.05-003].

54. Ibid., 2, 6, 7, 8, 10.

55. Ibid., 6–8.

56. Ibid., ("based on the premise," 9; "the public response" and "what is believed," 1).

57. Ibid., 11.

58. NPS, 1971-09 Wilderness Recommendations for MEVE, 20–33.

59. MEVE, 1972-02-11 DEIS MEVE Wilderness Proposal, 8.

60. Nathaniel P. Reed, "Secretarial Order 2920" (June 24, 1972).

61. For recommendation, see Thomas F. Flynn, 1972-03-06 memo from Acting Director—to Legislative Counsel, through Assistant Secretary for Fish, Wildlife, and Parks—re: Wilderness recommendations, MEVE [RG03-01.05-002]. For planning directive, see Donald A. Purse, 1972-05-23 Planning Directive [RG1-02.03-005.13]. For map, see NPS, 1972-09 Wilderness Recommendation for MEVE [RG03-01.05-003].

62. For draft bill, see Associate Director, 1973-01-05 memo from Associate Director, NPS—to Legislative Council—through Assistant Secretary—re: Wilderness Recommendations [RG01-02.07-086.1]. For "unresolved," "Archeological research," and "These units," see Associate Director, 1973-01-15 memo from Associate Director, Legislation—to Regional Director—re: Mesa Verde Wilderness [RG03-01.05-004].

63. David A. Breternitz, 1973-04-23 letter to Ronald R. Switzer, Superintendent [RG01-02.07-002].

64. Stephen H. Hart, 1973-06-26 letter from Colorado Historic Preservation Officer—to J. L. Dunning, Colorado State Director, NPS—re: Wilderness proposal, MEVE [RG03-01.05-004].

65. For "Predominantly surface,' see David A. Breternitz, 1973-07-28 letter from Director, Mesa Verde Research Center—to Stephen Hart, State Liason Officer, Colorado State Historical Society [RG01-02.07-002]. For wilderness portion, see David A. Breternitz, 1973-11-13 letter from Director, Mesa Verde Research Center—to Dr. Wilfred D. Logan, NPS, Denver Service Center [RG06-02.01-010].

66. Jack E. Smith, 1974-03, "Summary of the 1973 Season of the Mesa Verde Archaeological Survey." [RG06-05.01-004].

67. For "Very large pueblos," see Smith, "Summary of the 1973 Season." For consequence of wide canyons, see Smith, *Mesas*, 31–32.

68. Smith, *Mesas* ("No doubt" and "is often sparse" 62; most of the sites, 52–57). For correlation between the Mesa Verde phases and the Pecos classification, see Alden C. Hayes, *The Archeological Survey of Wetherill Mesa, MEVE; Archeological Research Series No. 7-A* (Washington, DC: USDI, NPS, 1964), 88.

69. J. Leonard Volz, 1973-09-20 letter from Regional Director—to Robert Garvey, Executive Secretary, Advisory Council on Historic Preservation [RG01-02.07-002].

70. USDI, 1973-11-27 Transmittal Letter from the Secretary of the Interior—to the President [RG03-01.05-004].

71. See Martin Nie, Christopher Barns, Jonathan Haber, Julie Jolie, Kenneth Pitt, and Sandi Zellmer, "Fish and Wildlife Management on Federal Lands: Debunking State Supremacy," *Environmental Law* 47, no. 4 (2017): 888–93.

72. For "severely handicap," see Ann Webster Smith, 1973-12-18 letter from Director, Office of Compliance, Advisory Council on Historic Preservation—to

J. Leonard Volz, Regional Director [RG03-01.05-004]. For "We understand," see Merrill D. Beal, 1974-01-14 letter from Acting Regional Director to Robert Garvey, Executive Secretary, Advisory Council on Historic Preservation [RG03-01.05-004].

73. Ann Webster Smith, 1974-03-14 (rec'd.—undated sent) from Director, Office of Compliance, Advisory Council on Historic Preservation—to Merrill D. Beal, Acting Regional Director [RG03-01.05-004].

74. Merrill D. Beal, 1974-01-02 memo from Acting Regional Director—to Assistant Director, Development—re: Wilderness Act, Protection and Preservation of Archeological Resources [RG03-01.05-004].

75. MEVE, 1974-01-24 Management Objectives—A Statement for Management and Planning ("Backcountry use" 3; "Study" 10) [RG01-02.03-011.2].

76. Switzer, 1974-02-04 memo to Division Chiefs, MEVE—re: Management Objectives [RG01-02.03-011.2].

77. Switzer, 1974-02-27 memo to Chief, Wilderness Studies—re: Statement of Important Issue, MEVE Wilderness, 1 [RG03-01.05-004].

78. Ibid., 2.

79. Ibid., 3.

80. Ibid., 4–5.

81. Ibid., 5.

82. Public Law 93-632, Sec. 2(c).

83. Nash, 203.

84. Switzer, 1974-02-27 memo, 5–6.

85. Ibid., 6–7.

86. Ibid., 8.

87. Ronald H. Walker, and Ronald R. Switzer, "Statements of the Director and Superintendent before the Subcommittee on National Parks and Recreation, House Committee on Interior and Insular Affairs on H. R. 13562 and H. R. 13563" (March 22, 1974): 5 [RG03-01.05-004].

88. Ibid., 7.

It is not clear why the testimony for the two important NPS cultural units in this legislation had such different opinions on potential wilderness designation. Bandelier was designated for a similar purpose as Mesa Verde. Proclamation 1322, February 11, 1916, designated the Monument to preserve "certain prehistoric aboriginal ruins . . . of unusual ethnologic, scientific, and educational interest . . . with as much land as may be necessary for the proper protection thereof." The area of Bandelier is similarly important to various Puebloan people and is believed to have been populated even more recently than Mesa Verde (https://www.nps.gov/band/learn/historyculture/ancestral-pueblo-people.htm (last visited 2024-07-05)). Perhaps the material difference was the Superintendents themselves. Despite Regional Director Kowski's memo (1968-01-24 [RG03-01.05-001]) to Superintendent Guillet informing him that the decision on whether Wilderness would be designated in Mesa Verde was not either of theirs, Park Superintendents wielded a tremendous amount of power. Guillet would do whatever he could to forestall designation in "his" Park, and Switzer, as far as he was able—temperamentally or politically—would attempt to follow suit.

89. MEVE, 1974 Final Environmental Impact Statement [FEIS]—Proposed Mesa Verde National Park Wilderness [RG03-01.05-004].

90. Ibid., 3.

91. Ibid., ("Public use," "No public use," and "Once permitted,"3; "Wilderness areas," 4; "If public," 27).

92. MEVE, 1976-12. Mesa Verde Wilderness—Description of Boundaries as Designated by Public Law 94-567 [RG03-01.05-004].

93. FEIS, 7.

94. David A. Breternitz, 1973-07-28 letter from Director, Mesa Verde Research Center—to Stephen Hart, State Liaison Officer, Colorado State Historical Society [RG0-02.07-002].

95. FEIS, 13.

96. Smith, *Mesas*, 58–59.

97. FEIS ("100 or more" 7; "80 per" 23; "many pithouse villages" 13).

98. Smith, *Mesas*, 65–77.

99. Breternitz, 1973-07-28 letter to Stephen Hart.

100. FEIS, 43.

101. FEIS ("prehistoric agricultural" 18; for other examples see 17–18, 22–24, 30–31).

102. FEIS, 21.

103. FEIS, 21.

104. FEIS, 23.

105. FEIS, 21.

106. FEIS, 24.

107. FEIS, 22, 24.

108. FEIS, 25.

109. WAct, Sec. 4(a).

110. FEIS, 25–6.

111. FEIS, 27.

112. FEIS, 26.

113. FEIS, 26.

114. FEIS, 30.

115. WAct, ("as necessary" Sec. 4(c); "historical value" Sec. 2(c)(4)).

116. FEIS, 32.

117. FEIS, 33.

118. FEIS, 34.

119. WAct, Sec. 2(c).

120. FEIS, 34–35.

121. FEIS, 35.

122. FEIS, 35.
123. FEIS, 35–38.
124. FEIS, 44, 46, 49.
125. FEIS, 39–40.
126. FEIS, 46.
127. FEIS, 47.
128. Stephen H. Hart, 1974-07-30 letter from Colorado State Historic Preservation Officer—to Lynn H. Thompson, Regional Director [RG03-01.05-004].
129. Lynn H. Thompson, 1974-08-07 letter from Regional Director—to Stephen H, Hart, Colorado State Historic Preservation Officer [RG03-01.05-004].
130. Philip H. Schmuck, 1974-08-13 letter from Director, Colorado Division of Planning—to Lynn H. Thompson, Regional Director [RG03-01.05-004].
131. David A. Breternitz, 1974-09-19 letter from Department of Anthropology, University of Colorado—to Office of State Archeologist [RG03-01.05-004].
132. James J. Hester, 1974-09-23 letter from State Archeologist, State Historical Society of Colorado—to Lynn H. Thompson, Regional Director [RG03-01.05-004].
133. Richard A. Strait, 1974-11-14 letter on behalf of Regional Director—to Robert R. Garvey, Executive Secretary, Advisory Council on Historic Preservation [RG03-01.05-004].
134. Lynn H. Thompson, 1975-01-31 memo from Regional Director—to Chief, Midwest Archeological Center, and Superintendent—re: Proposal of the NPS for use by the Advisory Council on Historic Preservation in completing a Memorandum of Agreement for the MEVE wilderness proposal [RG03-01.05-004].
135. Switzer, 1975-02-11 memo to Regional Director—re: Proposed Memorandum of Agreement—Mesa Verde Wilderness [RG03-01.05-004].
136. Lynn H. Thompson, 1975-02-24 letter from Regional Director—to Robert Garvey, Executive Secretary, Advisory Council on Historic Preservation [RG01-02.07-002].
137. Switzer, 1975-03-10 memo to Team Captain Midwest and Rocky Mountain Planning Team, DSC, through Deputy Regional Director—re: Status of Wilderness Legislation, MEVE, 1 [RG03-01.05-004].
138. Ibid.
139. Ibid., 3.
140. MEVE, 1975-12-02 Statement for Management, 1, 3–4 [RG01-02.03-011.2]
141. Ibid., 4.
142. Ibid., 7.
143. Ibid., 5.
144. MEVE, 1976-07-09. Summary of Public Comments Concerning the MEVE General Management Plan Assessment [RG01-02.03-011.2].

145. Sally Ranney, 1976-06-09 letter from Wilderness Coordinator, The Wilderness Society—to Superintendent, MEVE [RG01-02.03-011.2].
146. Lynn H. Thompson, 1976-08-04 memo from Regional Director—to Associate Director, Legislation, WASO—re: Statement for Management, MEVE. [RG01-02.03-011.2]
147. For "National Park wilderness," see U. S. Senate, "S. Rept. 94-1357—Wilderness Designations Within Units of the National Park System" (September 29, 1976), 3. For "When the imprint," see U. S. House of Representatives, "H. Rept. 94-1427—Designating Certain Lands Within Units of the National Park System As Wilderness; Revising the Boundaries of Certain of Those Units ; and For Other Purposes" (August 13, 1976), 3.
148. For "The Committee," see H. Rept. 94-1427, 6. For "recognizes that substantial," see S. Rept. 94-1357, 6. For "It is understood," see H. Rept. 94-1427, 6. For preliminary recommendations, see Chris Barns, 2020-12-31, memo from Volunteer Wilderness Specialist—to Superintendent—re: MEVE Wilderness Inventory [on file with author].
149. Doug Scott, "The Wilderness Act at Forty: Looking Back, Looking Ahead," *International Journal of Wilderness* 10, no. 1 (April 2004): 11.

Chapter Nine

1. For smaller scale map request, see Switzer, 1977-02-07 memo to Regional Director—re: MEVE Wilderness Map Review [RG03-01.05-004]. For changes in vegetation, see Donald A. Purse, 1977-07-27 memo from Assistant Manager, Midwest/Rocky Mountain Team, DSC—to Regional Director, Rocky Mountain Region—re: Topographic Map and Legal Description—Badlands, Black Canyon of the Gunnison, and Mesa Verde Wilderness [RG03-01.05-004]. For revised set of guidelines, see Associate Director, 1979-12-04 memo from Associate Director, Management & Operations—to Regional Directors—re: Wilderness boundaries [RG03-01.05-004].
2. Bud Martin, 1980-01-02 memo from Chief Ranger—to Chief, Division of Park Planning—re: Wilderness Boundaries [RG03-01.05-004].
3. Laura A. Kirn, "A Case for Storied Landscapes: Wilderness and Historic Preservation" (master's thesis, Goucher College, 2013), ("agency culture," 54; inertia, 75).
4. MEVE, 1977 Statement for Management, 5 [RG01-02.03-013].
5. MEVE, 1979-05. General Management Plan, 1 [RG01-02.03-198].
6. Ibid., 3.
7. MEVE, 1981 Statement for Management (World Heritage, 6; "Activity" and "Legislation," 13) [RG01-02.03-010.3].
8. Sellars, *Nature* ("Legislation," 284; "Such changes," 290); for more on the Vail Agenda, see 276–280.
9. Harold J. Smith, 1979-02-07 letter from Management Assistant—to

Robert C. Lucas, Project Leader, Wilderness Management Research Project [RG03-01.05-003].

10. Gilbert R. Wenger, *The Story of Mesa Verde* (Mesa Verde National Park: Mesa Verde Museum Association, 1980).

11. Louise Willcox, 1980-02 letter from Center of Environmental Studies, Williams College—to Superintendent, MEVE—re: wilderness rationing systems [RG03-01.05-004].

12. Heyder, 1980-03-11 letter to Louisa Willcox, Center of Environmental Studies, Williams College [RG03-01.05-004].

13. For access inquiry, see Jeff Nelson, 1988-01-04 (received) letter to Superintendent, MEVE [RG03-01.05-004]. For "Due to the steepness," see Heyder, 1988-01-29 letter to Jeff Nelson [RG03-01.05-004].

14. Heyder, 1992-07-07 letter to Jerry and Cora Jean Leenheer [RG01-02.01-093.2].

15. For Superintendent's concern, see Heyder, 1984-01-30 memo to Regional Director—re: BLM Planning for Weber Mountain, etc. [RG03-01.05-004]. For NPCA concurrence, see National Parks Conservation Association, "Boundary Study" (1988). [RG01-02.07-017.9].

16. Charles W. Quaintance, 1935-02-20 Supplementary Report: National Park Additions on sub-marginal land, 1 [RG01-01.07-050].

17. Switzer, 1977-07-05 memo to MEVE Division Chiefs and Director, University of Colorado Field School—re: SOP #77-3 employee visits to Wilderness, Backcountry Natural Areas, Undeveloped Ruins and Developed Ruin Sites [RG01-02.01-055].

18. For "There are many," see Heyder, 1979-08-30 memo to Chief Ranger, MEVE—re: Backcountry Management Plan, Visitor Use [RG03-01.05-004]. For Final Rule, see NPS, *Federal Register* Notice—36 Fed. Reg. 20511—Protection of Prehistoric Ruins and Visitors, Commercial Automobiles and Buses, and Hiking, Mesa Verde National Park (October 23, 1971). For "has outstanding opportunities," see WAct, Sec. 2(c)(2).

19. MEVE-SAR 1980, 29.

20. MEVE, Backcountry Management Plan. (ca. 1980–90?) [RG03-01.05-006].

21. Heyder, 1981-06-23 memo to all employees—re: Unauthorized entry into archaeological ruins. [RG01-02.01-054.1].

22. Heyder, 1981-07-02 memo to all employees—re: Damage to archaeological resources [RG01-02.01-054.1].

23. Heyder, 1982-05-06 memo to Regional Director—re: Management Appraisal [RG01-02.01-049.3].

24. Cecil Lewis, Eleanor Murphy, George Phillips, Tommy Cox, Bob Reynolds, and Bob Bendt, "Mesa Verde National Park Management Review, August 9–13, 1982" [RG01-02.03-005.16].

25. MEVE Chief Ranger, 1982-11-04 memo to Superintendent—re:

response to the August Management Review Report [RG01-02.03-005.16].

26. Jack E. Smith, 1982-11-18 memo from Chief, R&RM—to Superintendent—re: Management Review, August 9–13, 1982 [RG01-02.01-049.2].

27. Heyder, 1983-01-05 memo to Regional Director—re: Park comments on operations evaluation and management review of MEVE, August 9–13, 1982 [RG01-02.01-049.2].

28. MEVE-SAR 1982, 14.

29. For 1985 Annual Goals, see Heyder, 1985-04-11 memo to Regional Director—re: FY85 Goals Status Report [RG01-02.01-060.3]. For 1986 Statement for Management, see MEVE, 1986 Statement for Management [RG01-02.03-010.4]. For draft policy, see NPS, 1987-05-20 Memo from Associate Director, Policy Budget and Administration—to Directorate, Field Directorate, WASO Division Chiefs, Park Superintendents, and Area Managers—re: Review of Draft Management Policy on Wilderness Preservation and Management [RG01-02.01-049.3]. For "a draft reply," see Heyder, 1987-06-08 transmittal note to division chiefs—re: Review of Draft Management Policy on Wilderness Preservation and Management [RG01-02.01-049.3]. For "Mesa Verde," see Heyder, 1987-06-30 memo to Regional Director—re: Review of Draft Management Policy on Wilderness Preservation and Management [RG01-02.01-049.3].

30. For "September 1972" and "There is currently," see Heyder, 1989-01-04 letter to Steven C. Whitney, Director, National Parks Program, The Wilderness Society [RG01-02.08-027]. For direction, see NPS, 1988 Management Policies. U.S. Department of the Interior, chap. 6, 4.

31. Heyder, 1989-04-18 letter to Stephen F, McCool, School of Forestry, University of Montana [RG01-02.08-027].

32. MEVE, 1991 Statement for Management [RG01-02.03-010.5].

33. MEVE, 1991-12-04 Resource Management Plan [RG01-02.08-017.3].

34. For limiting employee use, see MEVE-SM 1993-05-24. For "Intrusion Detection," see MEVE-SAR 1994-5, 61. For closed to employees, see Linda A. Towle and Howard L. Dimont, 1995-07-07 memo to all employees—re: Closure of Three Backcountry Archeological Sites to Employees [RG03-01.05-006]. For backcountry hikes, see MEVE-SAR 1994-5, 128.

35. MEVE, 1996-10 Backcountry Use and Access Plan [RG03-01.05-007].

36. MEVE, 2000 MEVE Strategic Plan, Fiscal Years 2001–2005 ("to re-examine," 1; "manage and protect," 8) [B4-6-4].

37. For horse concession history, see Smith, *Shadows*, 186. For "The Service," see Phillip O. Stewart, 1978-06-16 letter from Assistant Director, NPS—to H. Paul Friesema, Associate Professor, Northwestern University [RG01-02.02-013.2].

38. For "The opportunity" and "Mug House," see Michael D. Snyder, 1988-02-17 memo from Acting Chief, Division of Planning and Compliance, RO—to Planning Team, Wetherill Mesa Development Concept Plan—re: Wetherill Mesa Development Concept Plan Alternatives [RG01-02.03-005.16]. For the

next plan, see John Kenoyer, 1992-10-13 Wetherill Mesa Trail Design Proposal and Mug House Operating Program—draft outline [B4-6-4]. For three alternatives, see MEVE-SAR 2001, 98.

39. For YCC, see MEVE-SAR 1988, 46–7. For Operation Raleigh, see MEVE-SAR 1992, 34. For the Park crew, see MEVE-SAR 1993, 24. For Colorado Outdoors, see MEVE-SAR 2002, 105. For Sierra Club, see MEVE-SAR 2005, 94.

40. Heyder, 1991-07-12 memo to Regional Director and Manager, Central Team, DSC—re: Request for Assessment of Potential Trail Use [RG01-02.03-015.10].

41. For "We feel," see Heyder, 1980-10-24 memo to Regional Director—re: Major Powerline in Mesa Verde Wilderness [RG01-02.03-112.8]. For "Overhead lines," see MEVE-SAR 1988, 5–6. For "With the removal," see MEVE-SAR 1992, 4. For northern overlook, see MEVE-SAR 1981, 48.

42. MEVE-SAR 1980, 29.

43. For ongoing effort, see MEVE-SAR 1997, 42. For terraces and waterbars, see MEVE-SAR 1997, 57. For silicone driplines, see MEVE-SAR 1998, 75.

44. MEVE-SAR 2004, 8–9; MEVE-SAR 2005, 18.

45. Smith, *Mesas*, 24.

46. For reconnaissance flights, see MEVE-SAR 1979, 17. For Rubenstein, see MEVE-SAR 1984, 19, 61. For Square Tower House, see MEVE-SAR 1994-5, 72–3.

47. For larger items, see for instance MEVE-SAR 1994-5, 71. For "evidence," see Douglas L. Caldwell, 1987-01-22 memo from Management Assistant—to Division Chiefs through Superintendent—re: Resource Threats Reporting [RG01-02.08-027]. For possible unreported collections, see Donna M. Glowacki, *The Mesa Verde Community Center Survey* (Spokane: Village Ecodynamics Project, Washington State University, 2012), 31 [B4-6-4].

48. For maintenance issues, see Jack L. Muller, 1987-12-22 memo from Acting Superintendent—to Regional Director—re: Annual Goals for FY88 [RG01-02 01-060.3]. For "The big problem," see Smith, *Shadows*, 198. For "All of these," see MEVE-SAR 1990, 22–3.

49. For fire impacts, see Julie Bell, "Fire and Archaeology on Mesa Verde," David Grant Noble, ed., *The Mesa Verde World* (Santa Fe: School of American Research Press. 2006), 119–121; Fiero, *Dirt, Water, Stone*, 156–7. For "Consultation," see MEVE-SAR 1997, 57. For photos, see Bell, 120.

50. MEVE-SAR 2001, 38.

51. For "For the first time," see MEVE-SAR 1991, 40. For "The Park received," see Heyder, 1991-10-16 memo to Regional Director, attn. Associate Regional Director, Operations—re: Summary Report on the Expenditure of Archeological Resource Protection Funds [RG01-02.05-103].

52. MEVE Backcountry Patrol Ranger, "1991 Annual Summary of Archeological Protection"; "1992 Annual Summary . . ."; "1993 Annual Summary . . ."[B4-7-2]; MEVE-SAR 1991–2006.

53. MEVE-SAR 1999, 28.

54. For inventory, see MEVE-SAR 2005, 23. For Extraordinary authorization, see unknown author. 2006-05-16 Camping Proposal [B4-6-4].

55. Lewis, et al. "Management Review, August 9–13, 1982."

56. For mesa-top vegetation and pollen analysis, see George S. Cattanach, Jr., *Long House, Mesa Verde National Park, Colorado* (Washington, DC: USDI National Park Service, 1980), 1, 401. For Douglas-fir, see Alden C Hayes and James A Lancaster. *Badger House Community, Mesa Verde National Park* (Washington: USDI National Park Service, 1975), 185. For the portions of the Park that were burned, see Smith, *Mesas*, 33.

57. For "further sophistication" and bighorn sheep, see Arthur H. Rohn, *Mug House, Mesa Verde National Park, Colorado* (Washington, DC: USDI National Park Service, 1971), 263, 261. For unworked bone, see Cattanach, *Long House*, 372. For PII/PIII comparison, see Hayes and Lancaster, *Badger House Community*, 185.

58. For elk at Mug House, see Rohn, *Mug House*, 102, 255, 261. For elk at Big Juniper House, see Jervis D. Swannack Jr., *Big Juniper House* (Washington: USDI National Park Service, 1969), 151, 161, 180. For elk in Badger House, see Hayes and Lancaster, *Badger House Community*, 69, 76. For elk as food and at Long House, see Cattanach, *Long House*, 4, 3, 372. For "Fewer than a dozen," see Marilyn Colyer, "Elk at MEVE" (February 1, 2007), 3 [B4-7-3].

59. MEVE-SAR 1979, 19; MEVE-SAR 1980, 39–40; MEVE-SAR 1984, 80; MEVE-SAR 2002, 92.

60. MEVE-SAR 1980, 40; MEVE-SAR 1984, 78; MEVE-SAR 2001, 65.

61. MEVE-SAR 1980, 40; MEVE-SAR 1983, 65; MEVE-SAR 1987, 51; MEVE-SAR 1990, 53; MEVE Research & Resource Management Division, "1993 Annual Report," 33 [RG03-01.01-010.1]; MEVE-SM. 1993-12-13, 2.

It is believed that as of late 2023 there are between 4 and 8 lions in the Park, and between 10 and 20 bears—though both species may roam outside the boundaries, especially to the south and west. Both species were heavily hunted outside Mesa Verde, but the relative ease in killing bears might account for too few individuals to populate the Park until the hunting regulations of the late 20th century allowed bear populations to rebuild. (Population estimates and comparative population theory from Nathan Brown, 2023-09-18 e-mail from Biologist/Wildlife Program Manager to the author.)

62. MEVE-SAR 1990, 53; MEVE-SAR 1993, 73.

63. MEVE-SAR 1984, 80; MEVE-SAR 1986, 44; Dave Stevens and Tom Smith, MEVE Bighorn Sheep Management Strategy (draft) (April 15, 1991) [B4-7-3]; State of Colorado and MEVE, "Joint Work Statement between State of Colorado, Department of Natural Resources, Division of Wildlife and MEVE, NPS, USDI" (October, 1991) [RG03-03.01-001.1]; MEVE-SAR 1992, 63–4; MEVE-SAR 1993, 71; MEVE Research & Resource Management Division. "1993 Annual Report," 33; MEVE-SAR 1994–5, 98.

64. Francis J. Singer and Michelle Gudorf, *Restoration of Bighorn Sheep Metapopulations into and near 15 National Park Units; Conservation Biology of a Severely Fragmented Species* (Fort Collins: USGS Biological Resources Division, 1997), 117 [RG03-01.01-010.2].

65. MEVE-SAR 2000, 75.

66. MEVE-SAR 2006, 100.

67. MEVE-SAR 1984, 78; MEVE-SAR 1987, 50.

68. MEVE-SAR 1986, 45; Matthew Johnson, Clint Francis, George L. San Miguel, and Maureen Essen, *Determining Protected Activity Centers (PACs) for Mexican Spotted Owls at MEVE, 2004–05 Final Draft Report* (Flagstaff: USGS, Southwest Biological Science Center, 2004) [B4-7-3]; Nathan Brown, *The Wildlife of Mesa Verde, a historical and current perspective: lions, owls, and bears oh my!* (webinar) (November 10, 2021).

69. MEVE-SAR 1987, 50; MEVE-SAR 1991, 60; MEVE-SAR 2002, 72; MEVE-SAR 2000, 72.

70. MEVE-SAR 1998, 55; MEVE-SAR 2000, 72.

71. For mink, see MEVE-SAR 1986, 44. For tracks, see MEVE-SAR 2000, 73. For crane, see MEVE-SAR 1983, 64.

72. Marilyn Colyer, "MEVE Faunal Species of Concern" (November 27, 2002) [B4-7-3].

73. MEVE-SAR 1992, 72.

74. MEVE-SAR 1983, 63; MEVE-SAR 1986, 46; MEVE-SAR 1988, 39.

75. MEVE-SAR 2006, 80.

76. MEVE-SAR 1986, 42.

77. Marilyn Colyer, "Plan to Control Musk Thistle" (March 2, 1987), 1 [RG01-02.08-079.1].

78. MEVE-SAR 1991, 54.

79. For the list, see Marilyn Colyer, "List of Non-Native Plant Species of MEVE" (February 6, 1997) [RG03-02.04-004]. For the most serious, see MEVE-SAR 1998, 51. For "The only," see MEVE-SAR 2002, 100.

80. MEVE-SAR 1998, 52; George L. San Miguel, "Progress Report of MEVE Invasive Species Control" (July 22, 2004) [B4-7-3]; MEVE-SAR 2000, 62.

81. San Miguel, "Progress Report."

82. Steven Dewey and Kimberly Andersen, *MEVE 2003 Invasive Non-native Plant Inventory* (Flagstaff: Southern Colorado Plateau Inventory and Monitoring Network, 2005) [B4-7-3].

83. San Miguel, "Progress Report," 3.

84. For goats, see MEVE-SAR 1981, 31. For emu, see MEVE-SAR 1998, 60.

85. MEVE, 1985-02-25 Draft Land Protection Plan, 1, 2–3, 3 [RG01-02.07-013.1].

86. MEVE Chief Ranger, 1979-01-12 memo—to Superintendent—re: Annual Report [RG01-02.01-20].

87. MEVE-SAR 1979, 18.

88. MEVE, Development/Study Package Proposal to Fence 14.5 Miles of Park Boundary (February 5, 1981) [RG03-01.03-001].

89. For "25 to 35" see MEVE, 1983-02 Natural Resource Project Statement [RG01-02.07-065]. For underestimation, see Colyer, "Grazing History" (draft), 32, 33 [B4-7-4].

90. Jack L. Muller, 1987-12-22 memo from Acting Superintendent—to Regional Director—re: Annual Goals for FY88 [RG01-02.01060.3].

91. Heyder, 1989-09-05 letter to Ernest House, Ute Mountain Ute Tribe [RG03-01.03-002].

92. Heyder, 1990-08-14 letter to Doug Frazier, Brand Inspector, State of Colorado, [RG03-01.05-006]; Heyder, 1991-02-06 letter to Doug Frazier, Brand Inspector, State of Colorado, [RG03-01.05-006]; Heyder, 1992-04-24 letter to Doug Frazier, Brand Inspector, State of Colorado, [RG03-01.03-002].

93. MEVE-SAR 1992, 32; MEVE-SAR 1993, 28; MEVE-SAR 1997, 62.

94. MEVE-SAR 2000, 67.

95. For centennial estimate, see MEVE-SAR 2006, 102. For "occasional small herds," see Colyer, "Grazing History" (draft), 30.

96. For air quality, see MEVE-SAR 1979, 4; MEVE-SAR 1984, 104; MEVE-SAR 2002, 90; MEVE-SAR 2004, 44–45. For water sources, see MEVE-SAR 1986, 47; MEVE-SAR 1993, 82. For night skies, see MEVE-SAR 2004, 46. For "Because of cuts," see MEVE-SAR 2006, 69.

97. Philip N. Omi, *Fire and Resource Management in MEVE* (Fort Collins: unpublished research study from Colorado State University, Forest and Wood Sciences Dept., 1979), ("tolerable trade-off," "fire may," and "carefully selected," 1; "Each fire," 4) [RG03-16.01-001].

98. For review focus, see Lewis, et al. "Management Review, August 9–13, 1982," 14. For "well aware," see Heyder, 1983-01-05 memo to Regional Director—re: Park comments on operations evaluation and management review of MEVE, August 9–13, 1982, 9 [RG01-02.01-049.2]. For "the need," see MEVE-SAR 1982, p. 2. For delay, see Douglas L. Caldwell, 1987-01-22 memo from Management Assistant—to Division Chiefs through Superintendent—re: Resource Threats Reporting [RG-01-02.08-027].

99. MEVE-SM. 1993-04-05; MEVE-SAR 1994-5, 3–4.

100. For seeding, see MEVE-SAR 2003, 75. For unsuccessful, see MEVE-SAR 2005, 91.

101. For study plots, see Karen R. Adams and Abigail R. Dockter, "Five Years of Fire Recovery in MEVE" (ca. 2012), 7–9 [RG01-16.01-015]. For "a minimum 300-year," see Omi, *Fire and Resource Management*, 2. For "[The fires have] given" and "All of us are excited," see Smith, *Shadows*, 218, 221.

102. MEVE-SAR 1987, 52.

103. MEVE-SAR 1989, 32; MEVE-SAR 1992, 73.

104. MEVE-SAR 2001, 65.

105. MEVE-SAR 1990, 47; MEVE-SAR 1991, 55.

106. MEVE-SAR 1998, 37; MEVE-SAR 1997, 42; MEVE-SAR 1999, 60.

107. For the fence, see Robert Ball, 1999-03-17 memo from BLM—to George San Miguel, MEVE [RG03-10.03-008.02]; Kent Hoffman, 1999-07-21 letter from Associate Area Manager, BLM San Juan Field Office—to Superintendent [RG03-10.03-008.02]. For buffaloberry, see MEVE-SAR 2000, 64. For "Cattle trails," see MEVE-SAR 2001, 64–5.

108. MEVE-SAR 1990, 47–8.

109. For beaver release, see MEVE-SAR 2004, 70. For leopard frogs, see MEVE-SAR 2002, 93.

110. MEVE-SAR 2004, 43.

111. For "It must be emphasized," see MEVE-SAR 2002, 83. For adjudication, see MEVE-SM 1992-11-??.

112. MEVE-SAR 1992, 41.

113. Linda A. Towle, 1993-09-28 letter from Chief R&RM—to Jayne Belnap, Canyonlands National Park [RG03-01.05-001].

114. George L. San Miguel, 1999-05-14 memo from Resource Management Specialist—to Members of the MEVE Park Research Committee [RG03-01.05-001].

115. George L. San Miguel, 2000-05-16 memo from Resource Management Specialist—to Members of the MEVE Park Research Committee—re: Proposal on the study Park Mesa for possible naming as a Colorado Natural Area [RG03-01.05-001].

Chapter Ten

1. NPS 6—Wilderness Preservation and Management, ("All lands" Sec. 6.2.1; "The superintendent" Sec. 6.3.4.2; "encourage and facilitate" Sec. 6.4), https://www.nps.gov/subjects/policy/upload/MP_2006.pdf (last accessed 2024-07-05).

2. The NPS manages fifty-four wilderness areas alone. (Seven are co-managed with another agency.) Of those fifty-four, as of 2023 only seventeen have completed Wilderness Management Plans. Among those that do not are eleven of the thirteen areas designated the same year with Mesa Verde. More important than having a Plan, however, is managing the designated Wilderness according to the Wilderness Act. Mesa Verde is anomalous in ignoring the law. (For a comprehensive list of NPS Wilderness areas, see "Advanced Wilderness Search," Wilderness Connect, https://wilderness.net/practitioners/wilderness-areas/search.php (last accessed 2024-07-05). Information on which units have Wilderness Management Plans was supplied by Roger Semler, NPS National Wilderness Stewardship Program Manager, in an e-mail to the author dated 2023-08-11.)

3. MEVE-SAR 2006, 128, 28.

4. MEVE-SAR 2007, 63–64.

5. MEVE-SAR 2007, 65–66. Colyer, "Grazing History, 45.

6. MEVE, Invasive Plant Management Plan (March 6, 2015), treatment priorities, 228; "there are no plans," 91 [B4-7-3].

7. For population estimates, see Bruce Lubow, 2012-04-16 memo to Paul Morey—re: Mesa Verde horse population estimate [RG03-05.03-002]. For trap placement, see MEVE, "Livestock Removal: Environmental Assessment" (April 2018), http://npshistory.com/publications/meve/livestock-removal-ea-2018.pdf (last accessed 2024-07-05). For removal timetable, see MEVE, "Livestock Removal: Finding of No Significant Impact" (March 2019), 1, https://parkplanning.nps.gov/document.cfm?parkID=79&projectID=60864&documentID=93688 (last accessed 2024-07-05). For 2023 status, see Nathan Brown, 2023-08-13 e-mail from Biologist/Wildlife Program Manager to the author.

8. See William H. Romme, Sylvia Oliva, and M. Lisa Floyd, "Threats to Piñon-Juniper Woodlands," in *Ancient Piñon-Juniper Woodlands: A Natural History of Mesa Verde Country*, ed. M. Lisa Floyd (Boulder: University Press of Colorado, 2003).

9. For "potentially," see Ibid., 357–58. For fire statistics, see MEVE-SAR 2007, 76–77, 126; MEVE-SAR 2008, 119; MEVE-SAR 2009, 92.

10. MEVE, "Fire Management Plan—Mesa Verde National Park and Yucca House National Monument—Draft Environmental Assessment" (July 2013), 91–96 [B4-2-1].

11. For the Plan, see MEVE, "Mesa Verde National Park and Yucca House National Monument Fire Management Plan—Environmental Assessment" (July 2023). For the FONSI, see "Finding of No Significant Impact: Fire Management Plan Mesa Verde National Park and Yucca House National Monument" (February 2024). For more on the process of a Minimum Requirements Analysis, see https://wilderness.net/practitioners/minimum-requirements-analysis/default.php (last accessed 2024-07-05).

12. MEVE-SAR 2007, 39–40, 44–45; MEVE-SAR 2008, 43–44.

13. MEVE-SAR 2007, 122.

14. MEVE-SAR 2008, 103; MEVE-SAR 2009, 69.

15. U.S. Senate, 2012. "S. Hrg. 112-274 (First Sess.), November 5. 2011."

16. R. Scott Anderson, Diana Anderson, Eric Herring, and Taylor Joyal, *Environments at MEVE during the Holocene and Anthropocene: An interdisciplinary study of vegetation, fire, humans and climate* (Flagstaff: Northern Arizona University, School of Earth Sciences and Environmental Sustainability, 2012), 3, 41–42 [B4-7-4].

17. G. William M. Harrison, Justin S. Tweet, Vincent L. Santucci, and George L. San Miguel, *Mesa Verde National Park: Paleontological Resources Inventory (Non-Sensitive Version)*, Natural Resource Report NPS/MEVE/NRR–2017/1550, National Park Service (2017), 30 [B4-7-4].

18. Lisa Floyd-Hanna, and Sasha Reed, "Characteristics of resiliency in

Pinus edulis-Juniperus osteosperma/Purshia tridentata woodlands of MEVE" (2015) [RG03-02.06-021].

19. For bighorns, see George L. San Miguel, "A Brief Summary on Bighorn Sheep at MEVE" (2011) [B4-7-3]. For CNA, see George L. San Miguel, 2015-04-20 Briefing Statement on Colorado Natural Areas (CNA) Designation at MEVE [B4-7-1].

20. MEVE, "Mancos River Restoration Project," Planning, Environment, and Public Comment project 97661, September 23, 2020.

21. Donna M. Glowacki, *The Mesa Verde Community Center Survey* (Spokane: Village Ecodynamics Project, Washington State University, 2012) [B4-6-4].

22. For extensive analysis, see Harrison, et al., *Paleontological Resources Inventory.* For "The purpose" and "may have been collected," see George S. Cattanach Jr., *Long House, Mesa Verde National Park, Colorado* (Washington, DC: USDI National Park Service, 1980), 294, 299. For burial accompaniment, see Arthur H. Rohn, *Mug House, Mesa Verde National Park, Colorado* (Washington, DC: USDI National Park Service, 1971), 93. For 139 catalog numbers, see Harrison et al., 45.

23. Unknown author, 2010-08-24, "VEOps" [B4-6-4].

24. Unknown author, 2010–11, "Compilation from site visits to Little Long House Overlook, Far View East/West, and Navajo Canyon," 1 [B4-6-4].

25. Ibid., 5.

26. Mesa Verde Foundation, "Spring Newsletter" (2020).

27. Unknown author, 2010 Backcountry Trails, MEVE [B4-6-4].

28. MEVE-SAR 2006, 109.

29. MEVE-SAR 2000, 67.

Leasing is discretionary, and the parcels in question could have easily been pulled from a lease sale. It is not clear whether Superintendent Wiese simply did not know this or if he was intentionally misled by the local BLM management personnel.

30. Bureau of Land Management, 2015-02-27, "Record of Decision for the Approved Resource Management Plan for the Public Lands Administered by the Tres Rios Field Office, Dolores, Colorado," II-118, https://eplanning.blm.gov/public_projects/lup/65211/78930/91207/Part_II_-_RMP_Chapter_2.pdf (last accessed 2024-07-05).

31. MEVE-SAR 2006, 109.

32. MEVE, "Mesa Verde National Park and Yucca House National Monument 5-Year Strategic Plan 2012–2016" (2011) ("Maintain" 15; "Create" 42) [MEVE non-public electronic files].

33. NPS, NPS Director's Order #41 (May 13, 2013) ("provide accountability" 1; "For every" 6.3) https://www.nps.gov/policy/DOrders/DO_41.pdf.

As noted above (see endnote2 in this chapter), many parks are not in conformance with the "two-year" window.

34. MEVE, "Foundation Document" (October 2015) [B4-7-3].

35. Ibid., ("protects" 5; "significance" 6; "fundamental" 8; interpretive themes 10).

36. Ibid., ("Mesa Verde" 11; Appendix 30).

37. Ibid., 44–45.

38. Ibid., 15.

39. WAct, Sec. 4(b).

40. Peter Landres, Steve Boucher, Linda Merigliano, Chris Barns, Denis Davis, Troy Hall, Steve Henry, Brad Hunter, Patrice Janiga, Mark Laker, Al McPherson, Douglass S. Powell, Mike Rowan, and Susan Sater, *Monitoring Selected Conditions Related to Wilderness Character: A National Framework,* General Technical Report RMRS-GTR-151, USDA Forest Service (Fort Collins: Rocky Mountain Research Station, 2002).

41. Peter Landres, Chris Barns, John G. Dennis, Tim Devine, Paul Geissler, Curtis S. McCasland, Linda Merigliano, Justin Seastrand, and Ralph Swain, *Keeping It Wild: An interagency strategy to monitor trends in wilderness character across the National Wilderness Preservation System,* General Technical Report RMRS-GTR-212, USDA Forest Service (Fort Collins: Rocky Mountain Research Station, 2008).

42. Peter Landres, Chris Barns, Steve Boutcher, Tim Devine, Peter Dratch, Adrienne Lindholm, Linda Merigliano, Nancy Roeper, and Emily Simpson, *Keeping It Wild 2: An updated interagency strategy to monitor trends in wilderness character across the National Wilderness Preservation System,* General Technical Report RMRS-GTR-340, USDA Forest Service (Fort Collins: Rocky Mountain Research Station, 2015)

43. Interagency Wilderness Steering Committee Chair, 2015-09-21 memo to Chair, Interagency Wilderness Policy Council—re: Interagency Wilderness Steering Committee's "Keeping It Wild 2" Recommendations; (approved by the Wilderness Policy Council Dec. 23, 2015), https://winapps.umt.edu/winapps/media2/wilderness/toolboxes/documents/WC/Interagency%20Wilderness%20Steering%20Committee%20and%20Policy%20Council%20endorses%20KIW2,%202015.pdf (last accessed 2024-07-05).

44. NPS, *Keeping It Wild in the National Park Service: a user guide to integrating wilderness character into park planning, management, and monitoring* (Lakewood, Colorado: NPS, 2014).

45. Joelle Marier, "Mesa Verde Wilderness: Wilderness Building Blocks 1 & 2—Wilderness Basics and Wilderness Character Assessment" (2014, rev. 2015) [B4-4-2].

46. Garry Oye, 2019-10-19 "Thoughts on visit to Mesa Verde National Park" [e-mail on file with author].

47. Suzanne Stutzman, 2019-10-12 "MEVE Wilderness Ideas" [e-mail on file with author].

48. Chris Barns, 2020-12-31 memo to Superintendent—re: MEVE Wilderness Inventory. This includes a rather weak rationale for excluding the area

south of Unit C to the Park border. The two rarely used routes, and the usually unstaffed fire tower, could easily be cherry-stemmed.

Conclusion

1. Ben H. Thompson, "A Wilderness-Use Technique," in George M. Wright and Ben H. Thompson, *Fauna of the National Parks of the United States, Fauna Series No.* 2 (Washington, DC: Government Printing Office, 1934), 39.

2. For "At Bandelier," see Mark Michel, "Lay of the Land—A Sordid Story at Effigy Mounds," *American Archaeology* 56 (Spring 2019): 2. For "The ongoing," see NPS National Wilderness Steering Committee, "Guidance 'White Paper' No. 1: Cultural Resources and Wilderness," November 30, 2002, http://npshistory.com/publications/wilderness/white-papers/1.pdf (last accessed 2024-07-05).

3. Dennis Milligan, 2020-01-13, e-mail correspondence with author.

4. Robert Powers, 2010 memo from NPS Southwest Region Chief Archaeologist (retired) (on file with author).

5. Jill Cowley, Peter Landres, Melissa Memory, Doug Scott, and Adrienne Lindholm, "Integrating cultural resources and wilderness character," *Park Science* 28, no. 3 (2012): 29-33, 38.

6. Yet as of 2024, the MEVE website still lists as part of its mission "Managing and protecting the *pristine* character of designated wilderness on 8,100 acres" (emphasis added), https://nps.gov/meve/learn/management/index.htm (last accessed 2024-07-05).

7. NPS National Wilderness Steering Committee, "Cultural Resources and Wilderness," 4.

8. John Muir, "The Scenery of California," in *California: Early history, commercial position, climate, scenery, forests, general resources* (California State Board of Trade, 1898), 16. Sigurd Olson, *Reflections from the North Country* (New York: Alfred A. Knopf, 1985), 83.

9. For an extensive exploration of the relationship between the "untrammeled" and "natural" qualities of wilderness, see Peter Landres, Chris Barns, Steve Boutcher, Tim Devine, Peter Dratch, Adrienne Lindholm, Linda Merigliano, Nancy Roeper, and Emily Simpson, *Keeping It Wild 2: An updated interagency strategy to monitor trends in wilderness character across the National Wilderness Preservation System,* General Technical Report RMRS-GTR-340, USDA Forest Service (Fort Collins: Rocky Mountain Research Station, 2015).

10. See "Minimum Requirements Analysis," Wilderness Connect, https://wilderness.net/practitioners/minimum-requirements-analysis/default.php (last accessed 2024-07-05).

11. Kenneth R. Wright, "Water for the Mesa Verdeans," in *The Mesa Verde World,* David Grant Noble, ed., (Santa Fe: School of American Research Press, 2006), 124.

12. For "To make," see Smith, *Shadows*, 189. For "Unfortunate" and "It does," see Donald A. Purse, 1972-05-23 Planning Directive for MEVE, 3 [RG1-02.03-005.13].

13. For "Looking," see Nusbaum, transcript of talk to The Denver Posse of Westerners at Bent's Fort, Morrison, CO, August 16, 1964, 9 [RG19-001-052]. For "Except," see Smith, *Shadows*, 214.

14. For "The feeling," see Lucille Bambridge, 1976-05-19 letter in response to Plan outreach [RG01-02.03-005]. For "wilderness landscapes," see Laura A. Kirn, "A Case for Storied Landscapes: Wilderness and Historic Preservation" (master's thesis, Goucher College, 2013), 1.

15. Joseph L. Sax, *Mountains Without Handrails: Reflections on the National Parks* (Ann Arbor: The University of Michigan Press, 1980), 79.

16. Alden C. Hayes, *The Archeological Survey of Wetherill Mesa, MEVE; Archeological Research Series No. 7-A* (Washington, DC: USDI, NPS, 1964), 12.

17. Joseph L. Sax, "America's National Parks: Their Principles, Purposes, and Prospects," *Natural History* (special supplement, October 1976), (not paginated).

18. Olson, *Reflections from the North Country*, 136.

19. Sax, "America's National Parks: Their Principles, Purposes, and Prospects."

20. Craig Childs, *Finders Keepers: A Tale of Archaeological Plunder and Obsession* (New York: Little, Brown and Company; Back Bay Books, 2013), 227.

21. Ibid., 239.

22. See, for instance, Michael Frome, *Regreening the National Parks* (Tucson: University of Arizona Press, 1992), 116. Frome cites Donald Madsen, Utah State Archaeologist, reporting that by 1980, of the 25,000 known sites in the state, 90 percent had been disturbed.

23. Douglas L. Caldwell, 1987-01-22 memo from Management Assistant—to Division Chiefs through Superintendent—re: Resource Threats Reporting.

24. MEVE, "Visitation Statistics," NPS, https://www.nps.gov/meve/learn/management/statistics.htm (last accessed 2024-07-05).

25. "Provoke," here, is used as by Freeman Tilden in *Interpreting Our Heritage*, cited above. "The chief aim of Interpretation is not instruction, but provocation," 9, 32–39.

26. Fiero, *Dirt, Water, Stone* ("stable and safe," 48; "The goal," xviii; "Although," 111).

27. For "Each structure," see Dan Simplicio, 2021-10-23 interview with author. For "The place," see Catherine M. Cameron, "Leaving Mesa Verde," in *The Mesa Verde World*, David Grant Noble, ed., (Santa Fe: School of American Research Press. 2006), 147.

28. Lloyd Burton, *Worship and Wilderness: Culture, Religion, and Law in Public Lands Management* (Madison: University of Wisconsin Press, 2002), 31.

29. For "Five thousand," see Hayes, The Archeological Survey of Wetherill

Mesa, 20. For "All artifacts," see MEVE Park Archeologist, 1957-05-24 memo to Superintendent—re: Information for Annual Report, 7 [RG01-02 01-001].

30. Arthur H. Rohn, *Cultural Change and Continuity in Chapin Mesa* (Lawrence, KS: The Regents Press of Kansas, 1997) (80 percent, 5–6; "The surface," 9; "a number," 27).

31. Sax, *Mountains Without Handrails*, 82–83.

32. Wilderness data in this chapter are from Wilderness Connect, https://wilderness.net/practitioners/wilderness-areas/default.php (last accessed 2024-07-05).

33. The question remains as to why Bandelier, Chaco, and Canyons of the Ancients are managed so differently. It is easiest to separate the BLM area from those managed by the NPS. The BLM has (somewhat smugly) referred to itself as "the agency of YES," while calling the NPS "the agency of NO." The differences in the management of the NPS units are harder to fathom. At the end of the day, it is likely to be simply a matter of past historical practices. See also endnote88 in "Mesa Verde Meets the Wilderness Act: The Fight over Wilderness Designation."

34. WAct, Sec. 2(c)(2).

35. Public Law 59-353, Sec. 2.

36. Several court cases over the last two decades have asserted the priority of the Wilderness Act over other laws with less specific mandates and clarified that Section 2(c) of the Act overrides any conflict in Section 4(a). The NPS may provide for other statutory purposes "only insofar as to also preserve its wilderness character" (*Olympic Park Associates v. Mainella*, No. C04–5732FDB, at *12 (W.D. Wash. 2005)). In addition, since "the Wilderness Act emphasizes outcome (wilderness preservation) over procedure . . . it is as close to a 'purist manifesto' as may be found in the area of environmental law" (*High Sierra Hikers v. U.S. Forest Serv.*, 436 F.Supp.2d 1117, 1138 (E.D. Cal. 2006)). For more detail on the legal nexus of wilderness and cultural resources, see Christopher Barns, "The 'Irreplaceable Heritage' in 'an Enduring Resource of Wilderness,'" in *Documenting the Dinétah: Papers in Honor of James M. Copeland* (Albuquerque: Archaeological Society of New Mexico, 2023), 13–21.

37. The exception is in the Olympic Wilderness in Washington (now known as the Daniel J. Evans Wilderness), where Public Law 112-97 removed 222 acres from a designated wilderness of over 875,000 acres.

38. Laura A. Kirn, 2021-02-24 interview with author.

39. For "Wild places," see Kirn, "A Case for Storied Landscapes," abstract. For "Wilderness is," see Doug Scott, *The Enduring Wilderness: protecting our natural heritage* (Golden, CO: Fulcrum, 2004), 12. For "Out of wilderness," see Doug Scott, "The Wilderness Act at Forty: Looking Back, Looking Ahead." *International Journal of Wilderness* 10, no. 1 (April 2004): 12.

40. For "many, varied," "harbors resources," and "agencies must," see Kirn, "A Case for Storied Landscapes," 250, 259, 279. For "The relationship," see

Leslie Marmon Silko, "Yellow Woman and a Beauty of the Spirit," *Los Angeles Times*, December 19, 1993. For "to be connected," see Burton, *Worship and Wilderness*, 169. Edith Warner quoted by David Brower in McPhee, *Encounters with the Archdruid*, 183.

41. Kirn, "A Case for Storied Landscapes," 9.

42. Chris Barns, 2020-12-31 memo to Superintendent—re: "'Solitude or a Primitive, Unconfined Type of Recreation'—Options for Visitor Opportunities in the Mesa Verde Wilderness and Backcountry" [on file with author].

43. For "The Indians," see Sellars, "A Very Large Array," 270. For "Some tribal," see Ari Kelman, *A Misplaced Massacre* (Cambridge: Harvard University Press, 2013), 167.

44. For "the reactionary," see Monte Mills and Martin Nie, *Bridges to a New Era: A Report on the Past, Present, and Potential Future of Tribal Co-Management on Federal Public Lands* (Missoula: Margery Hunter Brown Indian Law Clinic / Bolle Center for People and Forests, University of Montana, 2020), iv. For "Ensure," see Secretaries of Agriculture and Interior, Secretarial Order No. 3403, "Joint Secretarial Order on Fulfilling the Trust Responsibility to Indian Tribes in the Stewardship of Federal Lands and Waters" (October 15, 2021), Sec. 1(a), (b). For "Efforts," see Mills and Nie, 34–35; for "a fundamental objective," 85.

45. See "The 26 Associated Tribes of Mesa Verde," NPS, https://www.nps.gov/meve/learn/historyculture/upload/26meve_associated_tribes_508.pdf (last accessed 2024-07-05).

46. 436 F. Supp. 2d 1138 (E.D. Cal. 2006).

47. Washington Post Live, "'Field Trip' with Chuck Sams, Director, National Park Service," *Washington Post*, July 19, 2023, https://www.washingtonpost.com/washington-post-live/2023/07/19/transcript-field-trip-with-chuck-sams-director-national-park-service/ (last accessed 2024-07-05).

48. For the definitive discussion of the transformation of European "Old Roots" wilderness to the "*American* wilderness," see Nash, 8–96. For "Cup'ik ancestors," see Polly Napiryuk Andrews, "A Cup'ik Perspective," in "Wilderness and Traditional Indigenous Beliefs: conflicting or intersecting perspectives on the human-nature relationship?" Alaska Wilderness League, December 17, 2021, https://alaskawild.org/blog/wilderness-and-traditional-indigenous-beliefs (last accessed 2024-07-05). For agency wilderness acreage, see "Wilderness Acreage by Agency," Wilderness Connect https://wilderness.net/practitioners/wilderness-areas/summary-reports/acreage-by-agency.php (last accessed 2024-07-05).

In practice, the deeper meanings of wilderness have evolved even since the 1964 Act, evidenced in many of the cited works in the introduction.

49. See Dave Treuer, "Return the National Parks to the Tribes: The Jewels of America's Landscape Should Belong to America's Original Peoples," *Atlantic*,

April 12, 2021, https://www.theatlantic.com/magazine/archive/2021/05/return-the-national-parks-to-the-tribes/618395/ (last accessed 2024-07-05).

50. See, for instance, Fred Matt, former chairman of the Confederated Salish and Kootenai Tribes in northwestern Montana: "We were the first tribe that designated an area for wilderness. If there was no Wilderness Act, then we would've been the first ones to create a wilderness because we saw the value. . . . A lot of our tribal people who support the idea of wilderness, they may have not visited this area for years. Maybe the last time they were back here in the Missions was when they were very young. These places are there for not only ourselves, but we want to protect this area for our future generations." In *American Values: American Wilderness*, High Plains Films, directed by Christopher Barns, Drury Gunn Carr, and Doug Hawes-Davis, featuring Christopher Reeve, aired 2004 and 2005 on PBS, https://www.youtube.com/watch?v=H7IS9ZCRZHo (last accessed 2024-07-05).

51. Native Corporations were set up by a complicated selection process outlined in the Alaska Native Claims Settlement Act (ANCSA) of 1971 (P. Law 92-203). When Alaskan Wilderness areas were designated by the even-more-complicated Alaska National Interest Lands Conservation Act (ANILCA) in 1980 (P. Law 96-487), provisions for use were somewhat different from those under the Wilderness Act of 1964. This was due in part to the vast size of Alaskan designated Wilderness (the five largest areas, and fifteen of the twenty largest areas, are in Alaska), and the ongoing integration of Alaska Natives with the landscape. For wilderness data, see https://wilderness.net/practitioners/wilderness-areas/search.php#results and sort by size (last accessed 2024-07-05). For an overview of wilderness in Alaska, see Allin, 207–65. For a comprehensive analysis, see Theodore Catton, *Inhabited Wilderness: Indians, Eskimos, and National Parks in Alaska* (Albuquerque: University of New Mexico Press, 1997).

52. See *Keeping It Wild in the National Park Service.*

53. Henry David Thoreau, "Autumnal Tints," *Atlantic,* October 1862.

Index

Page numbers in *italic* text refer to illustrations.